Human Nature, Cultural Diversity,
and the French Enlightenment

PART ONE

THE PAST

FOREWORD

quests for information, and to thank Mrs. Rene Nielsen for typing the great bulk of the first and second drafts of the manuscript. Finally, I am indebted to the Proprietors, Investors' Intelligence, Ltd., Johannesburg, for permission to make use of the material contained in their monthly news-digest, *African X-Ray Report.*

Johannesburg and London   SHEILA PATTERSON

September, 1956

FOREWORD

Only half a century ago, the Boers were the heroes of Europe and America—the gallant little nation that went down before a mighty empire. Today, the greater part of the outside world regards the vocal majority of their descendants, the Nationalist Afrikaners, as the epitome of violence, race prejudice and Herrenvolkism.

In this study I have tried, as objectively as may be, to trace the development of Boer into Afrikaner, of oppressed nationhood into oppressive nationalism, and to see the reality behind the conventional stereotypes. Out of the medley of emotions, sympathy, exasperation, admiration and despair, that any contemplation of this historical development must evoke, came this book. If it gives non-Afrikaners sufficient material for a revision of their ideas, and provokes sufficient irritation amongst Nationalist Afrikaners to induce them to write more about themselves for outside consumption, it will have served its purpose.

It would be quite impossible to list here the scores of people who have given so generously of their time and knowledge during the two years that it took to write this book. I have thanked each one of them separately and here repeat my most sincere appreciation. I do however owe a particular debt of gratitude to Mr. Adrian Roberts, lately Union High Commissioner in Canada, for his invaluable bibliography, and to Professor Arthur Keppel-Jones, of the University of Natal, Dr. C. H. V. Sutherland, of Christ Church, Oxford, and Mr. Frans Deelman, for their valuable criticisms and factual corrections of various sections of the draft manuscript. Nobody but myself is however to be held responsible for any opinions or conclusions contained in this study.

I should also like to express my appreciation of the efficiency and courtesy with which the Union Bureau of Census and Statistics, the Provincial Administrations and the main Afrikaans-speaking voluntary associations have responded to re-

CHAPTER ONE

GENESIS, EXODUS AND CHRONICLES

'Wherefore come out from among them and be ye separate, thus saith the Lord'

(2 Corinthians, 6: v. 17)

'The importance of an historical event lies, not so much in the extent of its influence upon contemporary thought and action, as upon its propaganda value for a later generation'

(Professor Vincent Harlow)

THE birth-year of the Boer or Afrikaner nation was in 1657. In this year the Dutch East India Company, interested, as always, in penny-pinching, decided that a more economical method must be found of provisioning its Indies-bound ships at the Cape entrepôt, which had been set up five years earlier. The local Hottentots were not an agricultural people, and had proved demanding and capricious when pressed for a regular supply of cattle.

Accordingly, nine free burgers, all of Dutch or German origin, were settled in the Liesbeeck valley. The terms of settlement were sufficiently onerous to lay the foundations of subsequent strife between officialdom and the colonists.

The Company had no intention of creating a colony. The settlers, however, forced its hand by overflowing the Company's wild almond hedge and all the other boundaries subsequently set up, and moving steadily towards the interior. By 1660 the original nine settlers had become sixty, and by 1678 they had spread over the Cape Flats as far as the Hottentots Hollands Mountains. Thereafter followed three decades of assisted white

3

immigration and close European settlement, under a wise and far-seeing Governor, Simon van der Stel. It was a process that might, if continued, have altered radically the history of Southern Africa.

It was in this era that most of the ancestors of the Afrikaners of today arrived in South Africa. The original settlers had been easy-going and unfanatical ex-soldiers or Company servants, usually poorly educated Netherlanders or North Germans. The year 1688, however, saw the arrival of about 200 Huguenots, or roughly one-sixth of the free burger population. These new-comers were characterized by their knowledge of viticulture, by their industriousness and high capacity for organization, by a stern Calvinist fanaticism, and by a rejection of Europe and all her ways. The two latter traits at least were to become part of the Boer ethos. The Huguenots also brought with them the French language. This however was ruthlessly stamped out in the second generation by the authorities, who said firmly that they 'wanted no Quebec in the Cape'. Today, the French language remains only in the lovely, nostalgic names of the Western Cape wine farms, such as Bien Donné, Lorraine, and La Champagne. The Afrikaans-speaking descendants of these du Toits, Malans, Marais and du Plessis, were, however, to resist a century of anglicization with much greater success.

The contemporary Governor, Simon van der Stel, was deter-mined to ensure homogeneity in all spheres. He therefore dis-tributed his Huguenot settlers amongst Dutch and German farmers. Although they tended to group together later in the wine-growing districts of French Hoek, Stellenbosch and Drak-enstein, the Huguenots were soon integrated into settler society by intermarriage, though their darker colouring and stronger features often dominate the blonder northern strain to the present day. Another integrating factor was the growing community of interests and grievances which all settlers felt in opposition to the officials.

These grievances came to a head, and a settlers' front was achieved by the first decade of the eighteenth century. There had long been friction between officials and colonists. The rigorous conditions of the original settlement had been resented, and the Company's arbitrary fixing of grain prices and its ban on cattle-bartering were a continual irritation.

The climax came, and Afrikanerdom's first hero was created, when Simon van der Stel's able but ambitious son William Adriaan succeeded in acquiring for himself and other officials one-third of the colony's farm lands, and in cornering the colony's meat and wine contracts. This was not only strictly contrary to the Company's regulations, but had a throttling effect on the little colony's never too flourishing economy.

A wine farmer called Adam Tas, whose name is perpetuated today in the punning and provocative name of his wine farm 'Libertas', succeeded, despite imprisonment, in smuggling out a petition to the Company. The petition acquainted the Company with the Governor's actions and asked in uncomfortable and forthright terms for his recall. It was signed by sixty-three of the 550-odd adult male free burgers (the total adult population in 1707 was 803). It is worthy of note that half the signatures belonged to the smaller but more politically-conscious Huguenot group.

The colonists won this round and the younger van der Stel was recalled. Their victory was, however, an illusory one, for it confirmed the Company in its view that white colonists were troublesome. As a result, assisted immigration was stopped, and the Afrikaners have from then until the present day had to rely on natural increase and individual immigration for the augmenting of their numbers. A further even, more momentous consequence of the Tas episode was the D.E.I.C.'s official decision in 1717 to import more docile slave labour in preference to the unruly European immigrants.

Commissioner Verburg had reported in 1672: 'The Dutch colonists in the Cape of Good Hope bear the name of free men but they are so trammelled and confined in all things that the absence of any freedom is but too manifest.' Freedom was however a state for which the colonists hankered more and more. If it was not to be had near Capetown, it seemed to beckon them beyond the flats and mountains to the north and east. Uncertain markets, low prices, the labour shortage, were other factors which impelled the colonists on to the dry, sunbaked lands beyond. These lands were well suited to the cattle-farming that fulfilled the Cape market's only steady demand. They also offered a chance of evading officialdom and irksome restrictions.

Quite early in the eighteenth century, Cape society was divided into three sections; the townsmen, the plaas-boers and the vee-boers. First came the officials and company servants in Capetown (three of them to every eight burgers by 1740), and the townsmen who kept boarding-houses and canteens, and traded illegally but avidly. Near by, but separated by the bad roads and their distrust of official rapacity and urban sophistication, were the second group, the settled wine, corn and fruit farmers[1] of the fertile Boland. Each farm was, as Eric Walker described it, 'a state in miniature, producing little more than was needed for the maintenance of its inhabitants, but self-sufficing in everything save luxuries, articles of manufacture, and a few raw materials. But their vineyards, plough-lands and beloved oxen were for them a universe which was bounded by the flats and the mountains of Africa.'

The Boland farmer was no absentee landlord, although he might sometimes oversee his modest quota of slaves from the shade of his stoep. Solidity, moderation and piety were his recognized virtues, and the only hint of luxury was provided by the wedding-cake ornateness of the gables with which the Boland farmers decorated their solid farms after 1781–3, when the unofficial French occupation brought temporary prosperity to the settlement. Despite their early separation from the town, these plaas-boers were nevertheless part of the pattern of organized society. And in the next century they and the townsmen were to evolve a mature and tolerant plural society which was doomed to extinction once the Cape entered Union.

Neither the townsmen nor the plaas-boers were to determine the form of the South African society to be. This was left to the far-wandering vee-boer or cattle farmer, whose evolution will be described elsewhere. Here it must be stressed that this evolution owed much to the initial conflict with unsympathetic

---

[1]The term 'Boer' means farmer, but in the South African context it has rather the significance of 'land-owner'.

officialdom, and the fact that the vee-boers and trek-boers remained intolerant of authority and ready to remove themselves from it the moment it became irksome. The vee-boers came to regard the distant Government as an institution that should not tax but protect. This protection involved sanctioning the farmer's claim to unlimited land, ensuring an adequate supply of non-white labour and high prices for farm produce, and providing arms, ammunition, and if necessary troops to protect the farmer from Bushmen depredations and Kaffir raids. These views on government were later reflected in the Trekker Republics, which de Kiewiet describes as 'land-owning states which had fewer obligations higher than the encouragement and protection of their burgers and their right to land . . . From the beginning too, the power of government was limited by the refusal of burgers to accept any but the lightest restrictions or burdens upon their property.'

Meanwhile, the eighteenth-century gap between officials and colonists continued to widen. There was a petty and abortive rebellion in the north-west, when a landdrost summoned some burgers to court for looting Hottentot cattle while they were out on a forbidden cattle-bartering expedition. The rebel leader was a deserting ex-sergeant who accused the colonial authorities of tyranny and corruption and of favouring Hottentots above white men. More serious was the petition sent to Amsterdam in 1779 by 400 Cape Patriots, protesting forcefully against official venality and legal confusion, and demanding burger representation in government. These Cape Patriots were drawn entirely from the West. All of them lived within a day's ride from Capetown, and their action was not one of withdrawal but, like that of the American colonists, a demand for greater representation of their viewpoint in government.

In the next twenty years the Dutch East India Company drifted into bankruptcy, and the Boers in the eastern districts of Swellendam and Graaff-Reinet rose against its rule. Of the ideas of the French Revolution which had percolated along the long ox-wagon trails, liberty was stressed at the expense of equality and fraternity. The main issue, however, was that of the growing tension between Boer and Bantu on the frontier, exacerbated

7

by the attempts of an energetic landdrost to enforce the rule of law and the rights of both black and white on that frontier. The rebels were quelled by a show of military force when the British occupied the Cape for the first time, in the terms of their treaty with the refugee Prince of Orange. The same Boers rose again abortively in 1799. Between 1803 and 1806 the Cape came under the rule of the Batavian Republic,[1] and the ideas of a new, enlightened Europe entered the local scene.

Officialdom and its excesses or deficiencies were not the only factors to influence the evolution of the Boers. Even more important were the constant contacts, in peace or war, with the non-white peoples. In the white man peaceful contact produced a sense of superiority and the familiarity that breeds contempt, while contact in war bred insecurity, fear, and frequently hatred. These two sets of attitudes survive in uneasy combination in the Afrikaner of today, fixed and hallowed by the habits of generations.

The introduction of slaves into the Cape in 1658 was the first major turning-point in South African history. From then on there was no question of the Cape becoming a white man's country, as its climate and relative emptiness might have entitled it to do. Non-white labour became firmly integrated in the economic sphere and set the pattern for all future economic development in South Africa. Manual, and, for a time, even artisan labour, became the province of the slave, the Hottentot, the mixed-blood and later the Kaffir. Remuneration was non-existent or low, and work done for a master acquired a stigma which few Boers would incur. This occupational gulf was sanctified by custom and persisted long after slavery had vanished. When later the Boers grew too many for the land, the old division of labour stood in the way of their entry into modern indus-

---

[1] Under the terms of the Treaty of Amiens. The Batavian Republic was a mildly revolutionary 'client republic' of Napoleon's France—it entrusted the ruling of the former Dutch East India Company's territories to a Council for the Asiatic Possessions, one of whose members was the liberal De Mist. The liberal interlude was short-lived. In 1806 the British took over the Cape again for good, to safeguard their Indies route. The Cape was formally ceded to Britain under the general peace settlement of 1814.

trial life. This was the genesis of Poor Whiteism. A Poor White problem can only exist where poverty is by custom reserved for non-whites.

Reinforcing the economic colour-bar from the start was a religious sanction. Initially, the line had been drawn between Christian and pagan, and the few non-whites, mainly freed Asiatic slaves, who became Christians, were acceptable in white society. Perhaps the early shortage of white women contributed to this acceptability. The low cultural level of the Hottentots and the low status of the slaves soon, however, caused the three criteria of whiteness, Christianity, and superior social and cultural status to converge. By the end of the eighteenth century 'white man' and 'Christian' were synonymous terms; slave owners had ceased to favour conversion amongst their slaves; and farmers were objecting to the efforts by missionaries to convert and educate the Hottentots.

In succeeding years, Christianity spread to hundreds of thousands of non-whites, and the Christian-heathen and white-black dichotomies could no longer be made to coincide. The Christian-heathen dichotomy thereafter began to lose its force and Christian society acquired a hierarchy of pigmentation. This was reflected in the constitution of the Transvaal Republic, with its harsh stipulation that there should be no equality between whites and people of colour in Church or State. More recently, the Dutch Reformed Church theologians have evolved a concession to conscience, with their doctrine of vertical apartheid and separate chuiches for the different racial groups.

In the settled slave-owning areas the division between black and white and even between slave and free was never so rigid as it became on the frontier. After slavery was abolished in 1834, there evolved a complex socio-economic classification, based on European cultural determinants. In this the lower classes were coloured and the upper classes were largely white. This society drew no harsh lines. It was divided by an ill-guarded frontier area through which able, light-coloured individuals could pass upward, and ill-equipped whites could sink.

Slavery initiated the basic socio-economic division in South African society, but it was the frontier that made it sharp and irrevocable. There were various reasons for this. The frontier Boers were no longer meeting decadent and semi-Europeanized Hottentots and mixed-bloods, or the more cultivated slaves of the Cape. For a century they were exposed to the incessant depredations of the Bushmen, resentful at the loss of their immemorial springs and hunting-grounds. Of this period, the traveller Barrow writes: 'An inhabitant of the Sneeuwberg not only lives under constant apprehension of losing his property, but is perpetually exposed to the danger of being put to death. If he has occasion to go to the distance of five hundred yards from his house, he is under the necessity of carrying a musket. He can neither plough, nor sow, nor reap without being under arms . . . To endure such a life of constant dread and anxiety, a man must be accustomed to it from his infancy and unacquainted with one that is better.'

In the middle of the eighteenth century the Boers came up against the vanguard of an even more formidable foe. The energetic and robust Bantu peoples were moving southwards in quest of the same unlimited land that the Boer cattle farmers sought. During the next three-quarters of a century there were no fewer than eight Kaffir wars. These wars were in fact only the high spots of incessant contact and friction between the two peoples, whose way of life and economic aims were all too similar.

There is no object in examining here the rights and wrongs of the frontier struggle. What is important is the historical myth that the Boers built around the events of this period. This myth found its earliest expression in the writings of the 'Trekkers' historian' Theal. Like most myths it was not entirely divorced from reality, but had all the simplicity of an early American motion picture of cowboys and Indians in the Wild West. The heroes were the simple, peace-loving frontiersmen, anxious to defend their families and farms against the villainous Kaffirs, who were continually pouring over the border to raid, burn and murder. The auxiliary villains were the authorities, who would not defend the frontier adequately but thwarted the frontiersmen's efforts to defend themselves, and the missionaries, who maligned the frontiersmen to the authorities, and treated Hottentots and Kaffirs on an equality with Christian men.

The attitudes which the frontier Boers developed during this period of turbulence have persisted almost unchanged to the present day. Perhaps the most important and potentially dangerous of these attitudes is that which sees the African as an enemy on the other side of a frontier, and not as a member of society at all. It is this attitude that enables the most kindly and humane people to feel satisfied with a system which imposes taxation without representation, moves whole townships arbitrarily from one place to another, restricts the movements of labour-seekers, and in general treats the majority of the population as unwelcome aliens, despite the fact that inseparable economic links have been forged between black and white.

Mention has already been made of the friction between Boers and missionaries; firstly over the latter's attempts to educate and Christianize the Hottentots in the more settled west, secondly because they championed the 'noble Kaffir' on the frontier.

The missionaries were indeed the bearers of a new and explosive set of ideas which were to change the structure of the Cape Colony in a few short decades. The impact of these ideas was also to evoke an equally violent counter-reaction amongst a large section of Boer colonial society. This resentment outlived the missionaries and has since provoked measures designed to nullify their work.

The libertarian Christianity of the missionaries would in any case have percolated into the stagnant pool of the eighteenth-century colony. The effect would, however, have been gradual and possibly more effective in the long run. As it was, the ideas of these meddling missionaries and political parsons had the full backing of the British Colonial Government and of the affluent middle-class public in Britain. To the missionaries or to their allies in Britain could be directly ascribed the formal establishment of political and legal equality for the Hottentots and other free persons of colour, the promulgation of master-and-servant regulations that interfered with the farmers' traditional rights to deal with their servants as they thought best, the abolition of slavery and the emancipation of the slaves.

The effects of these radical and disruptive measures were

enhanced by the day-to-day activities and attitudes of the missionaries. The Boers considered that the missionary institutions interfered with their labour supply by providing a sanctuary where Hottentots could grow idle and insolent. They resented the missionaries' partiality for the heathen, and their much-publicized criticisms of established Boer customs. They were also shocked at the missionaries' impatient disregard of the accepted social barrier between white and non-white.[1]

On the black list of Nationalist Afrikanerdom, the 'meddling missionaries' hold the same high place as the anglicizing pro-consuls. The members of the London Missionary Society occupy the most prominent place and in their forefront stands the Kirk-caldy weaver's son, Dr. John Philip. According to Eric Walker he was 'stiff in opinions, given to hyperbole, and fully endowed with (a) love of disputation'. It was Philip who enlisted the support of Wilberforce and the English philanthropists for the Hottentots; the latter were technically free, but legally and economically in a worse plight than many slaves. Within nine years of Philip's arrival in the Cape his representations in London had secured the promulgation of the famous Ordinance 50 of 1828. This gave all free persons of colour a legal status and economic freedom equivalent to that already possessed by the white population.

Boer distrust of the missionaries was reinforced by a series of of later incidents and clashes in which the missionaries almost invariably figured as highly vocal protagonists of the non-white people against the Boers.[2]

For instance, there was Campbell of the London Missionary Society, who organized a miniature Griqua State on the Vaal River. This resisted the infiltration of land-hungry Boers for some years and, to the outrage of frontier opinion, even at-

---

[1]Dr. van der Kemp, the first representative of the London Missionary Society, married a freed slave girl many years his junior, while his successor Dr. James Read took a Hottentot to wife.

[2]Some American missionaries, and such observers as Mrs. Andrew Murray, Junior, felt indeed that the Boers were just as much in need of spiritual ministrations as were the 'heathen', and that the existing societies should devote some time and money to their plight.

tempted to exercise authority over those Boers who came within its territorial jurisdiction.

In 1840, a Wesleyan missionary living in the kraal of Faku, the Pondo chief, advised the latter to appeal to the British colonial authorities for protection, after the Natal Trekkers had sent a commando on a retaliatory raid on his neighbour's kraal. This incident, although it was not a root cause, influenced the British decision to extend Colonial protection to the tribes beyond the border, and led finally to the British occupation of Natal and to the end of the Natal Voortrekker Republic.

In the 1860's, John Mackenzie of the London Missionary Society incurred further odium for his Society by championing the Bamangwato and the Imperial connexion against repeated attempts by the Transvaal to extend its authority into Bechuanaland. David Livingstone, another member of the London Missionary Society, was suspected of having supplied powder and even guns to the Bakwena tribe, and was accused of having 'taught the tribes to kill Boers'. He himself, with his colleagues Edwards and Inglis, accused the Boers of being slavers, contrary to their own laws. This charge Eric Walker finds substantially justified, and it was one of the factors which led to the British intervention north of the Orange River. In the 1860's, the Free State Volksraad expelled the Paris Evangelical missionaries from Basutoland for politicizing. This action provoked widespread protest in London, and thereby strengthened the case for the British annexation of Basutoland.

Legislation in the Trekker Republics reflected their attitudes to the missionaries. The Nine Articles of 1837 forbade any contact with 'allen den Sendelings Genootscap van Engelant'. The Grondwet of the Transvaal excluded Roman Catholics altogether and discouraged all Churches not linked by the Heidelberg Catechism. Eric Walker gives evidence that the Boers' bark was worse than their bite, except where the London Missionary Society men were concerned. He does, however, mention that even the first Dutch Reformed Church missionaries in the northern Transvaal were very unpopular amongst the Boers there.

Whatever the contemporary Boer attitude, the missionary

from overseas has been built into almost a stage villain by the compilers of nationally-orientated Afrikaner annals. The mythical figure has been rounded out by the recent anti-apartheid activities of various Anglican clerics. The Reverend Michael Scott and Father Trevor Huddleston in particular have succeeded in attracting a world-wide audience for views which have greatly wounded Afrikaner *amour-propre*.

The liberal humanitarianism of the missionaries might, as has been said, have been less disruptive had it not influenced the British administration so directly. Taken by itself, the British administration represented a new and all-embracing system of government which would have proved sufficiently unpalatable to the colonists, and particularly to the frontiersmen, whose idea of government was based on the easy-going slothfulness of the dying Dutch East India Company. But, as Professor H. T. Strauss, Professor of Political Science at the University of the Orange Free State, said in October, 1953, 'the greatest calamity suffered by our nation was the appearance of human-ism on the soil of the fatherland.' Aided by the coming of the nineteenth-century British with their liberal traditions and nascent, revolutionary and democratic political ideas, human-ism had left a 'legacy of religious disaffection which even today causes nothing but trouble and sorrow'.

In addition to the measures designed to protect and improve the lot of the non-white inhabitants, the new rulers within twenty-five years reformed the currency (a step which always involves hardship for some individuals); initiated a vigorous programme of anglicization in Church and schools; planted 5,000 British settlers amongst the frontier Boers; attempted to stabilize the land-system and root the wandering frontier Boers by introducing optional quit-rent tenure in place of the loan-place system which had encouraged poor farming and wander-ing habits; established Circuit Courts which brought the law and its agents right up to the frontier; set up an independent judiciary and drastically reformed the local judiciary, abolishing the old unpaid local representatives and thereby incidentally doing away with the only representative body through which the Boers might have expressed their grievances.

The measures of the new rulers, however admirable and essential, were often modified and even distorted in their effects by such factors as the inconstancy of London colonial policy and the lack of officials and funds to carry out such measures in an undeveloped, impoverished and far-flung colony.

Two episodes occurred in this period of change which have in recent decades become keystones of Afrikaner mythology, exemplifying the most outrageous aspects of the new system. These were the Black Circuit of 1812, and the Slagters Nek Rebellion of 1815. The Black Circuit was the name given to the proceedings of the newly-created court that sat in Uitenhage and George in 1812. Here for the first time whites were hailed into court to answer for misbehaviour towards their Hottentot servants. This in itself was difficult enough to swallow, but the proceedings were embittered further by the large number of baseless or exaggerated charges brought by the zealous London Missionary Society representative, Dr. James Read, on behalf of his charges. He spoke irresponsibly of 'upwards of 100 cases of recent murders in Uitenhage', but, in fact, only twenty-two cases of all kinds were brought before the court. Many of these cases referred to events long past, and less than half were substantiated by a court which consisted of Cape Dutchmen. The shock to conservative frontier opinion, was, however, unbounded. A part of their resentment was directed against the authorities for putting them on a legal equality with their servants and against the missionaries for what was regarded as slanderous partiality.

In the Slagters Nek episode which followed soon afterwards, the missionary factor was lacking, but the essential elements were otherwise the same. The frontier Boer, Frederick Bezuidenhout, had for two years refused to answer a court summons on a charge of cruelty to a Hottentot servant. When a white officer and twelve Hottentot troops were sent to arrest him, he fired on them and was killed in the affray that followed. To many frontiersmen, this was yet another instance of the tyrannical excess of the new rulers. It was aggravated by the fact that the charge laid against the dead man had been made by a Hottentot and that Hottentot soldiers had been sent to bring him in.

15

Bezuidenhout's brother, Johannes, the influential Hendrik Prinsloo and a group of malcontents thereupon planned a rebellion. In this enterprise they were somewhat illogically prepared to make an ally of Gaika the Xosa Chief, although he was their erstwhile enemy and a Kaffir in addition.

Many Boers in the east did not support the plan, and the rebels finally rode out less than 200 strong. At the actual encounter at Slagters Nek, not a shot was fired. Most of the insurgents rode away and surrendered later. Johannes Bezuidenhout shot it out on his farm and died of wounds. Forty-seven prisoners were finally brought to trial under the old harsh unreformed Roman-Dutch Law. Thirty-two were banished from the frontier districts and six were sentenced to be hanged by the Cape Dutch judges who composed the special commission. One rebel was pardoned, but the rest were hanged on the spot where the rebel oath had been taken. The circumstances of the hanging were described by an eye-witness as 'horrid and distressing'. They supplied an additional goad to contemporary and later outrage. The rope broke, so that four of the five condemned men fell to the ground and had to be hanged all over again, despite their pleas for mercy.

This minor and half-hearted rebellion has, particularly in the last few decades, become one of the rallying-cries of Nationalist Afrikanerdom. Alleged relics of the gallows are still peddled and the non-participation of the majority of frontier Boers is forgotten. The Cape Dutch officials who defeated, tried and sentenced the rebels are regarded as traitors. At their head stands the Veld-Kommandant Nel, who, according to Cory, is thought to have induced the Boers to surrender by swearing that they would suffer no harm. The undocumented story ran that he watched the execution with a reprieve in his pocket, and that pangs of conscience drove him to suicide three months later.

Over the next twenty years, unrest and resentment grew amongst the frontier Boers. These Boers had by the last half of the eighteenth century become a very singular group, living a very singular and unchanging way of life. They had, in effect, become white Africans, or Afrikaners, as they sometimes called themselves. They had adapted themselves to the slow African rhythm of movement and to the semi-nomadic pastoralism and subsistence economy dictated by the African climate and soil. They did not dominate their environment, but like the Bantu made a successful adjustment to it. Only when the Boer and the Bantu clashed, and the supply of free grazing lands beyond the horizon dried up for both groups, did it become clear that the land could not support two such independent communities side by side.

Ecologically then, the frontier Boer lived the simplest of self-sufficient lives. Natural dangers were few, the climate moderate, and food and water were easily obtained. The frontier Boer's home was a thatched hut built of earth or reeds, or even a trek-wagon. His staple diet was meat, supplemented by the more settled and energetic with fruit and a little wheat. His clothes and shoes he usually made himself, and all he ever needed to buy was gunpowder, some cloth, coffee, brandy and various implements. These he paid for by the occasional sale of cattle, butter and soap to the roving butchers' agents. Regular markets were distant or non-existent and the frontiersmen had in any case been discouraged by the early monopolistic restrictions of the Company. Little of the land beyond the settled western Cape was suitable for intensive arable farming. The loan-place[1] system, with its relative insecurity of tenure, led to over-grazing and improvident farming. It also stimulated rapid dispersal and the restlessness which lay behind the 'trekgees' of later days. The frontier Boer was not deeply attached to any particular farm or building, but to his cattle, his way of life, and the land as a whole.

Wealth on the frontier was reckoned not in cash but in cattle and sons. Sons there were in plenty, but the constant Kaffir raids discouraged the accumulation of enormous herds. In a society where any men could acquire land for the asking, a

---

[1]The loan-places were great cattle-runs of 3,000 morgen or more, held on loan from the Company for a year at a time. In practice the grants were rarely resumed. The holder's heirs were entitled by law only to the value of the house and other improvements. The government made no charge at all until 1714, after which it levied an annual rent of £2. 10s. Many farmers held more than one such loan-place.

society which had come to regard 6,000 acres as every Boer's birthright, there were no hereditary class distinctions. All men were potentially equal, and few white men worked for a master.

Such a life could not fail to stimulate a spirit of self-reliance and independence. This made men intolerant of the distant demands of officialdom. Each patriarch administered his own law amongst his family, his Hottentot servants and his slaves (though relatively few families in the East were slave owners).

In time of war, the frontier Boers would assemble, not always enthusiastically, in the military unit evolved by them for frontier needs, the commando. This was under the command of a local official who was a farmer like themselves. When the danger was over, the Boers fell away again into their isolation.

In one aspect of life only did the frontier Boers dominate their environment. A law unto themselves they might be, but the great majority were not lawless. This was due to their profound attachment to their Calvinist faith. In the all too familiar phrase, the Boer went into the wilderness with a gun in one hand and his Bible in the other. This was usually the only book in a frontier household, but its influence was paramount. Predikants and churches were few and far between, but the Old Testament from which their initial Calvinism had been drawn now provided a manual of behaviour entirely suited to the frontier Boers.

As the historian Theal wrote so vividly, the frontier Boer lived 'under such skies as those under which Abraham lived. His occupation was the same, he understood the imagery of the Hebrew writers more perfectly than anyone in Europe would understand it, for it spoke to him of his daily life. He had heard the continuous roll of thunder which was as the voice of the Lord upon many waters, and had seen the affrighted antelope drop their young as they fled before the storm, when the great trees came down with a crash and the lightning divided like flames of fire. He knew too of skies like brass and of earth like iron, of little clouds seemingly no larger than a man's hand presaging a deluge of rain, and of swarms of locusts before whose track was the Garden of the Lord, while behind was a naked desert.'

In general then, the frontier Boers were independent, self-reliant, unimaginative, tenacious, enduring, roughly courteous, hospitable, devout, restless in their movements, but narrowly conservative in their thinking. Contemporary views of them ranged from the earlier judgement of the Batavian de Mist in about 1800 that these 'half-wild Europeans' were rebellious and unreasonable, and suffered from a 'complete corruption of their moral sense',[1] to the eulogies of Theal, and Sir Benjamin d'Urban's approving tribute to 'a brave, patient, orderly and religious people.'

On these frontier Boers, untouched by a century of European thought, and undiluted by any appreciable later addition to their numbers, there descended, from the second decade of the nineteenth century, the full impact of the new ideas and the new rulers. Liberalism and philanthropic negrophilism were buttressed by a centralizing authority. The rule of law was enforced, and an unsuccessful attempt was made to turn the roving subsistence farmers into intensive and settled agriculturalists. Rather than suffer these changes, most Boers were prepared to trek. A handful had already turned north beyond the Colonial border and moved over the Orange River.

Over and above these man-made inflictions, the frontier Boers were for the next decade subjected to a series of natural scourges. Drought, floods and Kaffirs plagued the eastern border, and the Government failed in Boer eyes to deal satisfactorily with the latter or to allow anyone else to do so in its place. In 1836, a particularly severe drought and the British Government's economy-minded decision to restore the newly-annexed territory of Queen Adelaide Land to the Kaffir tribes

---

[1]This judgement was later modified. General Dundas was, however, even blunter. He called them a 'troublesome and disaffected race', 'the strongest compound of cowardice and cruelty, of treachery and cunning, and of most the bad qualities with few, very few, good ones of mind', (Cory, p. 196). In general, the opinions of those hostile to the Boers tended to survive, and their continued immoderate tone may help to explain the deep resentment of criticism and sense of being misunderstood which the Boers developed and have maintained to this day.

touched off the mass movement of population which was to be called the Great Trek. Despite the later myth and grievances that grew around it, the Great Trek was, as de Kiewiet writes: 'In one sense but an acceleration on a large scale of the movement of expansion that had been going on for centuries. Since the end of the eighteenth century an important section of the population had been checked in its freedom of movement by the opposing native tribes . . . Tactically, the Great Trek represented a decision to give up the frontal attack and undertake an outflanking movement. When fully carried out, it was a manœuvre that carried the colonists beyond the range of British influence and enabled them to strike at the vital resources of the natives at numerous points.'

The leaders of the Trek left their own versions of the grievances that drove them to seek a new land without boundaries or irksome officialdom. Piet Retief published a Manifesto in the *Grahamstown Journal* in 1837. His first three points concerned the prevalence of coloured vagrancy (following the granting of equivalent legal status to Hottentots and other 'free persons of colour' in 1828); losses caused by emancipation (Retief was one of the few Voortrekkers who had been a slave-owner and the regulations affecting compensation were extremely irksome and petty); and losses caused by the 'continual system of plunder endured from Caffres and other coloured classes.' 'We are resolved' he wrote, 'wherever we go that we will uphold the just principles of liberty; but whilst we will take care that no one shall be held in a state of slavery, it is our determination to maintain such regulations as may suppress crime and preserve proper relations between master and servant.'

The grievances over vagrancy, plundering by Kaffirs and emancipation were stressed by most Trekkers who recorded their motives. Apart from the economic losses involved, there was widespread resentment at the sort of legislation which placed slaves on an equal footing with Christians and enabled Hottentots to run wild and to bring exaggerated charges against their ex-masters. Ordinance 50 of 1828 and Emancipation constituted a social revolution which struck at the whole Boer way of life.

Land hunger, economic and human losses,[1] insecurity and restlessness, the vexatious interference of officialdom and outrage at the attack on their established social system; all these were inflated and enhanced by a general feeling of personal outrage at the 'unjustifiable odium cast on us by interested and dishonest persons under the cloak of religion, to the exclusion of all evidence in our favour'.

By 1834, the idea was being whispered about the Boer farms of a mass trek to a land of their own where they might be 'left to themselves', to live in quiet, free and exempt from taxation'. Scouting parties were already out in 1835. These parties found Natal, land of milk and honey, and the inland plains, seemingly empty of tribes. The emptiness, though they could not know it, was a temporary phenomenon due to the devastations of Shaka and Dingaan. Later in the same year the two first important treks crossed the Orange River. They were followed during the next three years by some 10,000 to 12,000 Boers. The unit was the small trek party, under a patriarch or local official; each small party usually owed allegiance to one of the principal leaders. These pioneers alone are entitled to be honoured as Voortrekkers, although the Cape Boers continued to trek to the Republics for many years to come.

During that short period, as de Kiewiet points out, a thin layer of Boer settlement spread over the most desirable part of the interior, already settled by a virile Bantu population. This made the territorial segregation of the two races forever impossible, and linked the whole future of South Africa with the Boer race. In the interior, the Trekkers gained two more generations for their own way of life, beyond the reach of the Colonial authorities or the new ideas.

---

[1]"Seven thousand of His Majesty's subjects were in one week driven to utter destitution; 100 Europeans and Hottentots had been killed, 455 farms had been burnt, and many thousands of horses, cattle and sheep carried off, and, of the cattle taken or retaken, most had been eaten by the troops and commandos during nine months of war, and now many burghers were too impoverished to buy the remnant at auction, even with two months' credit. The total colonial losses amounted to perhaps £300,000.' (Eric Walker, *History of South Africa*, p. 194.)

The events of the Trek itself have passed into legend. This process was greatly facilitated by the paucity of written Trekker documents. The Trek came to be seen as the birth of a nation, as an Exodus with Retief as the Boers' Moses, and Natal as the Promised Land. In vain did the Dutch Reformed Church condemn the Trek as an Exodus without a Moses or the certainty of a Canaan, and refuse to send ministers to accompany the Boers in their flight from Pharaoh.

The frieze inside the Voortrekker Monument near Pretoria shows the main events of the Trek as they are remembered by the present generation of Afrikaners. Among its highlights are the Battles of Vegkop in 1836 and of Kapain in 1837, the second of which drove the Matabele north of the Limpopo and cleared the Transvaal for Boer settlement;[1] the trek of Retief's and Maritz's parties over the Drakensberg to Natal; Retief's negotiations with, and subsequent treacherous murder by, the Zulu King, Dingaan; Dingaan's slaughter of the Boers at the place which came to be called Weenen, the Place of Weeping; further disastrous encounters with the Zulus; the Vow taken by the Trekkers under their new leader Pretorius, at the battle which overthrew Dingaan at Blood River in 1838; the building of the Church of the Vow at Pietermaritzburg; Trekker women doing their men's work while the men were in the field; the murder of the fugitive Dingaan by the Swazis; the British occupation of Natal and the return trek over the Drakensberg to escape from British rule; and finally the Sand River Convention of 1852 which officially terminated the Trek, when the British acknowledged the independence of the 15,000 Boers beyond the Vaal.

In essentials, the modern legend of the Trek perpetuates the hostility, treacherousness and savagery of the African, the unwarranted interference and dog-in-the-manger attitude of the British authorities, and, as is only reasonable, the simplicity, piety, courage and endurance of Trekker men, women and children.

---

[1] Trekker myths do not usually stress the fact that the Trekkers, not then so delicate about arming black men as their descendants are today, allied themselves with the Barolong against the Matabele.

Courage and endurance there were in plenty, but the Trek was not perhaps so difficult nor so unique as it has been pictured, at least in comparison with the opening up of the far greater expanses of the North American West. The Drakensberg was the only considerable natural obstacle, and the formidable Zulu and Matabele empires were apparently broken within a few years. This does not of course mean that the Voortrekkers did not pay highly in losses of men and livestock, in insecurity, in discomfort and nostalgia.

The Trek has been divided into two stages. The first stage began in 1835; it took the Voortrekkers out of the Colony, Retief and Pretorius to Natal, Potgieter to Potchefstroom and Louis Trichardt on a *via dolorosa* as far as Delagoa Bay. The second trek began in 1843, the year of the British occupation of Natal. This occupation, followed by the annexation of Transorangia in 1848, drove all the most determined and irreconcilable elements over the Drakensberg and the Vaal into what was soon to become the South African Republic.

This second trek helped to differentiate the subsequent histories of the Orange Free State and the South African Republic. The former had already a substantial settlement of pre-Trek Boers, who had no quarrel with the Colonial Government and dissociated themselves very strongly from Trekker politics. These pre-Trek Boers were soon reinforced by the most stable and the least adventurous Trekkers, for whom one trek was enough, and by land-hungry newcomers from the Cape. Northward over the Vaal went the remainder of the Voortrekkers, a group of independent, unquiet, opinionated and factious individuals who were still far from being a nation. They were united mainly by their bitter resentment over the insidious British policy of following them up and reaping the benefits of Boer pioneering and endurance.

By the Sand River Convention of 1852 Britain recognized Boer independence north of the Vaal. In 1854, motives of false economy drove her to do the same in the territories north of the Orange River, despite the protests of a substantial section of its Boer inhabitants. This short-sighted move made it possible for Transvaal attitudes and policies to dominate a far larger area of

Southern Africa and thereby radically influenced future history.

Nevertheless, the Orange Free State, with its 'quiet pastoral people' and its proximity to the Cape, developed gradually but surely into a homogeneous little republic, where Boer, Briton and Jew lived in tolerance and harmony. As its motto it adopted the virtues: 'Patience and Courage'.

Across the Vaal the warring leaders continued to bicker, and the rank-and-file spread inexorably over the land, until this gave out in the 1870's. Each farm had a minimum area of 6,000 acres. Speculation was none the less rife. Some farms swelled to a quarter of a million acres, and a number of them were held by absentee owners. Much of this land was already owned by African tribes who had been driven off it temporarily during the 'Mfecane' (crushing) caused by Shaka the Zulu. Returning to find their land rights usurped, these Africans remained on it as squatters and labourers, an integrated part of the whole economy. Today Afrikaners are apt to defend themselves against outside criticism of their race attitudes by pointing out that their Voortrekker ancestors did not, like some other colonizing powers, follow the policy of extermination of the aborigines, and indeed saved these from further extermination by their own people.

The Transvaal Boers required little of their government but protection of their land rights; it was to be, and indeed by virtue of the population's composition had to be, a government of Boers, for Boers and by Boers.[1] In 1856 the factions came together sufficiently to draw up a rambling and highly flexible constitution; this could be and frequently was amended by a simple majority in the Volksraad. Anarchical conditions and centrifugal bickering between factions persisted however for the next quarter of a century. Political anarchy was accompanied by administrative inexperience and ineptitude, and conditions of economic chaos, verging on near ruin. An attempt by Marthinus Wessels Pretorius immediately after the ratifying of this constitution to unite the Boers south and north of the Vaal failed ignominiously.

---

[1] A land-owner acquired citizen rights easily, a landless man less easily.

The feeling of loose Boer community, south as well as north of the Vaal, developed into nationhood largely as a result of the alternation of fumbling vacillation and imperialistic leap-frog which characterized British colonial policy for the rest of the century. The penny-wise withdrawal from the Free State in 1854 was followed by London's rejection of Sir George Grey's bold federation plan to link the Free State, Natal and the Cape. In 1868, however, came the swing of the pendulum and the Free State was deprived of what it regarded as the fruits of victory by Wodehouse's annexation of Basutoland.

In 1870 the discovery of diamonds at what is now Kimberley gave added significance to the claim of Nicholas Waterboer, a half-breed Griqua chief, to the territory involved. The southern territory was claimed by the Free State on the grounds of occupation and prescription: by Waterboer, advised by an imperialist law agent called Arnot, on the basis of treaties with the Colonial authorities. North of the Vaal, the disputed territories were claimed on a reversed basis, the Transvaal depending on treaties, the Bantu tribes on occupation. Apart from its diamondiferous possibilities, the disputed territory was on the road to the north, the so-called Missionaries' Road. In Boer hands it could be used to check any British advance into the interior.

On arbitration the case went against the Transvaal in the north. In the south the Griqua chief appealed for British protection and Sir Henry Barkly, new High Commissioner, annexed the whole of Griqualand West to the British Crown. This latter action, coming as it did just after the discovery of diamonds in the area, deeply embittered the Free Staters and turned them back on the Transvaal. Some decades later, the historian Theal, who had lived through this event, thought the annexation had done more to alienate Briton and Boer than any other happening.

Federation, or confederation, nevertheless remained in the air, for reasons of order, economy and defence against the African. It found such supporters as the moderate President of the Free State, J. H. Brand, and J. H. Hofmeyr of the Cape. The possibility of federation was, however, effectively dispelled by

25

the premature annexation of the Transvaal, stage-managed between President Burgers and Shepstone. This action brought strong protests from Kruger and the mass of burgers, from the Free State, and even from Hofmeyr and other Cape leaders who had formerly supported federation. The annexation, indeed, helped to consolidate the Cape Dutch as a self-conscious political group.

After their early tame submission, the national feeling of the Transvaal Boers crystallized under the energetic leadership of Kruger, when the British failed to honour Shepstone's pledge to give the Transvaal self-government. The final British destruction of the Zulu military power which had menaced the Transvaal borders, and the new authorities' firm method of extracting taxes, gave the Boers an added incentive to rid themselves of their unwanted overlords. In December, 1880, over 5,000 Transvaal burgers came together at Paardekraal, decreed the restoration of the Republic and started the First War of Independence. The British were routed at Majuba, and the Transvaal's independence was recognized by the Pretoria Convention. The British Government, however, reserved its suzerainty over the Republic's external and frontier affairs, a step that was later to prove a considerable bone of contention. The Convention also defined the boundaries of the Transvaal on all sides, thereby for the first time setting a final horizon for the endless trek to new lands.

Majuba and the withdrawal from the Transvaal brought humiliation to the British, and imbued the Boers with a perhaps excessive self-confidence and a growing consciousness of nationhood. This consciousness now reached well beyond the Transvaal borders, and was summed up in the war-cry of the *Free State Express*: 'Africa for the Afrikanders'. Jan Hofmeyr wrote: 'The annexation of the Transvaal has taught the people of South Africa that blood is thicker than water. It has filled the (Cape) Africanders, otherwise grovelling in the mud of materialism, with a national glow of sympathy for the brothers across the Vaal, which we look upon as one of the most hopeful signs for the future'.

Meanwhile the Boer Republics were ceasing to be Britain's

personal problem. Germany, in particular, was moving into Southern Africa from the western seaboard. The danger was that she might join up with the Transvaal, and by occupying Bechuanaland cut the Missionaries' Road to the north. There was even a chance that Germany might claim the open Pondo coast south of Durban, or the north coast up to Delagoa Bay. These dangers were averted by the British annexation of the whole Natal coast and of Bechuanaland. German pressure eased for a while after the Berlin Conference of 1884–5. Within ten years, however, came Kruger's pro-German speech on the Kaiser's birthday, the appearance of German officers in the Transvaal and of German warships in Delagoa Bay, and, after the failure of the Jameson Raid, the Kaiser's over-exuberant telegram of congratulation to Kruger.

Apart from the ever-present danger that she might become a pawn in European power politics, the Transvaal's hopes of being left in peace after the Pretoria Convention were destroyed for ever by the discovery of gold on the Witwatersrand in 1886. Within a few years the gold rush had created an Uitlander population on the Rand which outnumbered the original Boers by two to one. The nearly bankrupt Transvaal soon grew wealthy on the taxes imposed on the mines and the Uitlander population.

Politically and socially, however, the Republic was totally unequipped to adjust itself to the new conditions and to the new inhabitants. The adjustment from an ox-wagon to a machine economy would have been difficult enough in a homogeneous society. Here the new economy and the new ideas were brought by aggressive and impatient outsiders, most of them speaking the language of the old oppressors. These differences were accentuated by Kruger's Dutch and German advisers, who had their own reasons for wishing to build an independent Boer national state across the path of British expansion in Africa.

The Uitlanders were a mixed bag of cosmopolitan adventurers, tough miners from England, and steady Dutch and English colonists from the Cape. To the stern Dopper President Kruger, sitting on his stoep in quiet Pretoria some thirty miles over the veld, Johannesburg might look like Babylon or Gomorrah. As mining towns went, however, it was not over-disorderly and was rapidly acquiring a stable population of skilled artisans and trained employees.

These Uitlanders had a number of grievances against the Transvaal administration. Most of them were genuine enough, but they were exaggerated by imperialists and politicians. The most bitterly felt grievances were the harsh naturalization and franchise regulations introduced after 1882, which made it virtually impossible for any immigrant to become a burger. Kruger, on the other hand, quite reasonably considered that if the franchise were granted to these alien newcomers, who outnumbered the original inhabitants seven to three by 1895, the Republic and the way of life for which the Boers had fought and suffered for so long must inevitably disappear.

Other Uitlander grievances concerned the lack of State support for English-speaking schools, the refusal of the right of public meeting, and the rough hostility with which the President often greeted deputations seeking peaceable redress. To one he said: 'Go back and tell your people I shall never give them anything; I shall never change my policy, and now let the storm burst'.

These were the grievances of the settled rank-and-file, most of whom were men of South African birth. To these grievances were added the irritation of the magnates, who were barely concerned with the franchise, at the inefficiency and corruption of the Republican Government and the irksome and discriminatory mining tariffs, monopolies and concessions, through whose agency Kruger milked the mining industry of its excess profits. However wise the old President's mining policy may seem to modern economists, it was greatly resented by the Randlords in 1895.

Even at this stage, events in South Africa might have moved to a peaceable solution. Opposed to each other were the obstinate old President, who as a child had taken part in the Great Trek, and who believed that the earth was flat, and Cecil John Rhodes, the magnate and imperialist, whose methods of achieving his grandiose ends could be both crude and unscrupulous, and whose impatience and recklessness were to increase as his life ran out. Kruger had always represented the extreme of Boer nationalism, and he was falling more and more under the influence of his German and Dutch advisers, the so-called 'Hollander clique', headed by Leyds. Rhodes, however, was still far from being the idol of the Jingo imperialists. His expansive vision of federation included Briton and Boer alike, and he was until the fatal year of 1896 working hand in hand to this end with the moderate Cape Dutch leader, Jan Hofmeyr, and his Afrikaner Bond.

In the Free State, President Brand had exerted his great moderation and wisdom in the direction of friendly relations with the Cape Colony and eventual confederation on a non-racial basis where whites were concerned. In the Transvaal itself, there was considerable Boer opposition to Kruger and Krugerism. This opposition was based on the resentment felt by many Transvaal Boers with Cape links and Cape orientation against the opinionated and arrogant 'Hollander clique'. The opposition included such individuals as Joubert, Schalk Burger, Louis Botha, Chief Justice Kotze, Eugene Marais of *Land en Volk* and Celliers of *Die Volkstem*. In 1892–3, indeed, Joubert was only narrowly defeated by Kruger in the presidential election. Under such men the Transvaal might have made the great and inevitable transition from the eighteenth-century veld to the modern capitalist world peacefully and gradually rather than by force.

As the first years of the 1890's passed, however, the moderating factors ceased to operate. Rhodes' impatience and Kruger's intransigence grew; the clamour of the Uitlanders, whether magnates or rank-and-file, swelled, and the Colonial Government became increasingly nervous about German intervention and the consequences of continued local Balkanization.

At the end of 1895 the interplay of these factors led to one of the most futile and unhappy events in all South African history —the Jameson Raid. The relative complicity of various British officials may remain in some doubt, but the significance of the Raid for the future of British-Boer relations was established immediately. As Dr. Jean van der Poel points out in her study of the Raid, the shielding of Chamberlain left the latter in power, a determined and temporarily discomfited imperialist, and aroused so deep a suspicion of the British Government in Boer minds as to vitiate the Boer-British negotiations that took place in the years between the Raid and the outbreak of war. These years were not, however, without genuine attempts at compromise by President Kruger, whose Hollander advisers were now yielding place to Cape Afrikaners, by Milner and even by the Rand magnates; these attempts were amplified by the sustained mediation of Hofmeyr, President Steyn and other Afrikaners from the Cape and Free State.

The immediate effect of the Raid was to strengthen both extremes. The Cape Colony was split apart on racial lines for years to come. Hofmeyr and other Cape moderates broke with Rhodes in sorrow and disillusionment. A young advocate called J. C. Smuts abandoned his British nationality and settled in the Transvaal, where he was soon to become State Attorney. The Free State turned northward for the last time, to ally itself to the Transvaal in a full military alliance. In the Transvaal itself, Kruger's hand was immensely strengthened vis-a-vis the more moderate opposition, and Britain became suspect, not only for her present actions but for all ambiguous deeds in the past. Lastly, the Raid arrested the slow move of all South African territories towards unity, without affecting the economic and political considerations that made such unity necessary and inevitable. Over the next few years Boer suspicions and bitterness were intensified by British attempts to conceal official complicity and to whitewash and even lionize Rhodes and Jameson.

At the centre of the storm, the Uitlanders' last condition was worse than their first. New laws were passed which seemed to threaten their precarious civil status still further. In 1899 some 21,000 Uitlanders petitioned the Queen for protection, thereby raising again the controversial issue of suzerainty.[1] At this stage Lord Milner, whose temperament was decisive and uncompromising, seems to have made up his mind to radical measures. He cabled London that the helotry of British subjects in the Transvaal was a matter of South African concern, and

---

[1] Twenty-three thousand however, signed a counter-petition in favour of the Government.

that to win the franchise for them would be a striking proof that Her Majesty's Government was not to be ousted from her rightful opposition in South Africa by heavily armed republics. Joseph Chamberlain replied that he was prepared to press the franchise issue and therefore that of paramountcy to all lengths.

At the instance of the mediators, a conference was held at Bloemfontein. This was rendered abortive as much by the unyielding character of the two protagonists as by their considerable differences of viewpoint. President Kruger had by then made up his mind that no concessions could prevent a further British attempt on Boer independence, and he was prepared for war, 'firm in the confidence that the God of Battles must be on their side'. A further attempt at concessions in August failed and both sides drifted into war. Feeling that time would only work against their side, the Transvaal Volksraad drafted an ultimatum demanding the withdrawal of British troops from their border, and the departure of all troops newly arrived in Africa or still on the high seas. So began the Anglo-Boer War, which the Afrikaners call the English War or the Second War of Independence. This war left as great a scar on the group memory of the defeated as did the War between the States. Of it one of its leaders, General Smuts, wrote: 'The Boer War was other than most wars. It was a vast tragedy in the life of a people, whose human interest has surpassed its military value . . . (It was an) epic struggle between the smallest and the greatest of peoples'.

An epic struggle it was indeed. The British put nearly 450,000 men into the field from first to last and spent £223 million. Against them the Boers numbered 87,000 men under arms. About 40,000 of these were Transvaal burgers and nearly 30,000 Free Staters. In addition there were some regulars, cosmopolitan volunteers, and over 13,000 Cape Dutch or Colonial rebels. The fact that there were no more of the latter, despite the strongly pro-Boer feelings of most Cape Dutch after the Jameson Raid, was probably due to the firm discouragement of disloyal activities by Hofmeyr and the Afrikaner Bond.

The problem of this divided loyalty has been immortalized in C. Louis Leipoldt's *Oom Gert Vertel* (Uncle Gert's Tale). This poem tells of the two young Cape Afrikaners who run away to join a Boer commando. They are caught, convicted and hanged; the same day two more follow their example. The older man, having tried to dissuade them, helps them as far as he can. Hofmeyr, who in both wars called upon the Colonial Afrikaners to show their sympathy by legal means and to contribute money to help the widows and orphans, fully understood this clash of loyalties. He had worked untiringly for conciliation in the decade before the war, despite accusations of disloyalty from both sides. Later he was both to advocate a general amnesty for the Colonial rebels and to issue a manifesto condemning the reverse process, the ostracism of the 'loyal Dutch' by Boer supporters.

The Anglo-Boer War was by no means the straightforward two-sided contest between Briton and Boer portrayed by later Nationalist historians. In the Cape, Schreiner's Government had made every effort to avert the conflict, and public opinion was obviously far from united. Even Rhodes, who was keeping in the background of Cape politics, at the end of the war's organized stage in 1900 warned the extreme anti-Boers that, while Krugerism had been overthrown, the Dutch remained and they would have to go on living together. In Britain itself there was strong opposition from the small I.L.P. under Keir Hardie, Snowdon, and Macdonald, and from such individual members of the Liberal Party as Wedgewood Benn, John Morley, Lloyd George and John Burns. The *Manchester Guardian* and Wickham Steed's *Review of Reviews* also attacked the Government. In the Khaki Election of August, 1900, seven votes were cast against Chamberlain's policy for every eight in favour. In the concentration camps which were set up for Boer women and children in the Republics, Emily Hobhouse and many other Britons worked indefatigably to improve the conditions which they regarded as a blot on their country's good name.

Apart from the continental volunteers on the Boer side, a fair number of English-speaking men living in the Republics joined the Boer commandos, and fought with them to the end. On the other hand, some Cape Dutch fought for the British, and a large number of Republican Boers took an oath of neutrality to the British after the first part of the war. Some 4,500 even joined the British forces as 'National Scouts' or 'Volunteers'.

The actual motives of those Boers who did not support the Boer cause were various and not always deserving of censure. Afrikaner national memory is however long and censorious, and the terms 'Handsopper', 'National Scout' and even 'Loyal Dutch' still carry the full opprobrium reserved for collaborators and quislings in Europe.

The war itself fell into two stages. The first was the regular campaign which ended with President Kruger's departure for Europe in August 1900, and Roberts' annexation of the Free State and Transvaal in May and September of that year respectively. The second was that of guerilla warfare, which continued until May 1902.

The first part of the war began with the Boer successes at Magersfontein and Colenso. At this stage the Boers outnumbered the British two to one, and should have invaded the Cape Colony to increase their strength by recruiting from the rural population, which was largely on their side. For this type of warfare, however, the Boer lack of an over-all command or of discipline in the field proved fatal. Denys Reitz writes of the siege of Ladysmith: 'Discipline was slack and there was a continual stream of burghers going home on self-granted leave, so that we never knew from day to day what strength we mustered'. The tide turned for the British with the relief of Kimberley, and the surrender of Cronje and 4,000 Free Staters at Paardeberg. After eleven months, Roberts considered the war over and sailed for home.

At this stage Boer individualism and self-reliance came into its own. Small, semi-independent commandos continued to fight for the next eighteen months, and the task of suppressing them drove the British into a policy whose consequences were to embitter Boer-British relations for decades to come.

At the beginning the British held the towns and the railway lines, which were defended by barbed wire and block-houses at frequent intervals. This was intended to cut the veld into compartments which would be cleared separately. The non-uniformed Boers, on the other hand, could rely on every farmhouse for supplies and information. Despite the protests of Milner, who was entrusted with the task of reconstruction,

Kitchener urged military necessity and applied a scorched-earth policy so indiscriminately that by the end of the war hardly a farmhouse was left standing, while crops were destroyed and stock driven away or slaughtered.

As an eye-witness, Denys Reitz, wrote: 'We rode over interminable plains devoid of human beings. We did not see a single homestead that was not in ruins, and at some places lay hundreds of sheep clubbed to death or bayoneted by the British troops, in pursuance of their scheme of denuding the country of livestock to starve out the Boers'. Elsewhere he qualifies this by referring to the 'unfailing humaneness' of the English soldiers, both officers and men. Contemporary accounts, indeed, abound with instances of chivalrous and comradely acts on both sides—despite the myth that has been built round it, the Boer War was in some aspects the last 'gentleman's war'.

The women and children and the farm servants whose homes were thus destroyed were hurriedly concentrated into canvas camps, mainly against their will. These camps were improvised and often badly run. The rations were usually those available for the army, and ideas of hygiene amongst both officials and inmates were rudimentary. The spread of epidemics amongs the Boers had been limited by their isolation. In the camps, typhoid, enteric and even measles fed on proximity, until some 26,000 women and children died. The death rate from fever amongst the British soldiers was heavy too, but the child mortality in some camps would have been sufficient if continued to ensure the extinction of the entire child population. Conditions varied from camp to camp and gradually improved, thanks to the importation of trained Anglo-Indian officials and the efforts of such individuals as Emily Hobhouse.

At the end of the war there were some 120,000 Boers and 80,000 Africans in separate camps, and the death rate was down to reasonable proportions, judged in terms of the normal high Boer infantile mortality rate. At this stage General Louis Botha expressed his thankfulness that so many of the Boers' families were in British hands, while the 'bitter-ender' President Steyn adduced the state of the camps as an argument for continuing the war.

The concentration camps were nevertheless to become the ultimate indictment against Britain. It is an indictment which persists to this day, in a form which permits national-minded Afrikaners who have experienced neither at first-hand to compare Heilbron and Vredefort with Belsen and Dachau. Ramsay Macdonald was right when he wrote after the war: 'I simply state the facts that hundreds of women fled before our columns for months and months, preferring the hardship of the veldt to the mercy of camps . . . We have to face this fact, which no one who knows the country dare dispute—that the camps were a profound mistake; that families on the veldt or in caves fared better and suffered a lower mortality rate than those in the camps; that the appalling mortality of the camps lies at our door (one of the saddest things I have ever seen in my life was a camp graveyard with its tiny crowded crosses: it looked like a nursery of crosses); that the camps have created a fierce bitterness among the women and the young generation; that when every other memory of the war will have faded away, the nightmare shadows of the camps will still remain'.

By May 1902 the Boer rank and file had had enough, although 21,000 of them were still in the saddle.[1] There was no further hope of a rising in the Cape Colony or of European intervention, but there was hope of a Liberal Government in England. The formerly pacific Free Staters resisted longest, but finally representatives of the two Republics met at Vereeniging and agreed by a vote of 54–6 to sign a peace treaty. The peace party votes were mainly those of the Transvaalers, such as Schalk Burger, Lukas Meyer, Botha and Smuts. They were joined later by Hertzog and de Wet of the Free State. President Steyn, bitterly resentful of the Transvaalers for dragging his Free State into a quarrel which was none of her making, and then expecting her to give up her independence, resigned rather than submit. Some 'bitter-enders' refused to take the oath of allegiance, and either remained abroad or emigrated to non-British

---

[1] Six thousand men were dead, and 32,000 were in prison camps in the Cape, the Bermudas, St. Helena and Ceylon. On the other side 22,000 men had died, a figure that was to pale into insignificance by 1915.

territories such as Portuguese Angola or the Argentine. In the former case they joined an existing Boer colony which had trekked from the Transvaal in protest against President Burgers' 'liberalistic' régime. Ultimately most of the 'bitter-enders' returned in poverty and disillusionment.

The peace terms were generous. Reconstruction went on apace under the unpopular but efficient Milner, and within five years both former Republics were granted responsible governments. Within eight years they and the former colonies of the Cape and Natal had entered a Union which seemed to realize the dreams of those earlier politicians and proconsuls who had dreamed of a wider unity.

Leading the reconstruction were Botha and Smuts, the Boer generals who considered that the British terms and granting of a responsible government had wiped out the 'century of wrong'. They saw the future in a Boer-British rapprochement, a 'single stream' of white South Africans. The intransigent voices of the 'bitter-enders' were hushed, or the outcome might have been different. Nevertheless, there was plenty of cause for bitterness —families had been bereaved, farms ruined, schools anglicized, and a whole way of life destroyed. The war had given a great impetus to the growth of the Poor White problem, and for many dispossessed and restless Boers there was little to look forward to but a lifetime of labour as a bywoner or a casual labourer in the English-dominated cities.

An unorthodox and perhaps unwelcome sympathizer of the Boer cause, E. S. Sachs, has written of the Anglo-Boer War and its aftermath: 'The older generation of South Africans still remembers the Boer War. Many of the new generation are sons and daughters of the Boer warriors. True patriots could have employed the glorious epic of the Afrikaner people and the moral courage, humanity and integrity of many Englishmen in South Africa and in Britain, to inspire a spirit of human greatness and nobility, a spirit of progress and tolerance, but unscrupulous petty politicians of the Nationalist Party perverted this glorious episode in the annals of the Afrikaner people and the human race in order to foist upon South Africa a policy of oppression, racial hatred, bigotry and intolerance'.

Even a cursory reading of modern Nationalist-inspired accounts of South African history confirms this observation. While many survivors of the Anglo-Boer War and the camps have long favoured co-operation and a wider patriotism, the trend amongst those who, by virtue of distance or youth played no direct part in the war, has been increasingly towards a narrow intransigence and a refighting of the Boer War.

An editorial in *Die Volksblad* in January, 1955, summed up the modern nationalistic version of the war succinctly: 'In the Second War of Independence, which was waged on the insistence of Jingoes in South Africa and Britain to "break the back of Afrikanerdom", not only were 4,000 burgers killed in the field but 26,000 women and children were killed in concentration camps, even if indirectly, armed non-Europeans by the thousand were used against white Afrikaners, among other things to chase women and children to camps after their houses were burnt down, the civilizing constructive work of half a century in the Free State and the Transvaal was razed to the ground and the whole nation reduced to beggary. After the Second War of Independence . . . those crushed Afrikaners who had just lost their political independence were obliged to send their surviving children ill-clad and half-fed to schools where they had the privilege of carrying round a placard with the words "I am a dunce" or "I must not speak Dutch" on committing the deadly sin of speaking their own mother tongue.'

This quotation is a good example of the simplified and partisan version of history which is all that most Afrikaans-speaking children of today have a chance to learn. In the mouths of national-minded teachers, preachers and politicians, history has become a tool to perpetuate the laager mentality of a minority group embattled forever against British imperialists, missionaries, Kaffirs, Communists, liberals and the world in general.

The highlights of this Nationalist version of Boer history or mythology are the Wars of Independence and the Great Trek, seen as 'the story of a people oppressed and misunderstood, fleeing into the wilderness to escape from a tyrannous imperial power.' Of this event, as a myth, Professor I. D. MacCrone writes: 'The annual celebration of that day (the Day of the Vow or Dingaan's day) at the present time, with its social, racial and religious implications, and its memories of "old, unhappy, far-off things", is an event calculated to reinforce the traditional attitude, not only by exciting emotions directly associated with those past contacts between the two races, but also by bringing into play the whole pattern of related attitudes. In such an atmosphere, group consciousness is raised to a higher and more emotional level, with a corresponding intensification of the exclusive group attitude against the Native as the traditional past enemy as well as the potential future enemy of the group. As an illustration of the power of a historical myth which has become part of the mental pattern and outlook of a group, to determine the attitudes of its individual members, it would be difficult to find a more beautiful example than that of the Great Trek'.

Nationalist mythology, in keeping with its highly subjective nature, has also set up a row of villains for general stone-throwing. Most of them have been or will be named in this study. On the British side, they include Lord Charles Somerset, Doctor John Philip, the Reverend John Mackenzie, Shepstone, Chamberlain, Milner, Rhodes, the Randlords and the Reverend Michael Scott. On the Dutch side, there are such alleged 'traitors', 'quislings' and 'collaborators' as Maynier, Stockenstrom, Cloete, Hofmeyr, Botha and Smuts.

Mythology must, however, have its positive side and its heroes in order to move the masses. This was realized by the national-minded in the late 1930's.[1] In 1938, they organized a giant ceremony on a sunny, bleak hill near Pretoria to commemorate the Centenary of the Great Trek. This was attended by 100,000 Afrikaners. Large columns of trek-wagons and

---

[1] In March, 1953, Dr. Otto du Plessis restated the principal names in this Nationalist Valhalla: 'President Kruger was a symbol of National Independence. President Steyn stood for Nationhood. General de Wet stood for Afrikaner Heroism on the battlefield. General Hertzog was the symbol of Sovereign Independence. Now we have a man (Malan) who stands for more than any of these—for the continued existence of White Civilization and Christianity—not only in South Africa, but throughout the length and breadth of the Continent of Africa.'

riders in Trekker dress converged on Pretoria and Blood River, the scene of Dingaan's final defeat in Natal. The ceremony and the press campaign that led up to it stirred the dormant national ardour of most Afrikaners. It led to the founding of the mass organization called the Ossewa-Brandwag and to the general identification of Afrikanerdom with political Nationalism.

The war caused some setbacks, but Nationalist ardour continued to grow. It was stimulated by the internment or imprisonment of a number of individuals who acquired martyr status by opposing the war effort and the British more actively than did the rank and file. The Nationalist Party, nevertheless, came to power in 1948 on a minority of white votes. Far too many Afrikaans-speaking voters were still not voting with the blood. Further campaigns were necessary to bring these 'loyal Dutch' or 'single-streamers' into the fold and to keep the flame alight amongst the 'ware Afrikaners'.

As in 1938, the cultural associations and churches set about organizing an ostensibly non-political mass rally, lasting four days, to celebrate the opening and dedication of the great £800,000 Voortrekker Monument that had been built over the foundation stone on the hill near Pretoria. This was an even more impressive religio-cultural festival than the 1938 ceremony. It was opened by dispatch riders, who carried lighted torches from all parts of the Union to light the lamp inside the sacred shrine. This struck a somewhat pagan note, the central sarcophagus being so constructed that a shaft of sunlight would fall on it at a certain hour, to illumine the words: 'We are for Thee, South Africa'. More than half of the £500,000 raised by public subscription for the monument is claimed by non-Nationalists to have been subscribed by the English-speaking group, mainly by large business firms. The shortfall of some £300,000 was made up by the Government.

The celebrations were attended by 250,000 people, many of them dressed in Trekker clothes, and sporting beards which had been specially grown for the occasion. They heard Dr. Malan thundering at them: 'Back to your people; back to the highest ideals of your people; back to the pledge which has been entrusted to you for safekeeping; back to the altar of the people on which you must lay your sacrifice and, if it is demanded of you, also yourself as a sacrifice; back to the sanctity and inviolability of family life; back to the Christian way of life; back to the Christian faith; back to your Church; back to your God'.

This particular ceremony could have little appeal to the English-speaking, or indeed to any other section of the population. 1952, however, was the 300th anniversary of the landing of Jan van Riebeeck at the Cape. This was an occasion that might be shared by all South Africans, white or black, English or Afrikaans-speaking. In fact, however, this pageant was early monopolized by the national-minded and was only prevented from becoming an entirely partisan demonstration by the fact that the main ceremonies had to be held in the non-national and liberal atmosphere of Cape Town. As the *Rand Daily Mail* pointed out, the original Nationalist intention was largely foiled by the common sense of the ordinary South African man-in-the-street; the pageant finally became a cross between a statement of unity, the Festival of Britain and a fun fair. This did not, however, prevent the Van Riebeeck celebrations from being boycotted by the majority of non-whites, for whom English-Afrikaner unity was too limited to have any meaning.

The next two occasions leant themselves much more legitimately to the expression of Afrikaner Nationalist sentiments. They were the Centenary of the Free State in 1954, and the Centenary of Pretoria, celebrated in November, 1955. Pretoria is now a modern city with some industry; it is also the administrative capital of the Union. But it holds preserved within its broad jacaranda-lined streets, like flies in amber, the seat of the Transvaal Volksraad, statues of the Boer heroes in Church Square and elsewhere, and the modest single-storey house on whose step President Kruger received his burgers, and in whose outhouses Mrs. Kruger sold the milk from her dairy cows. Now this house is a mausoleum full of pathetic personal relics, countless photographs of the President and dusty wreaths of immortelles sent to his funeral by European sympathizers.

The popular fervour aroused by such celebrations will be maintained by regular annual ceremonies at the Voortrekker Monument and all over the country, on such days as Dingaan's

Day or the Day of the Vow, which has since the Anglo-Boer War become Afrikanerdom's greatest religio-cultural festival. This fervour will also be fanned by constant harping on the past, by the unveiling of further monuments, by the wearing of Voortrekker or van Riebeeck dress at such public functions as Government garden parties and so on.

The objective of this positive myth propagation has been to arouse Nationalist ardour amongst the rank and file Afrikaners. If it continues it may ultimately have a similar effect on the Afrikaner who has always held aloof from Nationalism, but has found himself on the margin of the English-speaking world. Still more will such pageantry have an effect on the non-national Afrikaner's children, who are now compelled to attend Afrikaans-medium, Nationalist-dominated schools. The dynamic of this overtly non-political appeal is likely to be considerable, particularly now that the great single-stream Afrikaner leaders such as Botha and Smuts are gone.

It will be noted that the mythology now being propagated is a Voortrekker mythology. Starting with the wrongs of the frontiersmen, it proceeds via the Trek to the Anglo-Boer Wars, well-nigh ignoring the contribution of the Cape Dutch. Such is the dynamic of this mythology that the Cape Nationalists have accepted it and ignored their own fine history and fine tradition. The mythology has even forced its way into the English-speaking history books, so that today English-speaking South Africans are made to feel slightly ashamed of Britain's part in the building of the country, and to ignore the part played by their own group in the pacification of the frontier and the opening up of the mines, ports and railways.

A historical myth is undoubtedly essential to a minority group fighting for its survival. Implicit in the Afrikaner Nationalist mythology of today however is an undue preoccupation with the past and an ancestor-worship which do not seem to fulfil Kruger's last message to his people: 'Take everything that is good and noble from your past and build thereon your future'.

CHAPTER TWO

THE BIRTH OF A LANGUAGE

'We must win the language struggle. We shall win it. Without it, no contented people—no individual South African feeling of nationality—no enduring Federation—No English-Dutch Afrikander nation, sitting and working together in rest and unanimous unity, but a continual unhappy race division . . .'

(Jan Hendrik Hofmeyr, 1907)

'We must have a language in which we can dream, pray and love, and in the other we must become as proficient as we can.'

(Dr. W. Nicol, Administrator of the Transvaal, 1953)

'Afrikaans as the language of the original white inhabitants of the country will be the first official language. English will be regarded as a second or subsidiary language and will enjoy equal rights, freedom and privileges everywhere and whenever such treatment is judged by the state authority to be in the best interests of the State and its inhabitants'

(Draft Constitution of the Republic, Article 2, published by *Die Transvaler*, 23rd January, 1942)

AFRIKAANS, or South African Dutch, is the home language of over 1,500,000 white inhabitants of the Union of South Africa, or nearly 60 per cent of the total white population. It was by 1951 also the home language of nearly 700,000 Coloured people and even of 7,000 South African Indians, while knowledge of it amongst persons over 7 years of age was, according to the 1946 census query on official languages, professed by over 1,650,000 whites,[1] over 700,000 Coloured people, 30,000 Indians and over 1,200,000 Africans. Within the Union, it is therefore the most widely-spoken European language, even amongst the African population. Beyond the Union's borders, Afrikaans is spoken by an estimated additional 40,000, and is intelligible to those who speak Dutch, Flemish and certain North German dialects. It is one of the world's youngest languages.

As a language it has two aspects which will be considered in turn. One is concerned with its spontaneous or more purely linguistic development, the other with its rôle as the main instrument of group survival and national emergence.

The simplified spoken Dutch which is the basis of modern Afrikaans seems to have emerged in the first decades of settlement at the Cape. This development, which contrasts strongly with the ossifying process which occurred in French Canada, was natural enough in view of the heterogeneous structure of Cape society from its earliest days.

High Dutch was from the outset the language of officials and official documents. The original settlers, however, spoke various Dutch or German dialects in the proportion of 3 to 1. In the late 1680's, this proportion was materially reduced in favour of the non-Dutch elements by the arrival of nearly 200 French Huguenots. On the other hand, many of the latter had already lived some years in the Netherlands. They and those Germans who had been in the employ of the Dutch East India Company were thus presumably able to make themselves understood in Dutch before their arrival at the Cape. In addition, the mother's influence on the language learned by her children is generally decisive, and the great majority of the early white women settlers at the Cape were Dutch.

These factors, combined with the establishment of Dutch as the official language and the ruthless measures employed by the authorities against the French language, ensured that the language, and indeed the basic culture, of the white settlers was to be Dutch.

---

[1] 1,848,108 in 1951.

The settlers were not, however, living in a vacuum in their southern outpost. Although they were not to encounter the Bantu for a century, they were never long out of earshot of the complicated clicking talk or pidgin-Dutch of the Hottentots. Even closer and more constant were their contacts with the growing group of polyglot slaves. Most of these had at the outset some knowledge of the current *lingua franca* of the Indian Ocean, Malay-Portuguese. By 1780 there was nearly one slave to each colonist, so that the Dutch-speaking settlers were in a minority in relation to the total population.

None of these non-Dutch language groups seems, however, to have had any large-scale influence on the Dutch language. French influence led to the nasalization of certain vowels, while Malay-Portuguese, via the kitchen and the nursery, produced several characteristic constructions and a number of common words, including *baie* (very) *aia* (nurse) and *noi* (mistress). There is even a theory that South African Dutch, later to be called Afrikaans, arose as a bastard tongue out of a clash between Dutch and Malay Portuguese. More convincing, however, is the view that the rapid development and characteristic emphases and simplifications of Afrikaans are the outcome of the simplified versions of Dutch spoken by foreigners who had to learn the official language of the Cape, and of the simplified forms which the Dutch-speaking had perforce to use to the rest, and more particularly to their slaves and servants.

This new simplified spoken Dutch was therefore probably established before the middle of the eighteenth century. It was to absorb a fair number of words from the Bantu languages, particularly those which concerned the activities or objects which were new to the Dutch speakers, such as *donga*, *impala*, *mamba*, *tsetse* and *lobola*. At a later period, it was to face the dangerous infiltration of a new official language, English, with its tremendous literature, great flexibility and world-wide appeal. From this encounter with a language which was not dissimilar in form or vocabulary, simplified Dutch emerged not altogether unscathed in vocabulary, syntax or phonetic structure. But during the eighteenth and nineteenth centuries, at least outside the Western Cape, this South African Dutch de-

44

veloped spontaneously. The main forces in this development were geographical isolation, lack of formal education or reading matter other than the Dutch Bible, the normal diachronic distortion over the generations, climatic and environmental changes, occupational specialization and so on.

The new language acquired a whole set of usages to reflect the new hierarchy, with its sharp distinctions between slave and free, non-white and white, and its egalitarian relationship within the white group. Cape Dutch came to fit the Boer way of life like a glove, but it still remained the spoken language only. High Dutch was the hieratic language of the Bible and the Sunday sermon. It was also the language of officialdom until the British arrived in 1806. And when the spiritual renaissance of the Cape Dutch began in the last decades of the nineteenth century, their greatest leader, Jan Hofmeyr, saw this renaissance in terms of High Dutch and not Cape Dutch. He himself was in his younger years a powerful influence behind the growing Dutch press in the Western Cape.

Nevertheless, not all Cape Dutch leaders supported the claims of High Dutch. *Di Patriot*, a Cape Dutch publication, began to appear in Paarl as early as 1876. This and later periodicals played a great part in the establishment of Afrikaans, not only as a written language but as a literary language. The history of the Afrikaans-speaking press in South Africa is, however, so bound up with nationalistic policies and aspirations that it belongs more properly in the chapter on political life.

The same is much less true of the literary development of the Afrikaans language. Great poetry and prose do not spring only from political bitterness and cultural or national frustration. These provided the initial goad for many of the early Afrikaans writers, but a fair number found sufficient inspiration in themselves, their language and their environment to carry their work beyond the level of propaganda and stereotyped patriotism.

This has been particularly true of Afrikaans poets. Half a century ago they began to prove that the simple language of the countryside could be flexible, expressive and melodious; that it need no longer be regarded as the dialect of illiterate Boers and comical servants; and that indeed no work of lasting

THE BIRTH OF A LANGUAGE

literary merit could be achieved by writers cramped within the forms of what had become almost a foreign language.

The pioneers were the Rev. S. J. du Toit and the other poets of the First Afrikaans Language Movement, which centred round the Paarl and the Genootskap van Regte Afrikaners from 1875 until the Anglo-Boer war. Unfortunately the didactic and the polemic usually triumphed over the original and the poetic in their verse. The Genootskap period therefore produced nothing of lasting literary value. Indirectly, however, it served the cause of literature by achieving its main objects, the establishment of Afrikaans as a Kultuurtaal or cultural language into which the Bible could properly be translated.

This achievement was consolidated by a group of poets writing during and after the Anglo-Boer War. These men and their successors also benefited from the improved educational facilities in South Africa and from wider contacts with European culture. Epic inspiration came from the hard-bought triumphs and crushing tragedies of the war itself. Eugene Marais, Jan Celliers, Totius (D. J. du Toit, son of S. J. du Toit) and C. Louis Leipoldt became the bards of a nation's grief and bitterness. And because they were poets as well as nationalists and teachers, their work has helped to preserve that grief and bitterness in generations of Afrikaners who have never heard a shot fired in anger.

An instance of this is Totius' ironically-entitled poem *Forgive and Forget*. This tells of the little thorn-tree by the wayside over whose face rolled a wagon's heavy wheels. The thorn-tree's 'loveliness was shattered, its young bark broken through':—

> 'But slowly, surely upright,
> The stricken tree has come,
> And healed its wounds by dropping
> The balm of its own gum . . .
>
> The wounds grew healed and healthy
> With years that come and go,
> But that one scar grew greater,
> And does not cease to grow.'[1]

---

[1]Translation by Anthony Delius.

The early poets were popular poets, writing for a non-intellectual public about subjects which deeply moved themselves and their readers. It is not therefore surprising to find in their work a deep piety, and a profound love of nature and of the traditional Boer way of life.

Leipoldt was the first to transcend the purely national themes. His bitterness burned itself out and his later work pointed forward to the great developments of the 1930's, led by N. P. van Wyk Louw, his brother W. E. G. Louw, Uys Krige and Dirk Opperman. These poets began their journey in the national-minded camp, but soon sought escape in themselves, in metaphysical exploration and in the international scene. It is unfortunate that the language barrier should cause their work to be so little known even in the Union itself, although van Wyk Louw is held in great esteem in Holland and Belgium.

There is no space here for a detailed appraisal of Afrikaans poetry and its very notable achievements over the short span of seventy-five years. To the poets of the thirties, however, must be given the ultimate credit for the emergence of Afrikaans as a poetic language, direct, supple, idiomatic, rhythmic, alternately rugged and sonorous—and above all exciting in its freshness and constant growth. As Uys Krige once put it: 'Afrikaans is in a constant state of growth . . . every visit to the platteland or countryside becomes a linguistic adventure. Speaking with the farmers one is struck again and again by their capacity to create their own language.' The present academic schlerosis (as one poet described it) that has settled on the language to the consternation of the older generation of Boers is a necessary process of standardization. It is unlikely to be more than a phase in the thrusting development of this very virile young language.

Today, therefore, Afrikaans has won its battle for recognition. It is a language of well over 60,000 words, with a literature that is growing at the rate of several hundred books a year. It is never likely to become a world language, but it has survived generations of anglicization and the disrupting effects of urbanization and technological changes.

For the future the Afrikaans language has other and more insidious dangers to face. These dangers are those faced by

Afrikaans culture as a whole. The first is that of spiritual isolation from Western culture. This danger did not affect the earlier
writers, but is the product of the nationally-oriented education
and cultural life for which they strove.

Such cultural isolation has already resulted in a lowering of
standards in all spheres but poetry, where such pace-setters as
the magazine *Standpunte* keep standards high. Amongst all but
the most outstanding writers this isolation has also produced a
second dangerous factor, that of complacency.[1] This complacency, aided by an increase in the reading public, has produced
a flood of commercialized reading matter which has all but
swept away good prose-writing.[2] In the words of Dr. G. D.
Scholtz: 'Whatever is not intended to titillate is usually so
syrupy-sentimental in character that it has nothing in common
with real life.' He adds scathingly:—'The Afrikaner people
would be spiritually no poorer if 90 per cent of the novels of the
last decade were destroyed.'

While this criticism referred to contents as much as to style,
Professor Scholtz considers that this attitude of complacency is
a threat to the language itself. Condemning mispronunciation,
incorrect use of words, slovenly formation of sentences and the
constant use of anglicisms even amongst educated people, he
writes: 'anyone who loves the Afrikaans language has probably
asked whether a language that is so poorly spoken by some who
use it daily has any future'.

This low cultural level was condemned a few years ago by the
late Nationalist Minister of Education, Dr. Viljoen. He called
white South Africa a 'Standard Five nation, a nation of twelve-

---

[1]The award of the Hertzog Prize for drama in late 1952 provoked a
lively polemic between the Flemish lecturer in Afrikaans, Rob Antonissen,
a notable critic, who deprecated the fulsome praise there accorded to inferior work, and the Secretary of the S.A. Akademie. This developed into
a North-South intellectual battle, with Dirk Opperman, one of the editors
of *Standpunte* defending Antonissen and the South.

[2]A large part of this is sensational, suggestive and sexy, and goes by the
name of *prikkel-lektuur* (titillating reading matter). While this *prikkel-lektuur*
is relatively mild by American or French standards, it constitutes a perhaps
unduly large proportion of available reading matter and is purveyed by a
growing number of monthly illustrated magazines whose Afrikaner publishers are not well regarded by the Volk's spiritual and intellectual leaders.

year-olds.' Obviously every language and every culture has to face the threat of debased standards resulting from any increased demand for reading matter unaccompanied by high educational standards. Such a danger is however likely to be more acute, when it has to be faced by a recently enfranchised language, with a short literary tradition, a small store of literary achievement, and a limited cultivated reading public.

The danger is the greater because the more discerning reader is usually bilingual. He has therefore the means of satisfying his desire for quality in the large store of literature available to him in the English language. The Afrikaans writer, deprived of a discerning public, is then faced with the economic alternative of lowering his standards, or, if he is sufficiently bilingual, of adopting English as his vehicle for expression. This temptation to write in English is already a strong one, since, while the rivalry is keener, the writer may attain an almost unlimited reading public and an international reputation.

* * * * *

The survival of Afrikaans as a language is probably in the last analysis dependent upon the survival of the Afrikaners as a dominant national entity. But even this dominance, if continued, may have its dangers. The following extracts from the Court column of the Johannesburg *Star* of 15th May, 1951 perhaps illustrates the point most vividly:

'*Konstabel, jy maak* a liar *van die* court *en* a liar *van jouself*'— Coloured man on a dagga charge in E court.

'*Laat staan jou* speech-making *en vra jou vrae*'—Mr. H. S. de Wet, the magistrate.

Afrikaans and English remained reasonably pure in South Africa so long as the two groups remained geographically, occupationally and politically distinct. That time has now passed. Despite all dreams of apartheid it also seems reasonably clear that white and non-white will continue to live in increasingly symbiosis over the next generation or so. The urban Coloured people have long since developed their own pithy, vivid form of anglicized Afrikaans. Urban Africans show signs of evolving a pidgin-Afrikaans heavily loaded with Bantu and

English words. A pamphlet circulated in Sophiatown in early 1955 in protest against the Government's compulsory move of Africans from the Western areas ran as follows:

'Julle tyd het gekom vir *action*. Nou dar *julyt* (work) vir julle. Die mense kyk vir julle, die manne, *majijas*, die *motlanas* (parents and children). Dit is nou dit tyd om te *volunteer*. Julle moet nou antwoord vir die *mamlady* (ma) se reg. Sy is in *trouble*, is klaar *shandies* (difficulty), die tyd staan krom, en jy sit? Kom *meeting* toe laat ons verstaan hoe om te werk. Die *lanies* (white men) se ons moet *daak* (move) en ek jy se: Ons *daak* nie! Ons *pola* (stay) hier altyd vir *ever*. *Kofifie* (Sophiatown) is onse toun . . .'[1]

It has been shown how High Dutch preserved its Dutch character but underwent rapid changes and simplifications over a few generations when it became the language of a new and polyglot settlement in 1652. One may well ask what will happen to the language of the politically dominant minority if it becomes the official language of eight times that number of people, people who speak a wholly different group of languages and live mainly on a different and much simpler social and cultural level, which it is Government policy to maintain.

* * * * *

It has already been pointed out that the Afrikaans language has been the main instrument of group survival and nation-building. This is indeed the characteristic rôle of the language of any national minority group. The language therefore becomes the main target for the homogenizing endeavours of the authorities.

We are here concerned with two sets of linguistic opposition: the major one between English and Dutch, and the internal conflict between High Dutch and Afrikaans or Cape Dutch. The major conflict started with the British in 1806 and it has not yet ended. The minor conflict arose in the last decade of the nineteenth century and ended in 1925.

Under the Dutch East India Company there seems to have been no overt conflict between the language of officialdom and the Taal of the Boers. The latter was not yet a written language

---

[1] Non-Afrikaans words are italicized and followed by translation in brackets.

and could therefore voice no pretensions to higher status. In addition divergencies were not as great as they are today, when an Afrikaner may find it difficult to understand written or spoken High Dutch. The only event of significance was the ruthless and successful stamping out, in the early eighteenth century, of the French language spoken by the Huguenots. As Simon van der Stel said: 'We want no Quebec at the Cape.'

The British took over the almost entirely Dutch-speaking colony in 1806. They guaranteed the colonists all the rights and privileges which had been theirs before that date. In 1813, however, a determined policy of anglicization was begun. This was to continue in greater or lesser intensity for nearly a century, and its most earnest supporters, Lord Charles Somerset at the beginning, and Sir Alfred Milner at the end, earned themselves the foremost places in the rogues' gallery of militant Afrikanerdom.

The programme of anglicization began in 1813 with a proclamation making a knowledge of English compulsory for admission to the Civil Service, and urging the inhabitants to conduct all official correspondence in that language. At this stage, the Dutch population outnumbered the English 8 to 1, and barely 400 of the 60,000 could converse in English. The 1813 order was followed up in 1822 by a proclamation enacting that from 1827 English should be used exclusively in the Courts. Despite strong protests from the Heemraden of Graaff Reinet and the legal profession in Capetown the order was finally enforced by 1832. Anglicization had been long furthered in the public schools and churches by the importation of teachers and ministers from England. In 1839 it was announced that preference in appointments in the Dutch Reformed Church ministry would be given to those who could preach in English. The Church nevertheless remained the main custodian of the Dutch language throughout this period.

With the establishment of responsible Government in 1854, English was made the parliamentary language. In 1865 it became the sole official medium of education. The former provision led to the virtual disfranchisement of the rural Boers, although three-quarters of the population of the colony was

Dutch. Thanks to this and to their apathy in public life, the Dutch representatives constituted less than one-third of the elected members in the legislature until the 1870's, when group interests and loyalties began to quicken.

The credit for this change of attitude was largely due to the Dutch colonial press, and in particular to the old established weekly *De Zuid Afrikaan*, which had by then come under the powerful guidance of Jan Hofmeyr. This periodical had been going since 1830, following the successful struggle for the freedom of the colonial press. It was intended for 'All Africans, whether English or Dutch', but the Dutch language tended to predominate. During the next four decades *De Zuid Afrikaan* and the Dutch Reformed Church were probably the main purveyors of literary Dutch to the farmers who made up the great majority of the Cape's white population.

It was not, however, until the seventies, when the paper amalgamated with Jan Hofmeyr's *Volksvriend*, and came under his control, that the claims of the Dutch language began to be pressed more actively. It is from this period that one can trace the beginning of the rise of Dutch or Afrikaner group consciousness. Then, as later, it was to take one or two forms: the moderate and holistic patriotism of Hofmeyr and the exclusive chauvinism of the Paarl Genootskappers. In both cases the language was recognized as the paramount issue, although Hofmeyr supported the cause of High Dutch and the Paarl group that of Cape Dutch. National-minded Afrikaners have from the beginning understood that a national revival was more likely to succeed if it were based upon the spoken language of the people, and not upon a literary survival.

This Genootskap van Regte Afrikaners was set up in 1875 by the Reverend S. J. du Toit, with the backing of some teachers, predikants, and wine farmers. The object of the society was to 'stand for our language, our nation and our people'. One of its earliest activities was to set up a newspaper in Cape Dutch, *Di Patriot*, under the editorship of the Reverend S. J. du Toit's brother. Shortly afterwards came the publication of a Cape Dutch grammar and a history of South Africa.

The supporters of both forms of Dutch faced an uphill battle.

They were opposed not only by the authorities and the British settlers, but by many leading citizens of Dutch origin. In 1876 Lord de Villiers, who was later to become Chief Justice of the Cape, incurred a strong rebuke from *De Zuid Afrikaan* for saying that Cape Dutch was a 'barbarous mixture' and that English must eventually become the sole language of South Africa. Olive Schreiner relates how she was punished for using a single word of Afrikaans on the school premises, and this continued to be common practice up to Union. Even in the Transvaal, the Hollander Superintendent of Education, Mansvelt, thought Cape Dutch as monotonous as the Cape Flats, and promoted High Dutch in his single-medium schools.

The language issue, however, proved the most successful rallying-point in the political field. A Farmers' Protection Association (Boeren Beschermings Vereniging) had been started by Jan Hofmeyr in 1875 to protect the interest of the farming population, Dutch or English-speaking, in Parliament. In 1878 its Albert branch petitioned Parliament that the Dutch language might be used there. This initiative developed in snowball fashion, gained the support of the Dutch Reformed Church, and by 1882 an Act was passed making Dutch an optional language in both Houses of Parliament.

This was only the first step. In the same year a member for the Paarl succeeded in getting the school regulations modified. From now on the medium of instruction was to be left to the discretion of the governing bodies.[1] In 1884 Dutch and English were placed on equal footing in the magistrates' courts, and in 1886 Dutch became obligatory for all candidates for the civil service.

As an official language, English was in retreat all along the line. It seemed advisable to the more active Dutch leaders to consolidate the position among the general body of Dutch colonists by establishing an organization to champion the Dutch language. The Taalbond was therefore set up in 1890 with the support of Jan Hofmeyr. It had the joint aims of advancing 'the

---

[1]In practice, however, it seems that Dutch was not introduced as a school subject until 1892, and was taught through the medium of English.

knowledge of the language of the people and the awakenment of a developed feeling of nationality'.

It was decided by a vote of 48 to 37 that the Taalbond should champion the cause of High rather than Cape Dutch. By 1893 the Language Movement established its first landmark with the unveiling of a Language Monument at Burgersdorp, near Albert, whence had come the first parliamentary petition. At the banquet Jan Hofmeyr diplomatically toasted 'Our Language', including under this heading not only the Dutch of Holland but Cape Dutch, 'the language we had learned on our mothers' knees, in which our first religious impressions were communicated to us'. This close connexion between 'mother' and 'language' was constantly stressed in the poems and prose of the period.

Hofmeyr's words were perhaps an indication that the supporters of High Dutch were coming to accept the staying power of Afrikaans. His next move was, however, to advocate the simplification of written Dutch to correspond more closely to the spoken form. This he did at two language conferences held at Stellenbosch and Capetown, in 1895 and 1897. Their recommendations were finally agreed to by a pan-South African conference of teachers and other interested parties in 1904; they were accepted shortly afterwards by the University Council and the Education Departments.

As far as the Cape was concerned, the formal recognition of the Dutch language seemed won by the end of the nineteenth century. But the decade after the Anglo-Boer War brought a renewal of the policy of anglicization, with which is linked the name of Sir Alfred Milner. This policy was aimed particularly at the two former Boer republics, but even in the Cape it again became possible to enter the civil service without a knowledge of Dutch. It was at this stage, with group enmities and distrust inflamed after the war, that the Dutch language issue became unequivocally a 'racial' or national issue. It has remained so to this day.

The next years saw a great awakening of Dutch-speaking South Africans throughout the country to their own responsibility over the language question. While the 1880's had seen the Dutch language advance towards equality in education and public life, the ensuing decades had found many Cape Dutchmen too apathetic to consolidate these gains in their homes or schools. In 1905 there were still girls' schools in many Dutch rural areas whose pupils could barely write Dutch and who, though members of the Dutch Reformed Church, received their religious instruction in English. From 1905 onwards however this apathy was supplanted by an aggressive and chauvinistic enthusiasm. The process went so far that later in the century those Afrikaners who chose to give their children English-medium instruction were to become the object of official intervention and group condemnation.

The protagonists of Cape Dutch or Afrikaans had been far from inactive. Their successes had, however, been rather on the cultural side. Their increasing success in establishing Afrikaans as a language suitable for worship and literary effort has already been described. *Di Patriot*, the daily aimed at the general reader, was followed in 1896 by the weekly, *Ons Klyntji*. The new language acquired a heightened and patriotic value after the military defeat of the Boers. Ex-President Steyn set the note with his dictum: 'The language of the conqueror in the mouth of the conquered is the language of slaves'. In 1905 came the founding of the Afrikaanse Taalvereniging (Afrikaans Language Association) in Capetown, the Afrikaanse Taalgenootskap in Pretoria, and similar organizations in Potchefstroom and Bloemfontein. The S.A. Akademie vir Taal, Lettere en Kuns (S.A. Academy for Language, Literature and Art) was founded in 1909 to maintain and further both forms of the language, and to draw up spelling rules for Afrikaans.

The claims of Afrikaans, as the language must be called from now on, were further strengthened by the approach of Union between the Cape, Natal and the two former Boer republics, in which it was the language of everyday life. The years after the Anglo-Boer War saw the start of the Second Language Movement and the organization of about 200 Christian National schools in the ex-Republics. These were poor in staff and funds, but they did suffice to keep many children out of Milner's efficient but hated English school system.

Then came responsible government for the ex-Republics, and with it a revival of Boer interests. By 1905 most of these C.N.E. schools were incorporated into the Orange River Colony's system. In 1907 Smuts did the same for the Transvaal. By 1908 the reverse process had gone so far that Hertzog was able, to the outrage and the alarm of the English-speaking minority, to impose a rigid bilingualism on public schools in the Orange River Colony.

The Act of Union entrenched the equal rights of the English and Dutch languages. Dutch was enlarged to include Afrikaans by Act No. 8 of 1925, and Afrikaans thereby received its final formal recognition. It had become the primary school medium a decade earlier, and Chairs of Afrikaans were being set up in the universities by 1919. Since 1909, the Union of South Africa has, therefore, been in form at least a bilingual country with two official languages. This ideal has, however, been modified by such factors as economic interests, geographical isolation, social attitudes, differing educational policies and political factors. It would certainly not be true to say that South Africa is a genuinely bilingual country even today.

The main reasons for any continued bias in favour of English are economic. It is still the language of industry and commerce, internationally and locally. In addition, most cities have until recently been predominantly English-speaking. The purchasing power of the Afrikaans-speaking section has only lately achieved any significance.[1]

Against these factors, such indefatigable champions of Afrikanerdom as the F.A.K. and its economic offshoot the Reddingsdaadbond have striven for decades. Their methods have included the circularizing of business firms and professional men to demand bilingual treatment for Afrikaans-speaking clients, the provisions of technical dictionaries in various trades and professions, and the exhorting of national-minded individuals to demand service in Afrikaans wherever they might be, and to refuse their custom to establishments that did not meet this demand. In such matters, however, legislation or agitation

---

[1]Over £500 million per annum in 1952, according to the annual F.A.K. Report.

is far less potent than economic pressure and change. This is illustrated by an interview reported in the Johannesburg *Star* some years ago. 'At one of the busiest bazaars, the manager told me, proudly, that all their counter staff and most of the office staff were fully bilingual. He added that although about two-thirds of their customers were still English-speaking, the proportion was slowly decreasing. They would lose much goodwill and thousands of pounds in monthly trade if they neglected to cater for the increasing number of Afrikaans-speaking buyers'. As a rider to this, one should perhaps add that an increasing number of customers and staff are recently urbanized Afrikaners. Moreover, the jingoistic attitude towards bilingualism has decreased among English-speaking South Africans in recent years.

All the official business of the Union is conducted bilingually, starting with the Houses of Parliament. More Afrikaans than English is usually heard here, if only for the reason that members of the majority party are almost all of Afrikaner origin and that they almost invariably choose to address the House in Afrikaans. In the case of those who speak good English, this is presumably intended to demonstrate that they are the sole guardians of the Afrikaans language. The Opposition members, well over 50 per cent of whom bear Afrikaans names and who still represent about a quarter of the Afrikaans-speaking vote, usually speak in English. There is however an increasing tendency to speak in Afrikaans, even amongst English-speaking M.P.s. Many of the latter even spend their recesses taking intensive courses in the language. This may not be unconnected with the recent increase in the Afrikaans-speaking vote in the hitherto 'safe' English-speaking areas, but there is no doubt that it is in general a healthy trend.

Hansard, all legislation and other official publications, street-notices, railway-tickets and so on, are printed in both official languages, a costly process which should also be taken into account when the merits of bilingualism are being considered.

Bilingualism has been enforced in the public service since Union. The degree of its enforcement has however varied. Originally the public service tended to be staffed by English-speaking South Africans, and often by Englishmen. Indeed, this often remained the case at the higher levels until a few years ago. The bias was naturally in favour of the English-speaking, particularly in departments which had to deal with a mainly English-speaking public. Afrikaans-speaking South Africans entering the service found their way blocked, as it seemed to them, by a phalanx of English-speaking officials, non-national in sentiment and tending to interpret bilingualism as home-language English, with a smattering of Afrikaans.

Since the Nationalist Government came to power in 1948, this balance has been more than redressed. The Afrikaneriza-tion of the Public Service, already well advanced, has been speeded up. This time bilingualism has been increasingly inter-preted as home-language Afrikaans, with the amount of English that can be learned in a unilingual Afrikaans-medium school. For instance, the Public Service Commission Report of 1950 disclosed that nearly two-thirds of the clerks and apprentices actually appointed after taking the Public Service examinations in 1949 did not have 'a reasonable knowledge of the English language'.

Such a reversal would be fair enough, were it not for the fact that both overseas, and in the majority at least of economic transactions at home, the public servant has still to deal with an English-speaking public. The old system did not impede effi-ciency, but the new Afrikaans-oriented bilingualism is often applied at the expense of public efficiency. Amongst particularly obvious instances of this are the following cases.

The first involved the loss to the Transvaal Provincial Admin-istration in 1951 of a number of highly trained nurses, specially recruited in England, because they were unable to obtain pro-motion without passing bilingual tests; the Province pressed its bilingual demands despite a serious shortage of local nursing personnel. The second case concerned the grouping of railway administrative posts into three categories based on the degree of bilingualism required. This directive was issued in 1951; it was applied strictly to the letter where senior English-speaking officials were concerned; in one case an Afrikaans-speaking Opposition M.P. cited the case of a man who was refused promotion be-cause he could not name the bones of the hand in Afrikaans!

In the Statute Book and the administration of the law there is strict bilingualism. Natal Province has for obvious reasons been most lax in observing this provision. A recent amendment to the South Africa Act provided that all transactions, regulations in provincial councils must be in both languages; it gave local authorities until the end of 1955 to promulgate bye-laws and regulations in both languages; failing such promulgation, those bye-laws and regulations would be regarded as invalid.

A number of advocates in the cities do not speak fluent Afrikaans, because there is still no economic constraint on them to do so. Some judges have in former years been accused of speaking inadequate Afrikaans, but the present Government is redressing the balance by appointing a series of candidates whose bilingual qualifications at least are beyond cavil.

Protagonists of either or both languages in the Union have always seen clearly that the effectiveness of any language policy depends on what is taught in the schools. Primary and second-ary education have until now come under the Provincial admin-istrations, and their language policies have differed in accord-ance with the views of the majority on the Provincial Council. The attitudes of the two main parties on this question differ radically. The Nationalist Party believes in compulsory mother-tongue instruction to Standard VIII, or school-leaving age, the mother-tongue to be determined by the educational authorities. As Senator Verwoerd, Minister for Native Affairs, said in March 1953; 'The fundamental thing about education is not the wish of the parents, often a selfish wish, but the interests of the child'.

The United Party believes in mother-tongue instruction up to Standard V or the end of primary education, the language decision being left to the parent. Children from bilingual homes may attend dual or parallel-medium schools,[1] while single-medium schools should be available for those parents who prefer them.

In general, the position since Union has shown a gradual

---

[1]In dual-medium schools, pupils are taught in both languages. In parallel-medium schools, classes are duplicated in either language.

move from the bilingual ideal, as applied in parallel-medium schools, to the unilingual ideal, represented in old days by the opposition C.N.E. schools and today by the single-medium schools of the Transvaal.[1] There has also been an extension of compulsory mother-tongue instruction and a steady encroachment on the parents' right to choose the child's medium of instruction.

At present the Transvaal, with its Nationalist majority, is the pioneer of compulsory mother-tongue instruction. As this policy is, however, the stated policy of the Nationalist Party and of Christian National Education, it seems likely to spread elsewhere, whether or not the Provinces retain control of education.

From 1945 to 1949, provincial legislation initiated by the Transvaal United Party provided for mother-tongue instruction with parental choice for the primary education, and dual-medium education thereafter. After 1949, when the Nationalists gained the majority on the Provincial Council, mother-tongue education up to Standard VIII or the leaving age of 16 has been compulsory, and inspectors and school principals have the power to decide what the home language of the child actually is. This Ordinance applies to private schools, and business and correspondence schools, as well as to public schools. The only parents who at times have been able to exercise the right of parental choice have been immigrants who speak neither official language at home, and temporary residents. The children of

---

[1]Between 1946 and 1954 the following percentage drop occurred in the number of pupils receiving instruction in both languages in primary and secondary schools: Cape—4.48 per cent to 2.81 per cent; Transvaal 2 per cent to nil: O.F.S.—2.11 per cent to 0.09 per cent; Natal—2.98 per cent to 1.43 per cent. In the Cape, this represented an immense drop since 1925, when 48 per cent of pupils were receiving their instruction in both languages.

There are 176 Afrikaans-medium schools, 148 English-medium schools and 475 parallel-medium schools in the Transvaal. The large number of the latter is due to the fact that in country districts there are often insufficient children of one language group (usually English) for the establishment of a separate single-medium school. There is no doubt however that the Provincial Administration dislikes this system, which enables children to mix on the playground and in all school activities, and is doing its best to establish separate schools wherever this is at all feasible.

Dutch and German parents are, however, usually directed to Afrikaans-medium schools.

Nationalist views on parallelism in language instruction were aptly expressed by the Administrator of the Transvaal, Dr. W. Nicol, in 1955, when he condemned dualism in the family, religion or love, adding that in education 'it is cruelty to a child's mind and spirit comparable to a child being horse-whipped by its parents'. Mr. Harm Oost, Nationalist Member of Parliament for Pretoria District, declared during a language debate in 1952 that the bilingual child was not a problem child, but was considered a bad Afrikaner because he was 'neither fish nor flesh and had no national backbone'.

The real motive behind this educational policy is the drive towards what the Parliamentary Opposition has labelled 'white apartheid'. If Afrikaans and English-speaking children are kept apart in the classrooms and on the playing fields throughout their schooldays, they are the less likely to associate at home then or later. 'Bilingualism' then becomes the learning of the second language for economic or political reasons.

In the Transvaal this Ordinance has been applied with great stringency for the past six years. Inspectors have often seemed particularly concerned to drive the straying lambs of Afrikaans-speaking parents back from convents and other mainly English-medium schools to the straight path of Christian National Education. There has been a tendency to assume that children with Afrikaans-sounding names should speak Afrikaans at home. This had the anomalous effect in some cases of forcing purely Afrikaans-speaking families either to move to another province or to speak English at home, so that their children may be entitled to remain at an English-language school.

The same Nationalist language policy was in 1953 extended to schools in the Cape Province by a more subtle device. Previously mother-tongue instruction, more leniently interpreted than in the Transvaal, had been obligatory up to Standard VI, then the highest standard in the primary schools. In 1952, on a motion of the Nationalist-appointed Administrator, Dr. Olivier, Standard VI was transferred to the secondary schools. This brought the Cape into line educationally with the other provinces.

The United Party, which then had a majority in the Provincial Council, rejected the accompanying section which sought to raise the compulsory limit of mother-tongue instruction to Standard VIII, as in the Transvaal; instead, it substituted and carried a clause reducing the limit to Standard V. The Government, however, vetoed this section.[1] Subsequent United Party efforts to restore the deleted section proved in vain, as this Party lost its majority in the Cape Province in the 1954 Provincial Election.

The consequence has been that most parents, not wishing to change the medium of instruction after a year's secondary education, leave their children where they are. This ensures that more and more English and Afrikaans-speaking children are kept apart until they are 15 or 16. Missing, as yet, from the Cape scene, however, is the provision that officials should have the right to determine the child's home language.

In the Free State, which lost its one lone United Party Member of the Provincial Assembly in 1954, language-medium policy and education has gone a long way from the dual-medium schools of the nineteenth century. In this Province alone, the English-speaking minority shows a higher percentage of bilingualism than the Afrikaans-speaking majority, or the English-speaking people in other provinces.

In the Province of Natal, the reverse is true for the same reasons. In 1951 it was estimated that no fewer than 1,600 Afrikaans-speaking children were attending English schools in Durban alone. This anglicization is said to be accompanied by a drift away from Dutch Reformed Church membership, and is regarded with great concern by Nationalist leaders.

The linguistic result of this drive to segregate the national-minded sheep from the non-national goats is the continued production of young men and women who, despite the 1951 bilingualism figure of 73 per cent of the white population, are

---

[1]Mr. C. W. P. Swart (Nationalist Member of the Provincial Council for Worcester) justified this by saying that national unity would not be achieved by putting the children in the same schools. He then proceeded to quote the words of General Hertzog. 'You cannot put horses and quaggas in the same kraal'. (*Cape Times*, 5th June, 1953.)

unable to converse or write a simple sentence in the other official language. Worse still, perhaps, is the fact that such segregation permits of the teaching of entirely different attitudes to life, and can, therefore, perpetuate or even widen the division between the two language groups. While English-speaking children are taught a way of life which corresponds to that of the entire English-speaking world, the Afrikaans-speaking child is being increasingly quarantined within the laager of a Christian National world.

It is clear that Afrikaans has more than won its formal struggle for survival and equality with the English language. It has also won the lesser struggle by ousting Dutch and establishing itself as the language of all Afrikaners, in public and in writing as well as in private and in speech. Afrikaans has indeed passed over to the offensive and there seems little doubt that some of its more vehement advocates would like to see it become the Union's sole official language, in spite of the Government's re-entrenchment of the language clause in the South Africa Act in February, 1956, in an attempt to allay anxiety amongst the English-speaking section over the attack on Coloured voting rights, which were similarly entrenched in the Act.

This new and aggressive phase has its dangers. In the first place, Afrikaners who do not share the political views of the self-appointed champions of the Afrikaans language may be led to abandon their language in their efforts to escape regimentation; while the increasing identification of the language with a narrow political creed deters those English-speaking South Africans who were coming to accept the need for bilingualism in a 'one-stream' or 'two-stream' community.

Secondly, and more important for the mass of Afrikaners, the growing trend to unilingualism, even if it succeeds in establishing Afrikaans as the country's dominant language, can only cut off the Afrikaner from the main sources of his vaunted European culture, and from the great British and American trading and industrial world beyond the Union. There are signs that this danger is realized by some leading Nationalists, but the majority of politicians continue to ride the language hobby-horse long after its original goal of linguistic self-determination has been reached. The final consequence of this aggressive language policy can only mean the impoverishment of the language itself, the permanent separation of the English and Afrikaans-speaking sections of the society and the death-blow to any wider feeling of South African unity.

PART TWO

THE PRESENT

DEMOGRAPHIC NOTE

According to the 1951 Census, the total population of the Union was nearly 12½ million. Of this number, over 67.6 per cent were Africans, nearly 3 per cent Asiatics (Indians), nearly 9 per cent Coloured (mixed), and just under 21 per cent European or white. The latter group was divided in the rough proportion of 3 : 2 between the Afrikaans-speaking and the English-speaking sections. 1.4 per cent of the total white population gave both English and Afrikaans as their home languages (these were mainly urban dwellers), while 2.3 per cent gave some other language.

The relationships between the various ethnic groups have remained roughly constant over the four decades since Union. Within the white group, however, the Afrikaans-speaking group has shown a tendency to increase at the expense of the English section. The latter has maintained its numbers by means of steady immigration, but the Afrikaner birthrate was by 1951 reckoned to be one-third higher, and this group was stronger in the younger age-groups. The median age of the English-speaking group was 30, that of the Afrikaans-speaking group 23.

The white population in each of the four provinces was as follows: Cape — 926,948; Natal — 270,697; Transvaal — 1,164,575; Orange Free State—226,713. The provincial distribution of the two language-groups showed considerable variation—while the Cape Province and Transvaal distribution agreed closely with that of the Union as a whole, the Free State was predominantly Afrikaans-speaking and Natal was mainly English-speaking. Only one-seventh of the Free State's white population were English-speaking; while one-quarter of Natalians were Afrikaans-speaking.

The provincial distribution of the two language-groups did not differ greatly from that of 1936, the year when details of home languages first became available from the census returns. The Cape showed a small loss of Afrikaans-speakers, while this group increased in relation to the English-speaking group in the Transvaal and Natal. In the Free State there was a significant accession of English-speakers between 1946 and 1951, as a result of the development of the new goldfields.

Turning to the distribution of the two language-groups according to rural or urban residence, successive census reports show a steady and large-scale increase in the number of urban Afrikaners. The greatest invasion occurred in the Rand area, where by 1951 only Johannesburg itself remained predominantly English-speaking (100 : 48). In Cape Town and Port Elizabeth the proportion was approximately the same. In Kimberley it was even, while in the 'English' Eastern Cape and Natal the main cities showed the following ratios: East London and Pietermaritzburg—nearly 4 : 1; Durban 100 : 16.

The English-speaking group began in the towns and has remained there, (90 per cent in 1936, 91 per cent in 1951). On the other hand, the picture of the Afrikaner as a country-dweller has not been a complete one since the accelerated shift from the land in the 1930's. By 1936 only 48 per cent of Afrikaners remained in the rural areas. Of the others 27 per cent were in the small towns or dorps, and 25 per cent in the large towns. It was the large towns that exerted the greater pulling power. By 1946 34 per cent of Afrikaners were living in large towns, 30 per cent in small towns, and 36 per cent on the land. By 1951, the latter percentage had shrunk to 31 per cent, while the small towns had 32 per cent and the large towns 37 per cent of the Afrikaner group. In a preliminary report on the 1951 census returns it was estimated that the net loss to the rural areas was nearly 250,000, most of them Afrikaans-speaking. Curiously enough, the number of English-speaking rural dwellers between 1936 and 1951 actually went up by 7,000, or from 13 per cent to 16 per cent of the white rural population.

Bilingualism, or knowledge of the two official languages, English and Afrikaans, rose from 42 per cent in 1918 to 73 per cent in 1951. In the same period, the percentage of unilingual English-speaking whites declined from 30 per cent to 15 per cent, that of Afrikaans-speakers from 27 per cent to 11 per cent. The province with the highest percentage of bilingual whites was the Afrikaans-speaking Orange Free State (78.5 per cent)—while 'British' Natal came lowest with 55.5 per cent. Cross-classification between knowledge of official languages and rural or urban residence showed an equivalent degree of bilingualism amongst urban and rural residents over the age of 25, but more bilingualism amongst the younger urban age-groups. As could be expected, there were more unilingual English-speaking whites in urban areas, and more unilingual Afrikaans-speakers in the country.

English-speaking women, especially over 21, tended to be less bilingual than the men. There were no significant differences between the sexes in the Afrikaans-speaking group. The increased emphasis on mother-tongue instruction was shown amongst males and females in the Afrikaans-speaking group. While only 4 per cent of men and 5 per cent of women in the 21–39 age-group were unilingual, the corresponding percentages for the 7–20 age-group were 18 per cent and 17 per cent. In the English-speaking group, on the other hand, the figures were: males of 7–20, 9 per cent; males of 21–39, 10 per cent; females of 7–20, 9 per cent; females of 21–39, 13 per cent.

There has been no cross-classification between religion and home language since 1936. In that year nearly 6 per cent of the professed adherents of the main Dutch Reformed Church (N.G.K.) spoke English or English and Afrikaans in their homes. The majority of these were in the Cape and the Transvaal, and it is reasonable to assume that most of them were urban dwellers who had become integrated into the English way of life through intermarriage or for other reasons. On the other hand, the same returns show that a fair number of Afrikaners had retained their language but left their traditional faith[1]—(amongst the main groups were 14,825 Anglicans, 14,070 Methodists, and 25,732 members of the Apostolic Faith Mission). In all 10 per cent of Afrikaans-speakers did not profess adherence to any of the three Dutch Reformed Churches.

---

[1]Some of these non-Calvinists might of course be members of other white groups who had through intermarriage become integrated with the Afrikaner group in language but not in religion.

The two smaller Dutch Reformed Churches, incidentally, showed only insignificant defections to the English-speaking group, or to other Churches. Such defections were largely at the expense of the N.G.K., whose members then constituted over 81 per cent of the Afrikaans-speaking section.

This very useful cross-classification between home language and religion was later dropped. It would however be reasonable to assume that at least 95 per cent of the 1,402,703 persons who declared their formal allegiance to the three Dutch Reformed Churches in 1951 were Afrikaans-speaking, and felt themselves to be Afrikaners in the widest sense of the term—this would give a total of about 1,334,600.

The number of white South Africans whose home language was Afrikaans was however 1,502,898. This would mean that there were in 1951 nearly 170,000 Afrikaans-speakers who were not members of the three Dutch Reformed Churches—over 12 per cent of the total language group. At least 50,000 of these would be members of the Apostolic Faith Mission and other sects, and many more would regard themselves as good Afrikaners in the widest or even in the national-minded meaning of the term. These tentative computations do however suggest that the drift from the traditional Calvinist allegiance has not been arrested. It is also worth noting that there was in 1951 a disparity of nearly 17 per cent between the census total of adherents to the largest of the three Churches and the N.G.K.'s own statistics; this suggests that a fairly large minority of formal adherents are in fact lost to the Church and religious practice altogether.

Occupationally, there were great differences between the English and the Afrikaans-speaking sections. These were however tending to diminish. Between 1936 and 1951, for instance, the distribution of the Afrikaans-speaking group in various major occupations changed as follows:

1. Agriculture, Forestry and Fisheries
    86.44 per cent to 83.45 per cent.[1]

---

[1]All these percentages are related to the total of gainfully employed whites.

2. Mining and quarrying
    35.68 per cent to 52.95 per cent.

3. Manufacturing
    26.50 per cent to 44.54 per cent.

4. Commerce and Finance
    21.72 per cent to 32.15 per cent.

5. Transport and Communication
    52.26 per cent to 68.68 per cent.

These broad figures show that only in agriculture and transport was the Afrikaans-speaking group occupying a position proportionate to its size within the white group. In 1936, 56.94 per cent of those gainfully employed in public administration were Afrikaans-speaking, and although corresponding figures for 1951 were not available, there is no reason to assume that this proportion has diminished.

The following detailed analysis of certain professional and allied occupations by language-group in 1951 shows that in all but the teaching, nursing and social welfare professions the English-speaking group still had an absolute numerical lead. It is also evident from the analysis that Afrikaans-speaking women do not yet participate so readily in professional life as their English-speaking counterparts.

HOME LANGUAGE

OCCUPATION	Afrikaans			English		
	Persons	Males	Females	Persons	Males	Females
Civil Engineer	288	287	1	1,967	1,966	1
Architect	133	130	3	955	916	39
Mining Engineer	88	88	—	750	749	1
Mechanical Engineer	194	194	—	1,901	1,899	2
Electrical Engineer	211	211	—	1,751	1,750	1
Other Professional Engineer	289	288	1	2,208	2,202	6
Surveyor	506	506	—	1,120	1,117	3
Designer and Draughtsman	556	500	56	2,816	2,550	266
Quantity Surveyor	47	46	1	393	391	2
Technical Workers, Mechanical and Electrical	401	379	22	1,307	1,279	28
Chemist (Analytical)	292	281	11	967	917	50
Chemist (Dispensing)	359	294	65	2,266	2,026	240
Professor, Lecturer	530	449	81	610	469	141
Teacher	14,855	8,149	6,706	9,277	2,578	6,699
Scientist n.e.c.	735	702	33	961	835	126
Judge, magistrate	209	209	—	233	233	—
Advocate, Barrister	103	102	1	290	285	5
Attorney	713	708	5	1,997	1,954	43
Medical Practitioner	1,238	1,159	79	3,524	3,141	383
Dentist	207	203	4	612	594	18
Veterinary Surgeon	102	100	2	142	132	10
Midwife	410	—	410	350	—	350
Nurse	7,619	930	6,689	6,545	336	6,209
Author, Editor	353	300	53	924	744	180
Musician	358	96	262	1,122	472	650
Artist	288	216	72	1,522	963	559
Actor, Actress	112	88	24	205	140	65
Dancer, Dancing Teacher	12	2	10	231	38	193
Professional Athlete	74	66	8	638	594	44
Clergyman, Priest (Catholic)	25	25	—	375	375	—
Clergyman, Priest (other)	1,094	1,088	6	1,141	1,065	76
Social Welfare Worker	516	136	380	475	119	356

CHAPTER THREE

NATION AND PARTY

'The Volk desires to permit of no equality between coloured and white inhabitants in Church or State'
(Transvaal Grondwet of 1858)

'In die stem van het Volk heb ik gehoord de stem van God, den Koning der Volken, en ik gehoorzam'
(President Paul Kruger)[1]

'We are taking this step[2] because we are Calvinists who believe that God is sovereign and transfers that sovereignty to the legal rulers of the country . . .'
(Senator J. de Klerk, Minister of Labour, speaking at Linden in May 1955)

THE Afrikaners have since Union played a far greater part in South African political life than have the English-speaking South Africans. One obvious reason for this is their numerical majority, which has enabled them to dominate politics since 1910. In addition, like the French Canadians, the Afrikaners saw that through political action they could regain some if not all of the independence which they had lost through defeat and annexation. Finally, politics and the public service offered an alternative way of life for young Boers and French Canadians whose land was gone and whose entry into industry and commerce was initially all but blocked.

The political life into which the Boers entered, and which

---

[1]'In the voice of the people I have heard the voice of God, the people's King, and I obey.'
[2]The reconstitution and enlarging of the Senate.

they have all along dominated,[1] is however based on a system which national-minded Afrikaners regard as alien to the Afrikaner way of life. This was probably the main reason for their virtual disregard of the recent centenary of the founding of the Cape Parliament, which contrasts so very strikingly with enthusiasm over other 'national' occasions.

The ideal Afrikaner political system is based primarily on that of the Transvaal Republic. Its form was first and foremost that of a republic.[2] It was not theocratic, but like the Church was under the sovereignty of God. All its burgers were equal before God and therefore amongst themselves. The 1858 Grondwet (Constitution) of the South African Republic spoke of 'true burger-like freedom, equality and fraternity'.

The will of the people was held to be sovereign. This idea of the Volkstem or Volkswil was a compound of two earlier ones: the classical idea that the voice of the people was the voice of God, and that of the revolutionary Batavian Republicans, that the voice of the people was sovereign. Political or military leaders were entrusted with only limited authority and were constantly subjected to public control and criticism. Opponents of Potgieter's patriarchal sway in Ohrigstad complained that 'he treated them as if they were his subordinates'. Even Paul Kruger's strength lay less in his official powers than in his continued popular support. It was a far cry to the belief voiced in early 1956 by Professor H. J. Strauss of the Political Science Faculty of the University of the Free State: 'The Prime Minister is sovereign in the sense that he receives his authority from God; he merely uses Parliament, within the framework of the constitution, to endorse his legislation.'

In early days the Volkswil was heard directly at frequent

---

[1]Every Prime Minister since Union has been Afrikaans-speaking.

[2]Dr. E. F. W. Gey van Pittius of the University of Pretoria, writing in *Kultuurgeskiedenis van die Afrikaner*, Vol. II. The writer was a member of the Nationalist Party and was obviously considered sufficiently orthodox to contribute this chapter. In May 1955, however, he was one of the thirteen Pretoria University professors who signed a petition protesting against the Senate legislation on moral and constitutional grounds. For this deviation he was subsequently accused of 'liberalistic' views by Mr. Eric Louw, Minister for External Affairs.

Volksgaderings, often combined with the regular concourse of Boers for Nagmaal. The decisions of these popular assemblies were binding for the Volksraad. In the 1850's, this system was for geographical reasons superseded by a system of petitions and memorials, which flowed into the Volksraad and frequently caused projected legislation to be changed. Indeed, statutes only came into force in both northern Republics after some months, so that the Volk might have time to express its views.[1] In times of crisis however the Boers reverted to the Volksgaderings. An instance of this was the gathering at Paardekraal in 1880, which preceded the First War of Independence.

The legislative body in the ideal Boer republic is a unicameral Volksraad, elected by all burgers. A single chamber was felt to be adequate in the homogeneous socio-economic structure of the northern Republics. The Transvaal introduced a second Chamber in 1890 in a half-hearted attempt to propitiate the Uitlanders, but this second Volksraad was always subordinated to the first Volksraad. Dr. Gey van Pittius writes of it as at best a necessary evil. It may be that the lack of a bicameral system in the Boer political tradition has some connexion with the present Nationalist Government's willingness to degrade the Senate by packing it with their own nominees, in order to force through legislation to change the Constitution.

The Volksraad in both Boer Republics was elected by all burgers. Legislation however called for greater maturity, and a burger could stand for the Volksraad only after he reached a certain age, 30 in the Transvaal, 25 in the Orange Free State.[2] The Transvaal also demanded that candidates should be members of a Dutch Reformed Church, a stipulation that was

---

[1] The Volksraad could however legislate by *besluit* (resolution), a method that involved no delay whatsoever, and was used increasingly in the last years of the Republic to put through controversial legislation.

[2] Women gained the vote in 1930, a concession which was in part animated by the Government's desire to minimize the effect of the Coloured vote by doubling the white electorate. Afrikaner women are, despite their traditional assignment to the kitchen and the nursery, far from disinterested in politics. They tend however to be active in local organizations, and it was not until early 1956 that a Nationalist woman entered the Senate, nominated as a member of that now somewhat swollen body.

modified in 1889 to include all Protestant Churches. The Free State made no such requirement.

The Volksraad, as representing the will of the people, was sovereign. In the Transvaal even the Constitution, at least according to President Kruger's interpretation, could be changed by a simple majority. The Orange Free State however permitted constitutional change only by a three-quarter majority, apparently without regarding such a condition as a limitation on the people's sovereignty. Administrative and juridical functions were carried out by a combination of popular representatives and officials. Even officials had to receive burger approval, and the system, apart from its additional merit of economy, was satisfactory enough within Boer society. Its major weakness was the inevitable partiality of such burger officials in conflicts of interest between burgers and non-burgers, or at times between burgers and government.

The Transvaal's flexible constitution and direct form of democracy was suitable only to a socially and economically homogeneous people. The whole system was highly vulnerable once large numbers of newcomers with alien ideas and occupations entered the country as permanent residents. Initially, burger rights were easily acquired. Later the system was safeguarded by a barrier of restrictions through which it was intended that only those who were prepared to accept the Boer way of life should pass. The remainder were to be unrepresented, or to have some sort of second-class citizenship which could easily be revoked. All national groups naturally desire to safeguard their own way of life. Few have however found it possible to perpetuate the principle of taxation without representation where such large groups as the Uitlanders or the non-Afrikaner ethnic groups in the Union today are concerned.

Because of such safeguards, and of the relatively monolithic structure of society in the Republics, there were no organized political parties nor two-party system. The Boers however had their differences, and by the end of the Transvaal Republic there was evidence of emerging opposition to the patriarchal conservatism of Kruger and the authoritarianism of the so-called 'Hollander clique'. This healthy trend was however checked by the Anglo-Boer War, which drove Afrikaner politics back to the ethnocentrism which they have never since managed to throw off.

Today however it is still possible to detect the two conflicting trends in Afrikaner political thinking. These may be called the authoritarian trend and the libertarian trend, and they reflect a conflict within the Volk between the patriarchal or leadership principle and the desire for liberty and equality.

On the one side, we have the moderate nationalism of Dr. Gey van Pittius, who writes: 'It is unthinkable that the one-party system can successfully be introduced here from overseas, when one considers the religion, character and tradition of the Afrikaner . . .' On the other hand, there is the political ideology reflected in the Draft Constitution of the Republic. This Draft Constitution was published by the *Transvaler* on 23rd January, 1942, 'with the permission and on the authority of Dr. D. F. Malan'. Dr. Verwoerd was then editor of the paper, and Mr. J. G. Strijdom was Chairman of its Board of Directors. The Draft was drawn up, (on Christian National, neo-Kruger-ist lines) by a Policy Commission representing the leading Afrikaner organizations, O.B., Churches, F.A.K. and R.D.B. It has somewhat disingenuously of recent years been disavowed by Dr. Malan, Mr. Strijdom and the Nationalist Party in general, but it undoubtedly reflects the political ideal of the neo-Krugerist Nationalist wing. Article 11 of this document reads: 'The propagation of any State policy and the existence of any political organization which is in strife with the fulfilling of this Christian National vocation of the life of the people is forbidden'; while Article 3 gives the State power to prevent the various organs of public opinion, including political parties, from undermining the public order or good morals of the Republic, internally or externally.

To sum up, the two Northern Republics, and particularly the Transvaal, provide the Afrikaner with his ideal political system, and the one to which his political leaders are trying to revert. In essence, this ideal, which like most ideals presents history through somewhat rose-coloured spectacles, consists of an independent and democratic republic, based on Christian principles and aimed at maintaining and furthering the culture and well-being of the Afrikaner people. Such republics have existed and flourished in static and homogeneous societies at both ends of the civilization scale. They seem however doomed to failure in multi-racial, culturally-differentiated societies, or in circumstances of rapid economic change and development.

This was true of the Transvaal Republic and it is even more applicable to the Union of today. In both cases the homogeneous Afrikaner people is not the only group inhabiting the territory. There is a large minority of non-Afrikaner whites, and a majority of non-whites. The former endanger the Afrikaner ideal by their overseas links and their cosmopolitan views. They may however become acceptable as burgers if they break these links, and adopt the Afrikaner way of life.

For the non-white majority, however, all burger status is forever unthinkable. On this point, all Nationalists, even the most moderate, are in agreement. The ideal relationship between white and black is one of guardianship, and Biblical sanction for this was found by the Cape Dutch Reformed Church as early as the beginning of the eighteenth century. Dr. Gey van Pittius presents a somewhat idealized picture of the content of Boer attitudes and policy under the Republics:

'Their object was not to make a sort of half-hearted white man out of him (the native) so that they could then exploit him. They desired to preach the Gospel to him and help to civilize him so that he might preserve and develop all that was good and beautiful of his own.' The native was seen as having his own way of life, however primitive, just as had the Boer, and segregation was seen as the best protection for both groups.

This is a pretty piece of latter-day rationalization. It probably however does not in the least reflect the attitudes of the great majority of the Republican Boers, for whom the non-whites were either docile servants or savage enemies to be dispossessed and subdued. Nor indeed today does it reflect more than the views of a conscience-pricked minority of Afrikaner intellectuals and churchmen. It would be a mistake to suppose that this minority does not genuinely hold such views. On the other hand the ideals of the free burger republic and of separate development have, as will be seen, come to serve as a smoke-screen behind which some ruthless politicians are preparing a very different political order.

But to return to the present political system of the Union, which, despite its formally un-Afrikaans character, nationally-minded Afrikaners have increasingly succeeded in operating for their own ends. South Africa is a sovereign, independent state in which the British Monarch is the King or Queen of South Africa, represented by the Governor-General, who is advised by his Ministers. Sovereignty rests in the central Union Parliament, which is bicameral. What is essentially a two-party system prevails, as it does in Britain.

There is a universal franchise for white voters over the age of 21. In 1951, there were over 825,000 Afrikaans-speaking and nearly 700,000 English-speaking white inhabitants of the Union over the age of 21.[1] In the Cape, Coloured male voters who meet a property and literacy qualification are still eligible to vote on the common roll. Their franchise is however likely to be removed; the same applies to the communal franchise of certain qualified Africans, who at present elect three members of the House of Assembly and four Senators.

From the time of Union until 1936 the Senate consisted of forty members. In that year four were added to represent African interests, once the few African voters on the common roll had been removed; and another four were added after the incorporation of South West Africa in 1950. Senators were elected by the Members of Parliament and the Provincial Council of each province, eight senators to each province. Others were nominated or elected to represent non-white interests. The

---

[1] White British immigrants could formerly acquire citizen rights after two years residence. The large post-war influx of such immigrants could have constituted a formidable voting-group, but its effect was modified by the Nationalities Act passed by the Nationalist Government in 1949. This made citizenship contingent upon five years residence, the payment of an application fee, and the Minister of the Interior's agreement in each individual case. In consequence, only a few hundred Britons have applied for South African citizenship, with the result that the many remaining thousands of potentially anti-Nationalist voters are still disfranchised. Other aliens must wait seven years before applying.

Senate was intended to give support to minority rights, to the provincial principle, and to the interests of the four separate entities which had made the Union of South Africa. The Senate Act of 1955 ignored this intention, and set up an enlarged Senate of eighty-nine. The principles of proportional representation and the equality of representation of the four provinces were brushed aside, with the result that the strength of the provinces in the Senate after the elections in December 1955 was as follows: Transvaal—28 Nationalists; O.F.S.—8 Nationalists; Cape—22 Nationalists; Natal—8 Opposition Senators; S.W. Africa—2 Nationalists. In addition there were 18 Senators nominated by the Government. This reconstitution of the Senate was clearly not unconnected with the Government's desire to get a two-thirds majority of both Houses, in order to remove Coloured voters from the common roll.

It is conceivable that when this objective has been finally achieved the Government may discard this over-blown and embarrassing body in the hopes of gaining kudos for a belated concession to constitutionalism.

Senators must be white and over 30 years of age. Elected Senators must own immovable property worth £500 or more. Members of Parliament must also be white, but any registered voter may stand for the House of Assembly. Both Senators and M.P.s get £1,400 a year. These amounts were recently increased from £1,000 in both cases. One might perhaps comment here that such allowances make an appreciable addition to the income of, say, a professor or a small farmer, while they would not be equally attractive to individuals in the higher ranks of industry or commerce.

A particular feature of South African political life is the method of delimitating constituencies. At the time of Union, the interests of the sparsely-populated rural areas were protected by a 'loading' device, which entitled the Delimitation Commission to take sparsity or density of population into account to the extent of 15 per cent above and below the quota. This meant that an M.P. representing a rural constituency might represent up to 29 per cent fewer voters than an urban M.P. It was also felt, as in the Transvaal Republic, that the farmers were the true burgers, the backbone of the country, and that their views were more valuable than those of the fickle and flighty townsmen.

This system has consistently and increasingly favoured the Nationalist Party. In the 1948 election, the Nationalist and Afrikaner Parties won seventy-nine seats to the united opposition parties' seventy-one, although the latter received 140,000 more votes. Other voters who possess an even greater advantage than the rural voters are those in South West Africa. Here the constituencies contain about 4,000 voters, compared with 7,000 to 12,000 for the Union. Since South West Africa began to be represented in the Union Parliament in 1950, her mainly Afrikaans-speaking and German electorate has returned only Nationalist members.

The Union of South Africa, in practice though not in law, has two national anthems, 'God Save The King' (or Queen), and the stirring 'Die Stem van Suid Afrika'. The latter was written by C. J. Langenhoven, one of the fathers of Afrikaans poetry. Following a policy laid down by General Hertzog, both anthems are played at official functions and on non-Nationalist occasions. The Nationalist Party feels that the British anthem is a reminder of past dependence, and has for years tried to replace it by a single 'purely South African anthem', usually interpreted as 'Die Stem'.

The question of a national flag is at present regulated by the Union Nationality and Flag Act of 1927. This was actually piloted through Parliament by Dr. Malan as Minister of the Interior, after what General Smuts described as 'a state of turmoil such as we have not seen for many a day'. The Act states: 'The flags of the Union shall be (a) the Union Jack to denote the association of the Union with the other members of . . . the British Commonwealth of Nations, and (b) the National Flag, of which the design is set out in the following Section'. This second flag embodies the orange, white and blue of the House of Orange, with the Union Jack and the flag of the two old Republics imposed upon the white.

The national anthem, the flag and the coat-of-arms are all symbols to which national-minded Afrikaners have always attached great importance. In 1949 Mr. Havenga said: 'The Union Jack is not our flag. It is the flag of the conqueror . . . but as a concession to sentiment we gave way.' In 1951 *Die Transvaler* wrote that the Union Jack had entered the 'Republican territory' as a 'gatecrasher . . . by assault, burglary and robbery'.

In 1955, the Nationalist-dominated Provincial Council of the Transvaal decided to remove the Royal coat-of-arms and the Union coat-of-arms from the Provincial Council Chamber in Pretoria, and to put in their place a portrait of President Kruger and the Transvaal Republican coat-of-arms. During the debate, Mr. F. H. Odendaal, M.L.A., for Mr. Strijdom's constituency, said that it was time for people to stop 'wanting little bits of Britain in our midst. That is why we want a republic —to get rid of the pro-British sentiment and to have one flag, one anthem and one coat-of-arms.' In consequence of sentiments like these, the Union Jack is flown less and less, and unpleasant incidents sometimes occur where cinemas or theatres still show pictures of the Queen and the Union Jack, or play 'God Save The Queen'. The Draft Constitution envisaged that the Vierkleur of the old South African Republic would be the sole Union flag, with orange to replace the red band.

In general, there is a certain ambivalence in the attitude of many Afrikaners to the monarchy. This was well illustrated in the Nationalist Press after King George VI's death in 1952. The news was received with genuine sorrow, and good wishes were extended to the new Queen. It was nevertheless pointed out that, given a decision of the Volkswil, she might be the last Queen of South Africa. During the Coronation celebrations, the extreme Republicans attempted to prevent public money being spent on a 'person in England' and even protested against the attendance of Dr. and Mrs. Malan at the Coronation in London.

The monarchy as an institution is clearly still linked with alien domination and alien ideas of government. The Royal Family are however, particularly since their visit to the Union in 1947, highly esteemed as individuals by a large number even of Nationalist Afrikaners. It was like a breath out of Scotland to read in the Dutch Reformed Church's organ *Die Kerkbode* in 1953 an editorial criticizing both Princess Margaret for smoking in public and Afrikaans newspapers for publishing such photographs. 'So much is clear,' lamented the editorial: 'that our young daughters will infer that smoking is something that is desirable for a woman . . . It is . . . to be deplored that someone from a Royal household set such an example.'

As a result of the compromise reached at Union, South Africa is a country of two capitals. Pretoria, the old capital of the South African Republic, is the administrative capital, while the legislature meets in Cape Town. In addition, the Union Appeal Court sits at the Orange Free State capital of Bloemfontein. The material and technical disadvantages of such a system are obvious. Every year for five months or so the government in Pretoria packs up its files and moves itself and its staff nearly 1,000 miles to swell the congestion of Capetown in summer. On the other hand, non-Nationalists have since the time of Union felt that the older and more tolerant culture of the Western Cape exerted a beneficial influence on the wild men from the north. Some of them felt also that the sea breezes might cool the hotheads from the backveld better than torrid Pretoria. The champions of Capetown found additional support amongst the Cape Nationalists, either for geographical and economic reasons or because they themselves did not always see eye-to-eye with their more impetuous northern colleagues.

The descendants of the Trekkers, for their part, feel that the Western Cape is un-South African and 'jingoistic'. They feel ill at ease in a city where liberalism lingers to the extent that coloured people sit on the municipal council and on the same park bench or bus seat, where a motorist may be directed or even corrected by a coloured traffic policeman, and where a tourist may find coloured people using the same piece of beach or sea.

A northerner, Mr. Strijdom, has now taken over the Premiership from the Cape man, Dr. Malan. In general, political power has shifted from the liberal Cape to the extremist north, and from the less extreme Cape Nationalists to their more extreme northern colleagues. The transfer of the legislative capital to

Pretoria would only be a formal recognition of this shift, and one may expect it to happen sometime in the future.

Each of the four provinces has its own Administrator (appointed by the government), its elected provincial executive and its unicameral Provincial Council, elected by those who hold the parliamentary franchise. The position after the 1954 elections was that the Nationalists controlled the Provincial Councils of the Transvaal (45–23), of the Cape (30–26) and of the Orange Free State (25–0). Natal had 21 U.P. Members and 4 Nationalists. The Administrators of the first three provinces are now Nationalist supporters, though there was for some time an awkward situation because the Administrators appointed by the previous government survived the defeat of their sympathizers.

South Africa is a Union, and the provinces' powers are limited. Chief among them are primary and secondary education and general health. The central government has however firm control of revenue, and subsidizes 60 per cent of the provinces' activities. Seen impartially, the provincial system is costly, inefficient and even anachronistic, and the trend would inevitably have been towards greater centralization. A centralized republic is also the Nationalist goal, and there is constant encroachment on provincial authority. This authority is in any case based on a compromise arrangement made at the time of Union, which was made permanent in 1934, when a statute was enacted providing that no powers should be taken from the Provincial Councils except on their petition.

Local government from the township stage and above is carried out through elected boards or councils. The qualification for the municipal franchise is in all provinces ownership or occupation of property; in the two northern provinces only whites have the franchise. In Natal Coloured people may vote, while in the Cape the franchise is colour-blind. This has even led to the election of some Coloured councillors in Capetown and Port Elizabeth, and in general to the councils concerned pursuing a colour policy very different from that of the Union Government.

Recent years have seen attempts by the central authorities to bring straying local governments into line by financial and other forms of coercion. Perhaps the most serious inroads so far upon the rights of local authorities have been the taking over of local government of urban Africans by the Native Affairs Department, the Group Areas Act, and the Natives Resettlement Act of 1954. The latter enabled the Government to by-pass the recalcitrant City Council of Johannesburg, which had been stalling over the plan to remove about 57,000 urban Africans from the so-called Western Areas.

From spasmodic utterances by Nationalist speakers, it is evident that many in the Party do not regard the system of elected mayors and local councils with any great favour. On this point, Article 8 of the Draft Constitution of the Republic reads: 'Town or City Councils . . . are taken in charge by Mayors (Burgemeesters) who will be appointed as whole-time officials, and dismissed by the Administrator, subject to the approval of the Minister of the Interior. The powers of the Mayor . . . will include the rule over the whole of the local administration . . . as well as over local general activities which in the late Union of South Africa were carried out by the former Magistrates . . . Mayors are supported by local Advisory Councils, called Heemraden (Country Courts), representing the economic, social and spiritual groups of interests for the . . . town and district'. As regards the Nationalist attitude to provincial rights, it is worth noting that the Draft Constitution provides for provinces 'or other division of the State territory'.

At the time of Union, the public service was largely English-speaking (nearly 85 per cent in 1912). Since then, it has been increasingly recruited from the Afrikaans-speaking group. Starting usually in the lower grades, Afrikaners have gradually moved up until they now occupy many of the leading posts.[1]

---

[1] But according to Mr. Paul Sauer, the Minister of Transport in 1952, 80 per cent of the South African Railways and Harbours personnel were Afrikaans-speaking, but 67 per cent of those in the £1,000 and over income-group were English-speaking. The Deputy Postmaster-General gave similar figures for the Post Office in December 1953. While 68 per cent of all officials were Afrikaans-speaking, they occupied only 40 per cent of senior positions.

The reasons for this were initially mainly economic. The public service was unable to compete with industry and commerce for the cream of English-speaking youth. The latter were in any case often deterred by the bilingual requirements. On the other hand, the young Afrikaner who had been pushed off the land found the public service easier to enter than English-dominated private enterprise. In cases where his qualifications were poor, he could still enter the lowest levels of the public service, in a job normally done by non-whites, because of the 'civilized labour policy'. This policy meant that a labourer was paid not according to his abilities but according to his needs as a 'civilized' person. It was in fact a concealed dole for impoverished whites.

In theory the public service is outside politics, but it is inevitable that in a small country there should be a certain amount of nepotism and party-political favouritism. On the subject of the latter, Leo Marquard writes in *Peoples and Policies of South Africa*: 'Appointment, and particularly promotion, of public servants goes on without regard to party-political affiliations until a fundamental difference of policy manifests itself, when it breaks down. During the last war, there was such a difference between the United Party under Smuts and the Nationalist Party under Dr. Malan. The Nationalist Party was totally opposed to South Africa's participation in the war, and Smuts could not take the risk involved in promoting known Nationalists to key positions. When, in 1948, the Nationalists came to power, they reversed war-time promotions, notably that of the General Manager of Railways, and recompensed public servants who had been interned and had, therefore, missed promotion.'

The South African Railways and Harbours, because of its size and large establishment of unskilled or semi-skilled white workers, has never been able to function in a political vacuum. In early years, the alleged grievances were all on the Nationalist Party's side. Now it is the Opposition that accuses the administration of putting bilingualism ahead of efficiency, of failing to promote non-Nationalists and English-speaking employees, and of moving railway depots and large groups of white workers to areas where their votes may influence a marginal result.

The South African Police began as a largely English-speaking body. In the course of time, however, it has become predominantly Afrikaans-speaking, for the reasons outlined earlier. Unlike most other branches of the public service, there is no provision for entering the Police at different levels according to qualifications: a provision which would ensure that various sections of the population are represented on the Force. As throughout the public service, the ranks of the Police Force are largely and increasingly drawn from the poorer rural and urban Afrikaans-speaking elements. This element may be generally described as the most chauvinistic, illiberal and unadaptable group in the Union. This increasing uniformity of personnel has its disadvantages in any public service in a multi-racial country. It is all the more regrettable in a service which is concerned with administering the law and protecting the whole multi-racial public, and which has been given increasingly wide discretionary powers by recent legislation.

In general it may be said that while the average white regards the South African policeman with indifference or mild aversion, the non-white views him with fear and hatred, refuses to give him any assistance, and regards him as the agent of the 'white man's law'. It would indeed be a remarkable body of men that could fairly administer a set of laws based on partiality and the colour bar; but little in the recent behaviour of white police towards non-white prisoners or demonstrators or even towards anti-government meetings organized by mixed groups leads one to believe in their genuine desire for impartiality.

The Boers were always liable to commando service, and every white citizen between the ages of 17 and 60 is liable to register himself to render in time of war personal service in defence of the country, in any part of Southern Africa inside or outside the Union. For eight years after his seventeenth birthday he is also liable to undergo a course of peace-time training. All citizens not accepted for training may join rifle-commandos, in which they are required to serve for four years, and they may buy government rifles at cost price. These rifle-commandos are three times larger than the earlier Defence Force Rifle Associations which were dissolved in 1948. They are strong in the rural areas, and according to a 1953 Nationalist Party election pamphlet they may 'play an important part in quelling internal disorder and riots'. All boys living in well-populated areas may between their twelfth and seventeenth year be required to undergo a course of cadet training, unless their parents object. The Boer prejudice against arming non-whites has increasingly triumphed, and non-whites now serve in the armed forces only as servants.

The prejudice against fighting in 'Britain's wars' made it necessary that any forces sent out of South Africa should be composed of volunteers. In fact, whether their motives were idealistic, economic or simply adventurous, a very large number of Afrikaners volunteered for such service in both World Wars. In World War II the Orange Free State with its 86 per cent Afrikaans-speaking population topped the recruiting list, Natal coming last; well over half of the armed forces were Afrikaans-speaking.

In both world wars, Afrikaner volunteers braved the hostility of their Nationalist families and neighbours. It was Afrikaners who put down the 1914 Rebellion; Afrikaners who, after 1939, went home to the dorps and farms wearing the orange flash which showed their volunteer status, and sometimes even heard the predikants denounce them as 'red lice'. The prejudice against 'British' uniforms in certain areas was indeed so violent that servicemen going on leave were instructed to wear civilian clothes.

After World War II, the Defence Force was still permeated by the spirit of those South Africans of both language groups who had served actively and victoriously at Britain's side. It was only natural that officers who had gained experience in modern warfare should be promoted over those who had opted to stay at home. This state of affairs was not however likely to be acceptable to the Nationalist Party for long. Political reliability and lack of British ties were greater assets in a 'national-minded' force, whose main task in any war would be to maintain the *status quo* in South Africa against all comers.

So the years since 1948 have seen a steady stream of measures designed to effect this changeover. From 1950 it was announced that bilingualism would be more strictly enforced. This discouraged many English-speaking South Africans, particularly Natalians, and was also successfully applied against those British artisans and specialists who had joined the permanent force on a contract basis.

The next years saw the steady by-passing or forced retirement of a series of high officers with war-time experience, most of them Afrikaans-speaking, and the promotion in their place of a clique of 'reliable' officers, who often had no war service at all.

The 'nationalization' of the Defence Force was not confined to personnel matters. In 1952 the Minister for Defence, Mr. F. C. Erasmus, issued details of new uniforms for the forces. The general effect was distinctly Germanic, and was received with aversion and protest by ex-servicemen's organizations. The cadets were given Afrika Corps-style caps, the letters 'H.M.' were dropped from the cap-tallies of the Navy, which was, it was said, to be known simply as the South African Navy. In the same year, nine new U.D.F. decorations were announced; the English-speaking section did not go entirely unrepresented, but the two bravery awards for bravery were named for van Riebeeck and Louw Wepener.[1] In late 1955, the rank of Chief of the General Staff was replaced by that of Commandant-General, 'in keeping with the policy of introducing the traditional military ranks of South Africa (i.e. of the Republics) in the Defence Force'.

The South African law is less alien to the Boer way of life than is the present political system. There have nevertheless been hints in the Nationalist Press and elsewhere that the South African law should be purged of all English influences. The law of the Union is, however, as far as the civil code goes, still in essence the Roman-Dutch civil law of the early Cape Colony, adapted and interpreted to suit local needs. The criminal law became largely English in the reforms of the late 1820's, as did the law of evidence, while the laws dealing with the frame-work of a modern industrial society also bear the English imprint.

---

[1] Louw Wepener was a Free State military leader who was killed in the Free State-Basuto War in 1865.

The judicial system, however, is the one with which the British administrators superseded the easy-going untrained confusion of landdrosts, heemraden and veldkornets, although the jury of nine members is common to the Union of today and to the Transvaal Republic. In practice the juries always consist of white male property-owners. Trial by jury is optional, and it has been found that whites accused of offences against non-whites tend to opt for a trial by jury. Non-whites on the other hand, if the other party in the case is white, will prefer a trial by judge and assessors.

The judiciary follows a pattern similar to the English one. Judicial independence is safeguarded by law and tradition. Judges may sometimes be appointed not for juristic distinction but for political services. In general, however, the judges' bench has had a high reputation for impartial administration of a set of laws which are increasingly unequal in their reference to non-whites. But while the judges usually manage to temper the social attitudes of the white group from which they come with the traditions and principles of their calling, this applies far less to the magistrates on whom falls the bulk of the judicial work.

These magistrates are paid officials who also perform administrative duties in their areas. As such they tend to be in constant contact with and to some extent dependent for promotion on good relations with the local white population.

In general, the law is one of the professions in which the Afrikaner, like the French Canadian, has always been prominent. This sphere has also on two occasions seen a major clash between Afrikaner and Afrikaner. In both cases, the issue arose between the advocates of an uncontrolled Volkswil and the champions of the rule of law. The first clash came in the Transvaal in 1897, between President Kruger and Chief Justice J. G. Kotze. The latter claimed the right to test the Volksraad's laws against the Grondwet. The clash ended with the abrupt dismissal of Kotze by the President in 1898.

Half a century later came a second and closely parallel case. The legal point at issue was that of parliamentary sovereignty and whether or not this could be said to exist if the courts had a testing right; or, as one Cabinet Minister put it more bluntly, whether or not the Volkswil was to be thwarted by a 'handful of old men in Bloemfontein' (i.e., the Appeal Court). The immediate political issue was the Nationalist Government's determination to remove some 50,000 Coloured voters from the common roll. This franchise was, together with the equal rights of the two official languages, 'entrenched' in the South Africa Act. The Appeal Court entered into the picture in 1952, when it unanimously ruled that the Act which abolished this franchise was null and void since it had not been passed according to the procedure laid down in the South Africa Act, i.e. by a two-thirds majority of both Houses in joint session. At this juncture another Nationalist Cabinet Minister implied that no better ruling could have been expected from 'a bunch of liberals'.

The somewhat sordid story of further Nationalist attempts to achieve their objective at all costs has been described all too often. As the matter now stands they have all but done so. The two-thirds majority has been assured by the 'winner-take-all' Senate Act of 1955. The recalcitrant Appeal Court was dealt with early in the same session by the Appellate Court Quorum Act. This enlarged the Appeal Court from five to eleven, and made a full quorum of eleven necessary in cases which concerned the validity of an Act of Parliament.

The appointment of judges in South Africa is in practice in the hands of the Minister of Justice. It may be coincidental that the majority of judges promoted since 1948 have been Nationalists, to the virtual exclusion of Jewish or liberally-minded candidates, and that the Nationalists appointed have usually had considerably fewer years of experience than non-Nationalists who were passed over. Commenting on this development, the Johannesburg *Star* wrote on 26th April that the Government had not disguised the fact that introducing the new Bill it hoped to get a Court that would reverse the 1952 judgement on the constitutional issue. 'What', it asked, 'would happen if the newly constituted Court reached the same decision as its predecessor? . . . There is nothing in the Government's mood to suggest that they would accept the situation even then, for it is fundamental to their position that it is intolerable that any Court should prescribe to Parliament what its procedure should be. It is an irony that they should nevertheless be compelled to use a Court to establish that position. Having failed by other means to eliminate the Courts, they now seek a Court that is prepared to eliminate itself.'

It should be stressed that a great number even of Nationalist Afrikaners are alarmed by the irresponsible way in which the Nationalist Government has dragged the highest court of the land into the political arena and thereby lowered its dignity in the eyes of overseas countries and of coloured South Africans. The latter still looked to the Appeal Court, as the Uitlanders did to Kotze's High Court, for some measure of protection against the full consequences of their political impotence.

The present alarming trend away from the rule of law is also shown in the increasing amount of legislation which leaves the individual at the mercy of the Minister concerned, with no appeal to the Courts against his decision. Recent instances of this process are the Riotous Assemblies and Suppression of Communism Amendment Act, the Public Safety Act, the Passport Act, and the increasing powers given to the Minister of Native Affairs to legislate for the reserves by proclamation. An analysis of this delegated legislation was published by R. P. Plewman, Controller and Auditor-General from 1946–54, in the *Forum* of February, 1956. He pointed out that whereas the numbers of Acts delegating powers to the Governor-General remained relatively static over five decades of three-consecutive-year periods, the number of Acts delegating powers to Ministers and others rose from two in the period 1912–14 to ten in 1942–4, and twenty-six in 1952–4.

The legal system of the Union is, as has been said, a 'white man's law'. It is made by white men to protect their privileged status. It is therefore natural that the provisions which it contains dealing with offenders tend to be deterrent or even retributive, and to reflect a master-servant relationship which is dying elsewhere. These attitudes are by no means confined to the Afrikaner group, but perhaps they find their most unselfconscious expression in a Nationalist milieu. It was, for instance, the Nationalist Minister of Justice, Mr. C. P. Swart, who in 1952, allowed himself to be photographed brandishing a cat-o-nine-tails, which he wished to show to members in the House of Assembly as 'the kind used in Republican days to punish labourers'. And it was Dr. Otto du Plessis, the rejected Nationalist Ambassador to the Netherlands and later Director of Information, who in 1953 told a questioner that whipping was in the Bible and so in the best traditions of Christian civilization. In general, corporal punishment occupies an important place in the Union's penal system, particularly as applied to non-white offenders who have threatened the persons or property of whites.

*　　*　　*　　*　　*

Party politics in South Africa have never developed along lines of socio-economic cleavage and temperamental oppositions, as they have done in countries with a homogeneous population. These forces have, of course, exerted a certain uneven pressure. Initially, they roughly coincided with the division between rural Boers and urban English, but it is the 'racial' issue that has dominated the scene.

Indeed, in its mildest form, the disciplined 'Christian National' democracy of neo-Krugerism has for a decade or more been supplanting more liberal democratic principles even amongst the moderate 'two-streamers'. Amongst the extreme racialists, however, the doctrines brought from overseas in the 1930's and 40's have left a buried treasure of totalitarian ideas which glint disquietingly under the shallow foundations of Nationalist unity. Conspicuous amongst such ideas are the advocation of a stricter censorship, of a ban on political parties advocating non-national programmes, and of the concept of citizenship, franchise and the possession of a passport as privileges rather than rights.

In the party-political sphere, Afrikaners are, broadly speaking, divided into those who favour co-operation with the English group and those who wish to dominate or even absorb the 'Brit'. The first group is sub-divided into those who would like to see white South Africa united culturally as well as politically: (Smuts' and Botha's 'single stream' or 'holist' policy), and those who would prefer Hertzog's 'two stream' policy, each group having equal political rights but retaining its separate culture, language and traditions.[1]

The first group is split on a party-political basis. The 'single-streamers' are with the English in the United Party; a small minority may be in other opposition parties according to their individual and socio-economic interests. This single-stream group still comprises perhaps a quarter of the total Afrikaans-speaking group, but it is now regarded as a group of 'renegades' and 'traitors'. Of the 'two-streamers', the majority are, how-ever, with the uncompromising racialists of the now reunited Nationalist Party.

Both sections of the first group share another equally funda-mental political orientation. They believe in the democratic process for all members of the white population. Extreme Nationalists tend inevitably toward authoritarianism. The Nationalist Party, therefore, consists of two sections; one is authoritarian if not totalitarian, the other moderate and democratically inclined. This division, incidentally, seems to reflect the patriarchal authoritarianism and the libertarianism of Kruger's day. Today, however, the authoritarian principle is much stronger than it was then.

The Nationalist Party, therefore, represents Afrikaners whose views on two important matters are more or less opposed. This is, of course, the weakness of all political parties which claim to represent a whole nation. It is further complicated by the in-creasingly heterogeneous socio-economic structure of the Afri-kaner group. One may doubt whether nationalistic and anti-British slogans alone could maintain party loyalty, were it not for the other force which moulds and indeed dominates all Union politics.

It has been said that all South African politics are native affairs. This is true in so far that all major political parties are basically concerned to ensure the white group's continued political and economic domination over a large and disfranch-ised non-white group. The axiom applies not only to Afrikaners

[1]By 1930, however, Hertzog himself did envisage the possibility that the streams might conceivably flow together in the far distant future.

but to English-speaking South Africans. Of the latter, it may be said only that their attitudes tend to be dominated by expediency as well as by the fear and aggressiveness that animate the great bulk of Afrikaners.

The policies of English-speaking South Africans are therefore less rigid and more adaptable to the economic and other needs of the moment. In the party-political sphere, however, these flexible policies have to be adjusted so as not to lose the votes of a large number of Afrikaners who vote against the Nationalists while fundamentally accepting the Nationalist policy of 'apartheid'. This accounts for the pathetic attempts of the United Party in recent years to outdo the Nationalists in its advocation of segregation. Though one may feel disgust at these antics, it has to be admitted that there is a tactical reason for them. The United Party has steadily lost Afrikaans-speaking voters to the Nationalists, not only in the platteland, but also in the towns; apartheid combined with the call for Afrikaner unity have proved far stronger issues than economic or constitutional ones.

Economic and constitutional issues are likely to become more important once Afrikaner Nationalism has gained the total victory. It is then that the whispered differences of interest between farmers and industrialists and workers will emerge clearly; then that the believers in freedom and the democratic process will find that they are being shepherded towards a one-party state. But the authoritarian Nationalists have foreseen this situation. They have the support of the Dutch Churches, the Nationalist Party being regarded as the only political expression of the needs of the national soul, and they are taking steps to ensure conformity and discipline in every other sphere of life. The black and red bogies are brought out periodically in order to close the ranks, and critics from within are already meeting the charge of disloyalty. Most important, the younger generation is already being educated in unquestioning loyalty and obedience to the ideals of the new Nationalism.

The party-political history of South Africa since Union has been one of uneasy coalitions. In these the ultimate weight has usually been exerted by the 'two-stream' group of Afrikaners, those who were not actively hostile to, but rather suspicious of, the English-speaking group. The way in which these two-streamers have moved has been dictated not only by slogans but by personalities. These very strong personal loyalties to leaders have until recently been a major feature of Afrikaner politics. They are a survival of the old commando and trek days, when men banded themselves together round an outstanding leader.

Botha, Hertzog and Smuts, the first three Premiers of the Union, were all Boer War leaders, each with their own personal following. As Denys Reitz wrote in *Commando*: 'I rode behind General Smuts as a boy with a rifle on my shoulder and I have followed since for forty years'. So indeed were the ill-fated de Wet and Beyers, many of whose followers came out in the 1914 Rebellion. A similar phenomenon occurred in 1952 when old Boer farmers and young ex-servicemen hastened to join the Torch Commando under the leadership of 'Oom' Dolf de la Rey and 'Sailor' Malan, ace pilot of 1940. Botha and Smuts could command a great deal more of this personal loyalty than can the young United Party leaders of today, and it may be that the defection of some of the Smuts and Botha men and their families has contributed to the higher poll of the Nationalist Party at the present time.

The general trend today is however towards parties and not personalities. In the United Party this applies because there are no individuals of sufficient personality. In the Nationalist Party it has been engineered because personalities in politics are dangerous and unreliable. From now on it is to be the Party that counts, and no efforts are being spared to make it into an efficient machine with which no individuals, however popular, can interfere at will.

In 1910 the centre of Afrikaner political equilibrium was farther away from the pole of authoritarian Nationalism. This was natural in a country of rural individualists, a country which had long been under British rule, and in which the Afrikaner had to fight even for the survival of his own language. It was only with growing political strength that the voice of extremism was heard.

At the time of Union, indeed, the voice of the 'single-streamers' under Botha prevailed, and the fears of a few carping Natalians and English-speaking politicians from the Cape were dismissed as ungenerous and jingoistic. Dr. Niemeyer in the Natal Parliament repudiated these fears with the words: 'We are all Britishers alike now. We have all accepted the British flag, and the majority of us . . . wish to form one nation with you, to the glory of the British Empire.'

Here spoke the authentic voice of the 'single-stream' Afrikaners. It was a far cry from the 1953 statement by Dr. Otto du Plessis, that the Act of Union was forced on the Boers, as they had been conquered and had no choice. There was however no doubt that it represented the genuine feeling of many leading Boers at the time. No discordant note was struck aloud by any contemporary Afrikaner leaders, although the poet Totius wrote that the self-sufficient, freedom-loving man of the veld was submitting to foreign servitude and endangering the traditions for which he had so lately fought. Had such a note been struck, it would probably have impelled the constitution-makers to move slowly, to entrench many more rights and possibly to adopt a federal rather than a unified form of connexion for the four colonies, as the great Afrikaner Bondsman, Hofmeyr, advised.

In the first Union elections the Afrikaner Parties in the Cape, Transvaal, and Free State gained sixty-six seats. The Unionist and Labour Parties, which were predominantly English, returned thirty-nine and four members respectively, but many English-speaking voters had supported the two Bonds and 'Het Volk'. The Afrikaner parties amalgamated to form the South African Party, led by General Louis Botha, who also formed the first Union Cabinet.

As early as 1914, however, the extremist and often anti-British nationalism which had seemed moribund in 1909 reared its head again. In 1912 General Hertzog had broken away from Botha to found the Nationalist Party, which was to stand for 'South Africa First', as opposed to the imperial connexion. In his famous De Wildt speech in December 1912 he said: 'The time has come when South Africa can no longer be ruled by non-Afrikaners, by people who have no real love for South Africa . . .

Imperialism suits me when it is of use to South Africa. Where it clashes with the interests of South Africa I am its inveterate opponent. I am prepared to stake my future political career upon that doctrine.'

A sizeable minority of Afrikaners, some of them 'two-streamers', others unreconciled Boer Republicans, followed General Hertzog into his new Nationalist Party. Their number was increased by Botha's refusal to remain aloof from 'Britain's quarrel', as it was called, in 1914. The strength of anti-British Republican feeling amongst the Boers became clear in the 1914 election, after Botha's Afrikaners had put down the armed rebellion of Maritz and earned themselves the name of traitors to Afrikanerdom.[1] Despite the participation of Beyers and de Wet, the Nationalist Party had officially frowned on the rebellion; the Party nevertheless became the rally-point of anti-Botha Afrikaners, polling 77,000 in the election to Botha's 95,000. Botha, left with fifty-four seats, was compelled to make even closer connexion with the English-dominated Unionist Party, which was a thorough-going war party.

In 1916, Botha made an attempt to regain the lost moderate Afrikaner votes by avoiding too close links with the Unionists, by releasing the rebel prisoners, and by calling for a great national celebration of Dingaan's Day[2] at Paardekraal. The Nationalists however held a rival celebration and the South African Party was driven back for support to the English. By the 1920 election, Nationalism had gained so much in strength that Botha's successor Smuts was driven to amalgamate with the Unionists, despite the possibility of alienating still more Afrikaner 'two-stream' support.

---

[1] The more moderate verdict of J. A. Wiid, writing in the *Kultuurgeskiedenis van die Afrikaner*, is that Botha was too conciliatory and colonial-minded. He accepted the British parliamentary system and shed the blood of Afrikaner brothers in 1914, says the writer, although the Afrikaners had no quarrel with the Germans.

[2] Afrikanerdom's greatest national day—16th December—the day on which Pretorius defeated the Zulus at Blood River and avenged Piet Retief's murder by Dingaan—the day on which the Transvaal Boers proclaimed their independence at Paardekraal in 1880 after the British annexation of the Transvaal.

In the ensuing years, the 'racial' issue was to some extent subordinated to social and economic issues in South African political life. Urban-rural and employer-worker conflicts cut across racial divisions, so that the United South African Party came to represent urban industrial interests and the wealthier farmers, while the Nationalists, representing the rural and urban Afrikaner proletariat and the new Afrikaner intelligentsia, formed a pact with the predominantly English-speaking Labour Party.

Such was the discontent with the Smuts Government in 1924 that a Nationalist-Labour Pact government came to power and remained there until 1933.[1] The Labour Party undertook to soft-pedal any socialist notes that remained after the breakaway of its left wing in 1915. The Nationalist Party on its side undertook to respect the British connexion. Following the Statute of Westminster in 1931, Hertzog professed himself satisfied with the independence enjoyed by the Dominions within the Commonwealth. It was indeed over this point that Hertzog was in 1940 to part company from his extremist republican followers.

The 1931 economic depression induced Hertzog and Smuts to form a coalition, which won an overwhelming majority of 136 in the 1933 election. This Fusion Government was to rule the country until 1939, but it soon ceased to include united Afrikanerdom. The pattern of 1912 repeated itself, with the breakaway of Dr. Malan and a minority of extremists to form the Purified Nationalist Party. Curiously enough, its members came mainly from the traditionally liberal Cape, but they included Mr. J. G. Strijdom, alone of Transvaal members. The Malanites were able to win twenty-seven seats at the 1938 election, but the 'one-stream' and most of the 'two-stream' Afrikaners remained within the United Party, which came back with 111 seats.

In the mid-30's it seemed possible that the foundations were being laid for a single South African nation. Urbanization,

---

[1]Results of 1924 election: Nationalists, 63; Labour, 18; United South African Party, 53; Independents, 1. In the 1929 election, the Nationalists came back with an overall majority of 78, but continued to govern with 5 members of the now split Labour Party. The other Labour Party section won 3 seats and the United South African Party 61. There was 1 Independent.

inter-marriage and bilingual education were blurring the old social and economic divisions. Hertzog felt that the Afrikaner had now achieved equal status and should go forward side by side with the English-speaking South African.

Meanwhile, however, some Purified Nationalists were impatiently embracing the prejudices and methods of a National Socialist Party elsewhere, while the remainder were building up Krugerism into a political ideology, in which the English and other non-national elements were either to be Afrikanerized or treated as second-class citizens. Within the Fusion Party itself the English tended to distrust Hertzog, while the two-stream Afrikaners distrusted Smuts.

The final split came as before with the outbreak of war. Hertzog and his supporters proposed benevolent neutrality; Smuts, who like Botha saw South Africa in relation to the global situation, chose full participation on Britain's side. South Africa entered the war on a vote of 80 : 67,[1] and Smuts with his rump United Party formed a Cabinet which included Labour and the British-oriented Dominion Party.

There followed an unsuccessful attempt to reunite Afrikanerdom.[2] The internecine warfare of the last five years between Hertzogites and Malanites had however been too savage, and the two leaders had moved too far apart on the republican and other issues. Hertzog was even more than ever convinced of the rightness of his egalitarian two-stream policy. He was prepared to leave the matter of a republic to time and the goodwill of the English-speaking section.

The Purified Nationalists however saw an immediate chance of establishing their Volk Republic with the goodwill of an inevitably victorious Nazi Germany. They regarded the two-stream policy as dangerous to the younger and slighter culture, as impractical, and as unnecessary in view of the Afrikaners' growing political strength. Hertzog had in fact, in his efforts to give the Afrikaner a feeling of self-respect and equal status,

---

[1] One-third of Hertzog's own party, the Fusion Party, and all the Malanites voted against entry into the war.

[2] This concept no longer included United Party Afrikaners, whose leader Smuts was labelled 'England's Quisling' by Malan.

raised a brood of Nationalist Frankensteins who were not prepared to stop short at equality. This was inevitable. The two-stream policy was not a practical end in the circumstances. It was however an essential stage on the road from British rule to national unity. Unfortunately the spiritual climate of the times was such that for many of its adherents Hertzogism led inevitably to the demand for Afrikaner domination.

The attempt at reunion persisted for a brief period largely because of its popularity amongst rank-and-file Hertzogites and Malanites. Hertzog finally found it impossible to agree with the projected programme and the growing authoritarianism of the new Reunited Nationalist Party (Herenigde Nasionale Party). He withdrew in disillusionment and with his faithful lieutenant Mr. Havenga founded the Afrikaner Party. Most of his former followers however remained with the Malanite group. Hertzog shortly afterwards retired from active politics, and died within the year.

During the war, the narrow chauvinism, pro-Germanism and Nazi undertones of the Malanite programme lost them some friends and failed to influence others. Until 1942 their ranks actually included the National Socialist 'New Order' of Oswald Pirow. In the 1943 Election Smuts came back with a higher total of eighty-nine, supported by nine Labour and seven Dominion Party members. The Nationalists' strength dropped to forty-three, whilst Hertzog's Afrikaner Party was wiped out.[1]

The Nationalists were not however dissatisfied with the trend of events. They now had about 68 per cent of the Afrikaner vote, instead of 60 per cent in 1938, when Hertzog was in the government. It was also noticeable that one-third of the members of the Union Defence Force (over 50 per cent Afrikaans-speaking in composition) had refrained from voting, while the fact that the Afrikaner birth-rate was considerably higher than that of the English-speaking group augured well for the future.

Once the war was over, economic and social problems and the very natural desire of democratic electorates for a change caused a considerable swing away from the Government, even

---

[1]Twenty-two of their seats went to Smuts and two to Malan.

amongst English-speaking South Africans. Dr. Malan, sensing the changing times, dropped the republican issue from his 1948 platform, went into coalition with Mr. Havenga's Afrikaner Party and elevated segregation to the level of an ideal under the name of 'apartheid'. The 'black peril' issue proved particularly successful in view of the well-known liberal views of General Smuts' lieutenant, Mr. J. H. Hofmeyr.

Dr. Malan collected the bulk of the moderate two-stream Afrikaner voters and even a few disgruntled English. With his seventy seats and Mr. Havenga's nine, he faced a combined Opposition of sixty-five United Party, six Labour Party and three Native Representatives. By 1951, the Afrikaner Party had merged with the Nationalists to form Die Nasionale Party, and except for the rump of the Ossewa-Brandwag and Mr. Pirow's 'New Order', all 'ware Afrikaners' were together again. Six safe Nationalist seats in South West Africa were added to the total, and in 1953 the Nationalist Party came back with an increased majority, winning ninety-four to the united Opposition's sixty-five seats.

The Nationalist majority was not fully representative of the voters' wishes, owing to the loading of country constituencies.[1] Counting in the unopposed seats, the Nationalists received less than 46 per cent of the total vote, or a minority of between 100,000 and 130,000 votes. This was however an improvement on their 1948 showing, when they received 4 per cent less of the total votes. Only after the 1954 Provincial Elections with their lower poll did the Nationalists even claim to reach parity in votes with the combined opposition. It seems probable that the great majority of the voters who changed allegiance were urban Afrikaners, but a few may even have been English-speaking South Africans, to whom the uncompromising toughness of the Nationalist native policy appealed. Nothing succeeds like success, and indeed it seems unlikely that the Nationalist Party can be dislodged from office by constitutional means for a very long time

---

[1] In the mainly Afrikaans-speaking Orange Free State, for instance, about one-third of the electorate is estimated to support the United Party, but it no longer returns a single United Party member to the Assembly or Provincial Council.

to come. Such dislodgement will be rendered all the less likely if the Nationalists proceed with their proposed enfranchisement of whites between the ages of 18 and 21, in view of the Afrikaner group's higher birth-rate.

Meanwhile, the years of victory saw a shift of balance within the Nationalist Party. As always, the former extremists aged and even learned to compromise under the responsibilities of office, and a new group of young extremists sprang up. This did not mean that the former extremists retraced their steps for any great distance. Dr. Malan never became a two-stream man, but he appeared to have accepted constitutional methods and gradual steps towards a republic. He also made great though unsuccessful efforts to ensure that his successor in December 1954 should be Hertzog's lieutenant Mr. Havenga and not the 'wild man of the North', Mr. J. G. Strijdom.

Rank-and-file Nationalism, reinforced by the young bulls of the Jeugbond and the Afrikaanse Studentebond, had however also moved towards the extremists. Why accept the two-stream compromise when total victory was at hand? And so the Broederbond nominees with their blend of Potchefstroom theocracy and National Socialism are now firmly in power, and there is no prominent leader left in political life to speak for those moderate Nationalists who may still exist. This is a rôle for which the United Party and the dissident Conservatives have cast themselves. So far however there are few takers, while they are alienating a good number of their English-speaking supporters.

It remains to be seen whether Mr. Strijdom will, like his predecessors in office, have to face pressure from a new and even more extreme group, or even a revolt from the moderates, who are showing increasing signs of restiveness.[1]

---

[1] In May 1953, thirteen professors and staff members of Pretoria University, all claiming to be members or supporters of the Nationalist Party, issued a petition protesting against the Senate legislation on ethical and constitutional grounds. The indignation which this protest aroused amongst Nationalist politicians was voiced by Mr. Eric Louw in an attack which included a suggestion that persons to whose salaries the State contributed had no right to criticize the Government's actions. It is as yet too early to estimate the chances of the 'South African Bond', set up in Pretoria by ex-Hertzogites in December 1955, and allegedly connected with some of these professors.

At present the economic sky is blue and the Union is moving through a period of rapid industrial expansion and even of rural prosperity. Prosperity has however its dangers. While depression usually sharpens extremism, boom conditions may blunt its fine edge and seduce the rank-and-file to more materialistic doctrines.

Turning to the political parties, their principles and their practice, we find that the Nationalist Party, whether under Hertzog, Malan or Strijdom, has always stood for Afrikaner nationalism, for independence from Britain, for a republic and for continued white supremacy in Africa.[1] Differences have arisen mainly in the methods advocated to achieve these ends, methods which have become progressively more uncompromising and authoritarian as final victory draws nearer.

Being based on nationalistic slogans, the Nationalist Party has continually moved away from the moderate and towards the extreme. The compromise inherent in any two-party system has inevitably been construed as collaboration and even treason, and leadership has passed to the men who could produce the purest form of nationalism.

Probably the most important characteristic of the Nationalist Party is its claim to be the only political organ of Afrikanerdom. This claim led to the outmanœuvring of Hertzog in 1940, to the victorious battle with the O.B. in the war years, to the outlawing of Pirow and to the engulfment of the Afrikaner Party in 1951. It gave rise to Dr. Malan's cry of triumph in 1948: 'Today South Africa belongs to us once more. For the first time since Union, South Africa is our own, may God grant that it will always remain our own.' Unfortunately the acceptance of such a principle means the end of the parliamentary system, while the Divine sanction with which it is invested makes deviation even more difficult.

---

[1]The difference between Hertzog and Malan was that the former believed that the two-stream programme would ultimately lead to a republic agreed to by both sections; Malan and the Purified Nationalists mistrusted the goodwill and South Africanism of the English-speaking section and thought that national unity could only be imposed on this section after a republic was established and its links with Britain cut.

As the political voice of the Volk the Party cannot be wrong. Conformity is essential and even criticism from outside is fiercely resented. Compromise is usually a betrayal, but if the Party is in power, it can at times be justified by the changing needs of the Volk, of whose political will the Party is the only voice. For instance, Nationalist Party leaders have during the last few years begun to realize that the Afrikaner cannot stand alone, and that their past hostility to the English-speaking section is depriving them of the support of a million whites who may be needed to defend white civilization in South Africa against the black tide. In consequence, the republican issue has been soft-pedalled and the Commonwealth issue dropped, while the merits of 'apartheid' are constantly stressed. The last years have also seen the ingenuous disavowal by Nationalist leaders of the 1942 Draft Constitution of the Republic, whose chauvinistic authoritarianism and anti-British tone are not today the best propaganda for any Nationalist-English rapprochement.

Nationalist attitudes to the English-speaking South African have in general been characterized by antagonism, or at the best cautious dislike. It has therefore proved difficult to switch the entire Party machine and the rank-and-file to uncompromising fraternalism. The Nationalist Party still remains almost exclusively Afrikaner in composition. A few English-speaking stooges are, however, retained in case of need in such areas as Natal and the Eastern Province. Two of these are actually in the Senate.

The 'Volkswil' of President Kruger has provided modern Nationalists with a convenient tactical weapon. It has also served to conceal from the ordinary Nationalist the growing regimentation within the Party and the increasing arbitrariness and expediency of its policy. The most glaring recent example of the latter is the long-drawn-out constitutional battle which followed the proposed abolition of the Coloured franchise. In this the Nationalist Government, in the name of the sovereign will of the people, has disavowed the 'dead hand of the past' in the shape of earlier pledges in which the Malanites participated, has overridden the Act of Union, has packed the Senate and has lowered the prestige of the Appeal Court.

As a slogan, the 'Volkswil' has the merit of flexibility. When applied to the Republican issue, it is said the Republic will come only when 'the broad basis of the Volkswil' wishes it.[1] At times this phrase has been interpreted as involving the acquiescence of most English-speaking South Africans. This was the attitude of Hertzog in the 1930's, and even of Dr. Malan some years ago. In general, however, the Purified Nationalists tend to interpret the 'Volkswil' as the will of Nationalist Afrikanerdom, expressed through its parliamentary party.

An even more flexible concept with an appeal not confined to Afrikanerdom is that of apartheid. This was first put forward as a political programme in the 1948 election, and it undoubtedly played a great part in ensuring the Nationalist victory. Apartheid can mean either separation or segregation. Of late its adherents have endeavoured to substitute the phrase 'separate development' when rendering it in English. Whatever apartheid may in fact mean, it is indisputably the opposite of the liberal or *laissez-faire* policy of integration, and its aim is to maintain white supremacy or baasskap.

The theory of apartheid and its practice have so far diverged sharply. As a theory it was put forward by national-minded churchmen and intellectuals who sought a way of reconciling the traditional segregation and continued white supremacy with their consciences as Christians. The argument was that continued integration and Europeanization of the non-European would lead to a demand for political rights which could not in fairness be refused. This would, however, lead to the swamping and disappearance of the white group. If, on the other hand, political rights were refused to the non-European, the ultimate result would be the same because the non-whites would revolt and sweep away the whites. The result of this reasoning was a series of blue-prints for apartheid, demanding complete territorial separation for non-whites, with eventual self-government, the encouragement of cultural self-determination or 'develop-

---

[1]The Nationalist Party Constitution contains a clause which states that a Republic outside the Commonwealth is best suited to South Africa; this Republic should, however, be attained by a plebiscite and not by a parliamentary majority.

ment along their own lines' and so on. Chief amongst the advo-
cates of this intellectual apartheid are the Dutch Reformed
Churches and SABRA (the South African Bureau for Racial
Affairs, based on Stellenbosch University).

As an election slogan, particularly when opposed to the
vaguer United Party policy of Christian trusteeship, apartheid
had great virtue. As a practical political policy, however, the
type of apartheid advocated by the Stellenbosch intellectuals
was hardly practicable. Afrikaner farmers, housewives and the
growing Afrikaner commercial and industrial class were by no
means willing to contemplate selling their land or losing their
native labour, or to face the prospects of black cheap-labour
States on their borders which could undercut them in local and
external markets. Nor were the majority of whites, whether
Afrikaans or English-speaking, disposed to modify their traditional attitude of superiority to the non-white and to accept the
fact that he was different but potentially equal, given adequate
guidance.

Apart from the views of the Nationalist man-in-the-street, the
advocates of total apartheid were faced by certain almost in-
superable economic difficulties. Chief amongst these were the
inadequacy of the existing reserves, which were to form the
territorial nucleus of an African national home, to support more
than 4 million of the 11 million Africans in the country; the
impossibility of acquiring much more land within the Union for
this purpose;[1] and the increasing demands for more labour
for industry, whose labour force is already 67 per cent non-
white. In addition the apartheid theorists were faced with the
existence of a permanently detribalized and urbanized African
population.

In practice therefore the negative and 'treat-them-rough'
aspects of apartheid, seen as segregation or horizontal apartheid,

---

[1] The present area of South Africa's Native Reserves is just over 10 per cent
of the total land area of the Union. The acquisition of the Protectorates (a
constant Nationalist platform cry) would bring this percentage up to 49 per
cent, but this would be an empty gain, as the Protectorates, but for Swaziland, are drought-stricken and poor in soil, and already export much of their
available manpower to the Union's urban areas.

have so far been the ones to be stressed. As an official of the State Information Department said without conscious irony in late 1955: 'The impression that apartheid was designed expressly for the benefit of the non-white people would be incorrect'. The resulting legislation[1] fell more heavily on the Coloured people, who still retain some rights, than on the Africans. In all non-white groups this legislation caused frustration and hostility and laid the foundations of anti-white unity. Meanwhile, Dr. Malan and other leading Nationalists began to warn their followers that while total apartheid was still the goal it was not practical politics for the time being.[2]

After Mr. Strijdom became Prime Minister, the supporters of intellectual or vertical apartheid rallied. Behind the Prime Minister stand his eminence grise, the apostle of intellectual apartheid, Dr. Verwoerd, and the advocate of economic apartheid, Senator de Klerk. In the last year or so, there has therefore been a series of legislative and other steps directed towards a more positive apartheid. These measures include the Native Building Workers Act, the Bantu Authority Act, the Native (Abolition of Passes and Co-Ordination of Documents) Act, the Bantu Education Amendment Act, the Bantu Urban Authority Act, and so on.

The basic trend of this legislation is to assign to the African a national home in the reserves, to stress that he has a language, culture and way of life which are essentially his own and which his education and institutions must encourage and develop, and to allot him the status of a migrant labourer with no political or freehold rights in the white man's areas. In practice this means a return to the decayed institutions of tribal government

---

[1]Population Registration Act, 1950; Group Areas Act, 1950; Prohibition of Mixed Marriages Act, 1949; Immorality Amendment Act, 1950; Reservation of Separate Amenities Act, 1953; Separate Representation of Voters Act, 1953.

[2]Party leaders were by no means unanimous. On the same day, 1st May, 1951, Dr. Malan told the House of Assembly: 'The Afrikaans Churches' policy of total separation between black and white is not the policy of the Nationalist Party'. Meanwhile, Dr. Verwoerd was informing the Senate: 'The Churches' policy and the policy of the South African Bureau of Racial Affairs of total separation is that of the Nationalist Party.'

and indirect rule. Such a regression can hardly hope to succeed with semi-tribalized, semi-westernized communities. Success is rendered the less likely because the Nationalist Government has failed to check the steady flow of Africans into the towns and cities, and into industry: nor indeed, while good times last, can it hope to do so. South Africa's economy is based on cheap non-white labour and Afrikaners have now won a sufficient share in the economic jackpot to fear radical racialist moves in the shape of directed industry and forced population shifts that will discourage outside investors and deprive them of labour and of the non-white consumer market. By late 1955, Mr. Strijdom too was repudiating the concept of intellectual apartheid; all the present generation could do, he said, was to work in that direction.

The new prosperity has come up against the old anti-capitalist strain in Nationalist thinking. This anti-capitalism was the legacy of a society without class or cash, which saw itself destroyed by the rapaciousness of foreign capitalists and given the jackal's share in the new economic system. Afrikaners have long resented their small slice of the economic cake, and deliberate attempts to build up Afrikaner economic strength have been made since the 1920's. These attempts are now proving successful, but the need to work within the framework of what the Nationalists used to call 'British-Jewish' capitalism has stimulated the rise of a class of Afrikaner capitalists, and its converse, a property-less urban Afrikaner proletariat.

Such economic differentiation is not conducive to national unity, and Nationalist planners are concerned to prevent its further development. Socialism and Communism are of course rejected, but the co-operative system is seen as a possible alternative. The Nationalist Party must from now onwards try to avoid the mistake of the United Party in allowing itself to be linked with big business, even if this be Afrikaner big business. As E. S. Sachs wrote: 'The balance of political power and the political future of South Africa lie largely in the hands of the Afrikaner workers of the urban areas. Platteland constituencies overwhelmingly support the Nationalist Party and its policy of apartheid. Some of the rural areas and most of the urban centres support the United Party and the balance of political power is in the hands of about fifteen or twenty constituencies where the workers' votes predominate. Some workers will vote for the United Party only because it is the lesser evil and others of the workers look upon the United Party as a party of capitalists. In the absence of a strong and influential labour party, tens of thousands of workers voted Nationalist in the last election'.

The Nationalist Party has for long been aware of the need to catch its members young. There is therefore a youth movement called the Jeugbond, with branches in most African-medium schools and universities. The Jeugbond is for young Nationalists between the ages of 12 and 17; it has its own junior movement, the Strydmakkertjies, for children under 12. These were the children who were mobilized to help in the 1953 General Election. The unruliness and growing hooliganism of young political partisans in the Union may well be attributed to the indoctrination that is received from these political youth organizations. The Nazi tinge which has coloured political Afrikaner National-ism for the last twenty years or so seems at its strongest here, and it may be that the neo-Krugerites are nurturing a brood of Frankensteins who will not be prepared to abide by the official brand of disciplined Calvinist democracy.

Nationalist Party action today is distinguished by qualities which are in most cases alien to or distortions of the traditional Boer character. Chief amongst these are an uncompromising ruthlessness as to ends, combined with a flexible immorality as to means, for which expediency is too mild a word: a suspicious-ness and fear of other peoples and nations; an inability to take criticism from any source, and an increasing tendency to claim Divine sanction for its actions and policies. To all of this the Nationalist rank-and-file appear to be submitting more tamely than one might have expected of the descendants of the sturdily independent and even factious Voortrekkers.

The increasing strength of the party machine and of party discipline can probably be attributed to the growing influence of the Broederbond. This is a genuine secret society about which information can only be obtained from the accounts of those who have left it and those who have suffered by not belonging to it, or from the occasional releases about its more innocuous activities which have from time to time been published.

The Afrikaner Broederbond was apparently formed in Johannesburg in 1918, with aims of fostering the Afrikaans language and of bringing young Afrikaners on the Reef together. At this stage it was an open society, and seems to have drawn a good proportion of its recruits from ambitious and nationally-minded young railway clerks. Members were supposed to wear a badge with the letters A.B. on it, and to insist upon speaking Afrikaans in shops and other public places. At that time city life and commerce were even more English-dominated than they are today. As more and more school-teachers joined, the scope of the organization increased and propaganda began to be made for separate Afrikaans-medium schools. According to a founding member, the social and religious activities of the Broederbond at this stage were very attractive to young Afrikaners. Even in the early years, however, its chauvinistic tone grew and those members who believed in Botha's single-stream policy found themselves in a minority and gradually withdrew.

In 1924 a majority decided that the fight for Afrikanerdom could best be carried on underground. From then on, the Broederbond's true nature and activities can only be surmised. A founding member, whose brother remained in the Broederbond and subsequently rose to be the General Manager of South African Railways, writes: 'I could only draw my own conclusions when in later years I saw members occupying key positions in newly created semi-political organizations'.

Undoubtedly the character of the organization changed after 1924 and it seems probable that it became an elite group with a master plan for Afrikanerdom. By its own admission it has inspired the setting up of most of the important organizations in various spheres of Afrikaner life, notably the F.A.K. in the cultural sphere, the Reddingsdaadbond in the economic sphere and the Volkskas in banking.

The Broederbond's aims are concerned with republicanism, Krugerist democracy, the severing of all links with Britain, the dominance of the Afrikaans language and of national-orientated

Afrikanerdom. These aims appear in more or less modified forms in the Nationalist Party platform and in a purer version in the Draft Republican Constitution.

Membership at present is said to be between 3,000 and 3,500, consisting of teachers, farmers, clergymen and lawyers, in that order of numerical strength. It is by invitation and is only conferred after very careful scrutiny on those who are or seem likely to become key men in politics, the Civil Service, the professions and business life. There are sixty or more Broeders sitting on the Nationalist benches in the House of Assembly, and six of the Ministers in Dr. Malan's Cabinet, including the Premier himself, were also Broeders. Dr. Malan is, however, thought not to have stood high in the Broederbond, and may in his last years even have incurred the suspicions of its Executive Council, known as the Twelve Apostles. The Brotherhood is even more firmly entrenched in Mr. Strijdom's Cabinet today, Dr. Dönges, the Minister of the Interior, being particularly high in its councils.

The present Nationalist Party is therefore probably the political arm of the Broederbond. Non-members in the Party claim that their way is blocked, that the choicest fruits of office go to the Broeders and that any mistakes the latter make are covered up by the Broederbond.[1]

The impact of the Brotherhood falls most heavily on the former Hertzogites. In 1935, Hertzog said of the Broeders: 'They are sworn not to entertain any co-operation with the English-speaking population and thereby they stand in direct racial conflict with our fellow English Afrikaners, and their striving by way of domination on the part of the Afrikaans-speaking section to put their foot on the neck of English-speaking South Africa . . . The Broederbond has become a grave menace to the rest and peace of our social community, even where it operates in the economic cultural sphere.'

---

[1]This is said to apply in the Civil Service as well. From 1944 until the Nationalists came to power in 1948 Civil Servants were forbidden to belong to the Broederbond, though it was difficult to prove such membership in most cases. In prohibiting the Broederbond Smuts called it a 'dangerous, cunning, political, Fascist organization'.

In the years since Hereniging in 1940, and the Nationalist Party's engulfing of the Afrikaner Party in 1950, there has been a steady trickle of disillusioned Hertzogites out of the party, or even out of political life. First and greatest of these was Hertzog himself. 1954 saw the departure of Mr. Havenga, rejected as Dr. Malan's successor in favour of the Broederbonder, Mr. Strijdom. Mr. Havenga retired into private life in pained and dignified silence. Others, such as the then Mayor of Bloemfontein, Mr. J. G. Benade, left the part in a flurry of disillusionment and joined the United Party. The same course was followed by Dr. C. F. van der Merwe, Professor of Medicine at Pretoria University; the latter added a pointed comment on the growing inefficiency of the medical service in consequence of the domination of the administration by a Broederbond clique.

Both in 1944 and recently, the Broederbond was goaded by outside criticism into publishing a defence of its activities. The main line of defence was that the Broederbond was being unfairly used as a political bogey; the organization was in reality a non-political organization concerned with the furthering of Afrikaner unity, culture and interests. Its proceedings were not published simply as a matter of efficiency. This was the gist of statements made by Dr. Malan in 1951, when he offered to order an inquiry into Broederbond affairs if the United Party agreed to a similar inquiry into the affairs of the Sons of England,[1] and of the 1951 report of the Dutch Reformed Church Council's Committee of Investigation. The latter's conclusion was that the Broederbond was a 'good and sound organization'. This may be taken at less than its face value when one considers that the Broederbond supplied the material on which the Committee based its findings and that many prominent predikants in the Dutch Reformed Church are generally believed to be Broeders.

An organization which despite its present eclipse merits

---

[1]The 'Sons of England' is a 'true blue', Pan-Commonwealth, nostalgic association mainly based on Natal and the Eastern Cape Province; its jingoistic utterances have mellowed with the years. Its main function today seems to be to act as a clay pigeon for Nationalist counter-attacks whenever the Broederbond comes under fire.

discussion is the Ossewa-Brandwag (O.B.). Whereas the Broeder-bond is a back-stage elite, the O.B. was at its peak a mass organization fulfilling the deeper emotional needs and desire for a visible unity of the Afrikaner masses.

The O.B., which means the 'Sentinel of the Ox-Wagon', was founded in Bloemfontein in 1938. Its original purpose was to embody and perpetuate the idealism which the centenary celebrations of the Great Trek had inspired.[1] The Movement was organized on a commando basis[2] with a semi-military programme of training, a storm-trooper style elite of 'Stormjaers' and a Commandant-General, J. F. van Rensburg, whose open belief in National Socialism probably gave the movement a direction it would not otherwise have taken. The O.B. was enthusiastically welcomed by the Volk. By early 1941, its strength was said to be between 300,000 and 400,000.

Unfortunately, the O.B., however much it might fill a gap in the Volk's organizational needs, had not been initiated by and was independent of, the Nationalist Party. Moreover, it claimed

---

[1]The declared aims of the Ossewa-Brandwag were: 'the perpetuation of the spirit of the ox wagon in South Africa; maintaining and providing and giving expression to the traditions and principles of the Dutch Afrikaner; protecting and promoting the religious, cultural and material interests of the Afrikaner; fostering patriotism and national pride, and harnessing and uniting all Afrikaners, men as well as women, who endorse these principles and are prepared to make energetic endeavours to promote them. The *modus operandi* is as follows: Celebrating Afrikaans national festivals and our heroes' birthdays, erecting memorials, laying wreaths at monuments, locating and keeping in repair places of historical interest as well as the graves of Afrikaners who perished on the 'Pad van Suid Afrika'; organizing gatherings such as target practice, popinjay and 'vulture' shooting, playing jukskei, etc., doing folk dances and singing folk songs, holding processions, regular gatherings of an educational and social nature, dramatic performances, lectures on our history, literature, debates, camps for men and women, etc.

[2]A second organization of this commando type, called the Handhawers-bond, but with even more aggressive and specifically political aims, was started in 1940 by Gert Yssel, an enthusiastic University lecturer from Potchefstroom. It was hoped that the Handhawersbond might serve as an action group within the Nationalist Party, but it too closely resembled the O.B. and early incurred the hostility of the police and of the Krugerites within the Nationalist Party. In consequence, it faded into insignificance within the year, although it does not seem to have been formally dissolved, and was mentioned as late as 1955 in the Press.

to stand for a national union on the widest basis, in contrast to the Nationalist Party's stand for sectional party unity. In consequence, when the O.B. moved into the political sphere, it was not prepared to submit tamely to Nationalist Party domination, nor would the O.B. moderate its strong-arm methods and uncompromising demands for a German victory and for a one-party National Socialist Republic, even when the fortunes of war were moving in favour of the Western Allies.

All this constituted a threat, not only to Krugerism but to the unique power of the Nationalist Party. After some years of intrigues and battles, followed by tactical reconciliations, Malan won a decisive victory and forbade Nationalist Party members to join the O.B. The O.B. thereafter receded into semi-obscurity, along with the Fascist Grey Shirts (dissolved in 1950) and the National Socialist 'New Order' of Oswald Pirow, an able Hertzogite lawyer, who had in the Fusion Government been Minister for War. Both these groups had, like the O.B., become an embarrassment to the neo-Krugerite democrats of the Nationalist Party, once the possibility of German victory had receded. All three had indirectly left a legacy of submerged totalitarian thinking amongst their former adherents.

But it was only the O.B. that had become a genuine mass movement, less because of its totalitarian implications than because it seemed to offer 'to every man—and at first also to every woman—the chance of an individual and ponderable contribution to the great task of unifying the Afrikaner nation. At braaivleisaande, at jukskei[1] meetings, at the local Kultuur-vereniging meetings, and even on occasion at church, Afrikaners could meet in that Trekker dress which was to be the uniform of the movement and feel a sense of community of

---

[1]Braaivleisaande—'evening barbecue picnics.' Jukskei is an old Voortrekker pitching game played by men after the evening outspan with a portion of the yoke. It was revived in the thirties by the national-minded, to give the Afrikaner a national game. It is played with great ceremony and often in Voortrekker costume. But an athletic Afrikaner who was asked for his views on it commented: 'Jukskei corresponds to the English game of bowls. It is all right for a summer evening after a heavy meal but one can't get very excited or patriotic about it. Rugby was and remains the Afrikaners' national sport.'

culture, of common heritage, of organized progress towards a great goal—a feeling which they did not always (or even perhaps often) experience within the framework of their political parties. The O.B. indeed, aspired to embrace the whole Volk . . . it was to be the highest common factor of Afrikanerdom, the negation of that volkskeuring with which the rival charioteers on the Pad van Suid Afrika were always charging one another.'[1]

Today, the O.B. lingers on, aggressively pro-republican, anti-British and anti-democratic, sniping at the Nationalist Party in its organ *Die O.B.* Its strength was depleted still further in 1951, following the amalgamation between the Nationalist Party and Mr. Havenga's Afrikaner Party, with which the O.B. had formed a loose alliance. The Afrikaner Party supplied the political representation (until it was wiped out parliamentarily in 1943), while the O.B. provided its supporters. This link-up may seem an incomprehensible one, in view of the O.B.'s Nationalist Socialist leanings, and general opposition to political parties. It was, however, based on political expediency tinged by a sentimental attachment to Hertzog. The Nationalist Party swallowed the Afrikaner Party, but refused to omit its discrimination clause. The Afrikaner Party rank-and-file members, of whom the majority were now members of the O.B., were thus left with the choice of political homelessness or of resigning from the O.B.[2] A considerable number took the latter course, and the strength of the Ossewa-Brandwag was further sapped.

The Nationalist Party thus remained in complete political control of the Volk as presently defined. There is, however, a sizeable minority of 'non-national' Afrikaners, probably about one-quarter of the total. Their political allegiance dates back to a day when most of Afrikanerdom followed Smuts' and later Hertzog's policies of Vereniging or unity of all white South Africans, whether upon a one-stream or two-stream basis. To-

---

[1] Roberts and Trollip: *The South African Opposition* 1939–45, p. 74.

[2] A small minority of these O.B. members actually found their way to the United Party. In 1953, this Party put up Advocate J. D. Jerling, the O.B.'s former Assistant Commandant General, as its candidate (unsuccessful) for the tough Afrikaans-speaking workers' suburb of Westdene, Johannesburg, and Mr. A. J. Bekker, a former leading O.B. member, for the seat of Beaufort West, Cape Province.

day, most of Afrikanerdom has turned to the advocate of Hereniging or reunion of all Afrikaners, and the stubborn believers in Vereniging are branded as traitors, renegades and quislings.[1] Their sin is all the graver because if they were to return to the fold the Union could be permanently dominated by the Afrikaans-speaking group, leaving the English as a permanent political minority.

This minority of Afrikaners has, perhaps by virtue of the difficulties it has always faced, been the most politically active and constructive group in the Union. These difficulties are barely appreciated by most English-speaking South Africans, who live snugly in their urban enclaves of like-minded people. The anti-Nationalist Afrikaner, on the other hand, usually lives amongst his political opponents. He shares with them the same religion and culture, but he finds politics and political intolerance penetrating so deeply into all non-political spheres that he and his children face coolness, and occasionally even ostracism, in church, social meetings, classrooms or on the playing fields. He may find that political bigotry affects his job or business, and as the Afrikaans-medium schools become more and more 'national' he may even lose the allegiance of his children.

This pressure is of course deliberate and it drives the less stubborn to outward or even inward acquiescence. One of the more stubborn anti-Nationalists wrote bitterly of 'the Nationalists' arrogance in exploiting the Afrikanership of thousands of anti-Nationalist Afrikaans-speaking South Africans for political and economic reasons. They have appropriated the Afrikaans language and churches as if every Afrikaner is a Nationalist . . . yet the Transvaal Provincial Council had to pass a law to compel anti-Nationalist Afrikaners to put their children into Nationalist-dominated Afrikaans-medium schools . . . I think it is time someone took the lead to form a united, anti-Nationalist front, irrespective of party, language, race or creed'.[2]

---

[1]Amongst the Afrikaners who have been so described by their fellow Afrikaners on these grounds are: J. H. Hofmeyr, leader of the Cape Afrikaner Bond, General Louis Botha, General Smuts, 'Sailor' Malan, Mr. J. H. Strauss, and even at various stages of his career, General Hertzog.

[2]Louis J. du Plessis, in the *Rand Daily Mail*, 5th October, 1951.

The great majority of these anti-Nationalist Afrikaners are supporters, if not members of, the United Party, and indeed they supply it with the majority of its leaders and parliamentary representatives. Despite their excommunication by the Nationalist Party, they remain Afrikaners, with the outlook and attitude of Afrikaners. It has, therefore, been no mean task to drive them in double harness with the mercantile and more flexible English-speaking section which makes up the other large body of United Party supporters.

The indispensability of the Afrikaans-speaking supporters, who number about 25 per cent of the United Party's strength, is reflected in the republican clause in the United Party's Constitution, in the constant hero-worship of Smuts and even of Hertzog, in the close correspondence between the United Party and the Nationalist Party policy in such matters as the feather-bedding of farmers, the maintenance of traditional segregation, and the supply of cheap non-white labour. The main difference between the two parties is that the United Party is a non-racial party as far as whites are concerned, and that it stands for the continuation of the Commonwealth connexion and for parliamentary democracy on the British model. In method it is essentially empiricist and flexible. As the only large-scale anti-Nationalist party, the United Party must provide a policy that is all things to all anti-Nationalists, industrialists, liberals, farmers and artisans. In office this was possible for a while. In opposition it is not, and the consequence is that minority groups representing various viewpoints have been peeling off to form parties of their own.

These splinter parties are: the Conservative or Independent United Party; the Liberal Party, and the Federal Party. The latter need not concern us here, it is based on Natal and its members are almost entirely English-speaking.[1] The Conservative Party has at present seven members in the House of Assembly. It represents both the two-stream principle as between Boer and Briton and a right-wing or near-Nationalist attitude

---

[1]The Federal Party claims that the spirit of Union has been destroyed and advocates a federal structure instead of the present unitary one.

in non-white policy. This party was born because a handful of Afrikaans and English-speaking United Party M.P.s in the United Party felt unhappy about what they regarded as the growing liberalism of the United Party programme and hoped to form the nucleus of a central party drawn from both sides. Perhaps secretly the Afrikaners amongst them also yearned to return to the bosom of Afrikanerdom. These prodigal sons might have been welcomed more warmly by the self-appointed political representatives of Afrikanerdom had they brought with them sufficient support to give the Nationalist Government its two-thirds majority to abolish the Coloured vote. As it is, the Conservatives hover between the Government and the Opposition, popular with neither, but lecturing both on the errors of their extremes.

The Liberal Party is represented in Parliament by one African Representative and one Senator representing the Cape Africans. Both of these are whites, but neither of them are Afrikaners. This parliamentary strength does not however adequately represent the strength of the Liberal Party. It is an organization theoretically open to all races, which receives its mainly white support largely from geographically dispersed professional people and intellectuals of both language groups. This party opposes the colour bar and stands for universal adult suffrage, to be introduced in stages by interim qualifications designed to produce an informed electorate. It is not therefore likely in the foreseeable future to have any political influence, other than as a possible nuisance group in a closely contested election in a few upper-income group urban seats, and possibly as a symbol of white sympathy which may moderate the worst excesses of anti-white feeling amongst black nationalists.

Although the Liberal Party itself is treated with scorn by Nationalist Afrikaners, some of the liberal views that it expresses are not. As Dr. N. J. Diederichs said in the House of Assembly in 1948: 'What is at issue is two outlooks on life, fundamentally so divergent that a compromise is utterly unthinkable . . . It is a fight between nationalism, which believes in the necessary existence of distinct peoples, distinct languages, nations and cultures, and which regards the facts of existence of these peoples and these cultures as the basis of its conduct. On the other hand we have liberalism, and the basis of its political struggle is the individual with his so-called rights and liberties . . . Nationalism is the standpoint of members on this side of the House; and we say that this idea of liberalism is unnatural and impossible and should it be achieved one day, which fortunately is not possible, the whole world would be the poorer for it'.

In mid-1955, the liberal wing of the United Party became restive as a result of the leadership's steady abandonment of principle and modification of its non-white policy in the direction of apartheid. As a result of answers from the party leadership which he regarded as unsatisfactory, one M.P. of well-known liberal views resigned his seat and announced that he would ask his supporters to return him as an Independent on this issue. This they subsequently failed to do by a small minority, returning a former Nationalist in response to an appeal for party loyalty.

This partial disintegration of the United Party is being viewed with some satisfaction by the Nationalists. The splinter parties can do no harm to them, and indeed their main effect is to prove to the marginal Nationalists that the United Party is, as the Nationalists have always maintained, a home for English jingoes, renegade Afrikaners, liberals and Kafferboeties (nigger-lovers). The United Party will probably eliminate the splinter parties in the next election, as the latter's supporters will be chary of splitting the anti-Nationalist vote. The inexorable movement of two-streamers towards the rising star of Nationalist Afrikanerdom is however likely to continue, despite the United Party leadership's Canute-like belief in an incipient split between moderates and extremists within the Nationalist Party.

The third of the old-established political parties is the South African Labour Party, now down to five representatives in the House of Assembly. This party is mainly notable here for the fact that it has so far failed to provide a political home for the Afrikaner worker. In other words, the Labour Party has failed to make these workers vote for economic issues rather than vote 'with the blood'. The reasons for this are threefold. Firstly, the South African Labour Party has since its establishment before World War I been 'British' in leadership and tradition. Only two Afrikaners, Martinus van den Berg and Manie Celliers, both miners, became Labour M.P.s; the former joined the Nationalist Party in 1946, and the latter left political life altogether. In the meantime, the white working-class has come to consist overwhelmingly of recently urbanized poor Afrikaners from the platteland, anti-African, anti-foreign and nationalistic. E. S. Sachs writes: 'The leaders of the Labour Party, although they always appealed to the Afrikaner workers to come into the Party, because of their British tradition never really understood the sentiments and problems of a nationally-minded agrarian people. The Afrikaner workers, because of their history and background, require an entirely different approach from workers who have had a long industrial tradition. For Labour leaders, who have always belonged to a ruling race and have never known the problems and aspirations of people who feel oppressed, the national and agrarian questions seem to have no place in their political consideration.'

Finally, the Labour Party has come up against the fact that the white worker is not a worker at all in the European sense. His job and his status depends on the existence of a large substratum of cheap black labour, against which he must protect his vested interests. The egalitarian traditions of the European labour movement have, therefore, given way to such slogans as 'Workers of the world, unite and fight for a White South Africa'. And any European-style Labour Party must fall between two stools to the detriment of its membership. To quote the same writer: 'The spokesmen of the Nationalist Party and large numbers of white workers launched violent attacks on the Labour Party for being "pro-Kaffir". On the other hand, many Leftists and Liberals make strong attacks upon the Party for having a reactionary native policy. For years now, the Labour Party has had to meet the cross-fire from the reactionary right and the progressive left, with dire consequences to the progress of the Party. Many progressive intellectuals and workers have remained outside the Party because it is too reactionary, and thousands of white workers have not come in because it is too progressive'.

Mr. Sachs concludes that a strong Labour Party is the only party that could win the support of the vital marginal industrial seats away from the Nationalist Party, and thereby break the latter's parliamentary power. Nationalist leaders are well aware of this danger, as their long-sustained attack on the orthodox, Socialist-oriented, trade union movement shows.

The South African Communist Party, with one member of Parliament representing Africans, was always too insignificant to merit the crushing penalties laid down in the Suppression of Communism Act of 1950, and its 1951 Amendment. The Communist Party of South Africa dissolved itself just before the Act was passed and went underground. Most of its leaders were English-speaking, but it attracted some Afrikaans-speaking workers and intellectuals, particularly in the 1920's and 30's. E. S. Sachs, from whose book *The Choice Before South Africa* the above quotations are taken, was himself a member of the Communist Party until 1931, when he was expelled for deviationism. In 1952 he was 'named' as a Communist and ordered to give up his post as Secretary of the Garment Workers' Union.

Many anti-Nationalists, English or Afrikaans-speaking, have suffered from a deep sense of frustration with the existing political parties. This frustration was enhanced by the malaise of ex-servicemen who had seen in the years overseas golden visions of a happier land, or who quite simply were bored with the peace. Out of this restlessness arose in 1951 another commando-type action front, the War Veterans' Torch Commando. Its immediate cause was the threat to the Constitution inherent in the proposed abolition of the Coloured vote.

The Torch Commando was, from the start, a political pressure group. Its leaders intended it to meet a constitutional crisis and to break up once that crisis had been satisfactorily met. Its aims were defined by one of its founders, the Battle of Britain ace 'Sailor' Malan, as follows:—

'1. To work for the satisfactory entrenchment of the rights of the South African people. 2. To combat Communism. 3. To combat authoritarianism. 4. To restore democratic government.

5. To maintain full partnership within the Commonwealth.
6. To work towards harmony and full co-operation between all races in South Africa.'

These aims were, in fact, a modernized version of Botha's and Smuts' 'one-stream' parliamentary democracy. The Commando had, however, a wider appeal. Its leaders were new men, not professional politicians nor politically ambitious. They spoke to their audiences with the straightforwardness of young military men, amidst a disciplined blaze of torches by night. Within three months 100,000 men and women had joined,[1] and within four months there was a paid-up membership of well over 200,000. Mass meetings were held all over the country and a 'steel commando' drove down from Johannesburg to Cape Town to protest against the Coloured Voters' Bill. As it went this commando gathered strength from towns, dorps and farms until it arrived to parade, 10,000 strong, through the evening streets.

A fair number of Afrikaners joined the Torch Commando. They included not only ex-servicemen and United Party supporters but ex-Hertzogites, a few former Ossewa-Brandwag members, disgruntled individuals and many ordinary citizens who had never mixed in politics, but who had a vague feeling that something was wrong in the country. The latter rallied above all to the name of the Vice-President, the former Boer War Commandant Dolf de la Rey, while dissenting Afrikaner intellectuals were reassured by the participation of the former Chief Justice, Mr. N. J. de Wet.

The Torch Commando's success soon attracted the hostile attention of the Nationalist Party. With memories of the O.B. and its potentialities, Nationalist Party leaders began an all-out campaign to smear the Commando as dangerous, pro-Communist, pro-Kaffir and in general as a subversive para-military organization. At the local level, Torch Commando meetings were enlivened, if not broken up altogether, by organized bands of hecklers and thugs.

Such forms of attack were, however, merely a stimulus. The Torch Commando was finally checked, as the O.B. had been,

---

[1]Membership ultimately became open to all, but office holders had to have seen military service.

by those who were officially on the same side. At the outset this organization had mirrored the liberal ideas of young ex-service-men on the colour problem, and orthodox United Party members had fought shy of it. Within a few months, however, not without some Nationalist prompting, the Torch Commando was forced to take a stand on the colour issue, and to decide whether it would or would not admit Coloured and African ex-servicemen. Influenced by its growing conservative membership, the Torch Commando evaded the issue. It retained a colour-blind constitution and left it to each branch to decide on its membership. Only one branch, in Capetown, decided in the affirmative, but even so Coloured ex-servicemen were not allowed to parade in the Torch Commando demonstration on Alamein Day in Cape Town.

At this stage United Party adherents began to join the Commando in ever-increasing numbers. In a word, the Commando had become respectable. Under discipline, however, the flame was to sputter and die. By the time of the 1953 general election, the Torch Commando, which had formed a united front with the United Party and the Labour Party, was no more than a United Party action front, concerned with canvassing, tracing voters and maintaining order at meetings. What was probably the final blow came later that year, when leading English-speaking Torchmen in Natal and elsewhere associated themselves with the formation of the new Federal Party. This came as a blow to many Afrikaner Torchmen and caused the resignation of the Patron, the former Chief Justice de Wet, and two National Vice-Chairmen, Lieut.-General G. E. Brink and 'Oom' Dolf de la Rey himself. Like all other pan-South African Movements, the Torch Commando had foundered on the twin reefs of Afrikaans-English relations and the colour question. Like the Ossewa-Brandwag, it still exists in name, but merely on a 'caretaker' basis.

*　*　*　*　*

The Afrikaans-language press has from the start been linked with Afrikaner nationalism. The first link, was, in the widest sense, that of the preservation and development of Afrikaner culture and group consciousness. Today, with the exception of a handful of weeklies, monthlies, and academic quarterlies, this press is entirely devoted to the cause of Afrikaner Nationalism in its narrower sense. An anti-Nationalist daily in Afrikaans has never survived, although several have been started and *Die Suiderstem* even flourished for some years in Capetown.

The Afrikaans press, as such, really came into existence after the language provisions of the South Africa Act and General Hertzog's two-stream policy. Prior to that there had been one or two publications in Afrikaans, notably *Di Patriot* and the literary monthly *Ons Klyntji* in the Cape. But the bulk of periodicals for Afrikaner readers were in High Dutch. Chief amongst them were *Ons Land* in Capetown, and *Die Volkstem* in Pretoria. Before Union both represented the Boer point of view. After Union they became organs of the one-stream South African Party, *Die Volkstem* being the organ of Smuts himself. Both went through difficult times and finally ceased publication. *Die Volkstem* switched to Afrikaans in 1922; it was the last to go under in 1951, after trying to carry on as a weekly. The same fate met the more recently founded pro-United Party *Suiderstem*, controlled by Unie Volkspers. This became a weekly in 1946, and went bankrupt in 1950.

The failure of these and other attempts to set up an anti-Nationalist daily in Afrikaans is due, mainly, to insufficient demand through the shrinkage of the marginal central group, to consequent financial difficulties, and to the fact that the hard-core anti-Nationalist Afrikaners are often bilingual and read the anti-Nationalist English-language dailies. Those who do want to read the news in their own language ultimately turn to the Nationalist press. There they are exposed, sometimes with effect on their political allegiance, to a high-pressure flow of appeals for Afrikaner unity, couched in a journalistic style that is more violent and hard-hitting than that of the contemporary English-speaking press.

The Nationalist press consists at present of the very influential Sunday paper *Dagbreek*,[1] and five dailies: *Die Burger* in Cape-

---

[1] Formerly part-owned by the 'Corner House' mining interests, *Dagbreek* is now under a board of directors headed by Professor L. J. du Plessis of Potchefstroom, one of the intellectual pillars of neo-Krugerism.

town, which generally represents the more moderate extremism of its former editor, Dr. Malan; with *Die Burger* are linked *Die Oosterlig* in Port Elizabeth and *Die Volksblad* in Bloemfontein; in Johannesburg there are *Die Transvaler*, organ of Mr. Strijdom and Dr. Verwoerd, its former editor, and *Die Vaderland*. The latter, which was the organ of Hertzog and Mr. Havenga, was able during the Nationalist-Afrikaner Party rift in 1940–51 to display a relatively objective and impartial outlook. Even now it purveys a less aggressive and truculent brand of Nationalism than its Johannesburg contemporary.

A recent survey showed that thirteen English dailies had an official circulation of 558,000, as against 116,000 for the Afrikaans-language dailies. It was however, claimed that each Afrikaans paper was read by an average of 4.5 readers, to the English newspapers' 2.8. Despite these figures, it is clear that the Afrikaner, whether through apathy or for economic reasons, is not as much of a daily newspaper reader as is the English-speaking South African.[1] This is particularly true of the country districts. *Die Transvaler*, which published the results of the survey, gave as an instance the remote Cape district of Gordonia, where only one person in forty reads a newspaper. The survey also showed that nearly 29 per cent of Afrikaners read English newspapers; this was actually about the same number as read Afrikaans papers. In view of these figures, which more or less correspond to the number of non-Nationalist Afrikaners, it seems strange that non-Nationalist newspapers in Afrikaans have so far been unable to survive. Such, however, is the case.

While English newspapers have usually relied upon outright newspaper production for their revenues, the Afrikaans press, being unable to rely on adequate advertising revenue, has often combined magazine production and bookselling as profitable sidelines. For instance, *Die Burger* (which is incidentally read

---

[1] 38.5 per cent of Afrikaans-speaking South Africans are untouched by dailies in either language, according to an article in the African Press and Advertising Journal of 1953/4. On the other hand, the English-language press has only three weeklies with a circulation of over 50,000, while the Afrikaans-language press has three weeklies with an aggregate sale of over 1¼ million, and a religious weekly readership of 200,000.

by 24 per cent of the total adult white population of the Cape) is closely linked with the family weekly *Die Huisgenoot,* and *Die Jongspan,* a children's paper. The same applies to *Die Vaderland* and *Die Brandwag.* The capital behind the Afrikaans press has come exclusively from local sources, and a great deal has been contributed by small shareholders.

In the running of the Afrikaans press, editors tend to have greater power than their English-speaking colleagues, who, of recent years, have tended to be overshadowed by their business managers. As Lindsay Smith writes in *Behind the Press in South Africa*: 'In the frame of the Nationalist press, editors are the powerful being that fiction would have us believe that all editors are. With a fine academic background, they control the papers for which they are responsible, and their word is law, so that the managers take their cue from them.' This editorial power may, of course, dim before the rising star of Afrikaner finance.

Members of editorial staffs on Afrikaans papers, again unlike their English-speaking colleagues, are encouraged to take part in public life (naturally in the Nationalist interest). In view of the paucity of other openings more economically inviting, the Afrikaans press has certainly a wider choice of good intellectual material; the English press has frequently had to import its higher editorial staff from overseas. Unlike the French-Canadian pressmen of Quebec, most Afrikaner pressmen remain aloof from the South African Society of Journalists, of which about 70 per cent of all English-speaking newspapermen are members, and which the Afrikaners regard as English-dominated and politically deviant.[1]

* * * * *

Now that they are assured of political domination south of the Zambesi, national-minded Afrikaners have begun to look further afield. South Africa, with her relatively large permanent white population and her economic advancement, has

---

[1]Curiously enough, the Afrikaans press has still to rely for news coverage outside its own area on the S.A.P.A., which is controlled by the Argus Printing Company Ltd., its greatest English-speaking rival. The reasons for this are technical and economic.

always been a logical leader for the areas of white settlement to the north. The Nationalists see no reason why this should not develop under their aegis, and indeed it is essential for the survival of Nationalist Afrikanerdom that it should not be totally isolated and by-passed in the development of Central and East Africa. Extension of Afrikaner Nationalist influence northwards, and into the Protectorates, would also enlarge the potential areas of African settlement and so increase the chances of realizing total apartheid.

The latter consideration is however a long-term and possibly a minor one. Of more immediate importance to them is, as Mr. Strijdom said in April 1955, 'The closest co-operation between all countries who have interests in Africa and interests in the preservation of white civilization'. At a Nationalist Party rally in the Transvaal in June 1955 Mr. Strijdom went further: 'We must convince all Europeans of our viewpoint (on apartheid) and then the suffering, sorrow and sacrifices will not have been in vain. We shall then attain what we believe God has put us here for—our influence to spread right through Africa.'

Nationalist Afrikanerdom's ambitions north of the Limpopo are enhanced by the existence of large groups of outland-Afrikaners in the Protectorates, the Federation, Kenya and Tanganyika. The origin of these minorities is various and spread over many decades. They include the old type of inveterate trekker, such as Kenya's Eldoret settlers, the miners and railwaymen of Northern Rhodesia, missionaries, fugitives from Nationalism, and Nationalists conscious of their imperialist mission. Unlike their fellow Afrikaners in the Union, relatively few are as yet in the Civil Service or the professions, and only a handful are in active politics.

The number of these outland-Afrikaners is difficult to gauge, as none of the unilingual British territories collect language or immigration statistics which would isolate the Afrikaners as a group. Various statistics concerned with Dutch Reformed Church membership suggest that the total figure for British Central and East Africa may be in the neighbourhood of 40,000. Of these a large number may be intermarried, semi-assimilated or anti-Nationalist by political conviction.

At the time of Federation, however, it was suggested that one of the reasons for the urgency shown by Northern Rhodesia was that the Afrikaans-speaking percentage of the white population was thought to be approaching the neighbourhood of 40 per cent or more, distributed so that the Afrikaners constituted a majority in several electoral areas. For instance, the mining district of Kafue is represented by a Rhodesian-born apartheid supporter called Guillaume van Eeden, who was expelled from Lord Malvern's Federal Party on this ground in 1955. The percentage of Afrikaners in the total population of Southern Rhodesia is probably only half that of Northern Rhodesia. The immigration screening regulations which were in operation between 1951 and late 1955 ensured that this proportion would not be enlarged; in practice these regulations made it more difficult for all immigrants from South Africa to enter the country. Nevertheless over 50 per cent of the immigrants to Southern Rhodesia in this period came from the Union;[1] an unknown percentage of them were of course disgruntled British settlers, English-speaking South Africans or Afrikaans-speaking refugees from Nationalism.

The Afrikaans-speaking groups in Kenya and Tanganyika are never likely to reach any appreciable proportion of the total white population. Their future would seem to lie in gradual assimilation to the English-speaking group, or in trekking on to more congenial territories. There are indications that some Kenya Afrikaners are considering a move to new farms in South West Africa, a territory which still offers bountiful pioneering conditions and vast empty spaces where no farmer need see the smoke from his neighbour's chimney. A letter from an Eldoret settler in *Die Suidwester* of Windhoek lamented:

'Real Afrikaners have lost faith in the Government of Kenya and Britain. The natives and Asians are steadily gaining ground on us and time is running out for the white man in Kenya.'

A fair number of these outland-Afrikaners have become assimilated or at least integrated in their place of settlement.

---

[1]Between 1945 and 1951, a total of nearly 50,000 persons left the Union for the Rhodesias; something over three-quarters of them were bound for Southern Rhodesia.

Many however are still Afrikaners first and Rhodesians or Kenyans second. This phenomenon originated in the linguistic, religious and economic differences between the old-time Boer immigrants and the usually more sophisticated English-speaking settlers and officials. The division was enhanced by the patronizing and often contemptuous attitudes of the British. These attitudes still persist. The stereotype to which they gave rise is exemplified by the following passage from *Tandalla* by Count Ahlefeldt-Bille, the chief game-warden of Denmark after World War II:

'While in English the natives of Holland are called Dutch or Dutchmen, this name is an insult in East Africa, and in referring to inhabitants of the Netherlands one therefore uses "Hollander". "Dutchman" is the term for a type of Boer that under pressure from the south trekked north right up to Tanganyika and Kenya, where he has settled down. They are usually rough and unattractive farmers, and everywhere they have come they have systematically cleared all the game in the district with a senseless bloodlust that has always been a Boer characteristic.'

Another attitude of which Rhodesian Afrikaners in particular complain is the hostility of Rhodesians to the Afrikaans language. The Rhodesians have however always been unilingual; the general attitude is that all immigrants are expected to learn the official language and not to expect special concessions for their own language. For instance, the Southern Rhodesian school system does not permit of the teaching of Afrikaans in the primary schools, although in districts with a large Afrikaans-speaking population it is policy to provide a fully bilingual staff where possible. At a later stage Afrikaans may be taught as a second language in the place of French. To qualify for state recognition and aid, schools must use English as the medium of instruction.

Unofficially, there is undoubtedly individual hostility to the Afrikaans language and to Afrikaners. This hostility may even be on the increase, due to the increasingly truculent attitude of national-minded Afrikaners in the Federation. Such truculence has been stimulated in turn by the deliberate attempts of the Dutch Reformed Church, with its Afrikaans-medium

schools, and of other national-minded organizations such as
F.A.K. and the Reddingsdaadbond, to reinculcate or intensify
national feelings amongst outland-Afrikaners. The latter are
made to feel that, while they owe loyalty to their country of
settlement, they are part not of a Rhodesian nation but of the
resurgent Afrikaner nation. As the Union's Governor-General,
the Hon. E. G. Jansen, told the N.G.K. congregation in Bulawayo in June 1953:

'Your loyalty to the country where you are now settled does
not have to detract from the maintenance of the spiritual possessions which are your own. It does not mean that the ties of
blood and tradition have necessarily been broken.'

Die Volksgenoot also expressed the same national-minded
sentiment in a leader wishing the Queen a long and happy reign,
and assuring her of the loyalty of Rhodesian Afrikaners:

'We are a part of the proud Afrikaner nation which has its
home in Rhodesia. We give our loyalty to Her Majesty—a
loyalty which is born of a true desire to work together with our
White brothers under the Crown. That is the highest we can
offer without giving up what we have won with sweat and
blood and without betraying ourselves.'

The survival of national feelings amongst outland-Afrikaners
has been encouraged not only by the successes of Afrikaner
Nationalism within the Union but by political developments
within the Federation and Kenya. Many outland-Afrikaners
are watching with alarm the trend towards a truly multi-racial
society, and look longingly towards the Union, whose government is proceeding in an entirely different direction.

In 1951, just before Federation went through, the alarm of
Rhodesian Africaners led a cultural group in the South to form
a Nationalist-oriented political party somewhat misleadingly
called the Democratic Party. This party was devoted to furthering the cause of apartheid and to the possible incorporation of
Southern Rhodesia within the Union. After Federation went
through these elements united with conservative English groups
which had been opposed to Sir Godfrey Huggins' long domination of the Rhodesian political scene to form the opposition
Confederate Party. This stands for white supremacy of the

old-fashioned type and for opposition to Huggins' racial partnership policy on which Federation was built. In the Federal elections of 1953 the Confederate Party polled one-third of the total votes, and there are indications that its strength may increase.

New-style Afrikaner Nationalism emerged at the end of 1955 in the person of Mr. Guillaume van Eeden. He won the Kafue (Northern Rhodesian) bye-election in a largely Afrikaans-speaking constituency, on a platform of volk-unity, territorial apartheid and partition. He also successfully exploited local Northern Rhodesian jealousies over the Federal decision to choose the Southern Rhodesian Kariba Gorge Scheme instead of the Kafue Hydro-electric Scheme. Behind Mr. van Eeden, who subsequently founded the new Commonwealth Party, was the national-minded Rhodesian periodical *Die Volksgenoot* and the tacit approval of the Confederates. The latter withdrew their candidate in a seat which they had won in 1953 in favour of Mr. van Eeden, but the alliance broke down in early 1956.

It seems likely that the opposition to Sir Godfrey Huggins, now Lord Malvern, and ultimately to Sir Roy Welensky will gain ground, first because of white Rhodesians' growing apprehension about black-white partnership in practice (whites are outnumbered by over thirty to one in the Federation), and secondly because of the normal democratic swing of the pendulum against the party in power. Even if a party openly devoted to apartheid does not come to power in the Federation, there is no doubt that the Nationalists' task in the Union would be eased by the existence in strength of such a party north of the Limpopo. The success of the partnership would on the other hand make the future of apartheid and Nationalist Afrikanerdom difficult if not impossible.

National-minded leaders within the Union, and indeed many outland-Afrikaners themselves, are curiously illogical in their attitudes to their own nationhood and that of other groups. For while English-speaking South Africans and British and other immigrants to the Union are constantly berated for not learning the second official language or being willing to cut their overseas cultural and emotional ties, the outland-Afrikaner's

main duty is said to consist in maintaining his ties with Afrikanerdom. Any attempts by Rhodesians or others to enforce the
use of English or apply the ordinary laws of the land to outland-Afrikaners in such matters as overseas war service are
greeted with cries of outrage by national-minded leaders and
newspapers within the Union. Such illogical indignation is
however typical of ethnocentric groups which have come to
equate ethnic and national affiliation and to demand full scope
for one nation only—their own.

* * * * *

The story of political developments amongst Afrikaners has
been the story of the victory of the extreme over the moderate.
It has been a victory of the Krugerism of the north over the
Cape Dutch Liberals and over its own moderates; the victory of
Hertzog's two-stream concept over the single-stream concept,
and of Malan's Calvinist neo-Krugerism over Hertzogism.
There are disquieting signs that the stream of extremist victories
is not yet at an end. Most political leaders of today tend to be
drawn from the rural and professional sections of the community, and the voices of the urban proletariat and the entrepreneur have yet to be heard in full.

This process was inevitable when the Afrikaner Nationalists
claimed for a party-political organization the exclusive right to
speak for the whole nation. In the absence of any common historical tradition that could unite all Afrikanerdom, the substitution of a political principle was probably inevitable. It has,
however, led to a position where deviation cannot be tolerated,
and where the ultimate logical outcome can only be a one-party
state. Such a state will become increasingly necessary as internal
ideological and economic differences emerge within the Afrikaner group itself, under the relaxing influence of political
victory and economic prosperity.

If Afrikanerdom is not to deviate from its chosen path as the
saviour of white civilization in Southern Africa, its political
leaders will be compelled to tighten their hold on the Volk still
further, and to deny political rights to all the non-national
elements in the country, white as well as non-white.

In its growing extremism and exclusiveness, Afrikaner Nationalism has given a great stimulus to the nationalism stirring amongst other groups in the Union. Its policy of apartheid has played a major rôle here. In its negative application of humiliation, inequality, arbitrariness and disregard for human rights, apartheid has probably caused more bitterness, disillusionment and hatred amongst non-whites than the British Government ever aroused amongst the Boers. In its rare positive application it can only stimulate group consciousness and pride. These reactions are swelled by the tide of non-white nationalism which is sweeping through Asia and Africa. It seems inevitable that South Africa will ultimately see a White Nationalism and a Black Nationalism meeting in mortal struggle for a land in which both belong but neither can co-exist.

CHAPTER FOUR

THE LEAN YEARS AND THE FAT YEARS

'Thou shalt beget sons and daughters, but thou shalt not
enjoy them; for they shall go into captivity. All thy trees and
fruit of thy land shalt the locust consume. The stranger that
is within thee shall get up above thee very high; and thou
shalt come down very low. He shall lend to thee, and thou
shalt not lend to him; he shall be the head, and thou shalt
be the tail'.

(Deut. 28: 41–4)

THE Afrikaner comes to the economic field, as to every
other aspect of social life, as to an eternal struggle against
the malevolent forces of nature and of man. Man was
originally represented by Government, as in the days of Adam
Tas and the Voortrekkers. Later he came to be seen as a many-
tentacled monster, known as British-Jewish capitalism and
personified by the bloated cartoon figure of Hoggenheimer.
Indeed, just before the Anglo-Boer War, General Smuts, who
later came to be accused by his Nationalist compatriots of being
Hoggenheimer's puppet, wrote in his anti-British chronicle, *A
Century of Wrong*: 'It is ordained that we, insignificant as we are,
should be the first among the people to begin the struggle
against the new world tyranny of Capitalism'. In his later
career, General Smuts came to appreciate the contribution of
capitalism to his country's wealth and status. And as the Afrikaner gets a bigger bite of the industrial apple today, there are
already some signs that other hitherto uncompromising Nationalist opponents to capitalism are going through a similar change
of attitude.

The development of the Boer's traditional way of life and of his economic attitudes has been described in an earlier chapter. Briefly, the Boer of the eighteenth and nineteenth centuries regarded the land as his birthright. Farming was the only proper occupation for a man, though restless or impoverished young men might for a while busy themselves with hunting or transport riding. The farms were usually huge tracts of grazing land, 6,000 acres or more. On these, large families lived a simple pastoral life on a subsistence level, surrounded by black and coloured servants and squatters. Cash was hard to come by and rarely needed, and differences in wealth were hard to see. But, as C. W. de Kiewiet points out: 'The "poor whites" of latter-day South African history already existed obscurely in eighteenth-century frontier society. The windowless hut of thatch in which some families dwelt, the bed of rough wood and raw thongs in which they slept, the poor variety of their diet and the ambitionless round of their days brought them closer to their native neighbours than, for example, to the industrious New Englander.' Economic enterprise was discouraged by the lack of markets or capital, by the depredations of the Bushmen and Kaffir wars, by the apparently boundless availability of land, by the inefficiency of cheap black labour and by the very ease of subsistence in the South African climate.

Included in the Boer's birthright was a plentiful supply of cheap and docile labour from amongst the descendants of Ham. Comparatively few of the Voortrekkers were slave-owners, but it was amongst their descendants that the concept of 'Kaffir work' was held most strongly. This attitude was born with the introduction of slaves, which produced a clear correlation of dark colour and low status. As early as 1716, a Dutch East India Company representative complained that 'every common or ordinary European becomes a gentleman and prefers to be served rather than serve . . . the majority of farmers are not farmers in the real sense of the word but plantation-owners, and many of them consider it a shame to work with their own hands.' This attitude was intensified on the frontier by cultural differences and by conquest; eventually it came to include all manual labour and even work done for a wage or for an employer.

The 'lekker lewe' and the 'Kaffir work' concepts were to cast their shadow over the Afrikaner and indeed over the whole economic structure of South Africa in the years to come.

Basically, the economic history of the Afrikaner has been one of poverty and struggle. In this it differs little from that of the Bantu and Cape Coloured people with whom the Afrikaner has fought for land and later for work. The great difference is one of skin colour, buttressed by political power. This means that, while black poverty is part of the accepted order of things, Poor Whiteism becomes a problem.

The Poor Whites were primarily the product of rural over-population and a shortage of land. As the greater part of the rural population was Afrikaans-speaking, 80 per cent to 90 per cent of the Poor Whites were also Afrikaners. The frontiers were fixed after the middle of the nineteenth century and many of the once lordly farms were, through the Roman-Dutch inheritance laws, gradually sub-divided down into uneconomic small-holdings, often not even adjacent to each other. One heir actually found himself entitled to one 148,141st share of a farm of 2,527 acres. Most smallholders and collective owners continued to farm with the old wasteful and primitive methods that had given them a subsistence on 6,000 acres. Most of the land was not in any case suited for intensive agriculture and it deteriorated still further as a result of over-grazing, veld-burning and deforestation. The process of impoverishment was helped on by ignorance and apathy, endemic disease and such natural scourges as drought and pestilence. For instance, between 1882 and 1925 there was one drought every six years or so. In addition, rural poverty was accentuated by the sudden influx of wealth elsewhere, as a result of the discovery of diamonds and gold, and by the rise in land prices as a result of prospecting and speculation.

The final causative factor of Poor-Whiteism in the Republics was the systematic British devastation of the land. However defensible from a military viewpoint, this had grave and irremediable consequences in the economic and social spheres. Despite Reconstruction, many farmers never regained their former prosperity, while the uprooting had induced a permanent restlessness in others. Eric Walker points out that many farmers, after the harvest failure in 1903, refused to allow bywoners to return to their farms; the fact that many of the latter had been National Scouts, or quislings in Boer eyes, was often made a pretext for such action.

'At the peace of Vereeniging,' writes de Kiewiet, 'not less than 10,000 individuals had been torn loose from the land which was their way of life and the pillar of their self-respect . . . the countryside's contribution to the town was not a class of sturdy yeomen thrust forth by laws. A large proportion were defeated men, unable to maintain their hold on the land, destitute in both wealth and energy, drawn into an unfamiliar world of reluctant opportunities and depressed wages.'

The first consequence of rural poverty was the rise of a new class, the bywoner or share-cropper. These bywoners were Boers who had been forced off their own land and who worked for a landlord for a share, whether of crops or of cattle. At the extremes, they ranged from superior labourers to the equivalent of farm managers, who might have grazing and cultivation rights over an entire farm.

Elsewhere these landless Boers might have become farm labourers. This field was however closed to them because farm labour was already the province of cheap and docile black labour. Pride of race and an habitual aversion to manual labour forbade the Boer to compete in this sphere. It was in any case a sphere where the wages were too low to maintain even minimum white standards of living. So the first move of most Boers who had been forced off their own land was to live on the margin of another man's land.

This stage was however only a temporary one. The bywoner was a product of an era of subsistence farming and he could not hope to survive as modern methods of farming came to be accepted. And as rural poverty grew, there was increasing competition between white and white within the bywoner class. This enabled the farmer to stiffen his terms of employment. The bywoner's share fell from two-thirds to one-half in many cases in the first fifteen years of the twentieth century, and the process of impoverishment was thereby intensified.

The next step for many impoverished whites was to move to the towns, particularly to the areas where gold and diamonds had been discovered. Here they found the black man had again preceded them and had gained the monopoly of unskilled labour at his own low wage rates. The ranks of skilled labour were already filled by artisans from Britain and elsewhere, and in the Western Cape by the descendants of coloured slaves. These artisans jealously guarded their skills and their high wages against all comers, but in any case the impoverished rural Afrikaner usually lacked both the training and the adaptability to enter the skilled labour field. His initial lot was worse than it had been as a bywoner. There, his employer had been a Boer who understood the need to maintain white prestige. In the towns the economic system was in the hands of non-Afrikaners who were concerned not with Boer prestige but with profits. The impoverished Afrikaner was in a strange world of alien ideas and values, a world where business was conducted in an alien language which he barely understood.

The dimensions of the Poor White problem were immense. It was well established by the decade before the Anglo-Boer War, particularly in the older-settled areas of the North and East Cape, where subdivision had proceeded farther than elsewhere. In the Transvaal also, the Volksraad debated the plight of the 'poor burgers', who sat round the President's stoep clamouring for loans, donkeys and mealies. Denys Reitz wrote of them: 'Our Commando had of late been receiving reinforcements of inferior quality, mostly poor whites from the burgererven, the slum quarters of Pretoria, a poverty-stricken class that had drifted in from the country districts after the great rinderpest epidemic of 1896—they had become debased by town life, and had so little stomach for fighting that their presence among us was a source of weakness rather than strength.'

The effects of the rinderpest in 1896 and of the Anglo-Boer War were augmented by a depression in 1906 to 1908, and in 1908 the Transvaal Government appointed an Indigency Commission to report on the problem. In 1917 the Minister of Agriculture gave an estimate, based apparently upon church and magistrates' reports, that over 105,000 people, or over 8 per cent of the total white population, were living in poverty; . . . of these nearly one-third were said to be in a state of 'absolute poverty'. Professor W. M. McMillan questioned the figures in his study of the South African agrarian problem. On the basis of detailed studies he suggested that between 8 and 15 per cent of the Union's white population could be described as Poor Whites. He stated that nearly one-twentieth of the total white population were in 'permanent, absolute poverty, many of them perhaps demoralized beyond redemption', while perhaps another twentieth or more were so placed that they could be dragged down to such poverty in present conditions.

By the late 1920's, the position had so far deteriorated that the number of 'very poor' was estimated, according to the Carnegie Poor White Commission, at between 220,000 and 300,000, or 12 to 16 per cent of the white population. This description did not of course entirely coincide with that of a Poor White.

This estimate was made before the great depression of 1930 to 1931, which gave further impetus to the process of impoverishment. The depression was incidentally augmented by the obstinacy of the Nationalist Government, which stayed on gold to show its independence of Britain, and thereby provoked a flight of capital from the country. By the early 1930's, the proportion of Poor Whites to the total white population had reached the alarming figure of one in five.

During these decades the Poor White had gradually become an urban even more than a rural problem. Impoverished Boers had been drifting into the dorps, the diamond diggings and the alluvial gold areas since the 1870's. But large-scale shifts of population first became evident in 1904, when the census showed a drop in the rural population of the Cape Midlands. This was an area where impoverishment had been at work longest. By 1911 the area of depopulation had extended into the Orange Free State. In 1870, there had only been twenty towns in South Africa with a population of over 1,000. Thereafter towns sprang up wherever there were diamonds, gold or the railways to serve them, and the drift from the rural areas became a steady flow. Between 1891 and 1911 the white urban population increased by more than 200 per cent, while the percentages of white urban dwellers to the total white population in 1911, 1931 and 1951 respectively were 52 per cent, 61 per cent and 78 per cent.

Whether he remained on the land as many did or migrated to the slums of the towns, the Poor White was distinguished by certain traits which a mere amelioration of his material lot could not remove. By economic definition, the Poor White was an impoverished white person of rural origin, the product of an outmoded economic system. Not all impoverished whites shared the psychological traits which came to be regarded as inherent in the term 'Poor White', whereas some 'potentially poor' people could already be described as 'Poor Whites'. Chief among these traits of the Poor Whites were, according to the psychological report of the Carnegie Poor White Commission, an undisciplined restlessness inherent in the 'Trekgees', or trek spirit; a nerveless clinging to farm life despite all subdivisions and difficulties; conservatism and isolationism, and a disinclination to co-operate with others; apathy and fatalism; ignorance and indolence; irresponsibility and thriftlessness; a lack of industry or ambition; a feeling of impotence which produced passivity and an inferiority complex; lack of self-reliance or self-respect, frequent pauperization and a blurring of moral standards.

With all these failings, however, the great majority of the Poor Whites still regarded themselves as superior to the poor blacks with whom they competed for work and amongst whom they often had to live. The fate of the small minority who gave up the struggle and 'went Kaffir' was however the writing on the wall to the leaders of the white group and to Afrikaners in particular. By the early 1920's it had become clear to them that economic equality must eventually lead to social equality between black and white.

The reaction of the white group to this threat to the barriers which defended its privileged position was to set the pattern for further economic development in South Africa. This pattern was based not on economic laws or expediency, but on white solidarity and prestige even at the cost of economic advantage.

Those in authority who had been concerned with the Poor

White problem at an earlier date had seen the solution in terms of relief schemes and later of rural rehabilitation and improved educational facilities for the rising generation. Neither relief nor rural rehabilitation proved more than a palliative, however, while education was too much of a long-term policy to show immediate results.

From 1924, however, the new Nationalist-Labour Coalition set out to give the white man economic security, as far as possible unaffected by the workings of economic laws. The Poor White's position was improved by the institution of the 'civilized labour policy'. This policy ensured the unskilled white worker a protected field of labour, mainly in such public services as the railways, and rates of pay which were related not to his productivity but his needs as a 'civilized' person. Under these conditions 'Kaffir work' became acceptable so long as it was not done for Kaffir wages or side by side with Kaffirs. The chief exponent of this policy was the South African Railways and Harbours, the country's largest employer of unskilled and semi-semi-skilled labour. White labourers had been employed on the railways from 1907. Between 1921 and 1928, however, their number had risen from 4,705 to 15,878, employed in separate gangs at 'civilized' wages of between 3s. and 5s. per day with free housing or a housing allowance. By 1948, the railways were employing more whites than non-whites. Of the 87,174 whites in regular employment, only 18,816 were salaried staff. In addition the railways employed a regular force of 46,420 non-whites and 10,891 whites, an additional 43,220 non-whites being employed on casual labour.

The civilized labour policy was uneconomic and costly. The replacement of 1,361 'uncivilized labourers' by 'civilized' ones had cost £73,508 by early 1926 alone. Nevertheless its adherents thought that money well spent. Thousands of Poor Whites had regained their self-respect; some even moved into the semi-skilled and skilled fields, while others were able to help their children to do so.

The civilized labour policy was only an intermediary plan. Along with it went long-term plans for improved educational facilities, health services and legislation designed to reserve a field of skilled and to some extent semi-skilled labour for whites only, and to maintain the unduly large wage differentials which have always been a feature of the South African labour market.[1] This colour-bar legislation was also enacted to meet the demands of the still predominantly non-Afrikaner skilled labour force. The latter had become alarmed by the threat to their privileged position from cheap non-white labour on the one hand and by the natural tendency of employers to exploit this cheap labour against them on the other. As the Afrikaner moved steadily into the mines and industry, this legislation, which had originally been the barrier set up by skilled workers against the unskilled, acquired all the emotional content of the Boers' frontier attitudes, now translated almost unchanged to the towns. Despite the obvious inter-dependence of whites and non-whites in the economic field, their inter-relations continued to be regarded in terms of conflict and struggle.

White poverty itself gradually ceased to be a large-scale problem. The effects of the official measures of rehabilitation were greatly augmented by the large-scale development of industry which took place in South Africa during and after the Second World War. This absorbed all but the old[2] and the unredeemables. But the legacy of Poor-Whiteism remains in the violent colour prejudice of those who were dragged back from the near-Kaffir status to which they had sunk; and in the narrow nationalism and distrust of orthodox trade unionism of those whose status was regained not through their own efforts but by party political assistance. The former Poor Whites and their children are now the inhabitants of those marginal urban areas whose vote decides who shall govern South Africa. So far, the majority of them have given unequivocal support to the party that reinstated them as white men.

*   *   *   *   *

---

[1] An average proportion of 3½ to 1 in 1935 (but 10 to 1 sometimes on the Witwatersrand) as compared with 2 to 1 or 3 to 2 for the rest of the Commonwealth.

[2] In 1952 an 83 year-old niece of President Kruger was found in the Johannesburg district of Troyeville, living in respectable penury in one room on an old-age pension of £8 a month.

The Boer was traditionally a man of the land, though not necessarily of the soil. Even today Afrikaners, who constitute 85 per cent of the farming population, are reluctant to accept the fact that this way of life is passing out of the realm of fact into that of myth. Nevertheless, over 78 per cent of all whites, and 69 per cent of Afrikaners, are now permanently living in urban areas. 37 per cent of all Afrikaners live in large towns, and of these many are young people who know the true Boer life only from occasional visits to farmer-relatives.

The depopulation of rural areas as a result of poverty has been resumed in recent years, but for different reasons. In the old days, poor men moved from one hopeless situation to another. Since the fantastic growth of secondary and mass-production industry, however, the towns have presented a sure avenue of lucrative employment for even the unskilled,[1] and above all for the women. In 1946, although there were 20,000 more white men than women in the Union, the female urban population outnumbered the male by 23,000. This meant a short-fall of women in the rural areas of over 40,000, which in its turn was likely to have significant social consequences and to provoke a further flight from the land. In addition, universal education and the popular press have made the younger generation on the farms aware of the attraction of urban life.

This flight from the land has been accompanied and at times even stimulated by the rise of a new class, mainly Afrikaans-speaking, of 'land barons' or 'morgenheimers'. This has entirely reversed the process of interminable sub-division which prevailed until 1937. The farmers' new-found wealth is the result of the high prices for farm products, particularly of wool, which have prevailed during and since the war.[2] These high returns have encouraged land speculation and forced up land prices and farm rents. Other 'land barons' are speculators or wealthy city dwellers seeking a safe investment, or quite simply a week-end

---

[1] In 1941, at the beginning of the war-time industrial boom, only 32.1 per cent of rural families had an annual income of £200 or more. The corresponding urban figure was 73.2 per cent.

[2] The net income of South African farming increased from £45.1 million in 1939 to £215 million in 1953.

home. In consequence young farmers have found it difficult to set up on their own, while tenant farmers have been forced off the land, and large blocks of land are being concentrated in the hands of the few. This trend was shown clearly in the 1952–3 Agricultural Census, in which nearly 87 per cent of the total farming area was taken up by farms of over 1,000 morgen and 13 per cent by 836 farms with an area of over 10,000 morgen each.[1] In many cases this process has led to large-scale absentee landlordism, which has in some areas risen to 30 or 40 per cent, according to a Dutch Reformed Church estimate.

In the main this land is farmed more productively than it was by smallholders, though some of it is apparently bought for purposes of income tax evasion, and is not therefore farmed to yield the maximum results. In either case, however, it means the displacement of the smallholder. Such farms are usually run by a trained white manager with African labour, and there is no place for the bywoner with his subsistence methods. Between 1946 and 1951 the number of bywoners declined sharply from 9,385 to 332 (according to advance figures supplied by the Bureau of Census and Statistics). The number of white male farmers decreased between 1936 and 1946 from 139,345 to 106,780.

The social consequences of this process within the formerly homogeneous Afrikaner group are regarded with apprehension by leading Afrikaners. *Die Transvaler* wrote in 1951: 'The depopulation of the platteland carries with it the danger of an Afrikaans proletariat. When the dispossessed Afrikaner in the towns begins to hate the handful of rich plattelanders with their extensive possessions in a way which the Communists could exploit and encourage, it will mean the end of the organic unity of the Afrikaner people'.

The views of correspondents published in *Die Volksblad* in 1952 suggests that these fears are not groundless. One wrote: 'In the Free State, there is one district . . . where fifty-seven farms are managed and controlled by natives. The owners will not

---

[1] There are 302.4 morgen to the square mile, and there were in all 119,198 European-owned farms in the Union at that date.

give fellow-Afrikaners an opportunity or, if they do, the conditions are often so severe that only a native can endure them . . . If we come to the cities, we often see the wife or daughter of an Afrikaner in a motor car which is driven by a non-European. Those natives easily raise themselves above poor Afrikaners.'

Another correspondent wrote: 'It was the poor who mainly put the Nationalist members of Parliament into power, and what happens now? The rich are loaded with higher salaries; Members of Parliament get an increase of £400; teacher receive higher salaries; the wool farmers are given a reduction of income tax; the mealie and wheat farmers are helped by means of higher fixed prices; all who are not in much need are being granted a rise of salary . . . But to the poor outstryders[1] who risked their lives and lost all, a pension is awarded that can scarcely keep body and soul together.'

Despite the recent increase in productivity, South African agriculture has always been a delicate plant, needing a cloche of subsidies and state assistance. To quote Leo Marquard in *Peoples and Policies of South Africa*: 'Agriculture in South Africa has many of the characteristics of a gigantic system of outdoor relief'. The basic reasons for this are climatic conditions and low soil productivity, but the effect of such adverse natural factors has been augmented by generations of inefficient, short-sighted and unenterprising farmers, white as well as black. Even today, after decades of feather-bedding by the State, and after the introduction of improved methods of commercial farming and marketing, agriculture in South Africa still moves basically at the pace not of the tractor but of the underpaid, uneducated and increasingly unwilling African farm worker, whose labour is so misleadingly described as cheap. The word unwilling is used here because the African is increasingly aware that he could get more interesting and lucrative work even at the lowest level in industry. Consequently he only remains on the land because he he is compelled to do so by the pass laws. Despite these restrictions, many Africans do escape and there is an increasing tend-

---

[1]Veterans—usually applied by national-minded Afrikaners to the Boer veterans of the Wars of Independence.

ency for farmers to resort to convict labour and even to build joint 'farm-gaols' from which gangs are hired out to subscribers with Government approval.

The Cinderella state of South African agriculture emerges when its yields are compared with those of various Western countries. For instance, the average wheat yield per hectare (of European-owned land) in South Africa in 1938–9 was 5.5 quintals; for the United Kingdom 25.6, for the United States 8.9 and for Australia 7.2. The maize yields for 1938 (maize is the staple diet of Africans) was 8.9 quintals for the Union, 17.4 for the United States and 13.4 for Australia (1937 figures). South Africa has, on an average, been importing up to 40 per cent of her wheat requirements. As regards individual output it is said that while one agricultural worker in Great Britain can produce enough food for ten people, and in Australia for twenty-five, it is doubtful whether a man engaged in agriculture in South Africa could even manage to feed two. In addition, costs of production are so high that 70 per cent of the population is too poor to be able to buy what it needs.

The weakness of South African agriculture shows up again when one relates agriculture's contribution to the net national production of the Union to the percentage of the total labour force employed in agriculture. In 1911–12 and 1948–9, this share was 16.1 per cent and 14.9 per cent respectively. The 1911 census showed that 24.56 per cent of gainfully-employed white males and 39.60 per cent of male Africans were engaged in agriculture (and fishing); the corresponding figures for 1946 were 23.7 per cent of white males and 57.5 per cent of the total African male labour force in each group.[1]

There is, of course, still a considerable group of Afrikaner farmers who are neither on the permanent margin of destitution nor up in the land-baron class. For them the last decade or so has brought increased income, with such material comforts and conveniences as the radio, telephone, home electricity and the

---

[1] Agriculture's share of the national production is, of course, brought down by the fact that so many of the Africans are subsistence farmers on their eroded and impoverished reserves.

motor car. In general, however, these improvements are super-ficial, and the basic economic position remains as it was in 1941, when Doctor C. W. de Kiewiet wrote: 'Agriculture in South Africa is poor and precarious. Much of it is beyond the reach of modern science and technical progress. The expenditure and effort required to overcome many of its handicaps are too great to be profitable. Indeed, South Africa is not an agricultural country'.

In 1953, Professors Jan Goudriaan and D. G. Franzsen, writing on economic factors in *The South African Way of Life*, estimated that less than 6 per cent of the country's total area was under cultivation, and that only another 9 per cent could conceivably be brought under cultivation. The maximum area that could be used for irrigation purposes was estimated at 1 million morgen or less than 1 per cent of the total area of occupied farms and agricultural holdings. The writers referred also to the looming menace of erosion, which may well prove to be South Africa's greatest national problem.

The traditional Boer way of life has almost passed away, and no amount of repining about its virtues by Afrikaner leaders can alter the fact that the Afrikanervolk is increasingly made up of townsmen who know the country mainly from week-end ex-cursions. Those owner-farmers who remain will be more and more agricultural businessmen to whom the land is a livelihood rather than a way of life, and who live and think like their cousins in the towns, thanks to the press, the radio, and the motor car.

The Afrikaners came into an alien urban environment at the lowest economic level, and there the majority of them remain today. The main avenues for advancement are still the public service and the professions, and such progress as Afrikaners have made up the commercial and industrial ladder has been largely in their own recently-established enterprises.

At the lowest levels, however, Afrikaner men and women probably form the bulk of the white labour force in industry, if not in commerce. In mining, the oldest of South Africa's in-dustries and the one which by revolutionizing the old pastoral economy ultimately brought the Boer to the towns, Afrikaners have now all but displaced the original labour force of Cornish-men, Hollanders, and other Europeans. In this industry whites form something under 12 per cent of the total labour force of nearly 500,000. The remainder are unskilled migrant African labourers.

In clerical and managerial work however the English-speaking South Africans still predominate, and the major mining groups are owned by British or English South African interests. A Mr. Boshoff has however been active in mining for some years and in 1955 an Afrikaner owned mining company, Federale Mynbou, with a capital of £1 million, gained control of a group operating in the old shallow-reef gold area of Barberton. This company also obtained an interest in some chrome deposits owned by Crown Mines in the Rustenburg and Lydenburg areas. *Die Transvaler* greeted this as a further step in the Afrikaner's struggle to gain his share of the Union's mineral wealth. It is perhaps worthy of note that the Chamber of Mines had a few months earlier donated £25,000 to the Engineering Faculty of Stellenbosch University, presumably with an eye on the future.

As the original agent of the destruction of the Boer way of life, the gold-mining industry has always retained its diabolic character for the majority of Afrikaners. This industry has, nevertheless, until the last decade or so, been the mainstay of the country's economy. It has in times of depression served as a stabilizer because of the fixed price of its product; it has provided an umbrella for the growth of secondary industry; and it has contributed more than its share to support a precarious agriculture and the whole uneconomic framework of 'civilized labour' and differential allowances, which were designed to perpetuate the colour cleavages of the frontier in the new urban economy.

The high contribution of the mining industry may help to explain the diminuendo in the Nationalist Party's demand for nationalization of the mines. This demand was voiced most stridently in the days when the Nationalists were in opposition. Little has been heard of it since they came to power in 1948. In July, 1955, the Minister of Mines, Dr. A. J. van Rhijn, said that 'the Union Government intended that the gold mining industry should remain in the hands of private enterprise . . . suggestions for the establishment of a State Mining Corporation were not acceptable; . . . without risking any capital the Government received large amounts of revenue from mining companies. If it invested money and lost large sums, such as some companies did, the Government would be accused of wasting the taxpayers' money'.

The gold and diamond phase of South Africa's economy lasted from 1870 until after the first World War. Then began an industrial and technological revolution which has in forty years made manufacturing industry the largest contributor to the Union's national income. In 1912 this share was a meagre 6.9 per cent; at 15.2 per cent in 1930 it had outstripped agriculture, and by 1943 it had also outgrown mining, its original creator and protector. By 1953, stimulated by the war-time and post-war boom, industry's contribution to the nation's income had risen to nearly 25 per cent, compared with 15.4 per cent for agriculture and 12.5 per cent for mining. This development took place mainly in the production of building materials, textiles and clothing, shoes and the engineering trades. The Union's industrial revolution has, according to Dr. H. J. van Eck, Chairman of the Industrial Development Corporation, progressed in several respects at about three times the pace of the nineteenth century industrial revolution in Great Britain, and there are indications that the years ahead may bring an even greater expansion.

It is therefore manufacturing industry that has been the main urbanizing factor over recent decades. The percentage of European and African males engaged in mining has shown little change in the last twenty years, but the percentage of European males in manufacturing rose from 17.6 per cent to 22.8 per cent between 1936 and 1946 (the number of white women declined, possibly because of the change-over before 1946 from a war-time to a peace-time economy). It is perhaps worth noting here that the number of Coloured males engaged in manufacturing rose from 21.2 per cent to 27.9 per cent over the same period (Coloured women 8.1 per cent to 16.5 per cent). The same applied in the case of Asiatics, but not of Africans, who have no formal rights of union organization and are not regarded as 'employees' in terms of existing industrial legislation. The great increase of non-white industrial workers has shown very clearly that the white population is increasingly unable to supply South Africa's manpower needs, despite the fact that so many white youths are, thanks to boom conditions, going straight into industry without troubling about apprenticeship and its formal qualifications.

Like agriculture and mining before it, manufacturing industry in South Africa has been compelled to base itself on non-white labour. This continuing process of economic integration has already brought the apartheid planners to the fork in the road marked 'prosperity or principle'. At present about 70 per cent of all industrial workers in the Union are non-whites. In view of the continuing expansion and a shortage of white labour this percentage may well increase. Nor are non-whites confined to the unskilled grades. A Wage Board sample published in 1948 showed that non-whites constituted over 16 per cent of all skilled employees and over 66 per cent of all semi-skilled employees. Only 1.5 per cent of unskilled industrial employees were whites; such unskilled white workers find easier openings in the lowest levels of the public service and particularly in the railways.

It seems likely that the Afrikaner section, whether rural or second-generation urban, has provided the bulk of the increased white industrial labour force. This new urban working-class differs less and less in its general way of life and recreations from the English-speaking urban workers about it. The differences show in more profound ways; for instance, in the sharper race prejudices borne of the frontier; in the frequent distrust of conventional trade union action amongst those who have been rehabilitated by direct State assistance; and in the greater tendency to violence and crime characteristic of groups that have suddenly been transplanted to an environment where their original set of values seem inapplicable.

Other main occupations of urban Afrikaners are commerce, the public service and the professions. Commerce is a relatively new field of employment to the Afrikaner. This is largely because there have until recently been comparatively few Afrikaner-owned enterprises catering for an Afrikaans-speaking public, while the English-owned establishments have required fluent English from their employees, particularly from those who deal directly with the public. An increasing number of bilingual Afrikaners are now being employed even in English-owned stores and offices. This is a consequence of both the labour shortage and the increasing pressure and vociferousness of organized Afrikaner purchasing power. It should however be added here that the growing tendency to unilingualism amongst more recent products of Afrikaans single-medium schools virtually limits their employment to Afrikaans-owned concerns. This is a serious limitation because the great bulk of the industrial and commercial enterprises are still and will long continue to be owned by English-speaking South Africans. In addition, this group still has the greatest purchasing power and can therefore call the tune.

Apart from the professions the public service is the oldest form of urban employment for Afrikaners on *all* levels of ability and skill. The 'civilized labour' policy of the railways in particular has already been mentioned. In the higher levels of the civil service, the natural processes of the bilingual ruling and of superannuation have been accelerated by deliberate Nationalist policy to ensure that the public service has become almost exclusively Afrikaans-speaking. The same applies to the police force and even in recent years to the armed forces. English-speaking South Africans on their side have kept aloof because of the greater opportunities available in commerce and industry, and because of their aversion to entering an increasingly hostile environment where promotion would certainly not come easily.

Amongst the professions, predikants and lawyers have always been easily the largest groups. A law degree was until quite recently regarded as the badge of an educated Afrikaner just as it was in some central European States before the second World War. Many so trained became public servants or politicians but the inherited litigiousness of the Afrikaner always provided a large number of Afrikaans-speaking lawyers with a livelihood in their own field. Today, the young Afrikaner professional finds an increasing number of openings in the growing numbers of Afrikaner-dominated business concerns, while the Afrikaans universities are expanding their activities to supply the necessary technical or commercial training. If only for linguistic reasons, the Afrikaner professional is sure of a livelihood amongst his own people, who represent 60 per cent of the white population.

The bulk of newly-urbanized Afrikaners did not, as has been suggested, take kindly to orthodox trade unionism. The reasons for this were various. In the first place, the old British-dominated craft unions, alert to ward off threats to their own privileged position, regarded the unskilled Afrikaners with almost as much suspicion as they did the unskilled non-whites who were flooding into the towns at the same time.[1] Secondly, it was the State that carried through the costly process of rehabilitation in the face of *laissez-faire* economics. Thirdly, the unions were for a long time dominated by non-Afrikaners, and in the Cape had non-white members; while the principles of working-class solidarity to which these unions paid increasing lip-service ran quite counter to the strict colour line of the frontier, which urban poverty had only sharpened.

Finally, the leaders of Afrikaner Nationalism, seeing the potential voting power of the new Afrikaner urban working-class, saw also that this voting power might be lost to them if this working-class were allowed to develop freely under the alien urban influences into a true socio-economic class, placing class interests before those of the Volk . . . In this opposition to orthodox trade unionism, national-minded leaders were at one with non-Afrikaner employers, who saw the danger of allowing white and non-white workers to perceive their common interests, and so greatly to augment the power of organized labour.

Not long after the end of its seven-year political alliance with the South African Labour Party, the Nationalist Party switched

---

[1] These suspicions were fomented by the action of mine owners who took on hundreds of low-paid Afrikaners in place of British miners during the 1907 miners' strike.

over to a sustained attack on the orthodox trade union movement. This onslaught has continued to the present day, gaining force after the Nationalist Government came to power and could add legislation to its arsenal.

Prior to this, the campaign was conducted mainly on two fronts. From 1936 onwards there was an attempt to infiltrate and disrupt the unions from within, and a series of direct attacks was set off by the F.A.K. and followed up by a number of ostensibly non-political organizations and by predikants of the Dutch Reformed Church. The main purport of these attacks was that the trade union movement was un-Afrikaans, materialistic, communistic and negrophile. The aim of the campaign was 'to save the soul' of the Afrikaner worker and to win him back to the Volk and to Afrikaans culture.

As Dr. G. D. Scholtz wrote in 1953, the second generation of urban Afrikaners were ripe for proletarianization. Their volk-gevoel (national consciousness) was giving way before a rising class-consciousness, and they were, under the influence of alien trade union leaders,[1] putting class interests ahead of country and nation.

At times this campaign against the trade unions overstepped the mark and brought successful actions for defamation upon its spokesmen. Mr. E. S. Sachs, the former Secretary of the Garment Workers' Union, was perhaps the most consistently successful litigant in this connexion. In 1939 he received £250 damages from *Die Oosterlig*, a Port Elizabeth Nationalist paper; and later £100 damages from Mr. Havenga's former organ *Die Vaderland*, for an article headed 'Foreign Exploiters amongst South African Workers'. *Die O.B.*, the organ of the Ossewa-Brandwag, next paid Mr. Sachs £250 plus costs without going to court. In 1941 he was awarded £600 and costs of several thousands of pounds against the Voortrekker Press for publishing a defamatory brochure called *Communism and the South African*

---

[1]In 1939 it was reported at the Economic Congress that, out of 118 trade union organizations, 100 had non-Afrikaner secretaries, though their membership might in some cases be 80 per cent Afrikaner. But Dr. Scholtz even regarded some of the growing number of Afrikaner trade union leaders as hostile to Afrikanerdom.

Trade Unions. This had been compiled by Dr. H. P. Wolmarans, a predikant and Professor of Theology at Pretoria University. The brochure was based on material collected by a special Commission of Inquiry appointed by the N.H.K. in 1937 to report on these matters. Mr. Sachs' victory was followed up by several other trade union leaders who considered the brochure defamatory, and who received hundreds of pounds in damages without the matter coming to court.

This set-back produced a lull for two years, but the campaign was revived in full force in 1944. This time the attack was combined with disruptive tactics, but Mr. Sachs was again able to take action against one of his ministerial assailants, Dr. A. B. du Preez, who had issued a defamatory circular to his congregation. Dr. du Preez was defended by Mr. Oswald Pirow, an able lawyer and ex-Cabinet Minister well-known for his pro-Nazi views. Nevertheless, Mr. Sachs was awarded £300 and costs, which came to over £11,000.

In late 1949 a publishing company was formed under the name of 'Die Werkerspers' (The Workers' Press). Among its directors were Dr. Albert Hertzog, son of the late General J. B. Hertzog, and a Nationalist M.P., and Mr. D. E. Ellis, Secretary of the Mineworkers' Union. The aims of this Company were described in evidence given in 1951 before the Transvaal Supreme Court by a Mr. Jan Gleisner, who described himself as the General Manager. They were to publish newspapers to serve the interest of the opposition element in the trade unions; these opposition elements he called 'nationally oriented', by which were meant groups favouring a strict apartheid policy.

'Die Werkerspers' began to issue three publications, *Die Bouwerker* (The Building Worker), *Die Klerewerkersnuus* (The Garment Workers' News) and *Die Mynwerker* (The Mineworker). The first two were aimed at workers in two industries which the Afrikaner Nationalists were anxious to win back for Afrikanerdom, while the third was the organ of the Mineworkers' Union, which had already been largely 'gleichgeschaltet'. The printers were the 'Voortrekker Pers', amongst whose directors are Dr. T. E. Dönges, Minister for the Interior, and Mr. C. P. Swart, the Minister of Justice.

In its short but lively career 'Die Werkerspers' paid £500 and costs to Miss Anna Scheepers, the President of the Garment Workers' Union, while the printers paid out £1,450 and costs to thirteen prominent trade unionists, several of them Afrikaners, without going to court. 'Die Werkerspers', which had a paid-up capital of £7, finally went into compulsory liquidation in August 1951 on a motion by Mr. Sachs. He and Mr. Peter John Huyser, an Afrikaner, and national organizer of the Building Workers' Industrial Union of South Africa, had in mid-1951 been awarded £2,900 and £1,800 damages respectively against 'Die Werkerspers', which the latter failed to pay. The 'Voortrekker Pers' paid Mr. Sachs an additional £300, plus another £1,000 and costs for a further six articles in *Die Klerewerkersnuus*.

The initiative in this type of attack then passed back to the old-established Afrikaans-language press. In August 1952, Johannes Jacobus Venter, President of the Trades and Labour Council, and secretary of the Johannesburg Municipal Transport Workers' Union, claimed damages from *Die Vaderland* over an implication of Communist connexions, and received a settlement of £400.

The second front of Nationalist Afrikanerdom was fought within the trade union movement itself. Since the early days of the century, when Afrikaner workers had hardly been welcomed in the British-oriented craft unions, Afrikaners had entered the unions on a large scale. Many had become active trade union workers and leaders, but a large part of the rank-and-file in many unions remained apathetic and even suspicious of orthodox trade unionism. It was on this latter element that the Nationalists relied for eventual support.

The first union to attract these attentions was the Mineworkers' Union. This union had come to be mainly Afrikaans-speaking, after the wholesale dismissals of miners which followed the armed crushing of the 1922 white mineworkers' strike. Thereafter the union fell gradually back into the hands of leaders unfamiliar with the aims and functions of orthodox trade unionism. These leaders failed to win for their members any appreciable share of the prosperity which came to the gold-mining industry after 1932. Their neglect and apathy left an opening for the national-minded, who in the thirties began their bid for the support of the mineworkers. Following the donation of £10,000 by a wealthy Nationalist landowner, Mrs. Jannie Marais of Stellenbosch, a 'Reform Organization' was set up under the leadership of a prominent Broederbonder, Dr. Albert Hertzog. This soon won a considerable following amongst mineworkers. It then proceeded to attack the group in power in the union, and at one stage a group of Reformers went so far as to seize control of the union's offices. Mr. E. S. Sachs, in his account of this struggle, says that the young Afrikaner who assassinated Charlie Harris, the Secretary of the Mineworkers' Union, in June 1939 had undoubtedly been influenced by the propaganda directed against the union's leadership.

During the war years there was a lull in this internecine strife, many of the national-minded having been interned. After the war, however, the Reformers returned to the fray, and found the majority of mineworkers dissatisfied with their leadership. Under the name of the United Mineworkers' Committee, the former Reformers called a strike against the ruling clique in 1947. By 1948 the new Nationalist Party Government ordered a ballot under Government supervision, and the Reformers' nominees gained control of the union. The new General Secretary was Mr. D. E. Ellis. He was described by a Government Committee appointed in 1950 to inquire into the Mineworkers' Union's affairs, as 'very much in the position of a dictator, ruling the Mineworkers' Union with a firm hand'. Soon afterwards Dr. Albert Hertzog was appointed to the Executive Committee of the union, but in 1950 he was forced to resign. In 1951 Mr. Ellis came out with a statement that Dr. Hertzog wanted to use the union to achieve his political ends, and that a move was afoot to expel Dr. Hertzog from the union, of which he was still an honorary member. At that time Mr. Ellis had just heard a Government Committee accuse him of corruption in the purchase of a building for the union, with union funds. No public charge has been brought, by the Government, despite Opposition prodding. A private charge made by a member of the Mineworkers' Executive resulted in a verdict of 'Not guilty' on a technicality, although the magistrate involved implied that the evidence seemed conclusive.

Whatever the outcome of individual rivalries, there is no doubt that a large section of mineworkers remain national-minded. The work of such groups as the Reformers is made especially easy in this industry, with its wide wage-differentials resting on an arbitrary legislative colour bar—(unlike most other trade unions, the South African Mineworkers have never accepted the principle of equal pay for equal work).

The other union to attract the main attention of the Reformers, was Mr. E. S. Sachs' Transvaal Garment Workers' Union. Considering the immediate social and economic background and prejudices of its rank and file and many of its leaders, this union had for years displayed remarkable energy in purely trade union affairs,[1] and an extremely liberal attitude to non-white workers. It was divided into two sections, the non-white section becoming the larger by the 1950's.

In his book *The Choice Before South Africa*, Mr. E. S. Sachs describes in detail how a strike was fomented at Germiston in 1944, ostensibly because the management took on nine Coloured women to help carry out some urgent war contracts; the aim was apparently to prove that the existing leadership was not prepared to fight the black menace. This diversion received immense and seemingly co-ordinated support from the Afrikaans-speaking press, social and cultural organizations and from various eminent predikants.

The Garment Workers' Union, however, proved a tougher nut to crack than the Mineworkers' Union. The leadership surmounted this particular episode and the attacks and attempts at mob violence that followed it. After a meeting of the Garment Workers' Union at the City Hall in Johannesburg was broken up in 1948, the Nationalist Minister of Labour, Mr. B. J. Schoeman, appointed a commission of inquiry into the union's

---

[1] The Garment Workers' Union has struck more than sixty times over the last two decades or so, and has won wage increases from under £1 to £6 a week, and working-hour decreases from seventy or sixty hours to forty hours per week.

affairs. Most of the main witnesses against the union are said to have been members of the Blankewerkersbeskermingbond (White Workers' Protection Union), an organization which also has under its wing the Reformers in the Mineworkers' Union. The chief witness was a Mr. G. H. van der Walt. This gentleman had been expelled from the Garment Workers in August 1948 for disruptive activities, and he was found by the committee to have 'contributed to the immediate causes of the disturbance'. This witness was apparently intended to become a new-style leader of the Garment Workers. Under cross-examination, he admitted nine convictions for offences ranging from attempted murder to petty theft.

In the early 1950's the national-minded elements, now banded together in the 'Action Committee of Anti-Communist Garment Workers', continued their activities within the Garment Workers' Union, with a new nominee, Mr. G. L. H. van Niekerk, as their leader. Their methods included intensive house-to-house visits, the encouragement of dissident local groups and protest petitions, and a series of public meetings addressed by Nationalist M.P.s and predikants. Despite these activities, however, the existing President and Acting General Secretary, Miss Anna Scheepers and Miss Johanna Cornelius, were in 1953 returned with large majorities of over 12,500 in each case, while their opponents Mr. C. Meyer and Mr. G. L. H. van Niekerk could not scrape up much more than 3,500 votes apiece. At that time non-white votes were in a majority in the union. Before the 1956 election, it seems probable that the 13,000 non-white workers will have been compelled by new legislation to set up their own organization. The re-election of the present office-holders will therefore depend only on the 7,000 white workers, and the vote will be a close one. Mr. Sachs recently estimated that about 40 per cent of the white workers were likely to vote for 'national-minded' candidates. Of this figure, about one in four constituted the hard core, while the remainder were subject to vacillation and demagogic appeals.

Such figures are no consolation to Nationalist leaders, who are fully aware of the increasing importance of the urban Afrikaner's vote. So far this vote has gone mainly to the Nationalists, but there is always the possibility that a re-oriented type of Labour Party might draw increasing numbers of de-nationalized workers. After its accession to power in 1948, therefore, the Nationalist Government initiated legislative measures whose effect has been to undermine the orthodox trade union movement. Chief amongst these was the anti-Communist legislation of 1950 and 1951. The provisions made there for 'naming' and 'banning' persons who were considered by the Minister to be Communists under the rather wide and retrospective definition in the Acts, had by the beginning of 1954 resulted in the compulsory resignation of twenty-seven prominent trade union leaders and the naming of forty-two others.[1]

Amongst those 'banned' were Mr. E. S. Sachs, who had been expelled from the Communist Party in the 1930's; Mr. P. J. Huyser, national organizer of the Building Workers' Industrial Union numbering some 15,000; Mr. D. J. du Plessis, former Vice-President of the National Union of Laundering, Cleaning and Dyeing Workers; and Miss E. S. (Betty) du Toit, General Secretary of the same union. Others affected were officials of non-European unions. The then Minister of Labour, Mr. B. J. Schoeman, made the Nationalist aim quite clear in October 1953; he told the Transvaal Congress of the Nationalist Party that the Government was determined to purge the trade unions of Communists, so as to protect union members, and urged Afrikaans-speaking workers to join the trade unions so as to ensure that the right people would occupy key positions.

With its two-stringed harping on the red and the black perils, Nationalism has undoubtedly had some success in its endeavours to weaken orthodox trade unionism. This is shown in the shifts and hesitations amongst unions and co-ordinating bodies since the Nationalists came to power in 1948. At that time, the only national co-ordinating body was the orthodox South African Trades and Labour Council. To this body were affiliated all-white, mixed and non-white unions. There was also the old-

---

[1]In the same period over 500 individuals were 'named'. The total number of those who were 'banned' and forbidden to attend meetings was 100. This 'banning' is equivalent to loss of livelihood in the case of most prominent people.

established Western Province Federation of Labour Unions in the Cape; in this group most of the affiliated unions accepted Coloured members but not Africans. There were also a number of unions which were not affiliated to either group. These included the Mineworkers' Union (which had left the Trades and Labour Council in 1947), and some colour-bar unions connected mainly with the iron and steel industry in Pretoria. In 1948 these Pretoria unions formed a national-minded Co-ordinating Council, which in 1948 had thirteen affiliated unions and a membership of over 30,000.

The Trades and Labour Council was however too unwieldy and its component parts too divided to withstand the concentrated assault of the Nationalist press and Afrikaner organizations from without, and of disruptive activities from within. It was easy to persuade more conservative trade unions that the T.L.C. was dominated by Kafferboeties and Communists. In consequence a further group of unions broke away in November 1950, largely because of the Communist bogey. The T.L.C. was then left with 127,000 members, mainly representing the secondary industries.

This breakaway group ultimately formed a group called the South African Federation of Trade Unions, which by the beginning of 1954 had twenty-three affiliated unions (some mixed) representing more than 100,000 workers, mostly in the artisan and higher wage categories. The T.L.C. was by then down to forty-five affiliated unions (five of them African) or just over 80,000 workers. The Amalgamated Engineering Union (21,000) and the South African Society of Bank Officials remained unaffiliated.

It was at this stage that most trade unionists began to feel concerned about the 'divide and rule' provisions of the new Industrial Conciliation Bill which was then before Parliament. An attempt was made to form a Council of Trade Union Federations to co-operate on uncontroversial issues, but the project met with a stumbling-block over the question of recognizing African trade unions, which may not be formally registered as such in the Union. Finally, a Unity Committee, composed of leaders of the Federation of Trade Unions, T.L.C., W.P.F.L.U.

and A.E.U. was set up, but despite energetic protests it failed to get the new legislation set aside or materially changed.

Toward the end of the year the process of isolating the pro-left and anti-colour bar elements of the T.L.C. reached its final stage. Its more conservative opponents voted the Council out of existence and joined in setting up a new body called the South African Trade Union Council, whose membership was confined to registered unions (i.e. unions with Coloured and Indian members were acceptable, but African unions were excluded). In March 1953 the elements that had disagreed with this step (including the Transvaal Garment Workers' Union) and the African unions that had been excluded, representing over 40,000 workers, set up a colour-blind co-ordinating body under the name of the South African Congress of Trade Unions.

Meanwhile, the right-wing South African Federation of Trade Unions, which had been strengthened by the accession of the Mineworkers' Union, submitted a memorandum to the Select Committee on the Industrial Conciliation Bill; this accepted the Government's apartheid policy and proposed ways of introducing such apartheid into 'mixed' trade unions.

The Industrial Conciliation Bill had by 1955 received its second reading in Parliament and was being considered by a Select Committee. Its provisions would seem intended to promote apartheid at all costs and to strengthen the paternalistic powers of the Minister of Labour vis-a-vis the unions. No further 'mixed' unions are to be registered, and existing 'mixed' unions (of which there are sixty with about 140,000 members) must form separate branches; if more than 50 per cent of the workers in a given occupation wish to secede from a 'mixed' union, this new union shall be separately recognized and they shall be entitled to participate in any closed shop agreements. The Minister's new powers will permit him to exempt certain 'classes of persons' from the provisions of industrial agreements or awards and to safeguard the economic welfare of employees of any race in any industry or occupation, by directing the industrial tribunal for which the Bill also provides to recommend when necessary that such employment should be reserved for members of a specified race (including Africans). The inevitable result of such legislation must be the discouragement of collective bargaining and the strengthening of partisan interests and splinter groups, and a further disruption of the orthodox trade union movement.

Like the African, the Afrikaner's rôle in the cities had been mainly that of a worker and employee. The industry and commerce where he found employment were the creation of men and capital from overseas, mainly from Britain. In consequence, English became and has remained the commercial language of the country, and the Afrikaner seeking work found himself at a disadvantage on more than one count. Even as a consumer his purchasing power was for a long time too low to earn his language or his preferences any consideration in the largely English-speaking urban centres. Even as late as 1952, a contributor to the Afrikaanse Studentebond's organ *Werda* claimed that in Johannesburg only 1.5 of the 70,679 Afrikaners had an income of £1,000 or over, while 51 per cent were earning less than £600 (37 per cent were non-earners). Corresponding figures given for the English-speaking group were 10 per cent in the £1,000 and over group, 40 per cent under £600 per annum and 34 per cent not earning. Of the 3,282 persons with an income over £3,000, only eighty-one were said to be Afrikaans-speaking.

Over the last decades this state of affairs has begun to change. The change would probably have come about anyway as a result of the increasing occupational diversification and the increasing purchasing power of the Afrikaner group. It has however been accelerated by deliberate economic action on the part of Afrikaner Nationalist leaders interested not only in organizing the Afrikaner consumer potential but also in entering the ranks of employers and financiers. Somewhat tardily, national-minded Afrikaners realized that it was not enough to win the struggle on the language and political fronts, so long as economic power remained in alien hands. As early as 1916 Dr. Malan told the Afrikaner to conquer the cities, and this theme was gradually taken up until in 1939 it became an organized movement.

The story of the Afrikaner's economic struggle—as in other spheres the words 'struggle' and 'striving' occur with monotonous regularity—has now achieved the status of an epic, albeit an unfinished one. This epic begins with the simple rural Boer economy of the nineteenth century, in which the only commercialist was the (usually Jewish) pedlar or smous and in which the Boer produced little more than would suffice for his own needs. In the more populous villages, thirty-one small local banks were set up between 1836 and 1862, but by the end of the century only the Stellenbosch District Bank survived. The spirit of nationalist protest was nevertheless stirring. In 1880 *Di Patriot* of the Paarl outlined a programme which began to be realized only half a century later: 'There must be no English shops, no English signboards, no English advertisements, no English bookkeepers. Then a national bank must be started to displace the English banks. Next, munitions of war must be started in the two republics . . . So must we become a nation.'

In the years before the first World War, a few small Afrikaner enterprises were set up, including two tobacco co-operatives and two printing firms. 1915 saw the establishment of the Nasionale Pers, the publishers of the New Cape Nationalist organ *Die Burger*. The industrial development of the war years was not shared in by Afrikaners, many of whom found themselves in financial difficulties as a consequence of their participation in the 1914 Rebellion. A Helpmekaar Fund was raised to help them and realized the surprising sum of £180,000 in two months. This gave an indication of the new possibilities of mobilizing Afrikaner financial resources for a national purpose. It was not until 1918 however that the future giants of the Afrikaner economic movement began life. These were the K.W.V., or Co-operative Winegrowers' Association, an insurance corporation called Santam, and the associated life insurance company Sanlam.

The period between 1918 and 1939 is described as the 'second economic movement'. It was a period rather of individual enterprise than of co-ordinated planning and action by national-minded groups, in contrast to the third economic movement which was to begin in 1939. The first decade after the First World War saw the setting-up of a couple of smaller platteland trust corporations; one very small burial society (A.V.B.O.B.)

and one small loan bank; two large and several small agricultural co-operatives; and a large number of small platteland
businesses. On the debit side the Afrikaner's part in industry was
still only that of an employee, nor was there an Afrikaner-
owned commercial bank, building society or investment
company.

The thirties were mainly a period of consolidation and development of existing enterprises. One notable exception was
the foundation in 1934 of the Volkskas or People's Bank. Its
original capital was £615, and it was a small co-operative loan
bank. Volkskas became a commercial bank in 1941. When it
celebrated its coming-of-age in 1955, its fixed property was
valued at £2,500,000, and its total assets at £50 million; deposits
were £44,572,000 and loans, £31,591,700. The number of
employees had risen from one man and a typist to over 2,000.
The period of maximum development was under the Nationalist
Government, deposits having risen from £16 million in 1948.

Volkskas has achieved its phenomenal growth by exploiting
Afrikaner sentiment with its claim to be the only real South
African bank, and by aggressive and somewhat less conservative
methods of doing business than the two great old-established
commercial banks, Barclays and the Standard Bank. Both of
these banks have their head offices in London. In consequence
of its less orthodox financial policy, Volkskas gets some business
from non-Afrikaners, particularly when it is a matter of fixed
property deals, which the other banks do not handle. This challenge by Volkskas has not yet however seriously hurt the two
giants. Barclays has deposits of £186,560,000, with loans and
advances at £112,560,000; the Standard Bank has deposits of
£163,870,000 and loans and advances of £104,440,000. Both
reported a marked growth of business in 1954-5.

The decisive campaign in this banking war may well be
fought in the growing field of non-white business. This business
at present takes the form of small individual accounts, which in
bulk and in potential represent an economic capital that is
largely unorganized and undeployed. Here the Volkskas, with
its definite associations with Afrikaner nationalism and its
apartheid arrangements, may have some difficulty in ousting

English-speaking competitors. The history of Volkskas may however provide an example for the growing African nationalist movement, which has so far concentrated more on abortive political action than on a mobilization of non-white economic power.

The 1930's also saw the entry of the Afrikaner into the urban general distributive trades, with the setting-up of Uniewinkels and Sonop in Bloemfontein. A number of new co-operatives were established, and the co-operative was propagated as a truly Afrikaner organizational form which might ultimately provide economic salvation for the Afrikaner against the alien capitalistic system. But, as Dr. M. S. Louw of Sanlam commented at the quarter-century celebrations of the F.A.K. in September 1954, the co-operative proved less satisfactory in the distributive trade and finance than in agriculture. As a consequence most consumers' co-operatives either went under or turned into ordinary companies. A few were successful because of good leadership or because they were built up under the protection of existing agricultural co-operatives. In 1954 there were 190 consumers' co-operatives with a membership of 107,058 and a turnover of £12,945,958.

The agricultural co-operatives themselves took a long time to win general acceptance. This movement began just after the turn of the century and was encouraged by legislation in 1922. In the late 1920's, however, the Carnegie Report commented on the continued lack of co-operative spirit amongst South African farmers. The Commissioners attributed this lack to such factors as individualism, conservatism, and ignorance of business methods. Even amongst members of the rural co-operatives the Commission found a lack of unified action, due sometimes to political or church differences, and a lack of understanding of the co-operative principle and of consistent loyalty.

In 1934 there were 338 registered co-operatives or societies, with a membership of 86,715, and it was only in the 1940's that the co-operative movement really took hold. By 1949 there were 240 farm co-operatives (mainly Afrikaner), only 15 of them still organized on an unlimited liability basis, with a total membership of 200,000. By 1954 there were 268 agricultural co-operatives with a total membership of 245,000. Turnover in respect of farm produce in 1947 to 1948 was £81.9 million, as opposed to £27.9 million in 1939 to 1940. By 1954 this turnover had more than doubled to £177 million.

1939 was one of the most important dates in the economic development of the Afrikaner. This was the year of the First Economic Congress, called by the F.A.K. in Bloemfontein to discuss the Afrikaner's economic position, still a black one owing to the persistence of Poor-Whiteism, and to co-ordinate his future economic development. This congress called into existence the Ekonomiese Instituut to serve as Afrikanerdom's economic planning council, and the Reddingsdaadbond (R.D.B. or Rescue Action). This was an organization set up within the F.A.K. to consolidate the Reddingsdaad committees which had sprung up all over the country a year earlier, in response to an appeal by the now legendary 'Father' Kestell.

The Rev. John Daniel Kestell was a Natal-born Afrikaner who served as a chaplain with the Boer forces, was one of the five translators of the Afrikaans Bible, and became Moderator of the N.G.K. of the Free State. From 1902 onwards he had been telling Afrikaners that economic salvation would come not from outside help or government charity, but by their own efforts. ''n Volk moet homself red' (a people must save itself). At the Voortrekker Centenary celebrations in 1938 he suggested that the most tangible way of honouring the Voortrekkers would be to do something for their 'sunken descendants', the Poor Whites.

At the First Economic Conference however, the concept of the rescue action was enlarged. To the R.D.B. fell the tasks, not only of uplifting the Poor Whites, but of keeping the worker Volk-minded by 'reforming' the trade unions, and of organizing the Volk's purchasing power and savings power towards the end of building up an Afrikaner capitalism. The guiding spirit behind this organization has from the start been Dr. Nico Diederichs, M.P., economist, company director, and chairman of the F.A.K. Economic Section.

The R.D.B. is not a very forthcoming organization, and does not publish annual reports, perhaps because it figures fairly regularly in the English-speaking press in a somewhat controversial light. It is listed in the *South African Year Book* as having nearly 56,000 members organized in 330 branches. It runs two Afrikaans-medium technical and commercial schools. The Labour Bureaux which the R.D.B. ran earlier were found to be unnecessary after 1949. Its monthly *Inspan* was discontinued recently owing to lack of advertisements. The constitution stresses its Christian National and traditional values, and its name appears from time to time in reports of campaigns to make Afrikaners 'buy Afrikaans', or to keep the worker Volk-minded in work and at leisure. An official said to the writer recently, in rebuttal of criticisms that had been made of the R.D.B.: 'We are not anti-anything, but pro our own. We admire the Jews for supporting their own people in business. We are not a boycott movement. We are accused of being political but our conscience is clean.'

The Poor White problem has in practice ceased to exist, but the R.D.B. continues to pursue its other aims with energy. As the Rev. J. Conradie said in his chairman's address in October 1952: 'The Afrikaner worker is today forced to subject himself to the existing trade unions so that approximately half of the Afrikaner nation is today ensnared in the powerful machinery of the trade unions . . . an enormous task awaits to rescue the Afrikaner nation from the claws of this unnational power . . .'

A further result of the Economic Conference was the setting-up of the Afrikaanse Handelsinstituut, to serve the Afrikaner businessman and to help solve his problems. This was however all preliminary work. To quote Dr. Louw again: 'The real aim was to strengthen already existing businesses and to found and build up new Afrikaner undertakings which would give employment to Afrikaner boys and girls.'

This plan was greatly facilitated by the Union's immense industrial development in the war and post-war years. The net national income rose from £394 million in 1939 to nearly £1,376 million in 1954. These boom conditions should probably share the planners' credit for Afrikaner development over the next decade. This development was not unduly hindered even by the quotas and permits of a war-time economy, operating in favour of older-established enterprises, most of which were 'English' dominated. According to a Handelsinstituut survey of 'turnover', the Afrikaner share in commerce rose from 8 to 25 per cent, in finance from 5 to 6 per cent, in manufacturing industry from 3 to 6 per cent, and the over-all total rise was 5 to 11 per cent. This figure was regarded as satisfactory but as showing the great distance that had yet to be covered.

It was in this decade that the planners[1] set about filling up some of the gaps in Afrikaner participation in the Union's economic life. Volkskas converted itself to a commercial bank in 1941; it then had a capital of only £1 million, which had by 1948 risen to £16 million. Sanlam, which has a stronger sense of mission than most insurance companies, took on itself the task of implementing the Economic Conference's resolution that an Afrikaner financial company should be formed to serve hitherto neglected fields. This led to the foundation in 1940 of Federale Volksbeleggings Beperk (Federal National Investments Ltd.); to support in 1943 for a young Afrikaner building society, Saambou, which is now one of the biggest in the Union, with funds of about £10 million, and to the creation in 1946 of another financial company, Bonuscor. The latter provided policy holders with an opportunity of investing their cash bonuses in the shares of a finance corporation, and made funds available for the development of further Afrikaner industries. Bonuscor's capital in 1954 was nearly £1,500,000 and it was paying a regular dividend of $5\frac{1}{2}$ per cent. By 1955, the total capital assets of the Sanlam group totalled well over £50 million.

The F.V.B., which was later to become the Federale-Groep, had begun in a small way in 1940. By 1954 however it had a capital of £3 million and an outside capital (buite-kapitaal) of a further £3 million, with total reserves of over £1 million. Its investments, like those of Bonuscor, went into Afrikaner

---

[1]Amongst the names which recur like a sort of Brains Trust in the Nationalist economic movement are those of Dr. N. Diederichs, of the R.D.B., Dr. Albert Hertzog, Professor A. I. Malan, all M.P.s; Mr. C. R. Louw and Dr. M. S. Louw of the Sanlam group, Professor C. G. W. Schumann of Stellenbosch University, and last but not least Mr. Anton Rupert of Rembrandt tobacco fame.

enterprises, mainly in the basic industries of coal and fisheries (Marine Products in 1942, Tunacor in 1948, and Namib in 1949). By contrast, a finance organization called Tegniese Beleggings (Technical Investments), with a capital and reserves of £2½ million, concentrated on the direct creation of manufacturing firms. Chief of these are the prospering Afrikaans-owned tobacco manufacturer Rembrandt, (founded in 1941), and the Distillers' Corporation of Stellenbosch (founded in 1945).

Other manufacturing enterprises were set up during this period without assistance from the finance companies. Chief among them were the Midde-Westelike Visgroep (1949), Volkshemde and Klerefabriek. Another contemporary enterprise was Wolnit, set up by a finance company called Nywerkor, which has so far not extended its activities further.

Uniewinkels and Sonop remain the only large Afrikaner foundations in the distributive trade, but a large radio and electrical equipment group came under Afrikaner ownership as a result of co-operation by Sanlam, F.V.B. and Bonuscor.

The most recent developments, in 1954 to 1955, have been the foundation of three new companies, through the co-operation again of Sanlam, F.V.B. and Bonuscor. These are the Pensioendienste en Onderlinge Beleggingskorporasie (Pension Service and Mutual Investments Co. Ltd.), intended to save private employers the trouble of setting up their own individual pension schemes; the Federal Trust Ltd., to act mainly as industrial bankers; and the Central Finance Corporation, which will serve as a short-term finance company.

1955 saw the formation of First National Tea and Coffee Factories Ltd., in which wives of prominent Nationalists form the Board of Directors. Behind this company is the investment company which promoted the Rembrandt group. The company has already begun a vigorous sales campaign, directing an aggressively nationalistic appeal to the Afrikaner housewife, and coaxing the non-Afrikaner consumer by lavish use of historical titles and cultural allusions.

In addition, the Langeberg Kooperasie, an Afrikaner canning company set up in 1940, has recently bought up the formerly Jewish-controlled Standard Canners and Associated Canners. This was a capital transaction of about £1½ million. As a result, Afrikaner interests now control 80 per cent of the South African fruit and vegetable canning industry. The latter industry depends mainly on exports to Britain, a market where a quota system until recently assured Dominion exporters a regular market, but where fierce competitive conditions are now likely to prevail.

This raises a problem which is confronting Afrikaner businessmen to an increasing degree; the fact that the proclamation of a republic outside the Commonwealth would bring an end to imperial preference, formal or informal, and probably cause the loss of a great part of the export market. In their search for increased markets, Afrikaners will also not fail to note the potentialities of the non-white consumer market, potentialities which cannot be fully exploited under total apartheid conditions.

In the period since the First Economic Conference, it has been estimated that the Afrikaner's share of the national income rose from £100 million in 1939 to £350 million or 42 per cent of the total national income for 1948/9. Side by side with the campaign to build up Afrikanerdom's share in production and commerce, therefore, went a campaign to make the Volk as a whole buy Afrikaans and invest Afrikaans. This campaign has had considerable success, but it is still felt that many rank-and-file Afrikaners are too apathetic and fail to realize the importance of their participation in this aspect of the nation's struggle: some wealthy Afrikaners have actually shown themselves afraid to invest their money in Afrikaans-owned concerns. One reason for this hesitation on the part of hard-headed investors is suggested by Professor C. G. W. Schumann, in an article written for the Ekonomiese Instituut in May 1955. 'It can be laid down almost as an axiom that the undertakings which made the strongest appeals of Afrikaner sentiment were the poorest in business skill and in sincerity of aspiration'.

The 'Buy Afrikaans' campaign runs concurrently with the much older campaign to make non-Afrikaans concerns provide a bilingual service under the threat of a loss of Afrikaner custom. An interesting development in this connexion has been the tendency for non-Afrikaner firms to court the increasingly important Afrikaner consumer by appointing Afrikaner directors or personnel. A speaker at the R.D.B. Congress in Port Elizabeth in July 1954 warned Afrikaner consumers to be on their guard against such insinuating devices by concerns which 'in other respects have no love of, or interest in the Afrikaner struggle in the economic, cultural, religious or political fields . . .'

The Afrikaner's growing participation in the whole economy of the country has undoubtedly helped to strengthen his political and cultural position. Increasing participation in economic life has however brought with it various problems, and is likely to bring still more, of a kind which may even confound the Nationalist planners.

National-minded leaders do not however feel that the economic position of the Afrikaner is secure. Dr. P. J. Meyer, head of the public relations department of the Rembrandt organization, was quoted by *Die Volksblad* in June 1955 as saying that Afrikaner political power stood on shaky foundations because of the Afrikaner's economic backlog, and that the tempo of development of Afrikaans business was too slow to counteract the growth and concentration of foreign groups against it. He spoke of the rise of an Afrikaner labour party which could do great harm to the national feeling, and called on the politicians to assist Afrikaner industry, which could not yet fend for itself without State support. This statement reflects the insecurity and the ethnocentric way of thinking that pervades Afrikaner life today.

The first of these new problems concerns the rank-and-file of urban Afrikaners. These children of the Poor White problem were nearly lost to Afrikanerdom through spiritual neglect and demoralization in the twenties and thirties. In the years of political triumph and material prosperity to come, they may be lost again and for ever to the seductive influences of the quasi-American culture which is being increasingly purveyed over the radio, at the cinema, and in the Afrikaans weeklies. Nationalist leaders, both religious and lay, are aware of this danger, but their methods of dealing with it seem inadequate and antiquated. In addition, the Afrikaner urban worker is in process of acquiring an economic class feeling. This is not yet sufficient to make him side with his class against his Volk, but there are signs that the class resentment which in the old days could be directed against the 'foreign' capitalist exploiters is now focusing on the wealthier elements within the Volk itself.

The second problem is that of this new class of wealthy Afrikaners. With such exceptions as the wool farmers, most of them came to wealth by exploiting Afrikaner sentiments and by catering to an Afrikaner public. Now, however, they have to face the fact that further expansion must be outside this protected field, either in the English-speaking or the non-white section of the internal market, or in the export market, which is mainly British. They may even have to look for investment capital, most of which still comes from non-Afrikaner and overseas sources. This is not a situation in which the individual businessman finds a narrow economic nationalism advantageous. Finally, Afrikaner business enterprise has been built up within an existing capitalist framework, and on a basis of integrated, cheap, non-white labour in the industrial areas. Those who have achieved success along these lines are all the less likely to welcome the risks of an apartheid economy.

In short, the economic movement seems likely to produce yet another class within the Afrikaner group, a class of Afrikaner businessmen who feel an increasing class solidarity with non-Afrikaner businessmen, who have a growing interest in the economic and capitalistic *status quo*, or ultimately even in improving the non-whites' economic position in order to establish a sounder internal consumers' market.

This whole trend runs quite contrary to the limited capitalism of the Calvinist planners. Worse still, however, it runs contrary to the economic apartheid of such planners as Dr. Verwoerd and the Minister of Labour, Senator de Klerk. The trend has, however, an increasing number of supporters amongst those who have already tasted economic success, whether they are employers or employees. In neither case is there any willingness to bear the sacrifices required by the implementation of full economic apartheid. This would involve for the first group a costly decentralization of industry, and for the second the compulsion to do without the non-white menial labour that has been part of the South African economy for three centuries.

This state of affairs was frankly admitted by a leader-writer in *Die Transvaler* in September 1955: ' . . . territorial separation . . . must have the result that the Europeans will have to perform all their labour themselves. This great ideal will have to be realized if European civilization is to be upheld in the southern point of Africa. It implies that the Europeans will have to resign themselves to great sacrifices. At the same time let it be stated now honestly and frankly that the majority of Europeans have not yet awakened to the realization that this is the only manner of rescuing their civilization here. The conception that the European is above such forms of labour and that the non-European is meant for this is so deeply rooted in them after three centuries that they apparently cannot imagine another state of affairs'.

So the educational process proceeds, and the non-whites taste apartheid mainly in its most negative and humiliating aspects. Meanwhile the process of economic integration goes on, as even Nationalists will admit. Mr. M. C. de Wet Nel, M.P. told the 1955 Congress of the Jeugbond that South Africa would become steadily blacker over the next twenty years, but that thereafter the stream of Africans towards the urban areas would be reversed. He added that the idea of a Bantustan (the alleged ultimate goal of the total apartheid planners) should be rejected because it was as dangerous as integration; he concluded on a 'have your cake and eat it' note that undoubtedly reflects the views of most South African whites: 'I still see thousands of Bantu on our farms and in our mines, in our industries and even as servants in our houses, with only this difference however that they will be there as a result of the offer and grace of the Europeans and not as a right. At best they would be visitors in the European areas'. This attitude does not differ greatly from the old-fashioned 'segregation', which both major white groups accepted in the 1930's and earlier, and which C. Louis Leipoldt defined as ' . . . segregation, which in practice means that the natives should nowhere compete with the white man but that the white man should where convenient make use of the native'.

The new-style Afrikaner businessmen[1] are not without support in high places. Chief amongst the orthodox economic thinkers are the Governor of the South African Reserve Bank, Dr. M. H. de Kock, Dr. A. J. R. van Rhijn, Minister of Economic Affairs and Mr. Ben Schoeman, Minister of Transport. It is also pointed out that in 1955 the new Minister of Finance, Mr. Eric Louw, presented a moderate budget which made no provision for raising the annual millions needed for the implementation of Dr. Verwoerd's great plan for decentralizing industry to four main areas near African reserves on an apartheid basis.

The leader of the planners, Dr. Verwoerd, is not however the man to be deflected from his task simply because the implementation of his policies would lead to economic risk or even large-scale unemployment. Like earlier Nationalist leaders, he feels that *laissez-faire* economics must bow to the higher social good, which in this case is the preservation of the Afrikaner Volk. His task would be made easier by a period of industrial recession, but there is no doubt that his views command a great popular following today. The latter-day Afrikaner tends to admire the man with a master-plan, designed to control and co-ordinate the unruly elements of mid-twentieth century life.[2] It seems probable that the future of the Afrikaner people, and indeed of South Africa as a multi-racial country, may turn on this internal tug-of-war between profits and principles.

---

[1]Now organized in their own local Sakekamers (Chambers of Commerce) which are affiliated to the efficient Handelsinstituut in Pretoria.

[2]In 1946, the Nationalist Party issued an economic plan providing for a Central Economic Council, a Central Licensing Board for industry, planned central control of all mining activities, a body to control trade licences and fix maximum profits, a Central Banking Council, a Labour Council and a Social Welfare Council.

CHAPTER FIVE

THE CHOSEN PEOPLE

'And I will establish My covenant between Me and thee and thy seed after thee in their generations, for an everlasting covenant, to be a God unto thee and thy seed after thee. And I will give unto thee and to thy seed after thee the land wherein thou art a stranger, all the land of Canaan for an everlasting possession; and I will be their God.'

(Genesis Chapter 17: v. 7–8).

'The history of the Afrikaner reveals a determination and a definiteness of purpose which make one feel that Afrikanerdom is not the work of man but a creation of God. We have a Divine right to be Afrikaners. Our history is the highest work of art of the Architect of the centuries.'
(Dr. D. F. Malan, quoted in Eric Robbins'
This Man Malan, p. 7).

'It is not wholly fanciful to say that on a narrower stage, but with not less formidable weapons, Calvin did for the bourgeoisie of the sixteenth century what Marx did for the proletariat of the nineteenth century, or that the doctrine of Predestination satisfied the same hunger for an assurance that the forces of the Universe are on the side of the Elect as was to be assuaged in a different age by the theory of Historical Materialism. He (Calvin) taught them to feel that they were a Chosen People, made them conscious of their great destiny in the Provincial plan, and resolute to realize it'.
(Professor R. H. Tawney, *Religion and the Rise of Capitalism*,
p. 129).

A T first sight it may seem curious that the stern and sombre doctrines which the good bourgeois of Geneva embraced with such zeal in the sixteenth century should have taken such firm root on the sun-swept, empty veld of South Africa. These doctrines, however, sprang from a reading of the

Scriptures, which chronicled the history and religious experience of a pastoral people far removed from the cities, but not from
the far-trekking Boers with their flocks and their herds, their men-
servants and their maidservants, and their patriarchal families.

To the Boers the Old Testament was like a mirror of their
own lives.[1] In it they found the deserts and the fountains, the
droughts and the plagues, the captivity and the exodus. Above
all they found a Chosen People guided by a stern but partial
Deity through the midst of the heathen to a promised land.
And it was the Old Testament and the doctrines of Calvin that
moulded the Boer into the Afrikaner of today. As a reader wrote
to *Die Transvaler* in 1950: 'Through the hearts of the massed
thousands did the one perception shudder, that God called into
being and empowered the Afrikanervolk to fulfil His plan. How
else could the incredible happenings be explained, that the
Afrikaner tribe (stam) of the expanded Cape Border decided
like one man, and trekked out to meet a dangerous and unknown future, merely under the star of the Almighty; in whose
name a whole sub-continent was tamed and won for Christian
civilization.'

The doctrines which the Boers took with them on their long
trek through the veld and the centuries were those of sixteenth
century Calvinism, reduced to their simplest form in the memory of simple men with only the Bible to guide them. Chief
among these doctrines were that of the 'elect' and that of predestination. Such doctrines were reinforced by the harsh facts of
life on the frontier and on trek. In the vastness of the veld,
amidst droughts, plagues, and clashes with primitive tribes, a
white skin became the badge of Christianity and of civilization,
and these doctrines acquired an even sharper and more fundamental significance for the Boers. Further, the Calvinist insistence on personal responsibility and discipline encouraged a race

---

[1]So close to them was the Old Testament that the cattle farmers who
reached the Fish River Valley in the 1770's, finding great heaps of stones
there, concluded that they must be monuments left by the children of Israel
in their wanderings, and called the place Israelitische Kloof. Later there
were the Jerusalemgangers of the Western Transvaal, who waited for the
signal to trek to Zion along the river which they called the Nile (Nylstroom).

of sturdy individualists, while its conception of a visible Christian society ensured that the expanding South African frontier never knew the full lawlessness of the American West.

This South African Calvinism grew out of the veld like an aloe, unmoved by the mellowing breezes of liberalism that blew from Europe. Calvinist churches elsewhere adjusted themselves to the vast social and industrial changes of the century. South African Calvinism moved straight out of the seventeenth century into the present day. Finding themselves in an industrial urban society, theologians turned back to the fountainhead for a pattern of life. They substituted for the individualism of the veld the rigorous Christian collectivism of Calvin's Geneva. Increasingly they came to regard themselves as the leaders of God's Chosen People and the prophets of God's pre-destined will for the whole of Southern Africa.

For more than a century, the Dutch Reformed Church was the only Church tolerated in the Cape by the Dutch East India Company. This was despite the fact that a minority of the original settlers were Lutherans, whose numbers were later reinforced by German ex-soldiers. For all this monopoly, however, the Church was allowed very little freedom of organization. Until the coming of the Huguenots there were only two congregations in the little colony. These were in Cape Town and Stellenbosch. The ministers were licensed by the Classis of Amsterdam, but were paid and supervised by the Company. Each congregation had a consistory of elected deacons and elders, with the minister in the chair. In addition the civil authorities appointed political commissioners; a system that was retained by the British until 1843. In such circumstances the work of the ministers, whether among Christians or the heathen, was thwarted and discouraged. A Scottish minister writing in the nineteenth century went so far as to say that the Company had reduced them to the level of paid chaplains.[1]

A third consistory was set up at Drakenstein at the request of the Huguenots. This request was not, however, granted with-

---

[1]Reverend John M'Carter, *The Dutch Reformed Church in South Africa*, Inglis, Edinburgh, 1869.

out opposition from the local authorities. Governor Simon van der Stel complained of 'the impertinence of the French', but was finally overruled by the Council of Seventeen. The Huguenots, more militant Calvinists than the original settlers, challenged the authorities still further when their second minister, Le Boucq, questioned the right of the lay arm to interfere in spiritual matters. In this instance, however, the Huguenots lost and their pastor was sent off to Batavia.

Attempts at this time and later to form a local Classis were viewed with distrust by the Company and the Amsterdam Classis. A short-lived Assembly was set up in 1746, but its efforts to assert authority brought its suppression in 1759. Thereafter and for many years to come, the Cape congregations were destined to remain what Eric Walker describes as '*disjecta membra* of the Church somnolent*'.

In the educational field, the Church made more headway. Schooling was intended to fit its recipients for Church membership. This meant literacy and a knowledge of the scriptures, prayers and the Heidelberg Catechism. From 1710 until the time of the Batavian Republic, prospective teachers had to be approved by the Church authorities, while each Church place had its elementary school, conducted by the parish clerk.

For the first two centuries of its existence the Dutch Reformed Church in South Africa suffered from a constant shortage of ministers. The pastoral work of the existing ministers was further hindered by the fact that their sheep were of a wandering nature and, when settled, liked to live at a great distance from their neighbours. The Reverend M'Carter writes of one minister, 'noted for his zeal', who succeeded in visiting some parts of his parish only once in every three years.

By the end of the eighteenth century there were seven congregations. Those at Roodezand, Swellendam and Graaff Reinet had been set up in the wake of the wandering Boers. But so far flung was the settlement that only the nearest came to the regular Sunday service. The majority trekked in to the quarterly Nagmaal (Communion). Some came only once a year, while the most remote settlers might not come until there were two or three children to be baptized. This custom persisted for nearly two centuries. The Carnegie Poor White Commissioners found a middle-aged woman who told them that when she had been baptized the minister asked all parents of children who were about to be baptized to stand; the whole congregation rose. The woman's parents were trek-boers, so she never went to school, but learned just enough at home to be admitted to the Church.

For the Nagmaal, a wagon-town would mushroom round the church-house from Friday evening to Monday morning or even longer. This was probably the greatest event in Boer religious and social life. Apart from the communal religious observances such as prayers, sacraments, catechism, religious instruction, weddings, and christenings, which set the tone for the gathering, Nagmaal gave the Boers one of their few opportunities of social intercourse outside the family circle.

In view of the checks set on them by authority, and of the difficulty of maintaining any close-knit parish life outside the settled Western Cape, it might be thought that the Dutch Reformed Church ministers would not have been held in particular esteem by the colonists. Visitors at the end of the eighteenth century were, however, struck by the high prestige of the ministers amongst the laity. This prestige was perhaps the reflection of the dominating rôle of religion in the life of the Dutch colonists, and of the educational and personal superiority of individual ministers. Nearly sixty years later, young Mrs. Andrew Murray wrote of the Bloemfontein congregation: 'There are no grades of society and people or peasantry of an English congregation here rank as equal, and yet they look upon their pastor and his vrouw as their father and mother and hold them in great respect'.

This high prestige of the clergy was even further enhanced by the Church's later rôle as the defender and cherisher of Afrikanerdom. It is only now being overshadowed by the rise of a new commercial aristocracy and of a secularized urban proletariat within the Afrikaner group itself. By the end of the eighteenth century, nevertheless, the Church seemed to have fallen on evil days. Its monopoly had been broken, first by the Lutherans, then by the liberal decrees of the Batavian Commissioner J. A. de Mist. These decrees, while confirming the

Dutch Reformed Church as the established Church, promised equal protection to all communities which worshipped 'a Supreme Being for the promotion of virtue and good morals'. Worse still, the new authorities struck at the foundations of the Christian state by allowing civil marriages to be solemnized, by authorizing secular public schools, and by tightening state control over Church government. Most serious of all, perhaps, was the increasing shortage of ministers.[1] In the absence of any local facilities, all ministers had either to come from overseas or to go there for training. Meanwhile, ministers of other denominations were arriving in increasing numbers, to enter the mission field which had lain fallow for so long.

When the Cape was finally ceded to Britain in 1806, the burgers and inhabitants were guaranteed their present forms of public worship along with all the rights and privileges they had enjoyed until then. In practice, this meant the continuation of state control until 1824. But the breaking of the official link with Holland also meant that the trickle of ministers from that source dried up and the Dutch Church faced the danger that it might cease to be Dutch.

Lord Charles Somerset has always been a major name on the black list of Nationalist Afrikanerdom. Certainly his action in importing Scottish preachers and teachers to fill the gaps in the ministry and the new public school establishment struck shrewdly at the main centres of Dutch colonial feeling. Both anglicizing ventures came near to success in the settled western districts. By 1837, thirteen out of the twenty-five Dutch Reformed Church ministers were Scots, and union with the Church of Scotland was actually debated in 1824 and again as late as 1918. The Dutch Reformed Church, then under limited Government supervision, supported Governor Napier's attempts to recall the Trekkers in 1837. It branded the Trek as

---

[1] Until very recently, the Dutch Churches have suffered from a chronic shortage of ministers. Even in 1931, the Carnegie Poor White Commission complained that each Minister of the N.G.K. had 1,918 persons to care for and each G.K. predikant as many as 2,505, there being one minister to serve every three parishes. The Anglicans in the same period had 556 adherents to each minister.

a venture without a Moses or the true certainty of a Canaan, and no Dutch Reformed Church minister went near the Trekkers for more than a decade.

What the anglicizing policy failed to take into account, however, was that the congregations might make Dutchmen out of the ministers who had been sent to anglicize them. This was what happened in the majority of cases. The most famous instance is that of the Reverend Andrew Murray, who produced two equally notable predikant sons and a whole lineage of 'ware Afrikaners'.

Denationalization was also checked by the setting-up of a Theological College in Stellenbosch in 1858. This college sent an increasing number of local men to the Ministry. By the 1880's the Dutch Reformed Church was in the forefront of the fight to achieve official recognition for the Dutch language and had set up a normal school for training Dutch teachers in Capetown.

The limited freedom from lay control granted to the Dutch Reformed Church in 1824 was exchanged for a fuller freedom in 1843, with the abrogation of de Mist's Kerkorde. The Church remained however a Cape Church, and its writ only extended as far as that of the civil government. It did not, therefore, follow up its lost sheep until British rule was extended to Natal and the Orange River Sovereignty, in 1843 and 1848 respectively. Thereafter, only the Transvaal remained independent.

Long before the Trek, the religion of the frontiersmen had become an intimate family affair of Bible reading and prayers, with the home as the House of God. The lack of spiritual care on the Trek was therefore less harmful than it might otherwise have been, and it is noteworthy that one of the first acts of settlement anywhere was to set up a consistory and to plan a church building. For decades these church councils without ministers were to be a feature of the Transvaal Republic. During the Trek the only spiritual guidance which the Boers received was from the ex-mission teacher, Erasmus Smit, and the Wesleyan missionary Archbell of Thaba N'Chu. In the Natal Republic, the Boers took as their first pastor the American, Daniel Lindley. The latter's views on his flock were at times tinged with impatience. In 1839 he wrote: 'I do sincerely believe that the cheapest, easiest, speediest way to convert the heathen here is to convert the white ones first'.

The negative attitude of the Dutch Reformed Church of the Colony during the early years of the Trek had its consequences. The Transvalers, who included the most diehard and unruly elements of the Trekkers, had come to regard the Cape Church as a collaborationist body that followed the British flag. They hoped to get ministers from it, but were unwilling to place themselves under its jurisdiction. This move could involve them politically with the British authorities and might also oblige them to accept the Cape Church's formal policy of permitting multi-racial congregations. It will be recalled that the Republican constitutions stressed that there should be no equality between black and white in church or state.

The Cape Church saw to it that so long as the Transvaal refused incorporation, no Cape ministers should answer the call from the Transvaal. Finally, a predikant, the Reverend Dirk van der Hoff, arrived from Holland and, despite some internal squabbles, the independence of the Transvaal Church was assured. This was the second of the present three Dutch Reformed Churches, the Nederduitsch Hervormde Kerk van Afrika, (N.H.K.) and it was the State Church of the South African Republic. Doctrinally, it differs little from the Cape Church, although it has always looked to Holland for its predikants and its spiritual orientation. Its historian, Dr. S. P. Engelbrecht, lays stress on its Nederduitsch character, as denoting freedom from Neo-Calvinism on the one side and from Scottish and American (Methodistic) and Revivalist influence on the other.

The N.H.K. was not, however, to have a monopoly of the Transvaal's religious life. In twenty years, it suffered two major amputations. One group seceded to form the Gereformeerde Kerk van Suid Afrika, generally known as the Doppers.[1] The

---

[1]The origin of this word is obscure. It has been connected variously with the words 'doper'—a baptizer or baptist, 'domper' (extinguisher used for church lights), 'dorper' (dorp is a small village), and with the 'dop' that was used as a form for cutting hair. 'Dop' may mean a shell, husk, or pod, also a tot or drink measure.

other break came when the Dutch Reformed Church of the Cape (N.G.K.) established itself in the Transvaal in 1866; it attracted a number of N.H.K. members, not without rousing great bitterness amongst those who remained behind. The N.H.K. suffered even more than the other Dutch Reformed Churches from a shortage of predikants; a local supply was only assured by the opening of a theological faculty in Pretoria in 1917. Today it has nearly 130,000 adherents; all these are in the Transvaal, but for a small minority in Rhodesia, South West Africa and East Africa.

Despite their relatively small numbers, the Doppers have had a considerable influence on Afrikaner life. President Kruger was one of the original seceding church members in the Transvaal, and the Dopper Church has been most closely identified with Christian National Education. Indeed, the University of Potchefstroom, which grew out of the old-established G.K. Theological School, is the only place of higher learning which is openly practising this system today. The Theological School itself is the second oldest in the country. It was opened in 1866 at Burgersdorp, Cape, transferred to Potchefstroom in 1904, and has turned out a stream of able conservative theologians for nearly a century.

The Doppers existed as an unofficial sect within the Cape Church before the formal break occurred. Their strength was mainly on the frontier, in areas such as Graaff-Reinet and Burgersdorp. They were distinguished by their plain dress and their austere customs, by their independence and their doctrinal conservatism. Young Mrs. Andrew Murray has left us a vivid though scarcely sympathetic account of her impressions of a Dopper community in the Orange Free State.

'During this last trip we stopped with a peculiar race of Dutch people called Doppers, they are a sort of Quaker. The women always wear hoods in the house, very like Quaker bonnets in shape. They are very primitive in their habits and will not permit of any worldly conformity either in dress or manners, consequently the men never wear straps nor the women stays; the former have their hair cropped close round their heads, the latter put in behind their ears. They speak in a drawling manner and with a nasal twang, are slow in their movements and have a peculiar way of sitting. The worst is they are unlike the Quakers in being dirty and untidy, thinking that much regard for that betrays a worldly mind.

The only people I don't like are the Doppers. They are really such a dirty obstinate race. They won't buy merino sheep because their forefathers did not have them nor build better houses . . . They won't have a lame man for a predikant because the priests were to be without blemish. If you remonstrate with them for marrying a second time so soon, they tell you Abraham only mourned forty days for Sarah. They are the strangest, most quaint of mortals, many of them very religious, but prejudiced and ignorant to a degree. Owing to the weather, I was obliged to sleep one night in a Dopper farmhouse. Mr. Roux arrived at the same house. I fortunately always carry sheets and our sheepskin blanket. In one large room were three beds with curtains. The old man and his wife tumbled into one, Mr. Roux and another man into another, we had the third. I contrived to smuggle my clean sheets and blanket in behind the curtains and quickly made our bed on the top of the one destined for us, which had evidently had many occupiers before our turn came. Besides this there were four children sleeping on the floor.'

This extract may serve to illustrate the lack of rapport between the masterful and reforming Scottish predikants and their more conservative charges. The feelings of those Doppers who did not trek were exacerbated by new doctrines and by the tactless attitude of various Scottish ministers. This dissatisfaction finally focused on one point, that of the singing of hymns in church. This custom had been introduced into the Dutch Church at the beginning of the century from Holland. The Doppers, however, rejected it on the grounds that the hymns were not Holy Writ and should not, therefore, be sung in church. On this question feeling ran high both on the Cape and the Transvaal. Church members in the north even threatened that blood would flow if the hymns continued to be sung (or not sung as the case might be).

In 1859, fifteen members of the Rustenburg congregation, including the future President, Paul Kruger, left the N.H.K. to form their own congregation. With them as their pastor went the Reverend D. Postma, a vigorous and strong-minded personality who had been sent out from Holland by the Christelik (Gereformeerde) Afgeskeie Kerk, to investigate a possible field of work amongst whites as well as blacks. Within two years the new church had four Transvaal congregations, one in the Orange Free State and two in the Cape. Between 1859 and 1904, the membership grew from 300 to over 12,000. Today the G.K. has by its own reckoning nearly 80,000 adherents.[1]

One of its recent historians, Dr. S. du Toit, commented on the G.K.'s present position with modest pride: 'The G.K. will readily admit that it consists of only a small part of the population, and that for the most part of "simple people", but on the other hand it has, even in its weakness, made its contribution. Of the greatest importance by itself is the fact that the G.K. has held the banner of Calvinism high in our land amidst all sorts of influences . . . In the sphere of the State, the Volk and society, "Dopperdom" was ever in the forefront . . . The G.K. and the Afrikanervolk are inseverably joined together. It has always stood strongly against foreign influence of a religious as well as a political nature'.

Alone of the three Dutch Churches, the G.K. seems to have escaped the violent controversies between liberal rationalism and conservative orthodoxy which raged within the Calvinist Church in the nineteenth century. The main purveyors of the new ideas in South Africa were predikants who had become infected with liberalism during their studies in Holland. They found some support amongst educated laymen in the cities, and, in the cases of the Reverend J. J. Kotze of Darling, and the Reverend T. F. Burgers of Hanover (later President of the Transvaal Republic), personal loyalty from their congregations.

In the Cape a battle raged through church councils, synods, law courts and the press throughout the sixties. It was ended by the nominal victory but actual defeat of the liberals. Their

---

[1]The 112,233 listed by the 1951 census should, according to the Bureau of Census and Statistics, be treated with caution; it may be due to confusion caused amongst respondents by the similarity of names of the three Churches. The same applies to the census total of 182,988 for the N.H.K.

wings were clipped by the institution of the *colloquium doctum*,[1] by the flow of orthodox graduates from a new theological seminary at Stellenbosch and by the secession of a notable liberal, the Reverend D. P. Faure, to establish a splinter Free Protestant Church in Cape Town. The main factors behind this successful defence of orthodoxy were the doctrines brought by the Scots predikants, the natural conservatism of the Boer temperament, and the fact that the Dutch Church was an institution of a people struggling to preserve its own way of life against all outside influences.

In the Transvaal, the remaining decades of the century were occupied by inter-Church bickerings and abortive reconciliations. The general outcome in all parts of South Africa was for seventeenth-century orthodoxy to triumph over nineteenth-century liberalism. This triumph has been a lasting one. In 1929, the Reverend Doctor J. du Plessis was prosecuted for opinions which would, according to Eric Walker, 'have passed for the mildest liberalism in Western Europe'. In consequence, 'liberalism' has become an ugly name which, when used in the political field, conveys an opprobrium scarcely less than that contained in the terms 'Communist' and 'Kafferboetie'.

By the time of the Anglo-Boer War, the Dutch Churches had surmounted the hazards of anglicization, liberalism and internal strife, to become the leaders of the Boer people. They were the pioneers of education and the champions of the Dutch language. Many of the nineteenth-century minority of English-oriented predikants had by then disappeared. True, there was a difference of opinion between the bulk of the ministry, who supported the claims of High Dutch, and such men as Dr. S. J. du Toit, who early saw that the language of the people had more chance of survival than the language of sermons and literature. This difference was not resolved until the decade after Union. The Cape Synod of the N.G.K. was the last to capitulate, accepting Afrikaans as its official language in 1919. By

---

[1]The inquiry into their beliefs to which all intending ministers of the Dutch Reformed Church of South Africa who have received their training abroad have to submit. For a general account of the Cape struggle between liberalism and orthodoxy see J. H. Hofmeyr, op. cit. pp. 44 *et seq.*

1933 an Afrikaans version of the Bible was published, the result of sixteen years of co-operative effort by the three Dutch Churches.

During the Anglo-Boer War most Dutch Reformed Church ministers in the Cape and Natal sympathized with the Boers. Two ministers of the G.K. seminary at Burgersdorp took a group of students to serve with the ambulances. After the war, the predikants were prominent in material reconstruction and the rebuilding of Boer morale. As modern Afrikaner Nationalism developed, many ministers went along with it as followers or, as in the case of Dr. Malan, as leaders. In the 1930's some even became imbued with the ideas of National Socialism. Others, as the victory of Nationalist Afrikanerdom drew nearer, began to think in terms of a theocratic Afrikaner State like that of the sixteenth-century Geneva.

Today, it is the original Cape N.G.K., with its four provincial synods, each under its Moderator, and its Federal Council, that dominates Afrikaner religious life. According to the 1953/4 *Year Book* this Church has 1,065,306 'souls' under its care within the white group; almost one half of the total white population. By virtue of its large non-white membership it is also the largest Christian Church in the Union, but the missionary aspect of its work will be discussed later. The organizational unit remains the congregation with its elected council of elders and deacons, who 'call' their own minister. State control and financial support have long disappeared.

The Dutch Reformed Church still has a fair number of adherents and even ministers who are non-Nationalist. It is hard for people to whom religion means so much to leave the Church of their fathers and to worship amongst strangers in a strange language.[1] The voice of these dissidents is however rarely heard,

---

[1] In 1944, the Reverend D. V. de Vos broke away from the N.G.K. and formed a Reconstituted Dutch Reformed Church (Hervormde Nederduits Gereformeerde Kerk) which by 1952 had a synod of eighteen ministers. The breakaway was on political grounds. Dr. de Vos claimed that the N.G.K. was dominated by ministers and elders who were members of the Broederbond, and that his opposition to this had been agreed with General Hertzog. This splinter-church would not appear to be of any great significance at present.

and the Church's influence is solidly behind the Nationalist Party. Leo Marquard points out that in World War II it was difficult to find Afrikaner chaplains for the forces, although well over half of the troops were Afrikaans-speaking. Indeed, during the Boer War and its aftermath, and in both World Wars, some predikants found it their duty to denounce and to deny Communion to such 'traitors to the cause' as the National Scouts and Handsoppers, the volunteers of 1914 and those who wore the orange flash in 1939.

The Dutch Reformed Church is concerned with both the private and the public life of its members. Its influence in the latter field was comparatively restricted until recent decades, but its authority in private life has always been immense. The Calvinist cannot hope to win personal salvation by godly behaviour, but he can by prayer and action glorify God and create a sanctified society. Such a society can only be achieved and maintained by an all-embracing discipline, particularly when it must survive amidst a host of barbarian heathen and the subtler temptations of an alien and world-wide culture. The application of this discipline is the task of the Church, its ministers and its elders.[1]

At the 1952 Synod, the Moderator of the Free State, the Rev. H. J. Reyneke, reminded elders that the time had come for each of them to take a personal interest in the lives of congregation members in his area, despite any rebuffs or scoldings he might receive. Such opposition, he added, merely showed the extent to which those people had deteriorated spiritually.

A study of D.R.C. statements over recent years shows that the ideal unit of private life remains the old-style Boer family, with its strong pattern of paternal authority. Large families are desirable, birth control is condemned and it is not thought advisable that the mother should go out to work. Marriage outside the Dutch Churches or outside the Afrikaner group is frowned upon. It is regarded as leading to denationalization or the entry of alien ideas into the group itself. Boys should be disciplined,

---

[1] The N.G.K. has a Secretary for Public Morality, whose pronouncements are frequently reported in the Press.

but trained for ultimate self-dependence, to counteract the de-moralizing effects of the present welfare state.[1] Divorce is frowned upon (thought not always to any effect), and the Afrikaans Churches have recently demanded that adultery should become a criminal offence, as it was under Roman-Dutch Law in the old days. In Calvin's Geneva, indeed, adultery was a capital offence. The old Boer custom of family worship and Bible reading should be maintained or revived and a strict moral censorship should be imposed on all reading matter. In general, the secular and frivolous influence of American films, songs and publications is deprecated. This is not without reason, since Americanization has now replaced anglicization as the main threat to Afrikaner culture and mores.

The Dutch Reformed Church has been successful in enforcing the ban on organized public entertainment on Sundays throughout the Union, by means of such legislation as the un-repealed Sunday Observance Law of 1896. It has not however been able to check the growing tendency of Afrikaners to spend their Sundays, and even such holy days as Dingaan's Day, on the beach, picnicking or in other forms of private recreation.

Apart from the Afrikaans volkspele, modern dancing is generally condemned by the Dutch Churches as heathen, degrading and promiscuous. In 1951, the Commission for Combating Social Evils of the Free State N.G.K. issued a memorandum which suggested that 75 per cent of divorce cases begin on the dance floor; 'Chastity disappears and the sexual desires are gratified by the promiscuous association of one sex with the other. What is only permissible within the bounds of monogamous marriage becomes common property on the dance floor'. The report continues with a reference to the contributory circumstances: 'The erotic music, the stimulating clothing, the use of strong drink, the intimate association of the two sexes, the late hours and so on'. At the same synod, the Afrikaans-medium

---

[1]The Minister of Labour, Senator J. de Klerk, voiced the views of his *alma mater*, the Christian National University of Potchefstroom, when he said in 1955, 'As far as possible I will kill pensions—they are alms and should only be given when people can't work any more.'

University of the Orange Free State was criticized for allowing its students to attend and hold dances.

Immodest dress has long been the subject of attack, first because it encourages sexual promiscuity and secondly because it lets down white prestige in a multi-racial community. There was even an abortive attempt by the Churches to propagate truly Afrikaner styles in women's dress. In general, the Afrikaner woman is encouraged to conform to the ideal of the Boer wife and mother; such habits as smoking, and still more drinking, are still discouraged for women.

Drinking is regarded as unequivocally evil. Here however, the Church has from the start been fighting a losing battle in a country that produces wine and brandy, and is further blessed with an abundance of sugar cane. The Dutch Reformed Church has nevertheless shown commendable courage in standing up to the wine farmers, most of whom are themselves church members. In 1930 the Church submitted a memorandum to the Cape Coloured Liquor Commission categorically opposing the tot system,[1] and in 1952 the N.G.K. Federal Council issued a statement reaffirming its view that alcoholism was not in the first instance an illness but a sin.

All attempts to introduce a state lottery have foundered on Church opposition spearheaded by the D.R.C. Gambling and betting are regarded as social evils. Money should, it is felt, be earned by the sweat of one's brow, and racing was recently castigated in *Die Kerkbode* as 'an ingenious game intended to undermine the thrift, industry and fidelity of the ordinary man. There are countless examples where horse racing totally destroyed the family.'

There are signs of a very recent date that the Dutch Reformed Church is modifying this total austerity in such matters as cinema-going, smoking and dress. This represents a belated attempt by the Church at adaptation to the different circumstances to which most urban Afrikaners have already succumbed. For a Church of the people, it has come dangerously

---

[1] The system under which Coloured farm labourers receive a tot of wine at prescribed intervals during the working day. The legal daily maximum is 1½ pints, but this is often exceeded.

near to losing a large part of its flock. An N.G.K. inquiry showed that the majority of nominal adherents on the mining and industrial area of the Witwatersrand 'seldom or never attend church any more'. Concessions are now being made to the new way of life, but it seems still to be hoped that through the increasingly Christianized and Nationalized Afrikaans-medium schools a new generation can be reared in more godly ways. Whether or not the Union can ever be made into a latter-day Geneva remains however in doubt.

Towards the end of the nineteenth century and for several decades afterwards, the Dutch Reformed Church faced an equally grave cultural problem amongst large numbers of its adherents. This situation too had its origin in the process of economic change which drove the Afrikaner to the towns. The earlier problem however was one of poverty and eventual moral, intellectual and physical degeneration. This degeneration might, it was feared, loosen the Poor White's feeling of community with his Church and his people; it might even cause him to 'go Kaffir', inter-marry with non-whites and be lost to the white group altogether.

The Church's measures to deal with the Poor White problem took the form of parish relief administered through the deacons, of farm settlements where poor rural families could be rehabilitated, of orphanages, institutions for the old and infirm and, after 1919, of indigent children's hostels. At the height of the Poor White problem in the 1920's these hostels housed 8,000 children in the Cape, and enabled them to get the education which would rehabilitate them. In addition, the Dutch Reformed Church did much to bring the plight of the Poor Whites home to the European population in general, by preaching the need for Christian charity from the pulpit, by representations to government and by calling successive conferences to discuss the problem.

By its energetic response to this challenge the D.R.C. undoubtedly retained its hold on the majority of Afrikaners. The continuing disparity between census and Church statistics would however seem to indicate that a fairly large minority have slipped out of the Church's reach. In 1926 for instance the census gave 831,713 adherents of the N.G.K., while the Church statistics of the same year showed only 658,905 adherents. This was a shortfall of 172,808 or 21 per cent of the total. Of this number about 42,000 were in the cities, 130,000 in the rural areas and dorps. In 1951 the shortfall on a census total of 1,107,482 was 186,454, or nearly 17 per cent. Even allowing for the small and decreasing number of trek-boers who are beyond the reach of any parish, and for the handful of intellectual agnostics, it still seems likely that the majority of these lost sheep are to be found amongst the former Poor Whites.

This partial failure on the part of the Church was attributed by the Carnegie Poor White Commission to such factors as ultra-conservatism, which made the Church slow and cautious in realizing new problems and adopting its methods to deal with them (for instance provincial synods were held only every three or four years); to the past tendency of the Church to look on poverty as 'part of God's plan, by means of which the people must be prepared for and encouraged to hope for a fuller, more perfect and more blessed state hereafter' and therefore to bestow too little attention to the amelioration of present conditions; to a tendency to mechanical charity devoid of personal interest and encouragement on the part of Church workers, which encouraged dependency and pauperism; and to an insufficient sociological training for ministers and inadequate staffing of the Church in general, especially in the urban areas.[1]

The Commissioners also felt that the Calvinist virtues of self-help,[2] thrift, temperance, fairness in labour relations and the social solidarity of the whole community, rich or poor, were not always sufficiently stressed by individual ministers in their preaching and practice. The farm settlements set up by the Churches were run on these lines with a high degree of success, but a number of Poor Whites in the towns were found to be

---

[1] As late as 1951, a predikant writing in *Die Kerkbode* complained that the N.G.K. was neglecting the new O.F.S. goldfields area, while other Churches had already built churches there.

[2] This observation seems to have borne fruit. In 1952, *Die Transvaler* reported a protest by the Synodical Poor Relief Commission of the N.G.K. against a proposed State 'social security code for all'.

resentful towards the Church. The Commissioners quoted such remarks as 'members of other Churches visit me more faithfully when I am sick than my own', and: 'the Church is a rich man's Church'. To such attitudes may in part be attributed the growth of sects amongst the urban Afrikaner proletariat.

The Church's original plan for the Poor Whites was to stop their trek to the towns and to rehabilitate them on the land. The flow could not however be checked, and the newer generation of national-minded predikants came to see its political advantages and to encourage it. As early as 1916 Dr. Malan, then editor of *Die Burger*, suggested that the time had come when Afrikaners should take their place in industry, commerce and the public service, so that the cities might be conquered by the Afrikaners.

With the growth of an Afrikaner urban working-class and also of a class of Afrikaner industrialists and business men, the Dutch Reformed Church has begun to move towards the position of Calvin's Church in the commercial stronghold of Geneva. In 1951 the Transvaal N.G.K. synod issued a code of social justice laying down the duties of employers and employees. Its provisions were as follows:—

'The employer must:

1. Give the employee a fair recompense for his work.
2. Give him, together with things temporal, also things spiritual, such as respect, interest, advice and encouragement.
3. Provide a decent living for the worker and his family, including a daily, weekly and annual rest period and accommodation.
4. Treat him honestly as a man and a brother.
5. Give him a fair share of the profits.

The employee must:

1. Give not the minimum, but all his labour, time, power and interest to his employer.
2. Show respect, obedience and trustworthiness in all things.
3. Further the interests of his employer as an honest collaborator.'

If such conditions were followed faithfully, it was felt there should be no need for trade unions in the Christian National State. This may have been one of the reasons for the Dutch Reformed Church's sustained attack on the existing trade unions and in particular on the South African Trades and Labour Council and such militant bodies as the Garment Workers' Union. Equally important reasons for this attack are of course the colour-blind policy of many unions which have accepted non-European members, the left-wing views of many leaders and the fact that in such unions as the Garment Workers' Union some leaders and most of the rank-and-file are newly-urbanized Afrikaner girls. Ministers have gone so far as to denounce the trade unions from the pulpit as being foreign to the Afrikaner spirit.

In 1936 an Afrikaans organization was formed by the Nationalist Party to 'Afrikanerize' the trade union movement, while in 1937 the N.H.K.'s synod appointed a Commission to investigate Communism in the trade union ranks. This enterprise produced a rush of successful defamation suits brought by irate trade union leaders who had hitherto regarded themselves as anti-Communists. In his book, *The Choice Before South Africa*, Mr. E. S. Sachs, the former secretary of the Garment Workers' Union, describes the active though abortive intervention of Dutch Reformed Church predikants in the Germiston clothing factory dispute of 1944, in which nine Coloured workers were taken on during a labour shortage. Apart from other measures, an enlarged Church Committee of fifteen predikants was set up by all three Dutch Churches, which issued a pamphlet under the title *White South Africa, Save Yourself.*

Where Dutch Reformed Church intervention in economic life has not been politically tinged, it has always been aimed at preserving the *status quo*, or even at returning to an ideal past, whether it be the lekker lewe of the old Boer Republics or the Christian polity of Calvin's Geneva. In education, it has been concerned with enforcing a uniform Christian National programme to ensure that the younger generation returns to the fold of Calvinist Afrikanerdom.

The Church's political activities as such seem to be of comparatively recent date. From the late nineteenth century various ministers of the Dutch Reformed Church have been closely identified with the language struggle and the fight for group survival. The Church was not however so closely committed to a political party as it was later to become. This was perhaps because the older generation of ministers were themselves European-born or trained, and had a stricter conception of their ministerial functions. Dr. Malan was the forerunner and the greatest of the new-style political predikants, of whom the younger generation were to be the product of the single-medium Afrikaans schools. In 1915 Dr. Malan left the pulpit to become editor-in-chief of the new Cape Nationalist daily *Die Burger*.

In the same year he was elected chairman of the newly-formed Nationalist Party in that province, on his cry of 'Africa for the Afrikaner', although he did not enter the House of Assembly until 1919. Another political predikant, Dr. William Nicol, the former Moderator of the N.G.K. of the Transvaal, is now Administrator of the Transvaal. It was he who just before the 1948 general election, when he was still Moderator, published an article in a religious magazine, *Die Voorligter*, counselling Calvinist readers to vote for the Volk's Party. The political appointment followed shortly afterwards. Numbers of lesser predikants serve on municipal councils and such bodies as school boards, which have now become party political arenas. The question of the Broederbond's infiltration of the ministry will be discussed elsewhere, but it is known that Dr. Malan and some hundreds of the more active political predikants are Broeders. Mr. Louis du Plessis of Krugersdorp, who was a founder member of the Broederbond, claims that several now influential ministers were members when the organization went underground in 1924.

Amongst rank-and-file members of the ministry, particularly in the Transvaal, there is a tendency to political bias in the pulpit itself. Good Calvinist Afrikaners are asked to prove their love of country and nation by supporting the only truly Afrikaner political party, and deviationists may be branded. After the Nationalist Party came to power, in 1948, one Dutch Reformed Church minister at least held a service which he called the

Oorwinnings Diens' (Victory Service). In general, the Divine sanction is invoked for the policy and activities of the Nationalist Party.

The amount of political bias within the ministry has certainly not decreased in the period since General Hertzog, himself a devout Calvinist, said in 1938:

> 'I have always held that our church is something sacred to us. We can no longer be oblivious to the fact that there are unfortunately predikants—persons who are paid by their congregations to cultivate the finest and deepest feeling of love and esteem towards one another—who are entangling themselves in party politics. Where they should cultivate humanity and love they join issue in politics, knowing beforehand that the moment they do this there is division and disaffection in their congregations. Dare we as a people or as a government allow this to proceed?'

It should be added here that not all ministers nor lay members of the Dutch Reformed Church yet accept the political activities of the majority; this is borne out by the letters of protest that appear from time to time in *Die Kerkbode* and the Afrikaans dailies.

It was in Hertzog's day that a minority of Afrikaner predikants, like some of their German Protestant brothers, began to be infected with the views of National Socialism. Notable were Dominees Kotze and Stander, successive chairmen of the Groot Raad of the Ossewa-Brandwag. By the later years of the war, however, Afrikaner Calvinist leaders had withdrawn from overt acceptance of Nazism to a form of neo-Krugerism. The modified democracy of Krugerism laid emphasis on the citizen's duties rather than on his rights; and the rule of law was made subordinate to the word of God, of which the Dutch Reformed Church was naturally the interpreter.

In 1951 the N.G.K. reasserted its adherence to its own version of Krugerism in an important report on the relationship between Church and State which was adopted by the Federal Council in Bloemfontein. The main points in this somewhat prolix and obscure document are: that the state has been created by God and exists apart from its citizens; that there is a particular form of Christian state suitable to each Christian people, which each people will itself evolve, but that such forms as Communism, National Socialism and 'revolutionary democracy' (which believes in the sovereignty of the people) must be rejected as displeasing to God, as must also the idea of a world State; that the authority of the state is derived from God and is indivisible, so that there can be no division of power between legislature, executive and judiciary; that the state must order harmoniously the different interests of its members, thereby obviating the need for such bodies as trade unions; and that, as the government receives its mandate from God and not from the people, the franchise is not an automatic right for all men[1] but 'a privilege only to be entrusted to those who have come of age and who are capable of exercising it with responsibility to God'. This would exclude the non-whites and those who 'openly rebel against God', such as the Communists. In a Christian State, therefore, the test of the franchise is not only maturity, but allegiance to Christianity. Political parties are necessary in a State, but, as, only the Christian political faith is valid, no adherents of an anti-Christian philosophy should be allowed to form political parties.

Commenting on this important statement, Leo Marquard writes in *Peoples and Policies of South Africa* (p. 216); 'Calvinism is a determinist creed which consorts naturally with conceptions of racial superiority and of national separateness . . . Calvin's beliefs were formulated in a middle-class commercial society. It is perhaps not fanciful to suggest that the statement of the N.G.K. could not have been made while the Afrikaner was still an agriculturalist with strong individualist tendencies; the statement became possible only after he had entered the world of business in a modern urban society. If there is truth in that, the Calvinist political doctrines are likely to become increasingly influential'.

---

[1] A few weeks earlier an N.G.K. Commission had drawn up a lengthy attack on the United Nations' Declaration of Rights. The attack centred on this Declaration's fundamental error in stressing man and not God as the measure, and re-asserted the principle of duties, not rights, and the God-ordained diversity and inequality of mankind.

Professor R. G. Tawney has pointed out that theoretical Calvinism has two political aspects. It is authoritarian when it
represents a majority in the State, as in Geneva or John Knox's
Scotland. It is individualistic and even revolutionary when it
represents a minority, as was the case of the Puritans in seventeenth-century England.

In South Africa, the Boers were for long in a minority position, and their faith and their life as farmers combined to make
them freedom-loving and intolerant of all authority. Today the
newly-urbanized Afrikaners dominate the political scene, and
Calvinist authoritarianism, not uninfluenced by a heavy after-
taste of National Socialist doctrine, is growing. The N.G.K.'s
statement is Krugerism with a difference. Kruger himself spoke
of the will of the people as being the will of God, while even
Dr. Malan continued to talk of the Volkswil as being the sovereign power in South Africa. On the other hand, the Church's
present view was echoed in 1955 by the statement of the new
Minister of Labour, Senator de Klerk: ' . . . we are Calvinists
who believe that God is sovereign and hands over that sovereignty to the legal rulers of the land'.

The tendency to authoritarianism in the Union is likely to be
increased by the fact that while the Afrikaners hold a majority
position in the white group, the entire group is a minority vis-a-
vis the disfranchised non-white majority. The N.G.K.'s strict
limitations on the franchise and the functioning of political
parties would also seem logically to lead to a one-party state, if
not to a theocracy. It remains to be seen whether the old Boer
spirit of individualism, or the new anti-clericalism or revivalist
sectarianism which is emerging amongst certain sections of the
urban proletariat, will be strong enough to counter the purpose
of what is still by far the most powerful institution of Afrikanerdom.

The Dutch Reformed Church has always been primarily the
Church of the Afrikaner people. It has, however, been active
amongst the non-white inhabitants of the Union and has played
a great part in determining recent state policy towards them.
This Dutch Reformed Church mission work is organized on a
separate basis in accordance with Calvinist doctrine.

The N.G.K. has often been attacked on this question of separate churches. In justification of the Church's attitude, the Reverend C. B. Brink, Moderator of the Transvaal Synod, wrote recently: 'it is therefore not only for practical reasons . . . that the N.G.K. . . . aims at the establishment of separate non-white Churches which must finally become completely independent. The missionary policy of these Churches has sufficient scriptural grounds for us to feel justified in saying that the creation of separate Churches is not only permissible but essential. . . the Christian Churches must be careful not to deprive the whole of Africa's nativedom of the privilege of making its own contribution to the development of Christian truths. The native people were able to teach us much of fatherhood, brotherhood, and respect for authority. These qualities they have already to a great extent lost as a result of the integration policy pursued also by some Churches and the consequent disintegration of their tribal life. To avoid this danger the establishment of separate Churches is the only way out'.

In April 1953 Dr. A. J. van der Merwe, Moderator of the N.G.K. of the Cape, put the matter rather more bluntly: 'The agitation for the abolition of difference because of reasons of race or colour finds its driving force for the most part not in the Gospel but in anti-Christ and anti-Church ideology which in practice is a relentless form of tyranny . . . if there should eventually be an amalgamation between churches for whites and non-whites, it does not need a prophet of exceptional calibre to foresee that such a fusion would be fatal, and would resolve in a split in comparison with which today's separation is as nothing . . . are we not sometimes in danger of identifying complete sentimentality with Christian love? Let there be opportunity for more mutual discussion and prayer. Let there be more opportunity for the planning of the united front to combat all the ethical and spiritual dangers which threaten our common heritage.'

In accordance with this separatist principle, the Dutch Reformed Mission Church was established for non-whites in 1881. In 1950 the N.G.K. began to establish the foundations of a Nederduitsch Gereformeerde Bantoekerk for Africans. The purpose of the latter was to carry separation further by concentrating all Africans who were members of the Mission Church in their own church, and to leave the Mission Church of the Cape as an exclusively Coloured Church. By the end of 1953, the latter had the care of nearly 240,000 'souls', while the Bantu Church in all four provinces and the Rhodesias had the charge of nearly 300,000 more.

The Mission Church and the Bantu Church are both off-shoots of the main N.G.K. The other Dutch Churches have not sufficient non-white adherents to merit a separate church organization.

Social relations between white and non-white missionaries, are, it would appear, somewhat limited—the Rev. P. E. S. Smith of the N.G.K. Mission Council of the Cape told a Commission in late 1952 that white missionaries of his Church received native preachers in their studies but not in their sitting-rooms, and that tea or a meal might be offered, but not in the presence of the white family.

The Dutch Reformed Mission Church has separate predikants who receive a lower stipend; most of them are white but there is an increasing number of Coloured ministers who are trained, not at the Stellenbosch Theological School, but at Wellington. The Mission Church has separate congregations, buildings, and church organization, but owing to the poverty of its congregations is still to a large degree financially dependent on its Mother Church.

The few Mission Church congregations that are able to support their ministers without assistance have recently tended to show a certain independence of the Mother Church, particularly with regard to its views on apartheid and white Christian trusteeship. The Chairman of the Wynberg Ring in Capetown, a Coloured minister called the Reverend I. D. Morkel, went so far in 1950 as to issue a statement condemning apartheid. Immediately afterwards he left the Dutch Reformed Mission Church with his congregation and set up, with no doctrinal change, the South African Calvinist Protestant Church. This has already attracted several thousand adherents and founded six predominantly Coloured parishes in the Western Cape.

In general, the term Mission Church is resented by the Coloured people. They have been Christians for well over a century, and regard themselves as entirely European in culture. The dissident members of the Rev. I. D. Morkel's congregation declared: 'The Church's policy of trusteeship is no longer acceptable to us, as we have already reached maturity'. The paternalistic separatism or 'Christian trusteeship' of the Mother Church has caused a drift to other Churches where the colour bar is less stressed. This drift has been mainly to the Anglican, Roman Catholic and Apostolic Mission Churches. Unlike the Africans, the Cape Coloured people feel themselves too close to the Europeans to set up the hundreds of flamboyant separatist splinter-churches which are such a feature of Bantu religious life.[1]

The late arrival of the Dutch Reformed Church in the missionary field may be attributed partly to strict Government control, partly to lack of personnel and funds, and partly to the fact that the Dutch Reformed Church is part of the structure of Afrikanerdom. As such, its attitudes not only influence but are influenced by the attitudes of its members. These deep-rooted attitudes were formed in early Cape days, through contact with Hottentot servants and black slaves, who were for the most part both heathen and primitive.[2] This ultimately led, as with most Protestant societies, to an equating of Christianity, civilization and whiteness, an equation which habit and economic convenience continued to buttress long after the Cape Coloured people and many Africans had become Christians.

In consequence of these factors the Dutch Reformed Church came late to the missionary scene. Its work there continued to be harassed by the same shortages and attitudes. The other missions, on the contrary, were able to forge ahead, assured of

---

[1] Nearly 1,350 in 1950 (81 officially recognized).

[2] The early notion that a Christian should not be held in slavery soon made baptism of slaves unpopular amongst their owners. In 1770 this concept, which had lapsed, was partly reinstated by a Dutch East India Company order forbidding the sale or alienation of baptized slaves. Though this order was repealed by Governor Cradock in 1812, only about 100 slaves were admitted to baptism in the next decade or so; this does not argue a widespread missionary zeal on the part of ministers or slave owners.

boundless enthusiasm and large contributions from their supporters in Britain and elsewhere, and also of the support of the Colonial Government. Mrs. Andrew Murray, wife of the first N.G.K. minister to the territories across the Orange River, gives a balanced contemporary view of the problem:

> Most severely has Andrew reproved, most earnestly has he endeavoured to resist that hatred for the blacks which is the dark curse of our people. We have missionary prayer meetings, missionary collections, missionary maps for conversations. In many a sermon has he referred to the unhappy prejudice, and by example and labour we try to do our best to overcome it. But bitter speeches, harsh judgement, reproach and contempt are not the way to overcome evil and this is the chosen way I am sorry to say of the English colonial public, and even of too many missionaries and English writers, the so-called philanthropists who it is to be wished would show as much philanthropy towards white as black skins, when there are as large claims for it. Much evil has been done by mistaken philanthropy, looking only to the one side, seeing all missionary enterprise through the rosy colours of romance.

Earlier in the same letter she writes:

> Nevertheless I do not approve of the severe way in which these poor neglected people are judged. Far more pains have been taken with the natives on their borders than with themselves. There is a larger proportion of missionaries to the native population of the colony than there are ministers to the Dutch and the Church is only just awakening from its sleep to a sense of its great and culpable neglect.

The British and American missionaries were, as may be imagined, far more outspoken in their view of Boer attitudes. The American missionary Champion wrote: 'As to the Boers, I am not prepared to say what I think about them as a field of labour. God is making use of them as scourges of the natives; and perhaps when they shall have accomplished this they will be mutual scourges of each other. Their ignorance, their parties, their ungodliness, make it improbable that they can unite in any good form of government'.

The Trekkers had already suffered under what their leader

Piet Retief called the 'unjustifiable odium cast upon us by interested and dishonest persons under the cloak of religion'. By this he meant the activities of Dr. John Philip and the London Missionary Society. It is not therefore surprising that in their Republics the Trekkers regarded further missionary activities with disfavour, even when these were initiated by the Dutch Church. One of the main reasons for the Trek was the desire to preserve proper relations between master and servant, and this was reflected in the constitutional provision against equality between black and white in Church or State. The hostility to missionary activities was further heightened by the constant warfare which accompanied the expansion of the frontier and by such myth-creating events as the murder of Retief by Dingaan and the disaster at Blood River.

Nevertheless local religious zeal began to grow slowly, and by 1896 the Dutch Reformed Church of the Cape had ten mission stations within the Cape borders and two beyond. In 1891 the Church opened the station of Morgenster near Zimbabwe. This became one of the largest in Central Africa, and later extended its activities to Nyasaland. In 1951 Dr. Malan, defending the N.G.K. against charges of race prejudice, claimed that it was spending nearly half a million pounds annually on mission work. The smaller G.K. has since the 1890's opened missions in the North Transvaal, and has two ministers engaged exclusively on mission work. It is however the main N.G.K. that is responsible for the great bulk of all mission work done by Afrikaners.

In mission work amongst a subject race, the problem ultimately arises of the proper treatment and status of converts. All white-dominated Christian Churches in South Africa have been faced with the obvious incompatibility of preaching brotherhood in Christ and practising segregation because their white flocks demand it. Other Churches have found their own more or less face-saving formulae. As a result they have seen the defection of large sections of their black sheep to form their own black separatist Churches. Only the Dutch Reformed Church has come out boldly with its plan for separate churches, based on God's plan for diversity in unity.

As in most conquest-states, the theory was evolved many decades later than the practice that it was required to justify. It was in 1857 that the Cape Synod was faced with a large accession of Coloured members. It proceeded, somewhat unwillingly, and 'as a concession to the weakness of some members', to make provision for the 'congregation assembled or to be assembled amongst the heathen to enjoy its religious privileges in a separate building'. In 1881 this segregation was perpetuated by the founding of the Dutch Reformed Mission Church, while the Bantu Church was started in 1951.

It was not however until recent years that the increasing divergencies between its views and those of the other Christian Churches in the Union, and the growing attack from outside, forced the Dutch Reformed Church to justify its actions on ideological rather than practical grounds. Prior to 1949, the Dutch Reformed Church had continued along the established lines of Christian trusteeship and segregation that suited the views of its white congregations. As late as 1939, the Federal Council of the N.G.K. voted in favour of 'segregation'; it was only towards the end of the next decade that the Church began to discourage the use of the word, in order to humour non-white susceptibilities.

Shortly after the Nationalist Party took office in 1948, it became evident that certain Dutch Reformed Church theologians were re-examining their ideas and their consciences with regard to the non-white problem. The first product of this spiritual fermentation was the statement on race relations issued by the Cape Synod in November 1949. This advocated 'separate vertical development for each group', according to its own character and needs, and in accordance with its past history and future development. This was the original blueprint for total apartheid which so alarmed Nationalist legislators, although it was intended to supply a moral basis for their programme.

The statement on apartheid was followed by a ten-page justification of vertical apartheid on scriptural grounds, which was adopted by the N.G.K. Synod of the Transvaal in early 1951. Amongst the references cited was one justifying the prohibition of mixed marriages. This contention, along with the general proposition, was however contested by Dr. B. B. Keet of the Stellenbosch Theological Seminary of the N.G.K., in a series of articles in *Die Kerkbode*. He pointed out that the Biblical warning against mixed marriages referred not to biological mixture but to unions between believers and unbelievers. Nationality, language, culture and race, he wrote, have a meaning only in their own sphere as a means of glorifying God; and he warned his readers against the danger of laying too much stress on the people's mission: 'That danger is not imaginary. We have only to think of National Socialism and the Ku Klux Klan in the Southern States of America'.

The ferment amongst a number of Dutch Reformed Church leaders seems to have been increased by their recent realization that respected Calvinist theologians outside the Union disagreed both with their practice and with their theory on the race question.[1] The Netherlands Churches and those of the United States, including the ultra-conservative Christian Reformed Church, are all strongly anti-segregationalist in religious and other matters. This uneasiness was further strengthened amongst N.G.K. theologians after their delegates had participated in the World Council of Churches Assembly at Evanston, U.S.A. in 1954. Possibly as a consequence, the Cape and Transvaal Synodal Commissions of the N.G.K. took the lead later in the year in calling an inter-racial conference of church leaders in Johannesburg. This was a more ambitious version of the conference called in 1951 by the N.G.K. Federal Mission Council, the first joint conference to be held within the Church's history. Despite the fact that a separate part of the hall was allowed to non-white delegates and that refreshments were taken in separate rooms, such observers are Mr. Alan Paton felt that the generally urbane and gentle tone of the meeting showed that a real step forward had been taken in the œcumenical movement, although it might be asked whether there was time for such slow

---

[1]This realization was exemplified and sharpened by the publication in 1952 of *The Colour Crisis in the West* by Dr. Ben J. Marais, a brilliant scholar who is N.G.K. minister at Pretoria East. This writer took a long and objective look at the colour problem in North and South America, and drew some pertinent lessons for South Africa in the light of Christian teaching.

conventional attempts to find a common ground of Christian unity and action.

Some anti-Nationalists, despairing of the apparent impotence of the organized opposition in the white group, have come to feel that this spiritual stirring in some sections of the Dutch Reformed Church may offer the only hope of a peaceful solution to the Union's racial problems. Such spiritual unrest is also linked with the desire for outside approval and acceptance which is so often interwoven with Afrikaner isolationism.

It must however be pointed out that the traditional segregation is still accepted by the bulk of predikants and church members. The latter viewpoint was best expressed by delegates at the 1951 N.G.K. Synod. While accepting the report on the Biblical basis of apartheid, a group tried to add a rider to the effect that apartheid was in the interests of self-preservation and white civilization in future generations. A Pretoria University professor speaking on human relationships at a D.R.C. Youth Week meeting in late 1951 found it necessary to remind his listeners that the Native was a human being and had a soul as well as a body. 'We must not only be his master, but also his guardian and friend', he said. About the same time a Nationalist M.P., Mr. S. M. Loebser, commenting on the wage-differentials between whites and non-whites (1 : 5 : 12 for Africans, Coloured and Whites respectively in 1948), expressed his fear that the margin of difference might not be wide enough to enable the white to maintain his status: 'We must beware that our attitude towards the non-European is not so Christian that it becomes un-Christian towards ourselves and our children'.

Not all sections of the N.G.K. itself are consistent in their support of vertical apartheid. The Synodal Committee of the Transvaal N.G.K. decided in 1950 not to receive a delegation from the World Council of Churches, because the latter is a colour-blind organization and the delegation would have included coloured members. Finally, the views expressed in the N.G.K.'s *Fundamental Principles of Calvinist Christian Political Science*, with its emphasis on the immaturity of the African, do not encourage one to believe that vertical apartheid is viewed by the Church itself as achievable in the forseeable future.

A number of prominent Afrikaner politicians and professional men have lately become active in the Moral Re-Armament Movement, which professes a faith that should surmount barriers of class, creed or colour. M.R.A. has for the last five years spent enormous sums in missionary work in Africa, Dr. Azikiwe being its major conquest to date. Despite its multi-racial and universal structure (discreetly soft-pedalled in South Africa) M.R.A. is regarded with favour by the Nationalist Government because of its strong anti-Communist bias and because of its handful of prominent non-white converts, who have been converted from their 'black Nationalism' and Communistic beliefs to co-operation and acceptance of separate development. But while Afrikaners and Africans on M.R.A.'s globe-trotting teams show the world how they can fraternize, white M.R.A. supporters do little or nothing to support the cause of the 'Four Absolutes' by their actions inside the Union.

Other Christian Churches in the Union are increasingly in conflict with the Dutch Reformed Church in this matter of relations between black and white. In the other Churches there is often separation in the parish level, but the Churches are units and non-whites are gradually being integrated into their government. In addition, the other Churches have almost without exception roundly and repeatedly condemned the secular version of apartheid, as practised by the Nationalist government. This division between the Churches is enhanced by the fact that the others are mainly English-speaking, and in many cases have overseas links. In consequence the relationship between the Dutch Churches and the others, which in the 1920's was actively co-operative and cordial, has deteriorated with the growth of aggressive Afrikaner Nationalism. Today co-operation is restricted to individuals, and the Afrikaans Churches no longer belong to the inter-denominational Christian Council.

Relations are particularly strained with the Anglican Church, the Methodists, the Congregationalists and above all with the Roman Catholic Church. In the eyes of all Nationalist Afrikaners, lay or clergy, the first three have by their recent utterances and activities at home and overseas proved themselves public enemies in the tradition of Dr. John Philip and other 'imported political parsons' of the nineteenth century. A major factor in the present situation is the rivalry of Afrikaans and English-speaking Churches in the mission field, and particularly in the education of non-white children. Here the non-Afrikaans Churches have been teaching their charges ideas which conflict with Calvinist apartheid. This dangerous tendency was checked in 1955, when the state took over African education. It lingers on however in the minds of the African teachers, and in the schoolrooms of the Cape, where about 160,000 Coloured children are still receiving their primary education in mission schools; 42,617 in D.R.C. mission schools, 29,441 with the Anglicans, 19,075 Congregational, 14,020 Methodist, 12,352 with the old German missions, and 15,635 with the Roman Catholic Church.[1] The Roman Catholic Church in particular has in the last twenty years increased the number of its schools so as to treble the number of its pupils.

The attitude of the Dutch Churches to the Roman Catholic Church has always been one of definite hostility. This is based on general Calvinist attitudes, mistrust of the universality of the Roman Catholic Church,[2] and fear of the Roman Catholic Church's notably liberal colour policy, which is winning large numbers of non-white converts.[3] Finally, the Dutch Churches have taken alarm at the tendency of urban Afrikaners to send their children to convents because of the excellent education provided by the latter; it is feared that such children will be lured away from the Dutch Church and the Afrikaner way of life.

The campaign against the Church of Rome is therefore carried on systematically from the pulpits and in the religious and secular Afrikaans-language press. The N.G.K. of the Cape has a 'Committee for Vigilance against the Roman Catholic danger', and the Orange Free State N.G.K. Mission opened a fund to counter Roman Catholic efforts in that area in 1951. In

---

[1]Cape Educational Statistics, 1952.

[2]Many Afrikaner Calvinists belong to another universal organization, that of the Freemasons; the attitude of the Dutch Church is discouraging but not so far as to the point of an actual ban.

[3]There are over 4½ million Catholics in Commonwealth Africa, the vast majority of them being Africans.

1955 a D.R.C. deputation appeared before the town council in Kroonstad, near the Orange Free State goldfield, and opposed (unsuccessfully) an application by the Roman Catholic Church for a site to build a hospital. The deputation described the Roman Catholic Church as a 'threat' to the Protestant community. The admission of Roman Catholic immigrants even from the large Catholic communities in Holland and Germany is strongly deprecated by leading Nationalists; and a proposal to ask the Government to put a virtual ban on such immigrants and to stop subsidies to Roman Catholic schools was actually passed at a conference organized by the three Dutch Churches in Pretoria in 1950.

Various Church bodies protested most vehemently in 1949, when Mr. Charles de Water as Ambassador Extraordinary paid the usual courtesy visit to the Pope. In 1955, it was even alleged by the Roman Catholic periodical, *The Southern Cross*, that the banned pornographic book, *The Awful Disclosures of Maria Monk*, which originated 120 years ago in Canada and which 'purported to be the story of an unfortunately saintly girl who had entered a convent and undergone a series of terrible experiences at the hands of nuns and priests', had been translated into Afrikaans and was being 'pushed from numbers of pulpits of one of South Africa's biggest Church organizations'.

On its side, the Roman Catholic Church in South Africa has met this hostility with imperturbability and caution. In such minority situations, this Church has usually tried to compromise with the régime under which it has to work. Thus the Roman Catholic Church, while opposing apartheid in theory and in practice, has kept aloof from the recent flare-up of the constitutional crisis which produced the Senate Act. A leading article in the *Catholic Times* of South Africa in July 1955 explained that the Church, having 'a tolerance of the frailty of man born of 2,000 years of experience', did not condemn any form of government that operated in accordance with God's laws. The constitutional, Republican and Commonwealth disputes were not religious issues. Recently, the article continued, the Church had spoken on civil matters but only because reasonable exercise of her ministry was being disturbed. The Bantu Education

Act was prejudicial to her work of evangelizing the Africans and the Mixed Marriages Act had left out the Church's competency in a primarily religious affair.

In the vital issue of African education, it seems likely that the Roman Catholic Church may refuse to allow its mission schools to be taken over by the government, and will continue to run them without subsidies. At present there are some 2,000 schools with 200,000 African pupils. On the other hand, there is a possibility that the Church may make a deal with the government provided that it is permitted to retain control of religious instruction in the schools and in the Catholic teacher-training colleges for Africans. Meanwhile, the Canadian Order of the Oblates of St. Mary Immaculate is building a large seminary in Basutoland, just over the Union border, which will train 160 priests at a time.

The 1946 census showed 552,348 Roman Catholics in the Union. Of these 373,252 were African, 56,157 Coloured, 5,249 Indian and 117,890 Whites.[1] It is however impossible to say how many of these white Catholics were Afrikaans-speaking, as the cross-classification by religious affiliation and language was dropped. In 1936, there were nearly 5,000 Afrikaans-speaking Catholics, plus an additional 2,290 Catholics who were bilingual at home. This was nearly 8 per cent of the total white Catholic group.

The Roman Catholic Church is busy 'South Africanizing' itself, and priests are beginning to attend Afrikaans-speaking universities. It seems doubtful whether the tension between Calvinist Afrikanerdom and the Roman Catholic Church will actually come to an open showdown, but the Roman Catholic Church in the Union is facing an increasingly uncomfortable future.

The modern Nationalist definition of an Afrikaner is a white whose home language is Afrikaans, who is Nationalist in orientation and who is a Calvinist. Nevertheless the minority of Roman Catholic Afrikaners, some descended from Catholic Dutchmen and Germans, others from Irish and Portuguese who

---

[1] 141,330 in 1951.

merged with the Boers, still do not feel that their religion unfits them for membership of the Volk. This point of view was sturdily defended by letter writers in a correspondence on the Roman Catholic peril which enlivened the columns of *Die Transvaler* in March 1955. Roman Catholic Afrikaners are nevertheless fighting a losing battle. In the outcome, they may be forced to choose between their religion and their Volk.

In general, the growing identification between the Dutch Churches and a narrow political nationalism is driving some of the more liberal Afrikaners away from their faith. Some join another Church, while others are gradually lost to religious practice altogether. A recent N.G.K. census showed that more than 30,000 Afrikaners in Johannesburg and Pretoria had left the Church; thousands of respectable families were said to have become indifferent to religion and to have stopped home prayers, while 3,000 young people over 21 had been found to be unconfirmed. Other Afrikaners of the liberal persuasion do not secede from the Dutch Churches. Where provincial legislation still permits it, they do however attempt to spare their children the strong dose of Christian National Education which most Afrikaans-medium public schools now provide, by sending them to English-speaking schools or convents. There, as an article in the *Southern Cross* in 1951 pointed out: 'Experience has shown that conversions are effected by contact with other children and influences at the school'.

It may seem strange that Afrikaners should be members of the Anglican and other 'English' Churches. In 1936, however, the last cross-classification of this type showed that there were 32,859 Afrikaans-speaking persons in this group, and 17,154 from bilingual homes. Such non-Calvinist Afrikaners may be either the descendants of Afrikanerized English settlers, or of Afrikaners who changed their religious allegiance in the last century or later. This tendency of D.R.C. members to move to other Churches was deplored by Jan Hofmeyr in 1886, as an instance of lack of national feeling. In recent years the Anglican Church has been considering introducing Afrikaans for services in some platteland areas: while the Anglican Prayer Book and Hymnal are already being translated into Afrikaans.

A small number of Afrikaners are still members of the Lutheran Church, the second one to be established in the Cape settlement in the old Dutch East India Company days. After their early stubborn endurance, the Lutherans were overcome by the fissions of the mid-nineteenth century, and today are reduced to a congregation centred round the original church building in Capetown. Here each Sunday in one of the loveliest buildings in South Africa the 89-year-old pastor, who was originally a Dutch Reformed Church minister, preaches one sermon in English and the other in Nederlands, on humanity's steady march towards the Anti-Christ.

The Lutheran Church has however long since ceased to cause the Dutch Churches any apprehension. Instead, there is a growing challenge not only from the Roman Catholic Church but from such 'California-style' sects as the Apostolic Faith Mission. This latter challenge comes not amongst the better educated and the higher-income groups, but primarily amongst the growing Afrikaner urban proletariat. Many of them are Poor Whites or descendants of Poor Whites, whose contact with the Dutch Churches was loosened during their initial poverty, and possibly broken during their subsequent rehabilitation and consequent exposure to urban materialistic influences.

The Carnegie Poor White Commission commented on the growth of sects in urban areas as early as the 1920's. It cited as reasons for this growth the change to an urban environment; the tardy and insufficient action of the Dutch Churches; the attraction of such religious emotionalism for the religiously predisposed Afrikaner; and the way in which active participation in such emotional worship helped to assuage the Poor White's feeling of inferiority. The report also pointed out that between 1921 and 1926 the number of adherents to the Apostolic Faith Mission rose from 7,742 to 15,544. Of these all but 500 were Afrikaans-speaking or bilingual, and nearly 10,000 were in the Transvaal, where the greatest movement of population had taken place.

Today the hold of the sects on the urban Afrikaners has become even stronger. In 1952 the Reverend F. J. Hay wrote in *Die Kerkbode*: 'Our church has no lack of numbers, activities and material means, but of inner power and enthusiasm. A steadily growing stream of people leave the Church to join other religious bodies. Like vultures battening on a dead body the sects batten on the Church and grow steadily larger and stronger. Lifeless formalism and frigidity are nearly everywhere the mark of the Church'.

The Apostolic Faith Mission now has an estimated 70,000 white members, almost entirely Afrikaans-speaking, and over double that number of Non-European members; its general secretary is the Reverend A. J. Schoeman, who is the brother of the Union's Minister of Transport. Along with three other Pentecostal Churches, the Apostolic Faith Mission recently sponsored the visit of an American Evangelist, who drew crowds of over 50,000. Since then these Churches have planned a revivalist campaign to win 100,000 souls, black as well as white, in the next year. The 'Youth for Christ' movement started by Billy Graham was sufficiently successful to induce a group of Capetown N.G.K. ministers to issue a warning about it to parents.

The revivalist sects would seem to represent an even greater danger to the traditional faith and Church of the Afrikaners than its old enemy, the Church of Rome. With their high-pressure methods, colourful and emotional forms of worship, and active social work amongst the poor, the sects seem better adapted than the traditional Dutch Churches to cater for the needs of an urban proletariat. They may also represent a danger to Afrikaner Nationalism with their American-oriented universalism and their avoidance of politics. The Apostolic Faith Mission elsewhere even forbids its followers to vote, although it is difficult to say how such a ban can be applied in practice in large urban centres; the South African Mission authorities leave the matter to their members' discretion and conviction.

In considering the Afrikaner and his religion, the influence of the African social environment is often overlooked. A number of practising Calvinists both in the rural and the urban areas —like English-speaking non-Calvinists—have through many generations come to pay a half-ashamed tribute to Bantu and Malay magic, and to accept local ghosts and spirits. African and Malay doctors have until recently continued to attract large numbers of white patients from the poorer or less sophisticated classes, who considered that their 'European' skills were enhanced by their ancestral knowledge. It is impossible to say how far such beliefs have helped to rot the harsh fabric of Calvinism.

* * * * *

To sum up, the Dutch Reformed Church, to which most Afrikaners belong and which exerts the major social influence in Afrikaner life, faces two major threats from two separate directions. The first threat is to the Dutch Church's hold on its own people—the second to its missionary influence amongst the non-white majority, without whose acquiescence Calvinist Afrikanerdom cannot ultimately survive. In the latter sphere the Dutch Reformed Church seem to be fighting a losing battle. The liberal and universalistic ideas which it abhors have penetrated too far. It is doubtful whether the new Bantu 'apartheid' education can perform more than a Canute-like rôle against the tide.

It remains to be seen whether the Dutch Reformed Church can retain its hold on its own people by such measures as adjusting its ideas and methods to the new urban environment; by inculcating a stricter Calvinism amongst the young through Christian National Education; by moving towards a corporate Calvinist republic, in which only the 'nationally constructive' or elect will have a voice. At present Afrikaner nationalism and Afrikaner Calvinism are riding the full tide of success. As Arnold Toynbee has pointed out, however, a determinist creed stimulates group morale in success but saps it in adversity. This dualism may account for the ancestral and prophetic voices of doom which occasionally whisper through the applause for each new success of Boer over Briton—the voices which speak of the fear flickering in the vast black shadows beyond the firelight, and call upon the defenders of White Christian Civilization in South Africa to perish rather than surrender or even compromise.

CHAPTER SIX

UPBRINGING AND EDUCATION

'Ye shall fear every man his mother, and his father, and keep my sabbaths: I am the Lord your God'.

(Leviticus, 19: 3).

' . . . 'The Volk is seen as a Divine work of creation with its acknowledgment and emphasis on its own national world-outlook and religion; and the State as its natural form of authority, and maintainer and protector of its being and development. Consequently upbringing and education must be regarded as a volk-oriented (*volkseie*) and creative means towards individual and volk development, and the school as a national institution.'

(T. de W. Keyter, *Kultuurgeskiedenis van die Afrikaner*, Vol. II p. 293).

THE Afrikaner child is the product of his home background and natural environment, quite as much as of his formal education. Indeed, the ideal Boer education was based mainly on home and informal instruction, although the Afrikaner of today is often characterized by his eagerness to acquire as good a formal education as possible.

The ideal Boer upbringing, whether in the frontier districts or in the Republics, conformed more or less to the classic Persian ideal. The young Persian nobles were taught to ride, to shoot with the bow and speak the truth. The Boer who set forth into the wilderness with his Bible and his gun needed, and got, little more instruction.

The Boer child of old got his training for life within the family circle. This was a patriarchal one, in which the functions and authority of the parents were strictly distinguished. The Boer father was a stern father and his word was final. In general, older people were to be obeyed and respected, as the Bible enjoins, and children were to be seen and not heard. From his father the Boer child learned the technique of hunting and the rough skills needed on a self-sufficient farm. From his mother, who was usually closer to him, he learned his prayers and his manners, which included at least gentleness towards women.

Through his close contacts with the black and coloured house servants, he acquired the kindly but uncompromising authority which marked the Boer's ideal attitude to the non-white peoples. He also learned the ways of game and weather, modified his language and became increasingly an African at heart. As a member of a large family, living on the wide veld in a magnificent climate, he was less influenced by his family and more by his natural environment than urban children are. So he became independent and responsible at an early age. His house was, however, more than a dwelling-place. It was the church of every day, in which prayers were said morning and night and the Bible was read regularly.

This was the ideal upbringing of the Boer child, though it seems likely that some of the poorer farmers and bywoners did not pass it on to their children. When the impoverished Afrikaners moved into the towns, this type of upbringing proved insufficient. It also proved inadequate to withstand the sudden pressure of new distractions, such as films, sports and comic books. Afrikaans usually continued to be spoken in the Afrikaner urban home, but the way of life there bore an increasing resemblance to that of the English-speaking urban proletariat. The Church, and religion generally, became less important in Afrikaner home life in the towns, while in the inevitable absence of one or both parents at work, parental authority and responsibility gradually devolved on the schools. Noting this trend with alarm, Afrikaner Nationalists decided to ensure that the lapses of the home should be made good in the schools, and that the authorities should enforce a Volk-upbringing even on the children of backsliders.

Formal instruction had for generations been identified with the preparation of children for Church membership. The sixteenth-century struggle for religious freedom in Holland left the Dutch people religious-minded in all spheres of life; and it was their attitude, enforced by Huguenot zeal, that was to prevail in the new colony. The first school in the Cape was not in fact for European children at all, but for slave children. These, so that they might be more useful and amenable servants, were to be instructed in the Dutch language and the Christian faith.

European children, however, soon began to receive instruction in the three R's, their main reading matter being the Bible and the Catechism. This type of Bible education, whether administered in State schools, by private 'meesters',[1] or by the parents, was that received by the majority of Boer children in the frontier districts until well past the middle of the nineteenth century. It was the educational system that accompanied the Boers on the Great Trek and persisted during the South African Republic. Even in the 1920's, some remote farmers were still said to regard any additional education as suspect. The main elements of this system seem to have been its religious bias and its emphasis on the parents' responsibility. It is only in recent years that the Nationalist State has usurped that responsibility.

Afrikaner historians maintain with justice that this Bible education enabled the Boers to resist the spiritual and cultural degeneration that their isolation and primitive life might otherwise have brought about. On the other hand, it produced a community whose members were fitted only to be farmers on a not excessive level of efficiency, and who in their Trekker Republics were for decades unable to staff an efficient administration of their own. And when economic conditions changed, this Bible education left the Boers stranded in unskilled jobs in the urban labour market.

A more varied and secular type of education was however slow in arriving. In the first place there was little need for it amongst an almost exclusively farming population, many of

---

[1]These 'meesters' were a motley crew. Some were semi-literate discharged Company servants, others were actively disreputable characters. They were held in low repute locally in consequence, but were tolerated because of their easy-going ways, willingness to help with farm tasks, and the lack of anyone more suitable.

whom lived a month or more's journey from the nearest government schools.[1] In the second place, after the British occupation of the Cape, the free state schools with their imported and often prejudiced Scottish teachers became instruments of anglicization and consequently suspect. As one Afrikaner educational historian writes: 'The school became an alien institution which stood outside the life of the people and which served alone the alien ruling elements; only in some places was it supported by those who were either willing or forced by economic circumstances to desert their national life and serve a foreign culture'. The private Dutch-medium schools which sprang up in protest could serve only a fraction of the Boer population.

Between the Great Trek and Union, formal education in South Africa developed along two separate paths. In the South the trend was towards systematization and Anglicization. Secondary and higher education, mainly geared to the British system, were introduced in the Western Cape and along the coast. Those Dutch who wished to play any part in public life did so within an increasingly English framework,[2] while the remainder withdrew even further into rural life. For most of these Boers, a year or so of inefficient primary education from meesters, farm schools or mission schools was the most that they could hope to receive. Despite the national revival led by such Cape Afrikaners as Jan Hofmeyr and the Paarl Genootskappers from the 1870's, Dutch was only re-introduced as a public school subject in 1882. Even then it had to be taught through the medium of English.

Cape education was disorganized as a result of the Anglo-Boer War. Some teachers, then as now in the forefront of political activity, left the schools to join the rebellion. Others were found to be teaching South African history from a point of view

---

[1]In 1820, under 3 per cent of the children in the Graaff-Reinet area had ever been to school.

[2]By 1865 the teaching of Dutch had in practice dwindled to almost nothing in the public schools. Even in the private schools set up to further Dutch interests, such as the Good Hope Seminary in Capetown, the Stellenbosch Gymnasium, and the Huguenot Seminary in Wellington, English was often the most important language.

unsatisfactory to the authorities. Compulsory education was introduced as a principle in 1905, but could not be put into practice for some time, owing to the great distances, the shortage of teachers, and the lack of funds.

Regarded objectively, the better Cape schools produced an impressive series of intellectual and political leaders, both Dutch and English. They also produced the Cape tradition of liberalism, tolerance and an eclectic culture, a tradition that seemed to offer a common ground for Dutch and English, and ultimately even for the other inhabitants of the land. This tradition is however a dwindling one, cut off from the main stream of Christian National educational theory. It is the latter that must be considered here in more detail, for it animates the teaching that is being given to an increasing majority of young Afrikaners today.

The origins of Christian National Education are traced to the informal religious instruction which the Boer child received at his mother's knee. It did not however emerge as a movement until the end of the nineteenth century.

Prior to that, education, like other public services in the northern republics, and particularly in the South African Republic, suffered from lack of funds and skilled personnel. By 1867 there were only twenty-five teachers, thirteen of them in the rural areas, and the Transvaal budget for education was £1,750. This however represented about 6 per cent of the country's total net expenditure.

Geographical distance and parental apathy were other factors which had to be contended with. By 1876 there were only fifteen State schools, with 442 pupils, or about 8 per cent of the total number of children of school age. This was perhaps also a consequence of the secularizing reforms carried through by President Burgers in 1874. Like other plans of this gifted but unstable man, these reforms were decades in advance of their time. In 1881, when the religious basis of education was reaffirmed by the new Superintendent of Education, the Rev. S. J. du Toit of Paarl 'Genootskap' fame, the relief of Boer parents was reflected by a record rise in attendance. By 1888 there were 7,000 pupils attending 300 State-subsidized schools, only thirty-four of these schools being in the towns. This tendency persisted up to the Anglo-Boer War. By 1898 there was an attendance of 13,561 pupils, 92 per cent of them being in primary schools.

In the same period (1892–98) the number of teachers more than doubled. The shortage of teaching personnel had been partly met by importing large numbers of teachers from Holland. By 1898 as many as 300 of the 836 teachers were Dutch. The ubiquity of the Hollanders in Transvaal public life constituted—in education as well as in politics—a frequent source of friction. Many other teachers were Cape Afrikaners, who had themselves been taught in English and who knew the High Dutch in which they must teach only as a learned subject. The Dutch group were opposed to the English influence in language as much as in politics.

Many Transvaal Boers seem to have shared the utilitarian views of the Cape Afrikaner teachers. Then as now they regarded a thorough knowledge of English as useful if not essential to their children's future. Considerable numbers of Afrikaans-speaking children attended the English private schools which sprang up in the towns and villages to meet the needs of the Uitlanders. The 1884 Act had correctly interpreted Boer wishes over religious education; it had however gone too far with its insistence on single-medium Dutch schools.

This chauvinistic trend was continued in the 1892 Education Act moved by the new Hollander Superintendent of Education, Dr. Mansvelt. This Act was openly designed to foster Christian National Education. All teachers were to be members of a Protestant Church and school books were to be in Dutch only. This meant that such groups as English-speaking Uitlanders, Jews or Roman Catholics would be unable to benefit by free state education at all, although in practice they were paying most of the taxes. Vocal criticism produced modifications to meet the English point of view. The latter however continued to object, somewhat unreasonably, to the continued need to learn some Dutch. With perhaps more reason they complained of doctrinaire religious instruction and partial presentation of South African history. In 1896 they set up a Council of Education which was by the end of 1897 providing education for 819 children; but for the Anglo-Boer War, this Council might have set up opposition schools on the same scale as the Christian National Education movement was to do under the Milner régime.

One of the few positive by-products of the concentration-camp system in the Anglo-Boer War was the creation of schools in each camp, although these schools were naturally regarded as instruments of anglicization by most Boers. They were staffed by interned Boers and by as many as 300 British volunteer teachers. Religious instruction was given in Dutch, the remainder in English. By 1902 the enrolment was up to 17,000 in the Transvaal, and 12,000 in the Orange River Colony; this embraced four out of every nine children of school age.

Education in the Orange Free State had been earlier stabilized than in the Transvaal. Its orientation, though strongly religious, was less chauvinistic. The influence of Scots such as Andrew Murray was strong; in addition, secondary education was furthered by grants from the Cape Governor, Sir George Grey. Bilingualism, with parental choice, was the ideal, while the 1872 Act introduced the voluntary principle as regards religious instruction, though prayers and scripture-reading were retained at the beginning and end of each school day. For the last twenty-five years of the Orange Free State's existence, the Chief Inspector of Education was actually a Scottish teacher, Dr. John Brebner.

In the Free State however, as in the Transvaal, the Anglo-Boer War left a legacy of racial bitterness and antagonism. On the Boer side this was accentuated by the anglicizing educational policy of Milner. This was applied equally to the two former Boer Republics.

Under the new administration, education was to be highly centralized, little voice being left to local bodies. Instruction was to be in English, though for three hours a week Dutch might be studied as a language, and for an additional two hours Bible history might be taught in Dutch. Of over 900 teachers, 400 came from overseas, but this time most of them had come from England.

However excellent the medicine, it is not always possible to force it down a patient's throat against his will. By the end of 1903, 27,000 children were attending public schools in the Transvaal. On the other hand 5,000 were attending 115 C.N.E. private schools, staffed by 150 teachers and organized with the support of Botha, Smuts, Steyn and various prominent Dutch Reformed Church ministers. The curriculum was said to be on the same level as the Government schools. Funds were supplied by the Boers themselves and by well-wishers from overseas.[1] This period of anglicization left a legacy of bitterness amongst many Afrikaners who experienced it in all parts of South Africa, deviation often being summarily punished by the wearing of placards or dunces' caps labelled 'I spoke Dutch'.

When the two former Republics were granted responsible government, in 1906 and 1907 respectively, the Boer majority returned to power. The next step in both cases was to incorporate the C.N.E. schools in the public school system.

In the Transvaal this was done by means of the Smuts Education Act of 1907. This gave back considerable powers to local school committees and boards, thereby reverting to the old Boer system: it also provided for non-denominational religious education, and accepted the C.N.E. principle of mother-tongue instruction. On the other hand, the system was weighted on the English side. English had to be taught in every Dutch-medium school. It was the medium of secondary education and proficiency in it was made a condition of promotion of pupils. Dutch was to be taught to every child unless the parents wished otherwise. As an Afrikaner educationalist put it, the Smuts Act meant that every child might learn Dutch, but that he must learn English.

The history of Transvaal educational legislation from 1907 to the present day has shown a steady move to place the two languages on an equal basis, and to whittle away the parental right of choice. The Smuts Act was not however received with great

---

[1] There were about eighty-five such schools in the Orange River Colony; these were incorporated in the Colonial system in 1905. In the heyday of the C.N.E. schools, about £1,500 a month was coming in from Holland. This was their main source of support.

alarm by the English-speaking group in the Transvaal. On the other hand, the formerly liberal and tolerant Free State, given its head under responsible government, raised a storm of protest from the English-speaking minority over the Act put through in 1908 by General Hertzog. This Act imposed compulsory mother-tongue instruction up to Standard IV, with the gradual introduction of the other language as a second medium; in the higher standards, children were to be taught in either or both mediums. The Act embodied the 'two-stream' or 'white apartheid' principle.

After Union in 1910, primary and secondary education was left with the provinces, for a five-year period that has so far remained permanent, though there are hints that the Nationalist Government and the Dutch Reformed Church would favour increased centralization. Legislation was amended where necessary to meet the stipulation of equal rights for both languages laid down in the South Africa Act. Four years later, Afrikaans replaced Dutch as the official medium of instruction in primary and secondary schools in all four provinces. At last, Afrikaner children were able to receive instruction in a language-medium they fully apprehended, rather than through the semi-opaque media of English or High Dutch which had caused so much retardation and aversion to learning in the past.

The battle in the educational sphere now shifted to another ground. Afrikaner children might, indeed must, now receive instruction in their own language. In some cases however they were doing so in parallel-medium or dual-medium schools, where they played with or even sat side-by-side with English-speaking children. This was a more subtle menace to national identity than the earlier enforcement of the English-language medium. It also made it more difficult for nationally-minded teachers to instruct the children in the proper national spirit, for fear of complaints from English-speaking parents and school committee members.

Clearly, the Afrikaans single-medium school was the only type in which the Afrikaans-speaking child could receive a proper Christian and National education. The single-medium or language-apartheid school, where Afrikaans, English, or a Bantu language is the medium, is therefore the ideal form that national-minded Afrikaner educationalists have set out to achieve. It is however an ideal which not all parents in a given language group share. So the old Boer principle of parental choice has had to yield to the view that 'the State knows best'.

Christian National Education has since 1939 been the goal of Afrikaner Nationalists in education. Its modern form, as propounded in 1948 by the F.A.K., goes very much further than did the C.N.E. pioneers in the first decade of this century. The fight then was for recognition and equality; now the aim is absolute domination. Today C.N.E. stands for purity of language, culture, religion, and race; for a Christian education, defined as education 'based on Holy Scripture and expressed in the Articles of Faith of our three Afrikaans Churches'; for a National education, imbued with a love for everything that is our own', in particular 'our country, our language, our Church, and our culture'; every subject (including science) must be taught on fundamentalist principles (the theory of evolution is condemned as being opposed to predestination); geography must be taught on the basis that 'every people and nation is attached to its own native soil, allotted to it by the Creator'; history 'must be viewed as the fulfilment of God's decreed plan for the world and the human race', and must teach that 'God . . . willed separate nations and peoples, and He gave to each separate nation and people its special vocation, task and gifts'. It is the task of the Dutch Churches to see that these educational principles are carried out. A further somewhat sinister stipulation lays down that it is also the Churches' task to 'exercise disciplinary measures when the need arises, with reference to the doctrinal opinions and lives of the teachers as members of the Church': (members of the Church the teachers would of course have to be.) It may incidentally strike English readers as curious that the protagonists of C.N.E. also regard co-education as an ultimate desideratum.

In essence, C.N.E. rejects the generally accepted European view that the interests of the child are supreme. Instead the child is regarded as an instrument to further the interests of the Volk. This C.N.E. programme raised a storm of protest, which was by no means restricted to the English-speaking section of the white population. It has therefore still to become official policy in any province. In practice, however, C.N.E. principles are already being applied in many predominantly Afrikaans schools. This is particularly true of the rural areas, where Nationalist feeling is strong and the predikants' influence most powerful.

Education is obviously not a matter only of theory and legislation. In the last analysis it is the product of the individuals who are concerned with it. Most important of these are the teachers. As in other professions, Afrikaans teachers are grouped into separate provincial organizations.[1] From their foundation, the Afrikaans-speaking teachers' associations have been out in the national arena. It was the Transvaal Onderwysersvereniging (T.O.) that staffed the original C.N.E. schools after the Anglo-Boer War. Today with its 5,000 or more members it stands firmly behind the 'new look' C.N.E. programme. The Cape S.A.O.U. still purveys a milder brand of nationalism than its fellow-organizations, and has since 1916 maintained a Joint Council with the English-speaking S.A. Teachers' Association. Co-operation is close but the two partners have agreed to differ on the principle of compulsory mother-tongue instruction. The four Afrikaans-speaking teachers' associations were formerly linked in a Federal Council, but this broke up in 1953 over an 'ideological' difference concerning the representation of Non-European teachers on a proposed registration Council.

Deviation from the current orthodox views on Volk education is difficult for the Afrikaner teacher. In the first place, he has usually been trained in an Afrikaans-medium normal college or university, pervaded with the same type of thinking. Should he still have any humanist doubts, he is not likely to voice them for fear of offending the predikants and national-

---

[1]With the exception of the Free State, where there are very few English-speaking teachers. Not all teachers belong to these organizations. For instance, there are about 5,500 Afrikaans-speaking teachers in the Cape, of whom a little more than 4,000 belong to the S.A.O.U. Of the non-members, many are women primary school teachers, and teachers in urban areas where there are other distractions.

minded parents who make up most school committees; and ultimately for fear of losing his job. This fear will be enhanced if the education authorities ever agree to leave teaching appointments in the hands of the language community concerned. This request was actually made by the T.O. in 1951. It would of course have the effect in present circumstances of ensuring the appointment of national-minded teachers and no others in Afrikaans-medium schools.

This book is concerned with the Afrikaans-speaking group only. It is however interesting to note that the shortage of English-speaking teachers has led to the posting of Afrikaans-speaking teachers to English-medium schools. In the Transvaal, one-third of the teaching staff in English-medium schools were Afrikaans-speaking by early 1955, a trend that was approved by Nationalists as fostering a 'purer Afrikaans spirit in the English schools'. Presumably not all of these teachers are believers in Volk education; or if they are, they are probably more circumspect in their advocation of it in such a milieu. They nevertheless represent an influence from outside the group which is almost entirely lacking in the Afrikaans-medium schools.

This influence is also seen in the presentation of such subjects as South African history. While early English text-books were clearly jingoistic and unsympathetic to or ignorant of Boer aspirations and achievements, the balance has today been more than redressed. At present, it would seem that the English-speaking child is being increasingly educated to regard himself as part of a larger white South African group. The Afrikaans-speaking child on the other hand is being taught that the Afrikaner is the only true South African.

At times, it would even seem that the English-speaking child is being educated to believe that the Boer was always in the right and was grievously wronged by his own British forbears and the country from which they came. For instance, a children's newspaper called *Die Jongspan*, in which the Dutch Reformed Church has an interest, has been approved by the Transvaal Education Department for use in schools in order to further bilingualism. Its articles cannot be said to present the sort of objective history which would promote inter-racial understanding or moderate old prejudices in a bilingual country. In addition somewhat premature items like the following are printed: 'The Union Flag is the one and only flag of South Africa. There are people who say that this country has two flags, the Union Jack being the other. But this is not so. When the Union Jack is seen from public buildings, this is a concession allowed only on sentimental grounds'.

The ethnocentrism of this publication, which has a circulation of over 60,000, emerges even more clearly from the fact that it rarely devotes any space at all to countries or events outside South Africa. Of seventy-five column inches in two recent issues, seventeen were actually devoted to the Kaffir Wars, and thereby to the perpetuation of the myth of the treacherous and savage black men. *Die Jongspan*'s views on modern politics are illustrated by the fact that it found seventeen words adequate for the announcement of the death of General Smuts.

Behind the teachers and the Education Departments stand the school boards and committees. These have always been a happy hunting ground for the Afrikaner Nationalist; first in the struggle for group and language survival, later in the attempt to bring Christian National influences into the provincial educational systems by the back door.

The Transvaal provides the best illustration of this state of affairs. The importance of the boards is due to the fact that they recommend school staff appointments and promotions to the Provincial Education Department, and that the department may not vary these recommendations without reference to the board concerned. They advise the department on various subjects including educational policy and can exercise influence in their own districts on the administration of such matters as the Language Ordinance. Two-thirds of the members of any board are elected, all registered parliamentary voters having the right to vote. The remaining one-third are nominated by the Administrator of the Province.

The power of the school boards depends entirely on the energy of their members, and the interest taken by the general public. Until recently, the non-Nationalist electorate remained apathetic and complacent, while Nationalist candidates continued to gain control of what were ostensibly non-party political bodies. In 1947 however the Skakelkomitees, representing the Afrikaans cultural organizations and Dutch Reformed Churches in a given area, began to put up full tickets of candidates throughout the Transvaal, with the intention of achieving a racial monopoly on the Board.

This move served to alarm the non-national elements, whether English or Afrikaans-speaking. Full opposition tickets were put up by parents' groups representing these elements, and by the 1951 elections sufficient public opinion was aroused for them to give a decisive check to Christian National aspirations in the major urban areas. The effects of this check were in part negated by the Administrator. His nominations for the remaining one-third of board seats consisted almost entirely of defeated Skakelkomitee candidates.

The Administrator was within his legal rights in making these appointments. It was nevertheless not well received by voters, who thought that they had made their intentions clear by their votes. In some cases, where the non-national groups had not gained all the elected seats, the nominated and elected Skakelkomitee members constituted a majority. At Vereeniging, for instance, the defeated candidate returned to the Board as a nominated member and was actually elected Chairman. The Nationalists too showed indignation over the results of the elections, calling for a revision of the school-board election system.

The vote was relatively large,[1] and many of the victorious opposition candidates were themselves Afrikaans-speaking. This suggests that a fair number of Afrikaans-speaking parents were sufficiently disquieted by the authoritarian and narrow sectarian creed of C.N.E. to vote against those who claimed to represent the Volk.

It is interesting to note that a large number of Nationalist readers of *Die Transvaler* wrote to that paper to complain about

---

[1] Forty-four per cent on the Witwatersrand. 117,676 voted for the Skakelkomitee candidates, all of whom were defeated, and 485,124 for the opposition candidates.

the 'unfortunate choice' of so large a number of predikants as Skakelkomitee candidates. Some even attributed the loss of the elections to this fact. As one reader wrote: 'Myself and many other Nationalists refused to vote for predikants, because some of them abuse their powers, and also because some of us are against the Church'. A teacher's wife advised the predikants: 'Shoemaker, stick to your last'. Five out of ten defeated candidates on the West Rand were predikants, and three out of nine on the East Rand.

This then is the educational climate in which the Afrikaner child of today grows up. Although there are undoubtedly many parents, teachers and predikants who do not inculcate a narrow nationalism, the trend is against them. Just as Afrikanerdom has become the province of the Nationalist Party, so the political upbringing of young Afrikaners has been taken over by the national-minded, and deviation is less and less tolerated. If the new generation of Afrikaners can be won for Nationalism, the group will be assured of permanent domination of the South African political scene as it stands today. The next step is likely to be the transfer of white education from the Provinces to the Union Government, a move towards uniformity that is favoured by the Dutch Reformed Church.

The results of this nationalistic educational policy are already evident. Students at an Afrikaans-medium university, questioned on their attitude to other groups, in many cases admitted that their prejudice against English-speaking South Africans was formed or crystallized by what they were taught at school. One student even said that she could make no progress in learning English because to do so had been made to seem a betrayal of her people. On the other hand, another girl said that her teachers taught her to love the language and to welcome friendships with English-speaking South Africans, although she had learned from her history teacher that the Englishman was a selfish imperialist. The great majority had been taught to despise those Afrikaners who had 'English hearts' i.e. those who followed Smuts and the United Party, married English-speaking South Africans and so on.

It is indeed such non-conforming Afrikaners and their children who have to bear the brunt of the present chauvinistic trends. The English-speaking child, unless he lives in a country district, does not attend schools where these trends are most evident. The non-Nationalist Afrikaner's child may however have to face coercion from teachers and mental or physical bullying from fellow students, although such coercion and bullying are still not frequent enough to have crystallized into part of the group's mores. In urban areas, children may be able to conceal their parents' political views, but in rural areas everyone knows everyone else's business and this is not possible. A political organizer for the Junior United Party, himself Afrikaans-speaking, reported resignations from this group because of the ostracism such boys had to face. He claimed too that United Party sympathizers were often left out of school sports teams and ignored at social functions.

Undoubtedly, Afrikaans-medium schools have been penetrated to the lowest standards not only by narrow race-consciousness but by party politics. This has occurred despite the official ban on active participation in politics by teachers. Informally active in these schools, and particularly in the north, are the Nationalists' Party's youth movement Die Jeugbond, and its junior adjunct the Strydmakkertjies (little comrades-in-arms). Political awareness cannot, it is thought, start too young, and the task of the Nationalist Jeugbond is, according to the Prime Minister Mr. Strijdom, to breed the leaders of the future.

The fruits of decades of political indoctrination of youth were clearly seen in the 1953 election. Before that election the Transvaal Board of the Strydmakkertjies made an appeal to children over 6 to give some time to acting as guards of honour at meetings, distributing pamphlets and tracking down lost voters. 'Every Strydmakkertjie, every child whose heart beats only for South Africa, will have to give up a few hours to help', said the appeal. Many children did not however confine themselves to these relatively innocuous activities. Large groups of them attended political meetings, where their usual practice was to sit in blocks and to heckle the speaker, or even to prevent him from getting a hearing at all.

The writer was forcibly confronted with the consequences of this indoctrination during the same election. She was being driven through a predominantly Afrikaans working-class area in Johannesburg in a car with a United Party label on the windscreen, when it was stoned by a group of very young children. These children left the passengers in no doubt of their Nationalist sympathies. Nor is it easy to forget the set and fanatical expressions on the faces of a large guard-of-honour of youths and girls dressed in white, who preceded Dr. Malan to his first election meeting in the Stellenbosch Town Hall in that year. The banners read: 'We honour our Volk-leader, you lead, we follow'.

The trend towards racial kraals is continued into higher education. The promising national-minded student usually proceeds to one of four Afrikaans-medium universities. These are: Stellenbosch in the Western Cape, the University of the Orange Free State at Bloemfontein, the University of Pretoria, and the University for Christian National Education at Potchefstroom in the Transvaal. A considerable number of Afrikaans-speaking students still attend the English-medium universities. Some are non-national Afrikaners who feel more at home there. Others attend because they cannot yet get the relevant training in a particular subject in an Afrikaans-medium university; because they wish to perfect their English; or because they find it economically and professionally advantageous to do so, the degrees conferred by these universities being in general more acceptable in the outside world.[1] Afrikaners who wish to pursue a serious intellectual career usually go overseas for a higher degree, to Holland or even Germany if they find English universities too alien to their way of thinking.

The trend towards lowered standards is largely the result of

---

[1] Few English-speaking students now attend Afrikaans-speaking universities. This small number do so because they wish to study agriculture, or another of the subjects not available in English. In the past, a liberal minority of English-speaking parents sent their children to Afrikaans-medium universities to enable them to perfect their Afrikaans and to get to know their Afrikaans-speaking fellow-citizens. The atmosphere was less racially and politically tense then than it is now.

carrying Nationalism into higher education and of the cultural isolation produced by the success of the Afrikaans language movement. In one or two generations a predominantly seventeenth-century farming community has had to produce ministers, teachers, business men and a whole professional class. 'Scratch a professor or an insurance agent and you will often find a poor Boer's son who went barefoot to school', said an Afrikaner teacher to the writer.

From now on the trend should logically be towards improved teaching and standards. But this change may be slowed by three factors: the nationalistic desire to duplicate all courses available at the English-medium universities, so that Afrikaners may no longer have any excuse for ignoring their own universities; the stultifying effect of the strange C.N.E.-inspired doctrines, usually of a fundamentalist nature, which are increasingly offered as a substitute for rational inquiry to students in the natural and social sciences at more than one Afrikaans-speaking university; and the increasingly utilitarian approach to higher education amongst students themselves.

The University of Potchefstroom is at present the only institution of higher education which officially purveys Christian National teaching to its students. This institution was founded in 1869, as the theological school of the Gereformeerde Kerk at Burgersdorp in the Cape. Unlike the other Afrikaans-medium universities, which in their early days received some support from the British authorities, this school was solely supported by its founding church. In February 1905 it was transferred to Potchefstroom. Shortly after the First World War the Literary Department split away from the Theological School, to become a University College, and a constituent part of the University of South Africa. By 1951 it had become a fully-fledged university.

Alone of all the universities so far, Potchefstroom University has no 'freedom of conscience' clause included in its Charter. Such a clause means that no staff member need undergo interrogation as to his religious beliefs before appointment.

Potchefstroom occupies a very special place in the world of Nationalist Afrikanerdom. After it was elevated to university status, *Die Transvaler* wrote that Potchefstroom University was something more than a national institution: 'Its roots lie in the Afrikaner Volk's Christian conception of life . . . The best thing we can wish not only Potchefstroom but also the Volk is that our young university will sedulously maintain its Christian character and will produce men and women who will be like a leaven among the Volk to keep it on the old and tried paths'. This daily mentioned with some pride that Potchefstroom had shown its 'national' character even before the Anglo-Boer War, when it was known to the British as a 'rebel nest'.

Despite the apparent starkness and ruggedness of its task, Potchefstroom University makes a pleasing impression at first sight. It is situated in one of the oldest towns of the Transvaal. This town is built on a grid-iron pattern of broad green avenues lined with willows and oaks, with old one-storey houses, churches and modern schools. Life moves slowly and deliberately; there is time for quiet study and unpretentious hospitality, and girls and boys in light summer clothes bicycle to classes or stroll in pairs under the trees as they do all over the world.

Of Potchefstroom's 1,200 students about half come from Dopper families (as do 50 per cent of the staff). In early days there were more. A few bilingual students from local Jewish families attend, as do a handful of English-speaking students, mainly those enrolled in pharmacy courses. Social life is more supervised and less varied than elsewhere for the students, most of whom come from conservative and not too prosperous rural families. Wealthy and more sophisticated Afrikaner families in the north would be more likely to send their sons and daughters to Pretoria University or even to the English-speaking University of the Witwatersrand, both of which charge higher fees.

At Potchefstroom, with its homogenous population and lack of urban distractions, the students, most of whom live in residence, have little opportunity of hearing more than one point of view. Student life, though by no means devoid of private distractions, revolves round four associations, each concerned with a particular set of ideas and activities proper to the Christian National way of life. These are: the religious organization, the 'Korps Veritas Vincet' (K.V.V.) founded in 1894; the Afrikaanse Studentebond, to which all students are said to belong; and the co-ordinating cultural body, A.B.K.K. (Algemene Bestuur vir Kuns en Kultuur), which promotes interest in the arts, debating and of course volkspele, ordinary dancing being frowned upon in Potchefstroom. Last comes the Sentrale Sportsbestuur, 'muscular Christianity' being a firm tenet of Christian National education. In addition to more international sports such as boxing, rugby football (all South Africa's national game), hockey, athletics, tennis and even cricket and baseball, there is a club for the revived Boer game of jukskei.

Amidst all the eulogies it is difficult to assess the precise place of Potchefstroom in Volk life. The university has produced a number of theologians and other scholars, but its contribution to more worldly spheres has so far been limited. Senator de Klerk, the present Nationalist Minister of Labour, is its only prominent alumnus in political life. At times it would seem that Potchefstroom's main function is to be the living symbol of the Christian National ideal of education, a trainer of predikants and teachers, while its larger and more worldly brothers produce the politicians, lawyers and industrialists who are to lead the Volk in the twentieth century. Perhaps too, the Potchefstroom brand of university education may serve as a prototype for the training of that increasing number of disciplined and well-indoctrinated adjutants whom the leaders will need if they are to achieve and maintain their Volk republic.

Pretoria University draws its students from a more heterogeneous background. It was started in 1908 as a branch of the Transvaal University College in Johannesburg, now the University of the Witwatersrand. Even now it maintains a relationship of friendly enmity in work and sport with that arch-liberal, mainly English-speaking body. Today Pretoria, which became Afrikaans-speaking some twenty-five years ago, is much larger than Potchefstroom, and offers a far greater variety of instruction and distraction, being situated in the administrative capital, only thirty-five miles from Johannesburg. A minority of its staff and 5,000 students are open dissenters from the present Volk orthodoxy. The recent protest by thirteen professors and lecturers against the Nationalist

Government's Senate Act is a good illustration of this university's somewhat less conformist atmosphere.

The University of Stellenbosch is situated in the oldest and loveliest town in the Western Cape. Its classic buildings are interspersed with old white-gabled houses, built along the straight oak-shaded streets with their murmuring water-channels. Around the flower-filled town are the vineyard slopes and the blue silhouettes of the mountains. Only an hour's drive away is the windy bustle of Cape Town with its port and Parliament.

Stellenbosch University began as a gymnasium in 1866. In 1887 its authorities were sufficiently satisfied with the British connexion to change its name to the Victoria College of Stellenbosch. For some decades however it has been the cradle of intellectual Afrikaner Nationalism. Amongst its more distinguished alumni are:—Dr. Malan, Dr. Dönges, and six other members of the present Nationalist Cabinet. Of the non-Nationalists the most prominent were General Smuts and his great liberal-minded lieutenant, Jan Hofmeyr.

Today Stellenbosch professors are playing an increasing part in public life. In particular, the university's social scientists and theologians have combined in the South African Bureau of Racial Affairs (SABRA) to produce an intellectual framework and justification for apartheid. As the Malan régime became more established, practical considerations caused it to backtrack on the implementation of this uncompromising programme, but the intellectuals came back into their own with the rising political star of Dr. Verwoerd. Today SABRA officials shuttle busily to and from the government offices in Capetown, and apartheid-minded professors point with satisfaction to the growing pile of legislation aimed at unscrambling the racial omelette.

Like Pretoria, however, Stellenbosch University allows of minority deviations. It is after all in the heart of the traditionally tolerant Western Cape. To a decreasing extent non-Nationalist Afrikaners and English-speaking parents still send their children there, and there are sufficient political dissidents to reinforce the town's United Party and Liberal Party branches.

Student relations between Stellenbosch and the English-speaking University of Capetown are closer than those between Pretoria and Johannesburg. The teaching body contains a number of more or less vocal dissidents, one or two of whom are prominent liberals. The senior professor of the Theological Seminary, Dr. B. B. Keet, has consistently declared that apartheid has no Biblical sanction, contrary to the findings of many of his ministerial colleagues.

Despite these liberal flickers, however, the Afrikaans-medium universities are gradually moving towards full conformity with the Nationalist ideal, and deviation is increasingly penalized by loss of promotion or other means. The student bodies are increasingly regimented by the Afrikaanse Studentebond. There is a branch of this association in every Afrikaans-medium university and teachers' college, making a total of fifteen in all, with over 12,500 members. So far, however, it has been unable to set up branches at the English-medium universities, which do not allow 'closed membership' groups to function.

The first Studentebond was founded in 1916, and discontinued in 1933. The second A.S.B. was founded soon afterwards, but by 1942 it was successfully infiltrated by the Ossewa-brandwag, and several university branches, the University of the Witwatersrand, Pretoria, the University College of the O.F.S. and Huguenot College seceded because of this. In 1948 the present A.S.B. was set up on a Christian, National, and officially non-political basis: amongst its aims are the maintenance and furthering of Christian European civilization, as a bulwark against Communism, and the study of national problems in an academic way. The A.S.B. also stands for academic segregation and admits only whites, in contradistinction to its opposite number, the lively, liberal National Union of South African Students, in whose history an Afrikaner, Leo Marquard, played a prominent rôle.

This survey of the upbringing and education of Afrikaners shows certain conflicting trends. The traditional upbringing, which still persists to some extent in the isolated rural environment or in conservative urban families, and the deliberate policy pursued in schools and universities, are both working to produce the conformist, national-minded Afrikaner. On the other hand the majority of urban Afrikaners are brought up and live in an environment which is less and less distinguishable from that of their English-speaking neighbours. The Afrikaner child may not play with English-speaking children, but he goes to the same American films, reads the same comics and acquires the same economic attitudes.

This latter trend threatens group unity. As such it is strenuously combated by Afrikaner Nationalists. In their efforts to reintroduce artificially in the new environment a national feeling which grew naturally out of isolation, a homogeneous way of life and a sense of grievance, they are exposing their Volk to dangers of another kind. Chief amongst the latter are cultural isolation and inferiority, which may produce similar consequences in the economic field. In a world which is increasingly one world, it is very dangerous for a small nation to experiment with the minds of its children, particularly when these experiments involve putting the clock back a century or more.

CHAPTER SEVEN

SOCIAL STRUCTURE AND CULTURAL LIFE

'Family, blood and native soil—that is next to our religion and our love of freedom our greatest and most sacred national heritage.'

(Die O.B., 28th October, 1942).

EVERY people has its 'golden age'—its own picture of the optimum life. For some peoples this age lies in the future —not Eden but the Promised Land. For others, it lies in the past. For many Afrikaners, this ideal life still lies within the compass of an old man's memory. Even for town-bred Afrikaners this golden age is still represented as the 'lekker lewe' of the farmer, the Boer, in the old Republics; a life when land was there for the taking, where the veld grass grew tall, where the fountains never failed and the game thundered in uncounted herds. A life where men were strong and God-fearing, their women fair and brave and where the Kaffir knew his place. A life where the Boers could 'be left to themselves, to live in quiet, free and to be exempt from taxation'.

From this modern nostalgic mythology of the 'lekker lewe' and the somewhat less idealized contemporary accounts of travellers, missionaries and others, it is possible to get a composite picture of the old way of life for which Afrikaners today feel such nostalgia. This picture can even be verified in the remote country districts, where the old way of life survives nearly untouched by the insidious infiltration of urban values.

This old way of life dates back well beyond the Republics and the Great Trek. It was the product of Calvinism and a pastoral economy mingling on the frontier. Its main social unit was the patriarchal family.

The head of the patriarchal family was the Boer, in his rôles as husband and father, farmer, hunter, and frontier fighter. He was a somewhat aloof and formidable figure to his children, and especially to his sons. Only later to his grandchildren might he become more human. There was often some tension between father and son, which could be resolved only when the son married and was given his own farm, or when he trekked towards the frontier to take up new land. Later, when there was no more new land, all the sons stayed at home, waiting and scheming for their portion of the land that was left. Respect for both parents was reflected in the customary use of the third person singular as a form of direct address. The second person singular was never used.

In theory, the Boer woman's place was beside and a little behind the male head of the household. The household and family were her charge, and she knew nothing of emancipation. In fact, she was the mainspring of Boer life. She gave to a jolting ox-wagon or rough hut the warmth and intimacy of a home. She taught the children to read the Bible and heard their Catechism. She sent her man to war or on commando, and worked the land and defended the home while he was away. Usually she was no meek housewife but a spirited and strong-willed creature. Indeed, an observer in 1836 thought the women seemed even more determined to trek out of the colony than did the men. And it was the wife of Erasmus Smit, the mission teacher, who said to Hendrik Cloete after the British annexed Natal: 'Before we submit to English domination we would rather walk back over the Drakensberg barefoot'.

C. J. Langenhoven, writing nearly a century later, put these words into the mouth of his Voortrekker vrou: 'I must go to protect my man. There are dangers from wild beasts and rapacious, bloodthirsty barbarians. These my man will resist like a man. But there are other dangers. Other voortrekkers have gone among the savages, and have become debased, degenerate and interbred. They have forgotten their customs, their God, their white glory and nobility. I must go to protect my man against that danger. His body—my body—what are they? I must go so that with the help of God I may save my man's soul.'

At the turn of the century, the ideal was given new life by the Boer woman of the devastated farms, of the homeless trek wagons, of the typhoid-ridden concentration camps. This ideal is personified in the 'Rachel' of Totius' poem, and is also commemorated in the sculptures of the Voortrekker Monument at Pretoria. She stands outside in the place of honour, in her plain cloth dress and her kappie, gazing grimly into the distance, her son and daughter clinging to her skirts. Inside on the bas-reliefs she is portrayed as driving the ox-wagon, cooking, tending the children, loading rifles and exhorting her flagging menfolk. Looking at this Boer vrou and Boer mother, one wonders at the swift passing of the young Sannies, Saris and Annetjies of the Boer songs; of the girls with the yellow hair and blue eyes, who gaily dance to the accordion and meet lusty young men by the vlei at dusk. Yet the Boer girl and Boer vrou are both part of the picture, as daughter and sister, or wife and mother.[1]

About 26,000 women and children died in the concentration camps, and the Boer woman in her suffering came almost to be identified with the Boer nation itself. General de Wet's last words to his burgers before the surrender were: 'If today any one of you had stood bare-headed at the open grave of your mother you would at least have had the hope of meeting her in heaven; but this our dear native land and our own independence will never be ours again as we knew them. Wherever I have led, you have followed unquestioning and uncomplaining, but in this hour I know that I can lead you only one way. Lay down your arms and let us enter the dark waters together'.

On this subject even the bucolic satire of Herman Charles Bosman falls away: 'I was in the veld until they made peace. Then we laid down our rifles and went home. What I knew my farm by was the hole under the koppie where I quarried slate stones for the threshing floor. That was about all that remained

---

[1] In 1952 the Minister of the Interior, Dr. Dönges, rejected a suggestion that South Africa should have a 'Mother's Day' with the words: 'If we really wanted to honour our mothers properly we would need all the days of the year'.

as I had left it. Everything else was gone. My home was burnt down. My lands were laid waste. My cattle and sheep were slaughtered. Even the stones I had for the kraals were pulled down. My wife came out of the concentration camp, and we went together to look at our old farm. My wife had gone into the concentration camp with our two children, and she came out alone. And when I saw her again, and noticed the way she had changed, I knew that I, who had been all the way through the fighting, had not seen the Boer War.'

A strong element in the ideal picture of the vrou is the concept of her as a white woman, chaste and aloof amongst a coloured sea. This 'white woman' concept is found in most colonial systems. It would seem to be the outcome of a group will to self-preservation, combined with a strong feeling of cultural and social superiority. Today this ideal image of the 'white woman' is fiercely defended by white men, but it is obviously in the white women's interest that such an ideal should survive.

Whatever its origin, the 'white woman' concept is reflected in both law and custom in South Africa. Early legislation was largely concerned with the relations between white women and non-white men. In Natal there were provisions for mixed marriages, but there was a ban on illicit intercourse between a white woman and any 'Hottentot, Coolie, Bushman, Lascar or Kaffir'. In the Transvaal there was no provision for mixed marriages, and severe penalties for 'unlawful carnal intercourse between white women and any "native".' In the Cape and the Orange Free State, coloured and white people were free to cohabit with and marry whom they chose, but there was a ban on voluntary sexual intercourse between a white woman and an aboriginal native for the purpose of gain.

The 1927 Immorality Act imposed a single rule throughout the Union, by prohibiting all illicit intercourse between Europeans and Africans. The stable door was finally shut in 1949 and 1950, by legislation prohibiting both marriage and sexual intercourse between whites and all non-whites.

This legal defence of the white woman's rights and idealized status came somewhat curiously at a time when social sanctions against such miscegenation were stronger than they had ever been. In the period between 1925 and 1949 the number of marriages between whites and coloured people averaged seventy-nine, with a steady gradual drop over the last seven years. Of this number the proportion in which white women were involved ranged between 10 and 20 per cent of the total of mixed marriages.

In all cases of mixed marriage a white woman forfeits her membership of the white group. A man, on the other hand, might until fairly recently have succeeded in getting a light-coloured wife accepted in certain white milieus. As far as casual sexual relations between non-whites are concerned, Afrikaners, and indeed all whites, may admit that white men occasionally stray across the colour line, but consider it unthinkable that a white woman could be involved by choice. Any sexual passage between a white woman and a non-white man is therefore translated in terms of rape or assault. This leaves the 'white woman' ideal quite intact. The ideal is further strengthened by the draconian penalties which are applied to non-white offenders, ranging even to the death sentence. These sentences are in sharp contrast to the much milder sentences imposed by the courts on males, white or non-white, who rape or assault non-white women.

The idealization of the white woman is, of course, not confined to the Afrikaner people in South Africa. None the less, it was the frontier Boers and the Dutch slave-owners in the Western Cape who gave the ideal its purely South African flavour. This was devoid of the charm and languors of the Alabama belle or the Brazilian *senhora*. The mistresses of the elegant white-gabled houses of Capetown and Stellenbosch came nearer to this 'Southern lady' ideal than did the frontiersmen's wives. There was, however, always a characteristic moderation and austerity that precluded the growth of a white aristocracy on the Brazilian or Jamaican pattern. The traveller Borcherdts has left a typical picture of such a Stellenbosch vrou in 1861, seated for hours in the back hall at a small table, tea tray in front of her, regulating the household, acting as family scribe and dealing out home-made medicinal remedies.

It was not, however, in the lovely valleys and vineyards of the Western Cape that the Boer way of life evolved. There is an underlying unity of behaviour and institutions, but the Dutch settlers of the Western Cape developed a mellower culture and a tolerant liberal tradition which has since proved unacceptable to those Boers who trekked away.

Characteristic of the Boer family was its size. Girls married young and a family of ten or twelve was nothing exceptional. Widows and widowers rarely remained single, and multiple families were in consequence fairly common. Magdelena Retief, widow of the Trekker leader Piet Retief, in 1840 sent her brother-in-law Gideon an account of her family:

'Dear Brother, at your request I shall write to you how many children I have had and how many I still have. Of the late Jan Greijling I had nine children, three died in infancy, six I have brought to maturity; of these my Gertruijda was dead in child-bed, my second daughter Maria had heart palpitations, both were married, and my son Jan was murdered by the Kaffirs. He and his late father had to lose their lives there in the interior and their bodies had to be left to the wild animals . . . and here again I had to give the bodies of my brave husband Retief, my youngest son Pieter and my eldest son Abraham Greijling to the wild animals, because of the savage Dingaan . . . Of Retief's children, two others died in infancy, of Greijling's children I have still alive Piet and Barent, and of Retief's, Jacobus François—his wife and children are also dead—Debora, Jacoba—her husband and children also dead. And then I have Magdalena Margareta—her children are also dead; so I have of my fifteen children five still left.'

Boer society consisted of a relatively small number of large clans, each descended from the early Dutch, German or Huguenot settlers. Like the French-Canadians, the Boers increased not through immigration but through the cradle. A glance through the Pretoria or Montreal telephone books at the present time is sufficient illustration of this point. In the old days intra-group marriage occurred less because of religious or nationalistic sentiments—these seem to have been less pronounced in the past—than because of the isolation of the Boer group.

Inter-marriage later became exaggerated in some rural districts, either because of their remoteness or because excessive subdivision of land drove close relations to marry in order to 'keep the land within the family'. The Carnegie Report cited an instance of this process in the late 1920's; 'About twenty-seven miles from a large town a group of twenty-one families live in a valley about six hundred and sixty morgen in extent. All are related to one another, being descended from three brothers, who originally lived there—sturdy, industrious and progressive men. Their progeny, however, intermarried to such an extent that they deteriorated in every respect. Today only four families own a wagon and oxen, and are able to make a respectable living; the others exist in miserable conditions. Ten of the twenty-one families live on a plot a quarter of a mile square, of which only two and a half morgen are under cultivation. The diet is composed almost entirely of mealie meal, porridge (without sugar or milk) and black coffee. Living conditions are primitive; no furniture is to be seen in the houses. The children are very backward; the principal states that during the twenty-two years he has been there only four children had passed Standard VI (the end of primary school at that time) and all of these were from one family, allied by marriage to the rest.'

This excessive inbreeding is becoming less and less common, but the Boer community is still mainly composed of large groups of people bearing the family names of the early settlers. In recent years the cult of family has been revived, and various 'clans' have held reunions. Notable amongst these gatherings was the Malan reunion of 1951, attended by a member of the French branch of the family. There are about 6,000 Malans in the Union alone, and the committee collected sufficient contributions to enable it to establish a study bursary for a deserving family member. By far the largest clan, however, is that of the van der Merwes, estimated variously at 23,000 and 50,000. All are apparently descended from Schalk Willem van der Merwe, who established a farm in the Paarl district in 1692. The Pretorius clan is also estimated to run into thousands; it came together in style at the centenary celebrations of the city of Pretoria in November 1955.

There is a difference between this now somewhat self-conscious cult of family, which has even been extended to the tracing of family crests, and the old Boer familialism. In those days it was important to be the son or grandson of a well-regarded individual, and grandchildren were named for their respective grandparents, as a pious tribute and in the hope of perpetuating the desirable traits. There was no element of ancestor worship or snobbery in this attitude to the family.

The closely woven kinship web among the Boers helped to develop and maintain the egalitarianism which was for so long typical of their society. Other factors which worked to the same end were, of course, the similarity of occupation, the lack of conspicuous differences of wealth, and the feeling of fraternity in face of the non-whites around them. The egalitarian social relationship was expressed in familial terms. Older men and women were usually addressed as 'Oom' (uncle) and 'Tante' (aunt) and younger men or girls as 'Neef' and 'Niggie' (nephew and niece).

Contemporaries seem to have addressed each other as 'cousin'. Older people who were held in great affection and esteem by the community might be called 'Oupa' (grandpa) or 'Ouma' (granny). President Kruger was during his lifetime often referred to as 'Oom Paul', while in more recent times the late Mrs. Smuts was known even to the English-language press as 'Ouma'.

The exclusive content of these courtesy titles is shown by the fact that Afrikaners will not use them to non-whites. Older non-white men or women may as a sign of courtesy or affection be addressed as 'Outa' (old papa) or 'Aia' (nurse). These words date from slave days and as such are increasingly resented by non-whites.

The old Boer way of life, and its mainstay the Boer family, began to crumble when its economic bases failed. The patriarchal rule of the father could not be fully maintained by a landless bywoner or an itinerant digger or labourer. In cases where the father worked at a distance, the whole burden of authority and rearing would fall on the mother.

It was maintained in the Carnegie Poor White Commission's Report that the backwardness of the home was proportionate to the mother's confusion and ignorance with regard to her rôle within the family. In practice, the Commissioners reported that 30 per cent of the impoverished white families visited showed no signs of the most elementary social education or order. In some cases this was due to the number of other tasks outside the home that fell on the women (such as tending goats, harvesting, gardening) and the time taken to perform normal household tasks in the absence of any conveniences or manufactured goods. Other factors were isolation, ignorance, early marriage, lack of any reading matter, poor housing and constant child-bearing under primitive conditions.

The Report mentioned one fairly typical case of a mother in an isolated stock-farming area, who had been married seven years, had lived in thirteen different places and had four or five children, with whom she was, when visited, living in a little hut made of reed mats. The Report concluded that the 'strain of pioneer conditions rendered the mothers in isolated homes less and less able in succeeding generations (in proportion to the continuance of the isolation) to give their children normal social training. In other words they were less and less able to give them an idea of their normal relation to other communities, to other people, and even to other members of the same people. In this last and extreme case the lack of social sense would result either in disorder and irregularity in the home or in an exaggerated attachment to home and family. At the less backward stage it would result in incapacity for social intercourse, and inadaptability.'

These observations applied mainly to the rural poor. In the diggings and in the urban slums the evils of isolation were exchanged for the evils of proximity—proximity to the more urban practices of drink, gambling, crime and immorality, and above all proximity to envy-arousing wealth. In these surroundings, the mother was usually forced to go out to work to supplement her husband's wages. Consequently, she had no more time and energy for her children than in the rural setting. It was in the urban setting that the Church, the school, and the State began to take over many of the functions of the old patriarchal family.

In consequence, the pattern of urban Afrikaner working-class family life began gradually to approximate to that of the other white urban workers. A similar approximation was meanwhile occurring in the Afrikaner professional and higher income groups. Families became smaller and parental authority less. Marriages became more unstable and were often contracted only with a civil ceremony. As the man's responsibility and authority as husband, father and provider decreased, desertions and divorces became more frequent. Statistics co-relating divorce with home language are not available, but regular reading of the Divorce Court Reports suggest that the bulk of divorces fall within the Afrikaans-speaking group.[1]

The growing number of marriages outside the group also helped to break down characteristically Afrikaner family patterns, even when the non-Afrikaner parent became more or less assimilated to the Afrikaner side. National-minded leaders have not been blind to this trend and have been opposing it strongly from the pulpit and elsewhere. In 1951, Professor A. B. du Preez, of the Faculty of Theology at the University of Pretoria, said in an interview that an Afrikaner's marriage partner must 'take South Africa as his real and only home in the same way as the Afrikaner does' and should break all cultural bonds with any outside country—otherwise 'mixed marriages' were likely to lead to difficulties for both the partners and their eventual offspring.

In this, Professor du Preez did scant justice to the many thousands of children of such mixed marriages, who have in consequence developed a broader South-Africanism than existed in his philosophy. He was, however, quite rightly concluding that the majority of such children would not feel at

---

[1] The total number of white divorces in 1951 was 3,894 as opposed to 27,112 marriages. The 1935 figures were: 1409 divorces and 20,599 marriages. It is unfortunate that the result of a series of surveys carried out into urban family life under the direction of Professor Cronjé of the Department of Sociology, University of Pretoria, were not available at the time of going to press. These surveys will undoubtedly provide reliable data as to the nature and extent of changes due to urbanization.

home in a narrow racialistic culture, whether it were Afrikaans or English.

Poverty and its products were not the only factors to influence and change Afrikaner family life. For many poverty was succeeded by relative prosperity, which gave the former impoverished whites access to urban recreations, to the cinema, sporting events, bars and clubs of all kinds, and so lessened their dependence on the home. In the urban areas the women were often able to find factory and other work more easily than the men, because of the wage differentials for the sexes. This contributed not only to the loosening of urban family ties but to the break-up of rural life. The influx of women from the rural areas was so great that both in 1936 and 1946 there was a shortfall of at least 40,000 women in the platteland.

The women were as much affected by these new facilities as the men. 'The modern woman tries to imitate the man. She wants to be the equal of the man, and thereby she has sunk to his level. She smokes, drinks and works in offices. This has caused her to lose her gracefulness and charm and her health suffers'. This was the lament of Doctor A. J. van der Merwe, Moderator of the N.G.K. of the Cape, in 1953. He continued his account of the decline of the Boerevrou by an attack on beauty competitions where women were exhibited like animals: 'I see in this the undermining of woman's natural modesty, which she should never surrender if she is to remain a woman in the true sense of the word'.

A recent correspondent to *Die Burger* expressed even more nostalgic views in an approving comment on an earlier correspondent's statement that money was the cause of unhappy marriages and divorces: 'I appeal, therefore, do not give the wife money, even if she cries: "help! help! help!" . . . No, give me that farm girl who has no gloves, with those upcurling veldskoene, for whom her domestic duties are still her birthright, who does not hanker after the Woman—Woman movements, who is subordinate to her husband and, shoulder to shoulder with him, loses herself in the happiness and welfare of her family'.

This compulsive exaggeration of the traditional values and

patterns is in itself a reflection of the deep-rooted insecurity which has been evoked amongst Afrikaners by the radical changes of recent decades. More realistic views about the present have, however, gradually begun to be expressed. Clearly the working woman, and even the working wife, is there to stay. This new rôle was recognized by the compilers of the F.A.K. Silver Jubilee Book in 1954, in a graceful tribute to their secretarial staff over that period: 'Just as in many homes from which a man comes forward to serve his people and his fellow men a woman toils in silence to prepare everything for him so that he can perform his task outside unhindered, so in each office which renders service, there are some silent workers busy day after day performing their task, unseen and unheard, to the tempo of the clattering typewriters and the harsh sound of the telephone. Unseen and unheard, and yet not unseen and not unheard. Your silent work, your patient readiness to serve, your sacrifice, your cheerful service have not passed unnoticed . . . a grateful Afrikaner Volk pays grateful tribute to you all, ladies!'

Afrikaner social life, like the Afrikaner family, has changed under the influence of economic differentiation and the rise of socio-economic classes within the Afrikaner group. In the old days, social life was uniform, simple and egalitarian. The family was the main unit, and individual kin paid long visits to each other or assembled for weddings, christenings and funerals and such festivals as New Year's Day. The wider group as a whole, was, however, held together by two communal activities, those centering round religion and war. The main group assembled only for the quarterly Nagmaal, or the sudden call for commando service. These assemblies of course gave an opportunity for a whole set of lesser group activities, such as auctions, dances and meetings between young people of the two sexes.

In the Boer society of the frontier and the republics, there were until the end of the nineteenth century no inherited social distinctions. Prestige within the community depended upon the individual's worth, but even the most outstanding remained accessible and easily informal in their relation with fellow Boers. The aloofness and cold formality of the Hollander specialists imported by President Kruger to help run his country were amongst the main causes of their unpopularity amongst the Boers. Kruger himself, on the other hand, was always available to any burger who might wish to come and talk to him on the stoep of his house.

This accessibility and informality remained characteristic of South African politicians and officials even to this day. Thus dissatisfied citizens, particularly those of Boer stock, rarely waste times on letters or official channels. They are more likely to trek in to Pretoria or Cape Town and demand to see the minister concerned. More often than not they succeed.

A homogeneous egalitarian society was typical of the Boer as such. It did not, however, extend to the older Dutch settlement in and around Cape Town. Here there were almost from the outset inherited social distinctions based on land-ownership and wealth in slaves or trading goods.

Gradually there evolved a genteel social hierarchy, increasingly intermixed with British newcomers after 1806, in which economic factors might be less important than birth, cultivation, professional eminence, and the other determinants of social class in a sophisticated urban or peri-urban society. This western Cape Dutch society is the only Afrikaans-speaking society that most English-speaking people ever enter. Quite erroneously, they tend to identify it with Boer and Afrikaner society as a whole. In fact the limits of Cape Dutch society and of its influence are roughly coterminous with the line where the white-gabled manors with their wedding-cake mouldings, their libraries and their fine furniture end, and the plain whitewashed cottages or huts of the Boers begin.

Class distinctions began within the Boer group proper with the rise of the landless bywoner class and the gradual descent of many impoverished Boers to an 'uncivilized' and even 'Kaffir' level. Initially, while land was still plentiful, the wealthy farmer's attitude to his tenants was usually one of fatherly benevolence. As pressure on land increased, this attitude often changed for the worse. The Carnegie Poor White Report speaks of the selfishness, overbearing manner and contempt displayed by many wealthy Afrikaners towards the indigent:

'The bywoner and farm labourer are in many cases no longer received as social equals by the landowner and his family. They are very often allowed only in the kitchen of the house. The labourer's wife comes in the house only to work as a servant . . . H. A. is a farm labourer employed by a land-owner who has many white and coloured men in his service . . . He lives on one of his employer's farms together with some coloured families, and is responsible for the care of the owner's stock. The unsympathetic treatment he experiences has accen-tuated his feelings of inferiority, and through lack of intercourse with other Europeans he has been driven to associate with the coloured labourers on an equal footing. There is no longer any respect for him and his wife on the part of the latter. They no longer address them as "baas" and "nooi", but call them by their Christian names.'

This awareness persisted and deepened in those bywoners who went to the towns. In the urban setting, an economic class-hierarchy was already established before the influx of impover-ished rural whites took place. The determinants of the class structure varied. There was the Anglo-Dutch complexity of Cape Town, the British-Jewish plutocracy of Johannesburg, the Boer-Hollander administrative and professional hierarchy of Bloemfontein or Pretoria. Wherever he went, however, the im-poverished white found himself at the bottom of the ladder, with the mixed-blood proletariat and the black sea of detribalized Africans waiting to engulf him.

Class distinctions cut across in linguistic groups to a greater or lesser extent in Cape Town, Bloemfontein or Pretoria. In Johannesburg, however, with its blunt emphasis on wealth, and its English-speaking insularity, the rising class of Afrikaner pro-fessional men found themselves isolated and ignored. It is rare today to meet an Afrikaner at a purely social gathering in one of the wealthy northern suburbs. It must indeed be admitted that the wider English-Afrikaner social contacts in other cities have largely been due to the courteous readiness of bilingual Afrikaners to speak English and to meet English-speaking South Africans on the latters' own ground. Apart from the normal constraint produced by social contacts in a foreign language, these meetings have not always been devoid of slights and humiliation for the Afrikaner. Such slights have taken the form of insensitive jokes about the Afrikaans language, Calvinism and Afrikaner customs, of patronizing attitudes and lack of reciprocity, and even of direct snubs in such situations as election to social clubs.

Most educated Afrikaners were not likely, therefore, to feel at home in the existing English-dominated hierarchy. The natural tendency for them to evolve their own separate Afrikaans-speaking society in the cities was greatly stimulated by the growing aggressiveness and exclusiveness of Afrikaner political nationalism. The consequence has been that today there is less and less social mingling between English and Afrikaans-speaking South Africans, except in the official and diplomatic circles of Cape Town and Pretoria and the small liberal world of the universities and the arts. Instead, an exclusively Afrikaner urban class-hierarchy is replacing the old classless society of the Boers.

In the rural setting, land-ownership was the main determinance of status. And the endless availability of land was the guarantee of the egalitarianism of Boer society. Trading, apart from barter, was in the hands of the Jewish pedlar, whose participation in Boer society was largely limited to his economic rôle. There was, however, one other occupational group which was from the beginning accorded the highest social status amongst the Boers. This was the group of ministers, whose status was determined not by land or wealth, but by learning and culture. As the network of schools spread through the country, this status came to be shared by the new trained teachers who were replacing the old vagabond meesters.

Learning and culture, interpreted in terms of professional and academic eminence, became the main determinants of status in the fast-growing Afrikaner society of the towns and cities. A glance at the biographies of the present Nationalist Cabinet provides an interesting contrast to the careers of most English or American politicians. Out of a total of fourteen Ministers, all but two were born in small towns or in the country, and all but one have at least a B.A. degree (six of them in law) while three have a Ph.D. degree. Six out of the fourteen have at one time been teachers or university lecturers, five have practised law, four journalism and five have farmed.[1]

Undoubtedly professional or academic status still stand higher in the Afrikaner professional hierarchy than they do amongst English-speaking South Africans.[2] Of recent years, however, the spread of general education has tended to reduce educational and cultural differences within the Afrikaner-speaking group, and consequently to diminish the importance of learning and culture as status determinants. A contributor to the *Cultural History of the Afrikaner*, lamenting the decline of the Boer family and society, wrote: 'Our volk culture has now become a class or *élite*-culture'. This process has been speeded up by the Afrikaner's growing participation and success in the commercial and industrial world and by his unconscious acceptance of the 'English' and 'American' values current in this world.

At the present time, an Afrikaner social class structure based mainly on wealth is slowly rigidifying in the country as well as the towns. It is separate from but similar to the social hierarchy of the English-speaking group in its values, its snobberies and its affectations. This similarity is well illustrated in the two annual charity balls held in Johannesburg, one by the English-speaking group, the other by the socialite Maria van Riebeeck Club for Afrikaner women. At both balls, white-gowned young women whose families have a desire to figure in social circles are presented to the Governor-General and his wife. This originally Royalist ceremony has, since the appointment of the formerly pro-Republican Hon. E. G. Jansen to the Governor-

---

[1] The occupational breakdown of the 1953 Parliament reflects the social structure of a decade past or more. More than one-third are farmers (55 out of 158—most of them Nationalists); thirty-two are lawyers—again most of them Nationalists; ten professional party officials—all Nationalists; twenty-one business men (mainly Opposition); and about two dozen professional men (mainly Opposition)—there are no M.P.s representing the artisan group, and there are only four women.

[2] In 1952, Dr. de Vos, founder of the splinter Dutch Reformed Church, gave a detailed occupational breakdown of the Broederbond's membership as 357 clergymen, 2,039 teachers, 905 farmers and 159 lawyers (60 M.P.s).

Generalship, become even more obviously a local social event, filling a local social need.

There are occasional signs of friction between the intelligentsia and the growing *nouveau riche* class. In October 1955, for instance, Ignatius Mocke, a well-known Afrikaner writer, was reported by *Die Transvaler* as saying 'If some of our rich farmers, who paid up to £100 for Test tickets, were to think of investing only half of that in our culture. . . . Sport has its place, but today it is practically a religion for the South Africans. And it is one of the smyptoms of increasing superficiality which manifests itself also in other spheres, like the popularity of yellow-press reading matter and the Hollywood film.'

The growth of class-distinction amongst Afrikaners should not, however, be exaggerated. Sarah Gertrude Millin rightly points out that white South Africa is essentially a middle-class society and that the social range within the white group is narrow and fluid, compared with the immense gulf between white and black. The distinctions of wealth or culture which undoubtedly exist between Afrikaners today might prevent the closest social contact between the various levels, but in everyday life most Afrikaners, and indeed many English-speaking South Africans, tend to address and treat each other as equals, in the old fraternal style of the veld.

Afrikaner urban society has tended to approximate to the English-speaking pattern, not only in structure, but in its values and activities. And Afrikaner urban society is increasing in size as the old Boer society grows smaller. Its patterns are even being extended into all but the most remote country districts, through kinship ties and modern means of communication.

The differences between the life of Afrikaans and English-speaking town dwellers are those not of kind but of degree. Amongst the Afrikaners there may be more organized religious life and less sophistication, but both groups share the same informal, open-air life, and are exposed to the unifying influences of the Americanized cinema, radio and popular press.

Through such media, these influences reached the Afrikaner in his own language. This is particularly true of the recently introduced 'C' programme. This consists of variety shows, soap operas and other serials, usually American, interspersed with commercials. As most advertisers and sponsors are non-Afrikaners, the 'English' side has tended to be stressed. Shortly after the 'C' programme began, *Die Transvaler* pointed out that it was un-Afrikaans and was exposing Afrikaner homes to a blast of foreign influence.

According to an analysis published in the Johannesburg *Star* in 1953, an average listening week on the S.A.B.C. provided over twenty-five hours of light music, nearly eight hours of news, nearly six hours of programmes for young people and children, two and a half hours dance music and two and a half hours devoted to physical exercises. Afrikaans-programme listeners got more sport and serious music, twenty minutes more of religious broadcast and nearly seven hours of boeremusiek (folk-style songs and dances). English-speaking listeners got four hours more of feature programmes, three and a half hours more of drama, two and a half hours more of talks and two more hours of poetry. These figures provide some justification for the somewhat scathing observations on the present Afrikaner trend to triviality made by Dr. G. D. Scholtz in his book *Has the Afrikaner a Future?* He points out that the S.A.B.C has to make concessions to this trend, or Afrikaner listeners switch over to the English programme.

Prominent Afrikaner intellectual leaders like Dr. G. D. Scholtz are greatly concerned about what they regard as the threat to 'Afrikaans culture'. As always, this word 'culture' is used somewhat loosely, at times to apply to a general set of values and patterns of behaviour, at others in a more limited reference to a set of achievements in the worlds of the intellect and the arts. Taking the term in its more general sense, it can be said that the Boers on the frontier and in the Republics evolved a specific Boer culture. This culture still lingers on in the rural areas, although it is being gradually diluted in all but the most remote.

In the towns, however, Afrikaner or Boer culture is becoming less and less a distinctive way of life, and increasingly an imposed set of abstractions evolved and propagated by a clique of intellectual and political leaders, so as to prevent the mass of urban Afrikaners from mingling with their English-speaking neighbours. In its modern version, 'Afrikaans culture' is largely a nationalistic slogan designed to emphasize national uniqueness and national destiny, and to conceal from the ordinary Afrikaner his cultural similarities with the outside world. It reflects the belief that each race or ethnic group should have its own culture, just as it should have its own language, religion, territory and national organization.

Turning to the more restricted use of the word 'culture', in the sense of a group heritage in learning, literature and the arts, even the most ardent Afrikaner nationalist will admit that Afrikaans culture is young and fragile. In the field of scholarship individual Afrikaners have made considerable contributions, but with the exception of some theologians they have received their higher training outside the Union and have done their best work in a wider environment than the 'national' one.

The achievements of Afrikaner poets and writers in the last half century are described elsewhere. It is in poetry that the Afrikaner has so far reached his highest flights. But here, as in other cultural fields, the writer and his readers have suffered from the long association of the cultural and linguistic movement with political nationalism. As a result, particularly in the early period, writers have tended to concentrate on national themes, to be didactic and take themselves too seriously. Their work has all too often been received and criticized not according to its artistic merit alone, but as showing an Afrikaans or an un-Afrikaans spirit.

Some recent writers have liberated themselves from these shackles, but they face other problems. Chief amongst these problems is the growing cultural isolation of the new generation of Afrikaners, educated in single-medium schools which in practice cut their pupils off from the riches of Dutch, French, classical and even English literature. Such isolation generates a narrow self-complacency which does not stimulate in either the writer or his readers a critical sense or a striving for the highest standards.

Despite the present trend towards a wider South African or western spirit, Afrikaner writers have nevertheless laid the foundations of a literature that is distinctively Afrikaans. This cannot be claimed for Afrikaner achievements in the other arts, which are in any case, by virtue of their medium, more international. In music the only form which could be attributed to the Boers is that of the folk songs and dances called in their jazzed-up modern form 'boeremusiek'. Even here the Cape Coloured people must share the credit for many of the gayest songs. It is at present fashionable in more intellectual Afrikaner circles to despise boeremusiek, and its original media, the concertina and guitar. This type of music is also felt by the national-minded to be undignified and unworthy of the resurgent Volk.

South African composers have at times borrowed themes from folk music, but their work in general tends to reflect European influences and training. Until now, most composers in South Africa have either come from overseas or have received their final training abroad. Amongst the younger generation, the majority have Afrikaans names, and one of them, Arnold van Wyk, has an international reputation. His work does not, however, fall into the category of 'Afrikaans' music, and is neither well-known nor clearly understood in the Union as a whole.

The same Europeanizing trend is visible in art, though here there are some signs that the techniques have been digested and that a native school may soon arise. Most of these experimenting painters are Afrikaners by birth. Amongst the most prominent are Pierneef, Le Roux Smith le Roux, and Alexis Preller. They will not however form an Afrikaans school of painting but a South African one. These painters are concerned not with 'Volkskultuur', but with finding new techniques and idioms through which to express the South African scene.

In sculpture on the other hand a truly Afrikaans-oriented craftsman has emerged. This is Coert Steynberg, who is responsible for almost every national memorial. The Voortrekker Monument itself might presumably be cited as an example of distinctively Afrikaans architecture. In the field of architecture however, as in painting and music, overseas influences are paramount, and nothing specifically South African has been produced since the gabled Cape Dutch farmhouse.

Owing to the huge distances and the competition of the cinema, the live theatre in South Africa has been largely left to repertory or amateur companies. For the last few years, there has also been in existence a bilingual National Theatre, sub-sidized by the Department of Education. Its aims are to bring the theatre to all parts of the country, by means of touring companies, one Afrikaans-speaking, one English-speaking, and to encourage further indigenous playwriting in both languages.

The National Theatre's organizers are, however, animated by the sort of broader South Africanism which led them to write: 'A National Theatre in South Africa would be one of the finest weapons against racialism. True art knows no race discrimina-tion and in a National Theatre Afrikaans actors and actresses would be cast in English plays and vice versa, apart from each playing in their own language . . . A National Theatre would provide a common ground where the two sections could meet. It would be the pivot of a new cultural alliance between the two sections. It would knit both races together—not only the artist—but the audiences throughout the land'.

This brief account of 'Afrikaans culture' in its narrower sense suggests that there is and can be 'no such animal', except in so far as it is linked with its wider human and natural environment and stimulated by the general heritage of Western culture. But for 'culture' in general there is a profound and widespread yearning amongst Afrikaners as a whole, as the following com-ment on the above section suggests. It was written by a half-Afrikaner, who is himself something of a poet and who felt that the present account did 'Afrikaans culture' scant justice:

Admittedly there are some people trying to make a lot out of a very modest amount, and they are trying to do so from pretty shady political motives. But this must not lead one into slating the genuine desire for cultural achievement among so many Afrikaners and for the quite high standard which their poetry has reached. Perhaps very often the poetic ambition of the Afrikaner poet outstrips his performance, but it is not a mean sign this driving desire to overreach, and it is what urges people on so that now and then comes a talent which can make use of the vitality. The Afrikaner is full of a desire to write things large, he wants to be a full European, he longs to be utterly of Africa, he goes in for silly boasting on a ridiculous scale, there is no wrong done to anybody as big as a wrong done to an Afrikaner, he bristles like a porcupine with suspicions of inferiority, yet he regards himself as the superior of any other white man on the continent and certainly better than any black. He can apply himself to any topic or enterprise no matter how grand or despicable with astonishing obstinacy, and though he has no feeling for soil, he has a passion for country, for the great bones of scene, sweep, plain, mountain range, desolation, loneliness. You'll find it nearly all in his poetry, and in a more perverted way in his politics. His craving for culture is in all his history of the last 150 years, and maybe before.

*　　*　　*　　*　　*

In the old simple Boer society, the major social units were the family, the Church and the commando. It was only when the economic basis of Boer society broke down and the Boers moved to the cities that these types of social unit became inadequate. Part of their functions passed into the hands of the State, while others were taken over by a growing network of Afrikaans-oriented voluntary associations.

A network of voluntary associations already existed in South Africa, but these were usually so English-oriented and English-dominated (using 'English' in the wider sense of 'English-speaking South African' as well as 'English') that Afrikaners avoided them, either for political reasons or because they did not feel at home socially or in the language.

In the latter case the Afrikaner's feeling of 'not belonging' was often increased by the patronizing or aloof attitude of many English-speaking South Africans themselves. In the former case, Afrikaner avoidance might be attributed to a narrow nationalism or to the need to set up organizations to which by their very nature most English-speaking South Africans were unlikely to initiate or support. Such were the associations which aimed at furthering the use of the Afrikaans language, or at assisting those who were in need as a result of participating in what English-speaking South Africans might regard as hostile or treasonable activities. Sometimes too, the Afrikaners objected to the fact that some existing English-oriented organizations lacked a colour-bar and might even admit a few non-white members.

Political, economic, educational and religious organizations are described in the chapters devoted to these aspects of Afrikaner life. So too are the cultural associations devoted to further-ing the Afrikaans language. The Genootskap van Regte Afri-kaners of the Paarl is indeed one of the earliest Afrikaans organ-izations. These early organizations were mainly concerned either with promoting the Afrikaans language or with welfare. It was not until the 1930's that the network of Afrikaner volun-tary associations began to assume the diversity and richness that characterizes it today.

It is obviously impossible to describe the whole of this net-work, but an account can be given of the most important asso-ciations in each section.

Of the women's organizations the A.C.V.V. (Afrikaanse Christelike Vrouevereniging) of the Cape (and later of South West Africa) is the oldest. It was founded in 1904 to perpetuate the women's committees which were set up in the Cape Colony to work amongst Boer prisoners and in the concentration camps during the Anglo-Boer War. The A.C.V.V. has remained pri-marily a welfare organization, in keeping with the traditional rôle of the Boerevrou. It thus presents a certain contrast to the predominantly English-speaking National Council of Women. The A.C.V.V.'s motto is 'Vir Kerk, Volk en Taal', but it and the other provincial women's organizations show a certain interest in feminist matters, in so far as these affect family life and well-being (for instance, married women's property and custody of children).

Amongst the A.C.V.V.'s activities, have been the founding of local health committees and appointment of district nurses, the establishment of housecraft schools and an education fund, and of institutions such as boarding-houses, crèches, homes for the aged, marriage guidance bureaux, women's needlework clubs and children's clubs. The A.C.V.V. employs nearly forty social workers. With its sister organizations in the Transvaal (S.A.V.F.), Natal (N.C.V.V.) and Orange Free State (O.C.V.), it forms a Union-wide Federale Vroueraad, established in 1921, and representing a total of about 15,000 Afrikaans women. The A.C.V.V. publishes a quarterly called *Eendrag*, while the northern societies bring out a joint publication called *Vrou en Moeder*.

It may perhaps be an illusory impression that the Cape organization, while staunchly maintaining the general values of Afrikaner family life and culture, retains a more moderate and tolerant spirit than its northern colleagues on such matters as political Nationalism and co-operation with English-speaking organizations.

Other important Afrikaner women's organizations are associated with the three Dutch Reformed Churches. The N.G.K. has its Vroue Sendingbond (Women's Mission League), whose work, by reason of its nature, falls mainly outside the Union. The N.G.K. of the Transvaal has its Bond van Dienaresse, working in the Province; there are thirteen branches in Johannesburg alone. The N.H.K. has an active Sustersvereniging, with ten branches in Johannesburg. The Gereformeerde Kerk has its own Sustersbond.

Amongst secular organizations there are the large women's agricultural unions (V.L.V.) in each province. Their purpose is to promote self-help and better home management amongst women, mainly in the platteland areas. These organizations are officially bilingual and have an overseas connexion with the International League of Country Women. By virtue of their aims and area of activity, however, they tend to be mainly Afrikaner in membership.

A consequence of the growing class-differentiation amongst Afrikaners has been the institution of clubs with more purely social aims. Notable amongst these is the Maria von Riebeeck Club in Johannesburg. This has its own premises, where social functions and elections are held. So far, there are no separate Afrikaans-speaking associations for business or professional women (as opposed to men). Those Afrikaner women who have careers outside the home, unless they are teachers, still tend to belong to the existing pan-South African organizations, although these are often dominated by the English-speaking group.

Welfare has always been a prominent aim in Afrikaner organizational work, by virtue of the material situation of the Afrikaner people. An early general welfare organization was the Helpmekaar Vereniging. This was originally formed after the 1914 rebellion, to help defeated rebels and other Afrikaners, who might be victimized economically because of their race. The original aim was to raise £100,000, but this target was exceeded and £180,000 was ultimately received. With the surplus, Helpmekaar turned to the educational field. Here it continues to provide study-loans for young Afrikaners.

The emotional climate of this organization is perhaps best shown in the speech with which Dr. Malan, one of the original promoters, opened the 1955 Helpmekaar Congress in Paarl. He pointed out that while the need out of which Helpmekaar had been born no longer existed, the 'struggle' still went on in other fields; '. . . For instance, in the Eastern Cape cities, some of which are so unsympathetic to their Afrikaans-speaking minority. There is Natal with its brave but struggling Afrikaners . . . There are the two Rhodesias, where the most elementary rights in the cultural and educational sphere are still being systematically denied to a considerable Afrikaner minority. And there are Kenya and Tanganyika where the Afrikaner community does great credit to our people in every respect, but where they will be able to maintain themselves only under the most difficult circumstances and with the utmost exertion. They belong to us, and we to them. Is the Helpmekaar only for us, or for them, too?'

Welfare work of an all-embracing kind is done by the Dutch Reformed Churches in the parishes, through their women's organizations and their youth organizations. The main N.G.K. has a Federal Poor Relief Council to co-ordinate the more material and immediate aspects of this work in all four provinces.

A specialized service association which corresponds more or less to the St John's Ambulance is the South African Noodhulpliga (First Aid League) This was set up in 1935 as a result of a resolution passed by the annual congress of the Afrikaner Railwaymen's Cultural Organization (A.T.K.V.). The

Noodhulpliga, which has always retained a close bond with the A.T.K.V., was intended to satisfy the Afrikaner's desire to have 'his own first aid organization, one which had arisen out of the soil of (his) beloved fatherland, and could be set up in line with (his) national traditions and way of life. The Afrikaner also yearned for first aid instruction in his own beloved mother-tongue'.

The Noodhulpliga describes itself as a non-political, Christian, National, Afrikaans-speaking association. Only white persons are eligible for membership, but there are some separate non-white sections organized by the Dutch Reformed Churches. It provides ambulance and nursing services, training in first aid, home nursing, mothercraft, child welfare and so on. The Noodhulpliga's membership has soared over the last few years to over 4,000, but well over half of these are enrolled in the new branches set up within the South African Railways organization since mid-1954. Membership of its Junior League has also risen steeply, and an attempt is being made to establish branches in all Afrikaans-speaking schools.

The Dutch Reformed churches have their own youth organizations, with the usual religious and cultural aims. The N.G.K. has the Kerkjeugvereniging, with a membership of over 16,000, while the N.H.K. and the G.K. have their own Jonge-liedverenigings. The youth organizations attached to the political parties are described in the chapter on political life, and the Afrikaanse Studentebond in the section on education. The Students' Christian Association of South Africa is one of the oldest organizations in the country. It was founded in 1896 and still tries to maintain its non-racial atmosphere, although the English and non-white sections are in fact smaller than the dominating Afrikaans-speaking section.

More characteristic of the all-Afrikaner youth associations is the Voortrekker Movement. This was started in 1918 as an Afrikaans-speaking counterpart to the English-oriented, overseas-affiliated Scouts and Guides. In the 1920's the first Voortrekker Movement considered setting up a bilingual and truly South African organization with the Scouts. On the question of limiting membership to whites, both organizations agreed. Difficulties, however, were encountered over the Scouts' Promise and their flag. The Scouts were unwilling to abandon the Union Jack or to omit the reference to the King. Nor did they approve of compulsory bilingualism, although they supported equal rights for both languages. Finally the Voortrekkers decided to go their own way, but the parting was cordial. The Scouts trained the first Voortrekker leaders, while the Voortrekkers adopted a revised edition of the *Scout Handbook*. General Smuts was one of the first Voortrekker patrons; and the organization strove to keep itself above politics. During the war years it succeeded sufficiently to retain official permission to wear uniform and badges, in common with the Scouts, Guides and Students' Christian Association.

The total membership of the Voortrekkers at present is 22,000, more than half this number being in the Transvaal. Some troups are organized in the schools, and most members come from middle-class homes, perhaps because of the cost of uniforms and other similar considerations. Membership is open to boys and girls between the ages of 12 and 17. Those over 17 may become Staatmakers (State-builders), while younger children belong to the Penkoppe and Drawwertjies (equivalent to Cubs and Brownies). 'Brownies' is not a term which could be easily adopted in a colour-conscious country.

The Voortrekker Movement is, at the highest levels at least, not as chauvinistic as the bulk of Afrikaner organizations. It may be too that the Nationalist Party's Jeugbond channels off some of the more narrowly nationalist ardour amongst the rank-and-file of young Afrikaners.

A Voortrekker vows to do his duty faithfully to God, his Volk and his Country, and to serve his fellow-men at all times. The Voortrekker Code tells him to be pure in thought, word and deed, obedient and respectful to his superiors, to be helpful and friendly, to honour his language and to be a friend to animals.

The Boy Scouts and Girl Guides still have a number of Afrikaans members (about 8 per cent and 2 per cent respectively); these tend however to come from semi-anglicized or bilingual families. The total white Scout membership is a little less than 20,000.

Like welfare, culture has long been a main motif of Afrikaner voluntary associations. The early cultural organizations were concerned with defending the political rights of Dutch and Afrikaans, then with getting the latter accepted as an official and literary language. By 1920 this campaign was more or less won, and the emphasis shifted to the content and quality of the culture which had been so stoutly championed.

1921 saw the legal incorporation of the Suid-Afrikaanse Akademie vir Wetenskap en Kuns (S.A. Academy of Science and Art), which had been set up in Bloemfontein just before Union, under the auspices of ex-President Steyn. This Academy originally consisted of a Faculty of Language, Literature and Art. To this in 1942 was added a Faculty of Natural and Technical Sciences. Since 1909 the Academy has published a regular periodical. Its membership is limited by statute to 200, divided equally between the Faculties. In addition, it has several hundred assessor members and assistant members. The Academy performs all the functions of a learned academy for the Afrikaner world and the Afrikaans language. Recently, it has advocated the increased teaching of Dutch in Afrikaans schools, to combat cultural isolation. It has also set itself the task of drawing up lists of Afrikaans technical terms in the various sciences, so that Afrikaner scientists and workers may not have to continue using the English words.[1]

A more recent foundation on the academic level is SABRA —the Suid-Afrikaanse Buro vir Rasse-Aangeleenthede (South African Bureau of Racial Affairs). This organization was set up in 1949 by a group of Stellenbosch intellectuals, mainly theologians and social scientists, who advocate intellectual and cultural apartheid. Its function is the scientific study of race problems, and the instruction of the general public and the outside world in the essentials and possible solutions of these problems.

---

[1]Many Afrikaner scholars of course participate in such bilingual learned associations as the S.A. Association for the Advancement of Science, which publishes a bilingual monthly journal. In the welfare field, too, there is collaboration in such organizations as the S.A. National Society for the Blind and many others.

In practice SABRA provides an intellectual justification for apartheid, and acts as the opposite number of the older-established, multi-racial South African Institute of Race Relations, with its doctrines of liberalism and integration. SABRA's research is on a high level, although the total unanimity of its conclusions sometimes suggests a certain subjectiveness of approach.

At the other end of the cultural hierarchy are three popular associations intended to further Afrikaans culture and the Afrikaans language. These associations are perhaps unique in that they are confined to the workers in given sections of the public service. Two are very recent but the A.T.K.V. (Afrikaans Taal-en-Kultuurvereniging) was set up over twenty-five years ago for workers in the South African Railways and Harbours. Its growth has been amazing, and today it is the largest Afrikaner organization after the Churches and political parties. It has a total membership of 66,000, of whom 15,000 are minor children of members. This figure represents nearly 50 per cent of the total number of European railwaymen employed by the South African Railways—the railway authorities incidentally collect the 2s. monthly dues for the organization by stop-orders. The A.T.K.V. is said to be highly democratic, and not to reflect the occupational status of its members. It is also officially non-political, and any executive member who enters active politics must resign his A.T.K.V. office immediately. On the other hand, as an official commented: 'the Calvinist *weltanschauung* does not tolerate compartments—it sees life as a complete whole'.

A small number of A.T.K.V. members, perhaps 5 per cent, are English-speaking, but the A.T.K.V. is intended to serve Afrikaans-speaking railwaymen 'on a Christian National basis'. Its colours are green and orange, and its badge is a trek-wagon and a winged train-wheel.

The A.T.K.V. provides varied services for its members. In addition to such welfare services as a death-benefit fund, it gives educational loans to school-children and university students, and issues 8,000 copies of a popular family monthly magazine, *Die Taalgenoot*, which is distributed free to members. The

A.T.K.V. does not fulfil the normal functions of a staff organization, but makes frequent representations to the railway authorities in cases where it considers that the bilingual rules are not being properly enforced, or where incorrect Afrikaans is being used. The organization has its own seaside resort, which accommodates 10,000 to 12,000 holidaymakers a year. Local branch activities include lectures, Eisteddfods, picnics, handicrafts, volkspele[1] and jukskei. Many local branches are individually affiliated to Afrikanerdom's main cultural co-ordinating body, the F.A.K.

As one of the largest and most solidly established Afrikaner voluntary organizations, the A.T.K.V. has played a leading part in various Afrikaner national celebrations and events. Its first outstanding achievement was the organization of the symbolic 'Ox-Wagon Trek' of 1938, to commemorate the centenary of the Great Trek. This event evoked a wave of national sentiment and enthusiasm amongst the mass of Afrikaners, and led to the founding of the Ossewa-Brandwag.

In 1949 the A.T.K.V. organized the despatch riders who took part in the ceremonial unveiling of the Voortrekker Monument, while its Vrou-en-Moeder Movement undertook to provide a tapestry costing £10,000 for this edifice. The mail coaches which trekked from all parts of the Union in 1952 to take part in the Van Riebeeck celebrations in Capetown were also contributed by the A.T.K.V. In addition, 1,000 A.T.K.V. members took part in the 1954 centenary of the Orange Free State.

---

[1]'Folk dances'. The Volkspele Movement was initiated some fifteen years ago by the Reddingsdaadbond. Its aim was to fill the need of young people for some self-sufficient open-air relaxation belonging to the group itself. Volkspele are traditional melodies sung and danced in national costume. They are part of Boer tradition, but were only revived by Dr. S. H. Pellissier about 1914. The cult spread slowly, but after the general wakening of national-minded Afrikaners in 1938, volkspele became an accepted part of Afrikaner national ceremonies and life. They are increasingly taught in Afrikaans-medium schools; by 1955 7,000 volkspelers and 220 teachers were affiliated to the Movement. Volkspele fulfil the demand of the national-minded for a nationally-oriented and exclusive activity in the field of recreation as elsewhere. They also provide an alternative to the secular distractions of urban life, and as such are approved by the D.R.C.

Very junior brothers of the A.T.K.V. are the A.T.K.B. (Afrikaanse Taal-en-Kultuurbond), set up in December 1953 for Afrikaans-speaking white employees of the Department of Post and Telegraphs, and A.K.P.O.L. (Afrikaanse Kultuurvereniging vir die Suid-Afrikaanse Polisie) set up in 1955 for Afrikaans-speaking policemen. The aims of both organizations are very similar to those of the A.T.K.V. The A.T.K.B. already has its monthly *Die Bondgenoot* and nearly 10,000 members. Like the A.T.K.V., the two younger organizations are entirely Afrikaans-oriented, although the white personnel of the police and Post Office are not yet entirely Afrikaans-speaking.

The stirring of nationalistic sentiment amongst Afrikaners in the 1920's led in 1929 to a Language Conference, and to the setting-up of a Federation of Afrikaans Cultural Organizations (F.A.K.). This has grown to be the co-ordinating body for Afrikanerdom in all but the party-political field. The distance between party politics and cultural nationalism is not, however, a great one in the case of this body, which takes as its spiritual ancestor the Paarl Genootskap van Regte Afrikaners. As Leo Marquard points out, the F.A.K. 'may not unfairly be regarded as a powerful unofficial ally of the Nationalist Party'.

All national-oriented Afrikaner organizations are by now affiliated to F.A.K. on a national or local basis, to the number of 100 or more. In addition, there are over 250 affiliated church councils and 1,000 individual contributors. Local membership is either through local cultural associations (Kultuurverenigings) or local liaison committees (Skakelkomitees), representing the cultural, religious, social and educational associations in a given area. By the end of 1953, fifty cultural societies and sixty liaison committees were affiliated to F.A.K.

The liaison committees in the large cities have great influence in other than the purely cultural sphere. For instance, the Johannesburg Skakelkomitee, which represents ninety out of a possible 140 Afrikaner associations in the city, has over the last few years put up national-minded candidates for the Johannesburg School Board elections, produced a list of Afrikaner organizations for the information of immigrants who wish to become familiar with Afrikaner life, organized visits to many of these immigrants in their homes, particularly those who come from Holland and Germany, and issued a circular to 6,000 business establishments in Johannesburg, requesting the implementation of bilingualism behind the counter, on the telephone, in advertisements and in all printed matter. The last initiative was supported by hundreds of members of affiliated societies who demanded service in Afrikaans in shops and other business establishments, withheld their custom if they were not satisfied, and reported any shortcomings.

The local bodies take their turn on all matters of policy from the bulletins issued by the Executive Committee of the F.A.K. The broad outlines of policy are laid down by the Afrikaanse Nasionale Kultuurraad (Afrikaner National Cultural Council). This is composed of members of the Executive Committee, with representatives of the three Afrikaans Churches and of the main Afrikaans organizations. General policy has until now been dominated by the external struggle against anglicization. Recently, however, there have been signs that some Afrikaner leaders appreciate that this campaign is more or less won, and that the real danger is what one of them called 'the enemy within'. By this is meant the lowering of the old Boer moral values and the increasingly materialistic attitude of the mass of urban Afrikaners.

One of the most important achievements of the F.A.K. in the purely cultural field has been the collection and publication of a large number of Afrikaans folk songs. In education, F.A.K. has propagated Christian National doctrines, through an Institute created for that purpose after the Education Conference held in Bloemfontein in 1939. The Institute for National Welfare was set up at the same period to deal with such matters as the Poor White problem and national health. In the economic sphere, the F.A.K. was through its Economic Institute responsible for the setting up of the Reddingsdaadbond and the Afrikaanse Handelsinstituut, whose aims and activities are described elsewhere. It has also played a leading part in the attack on orthodox trade unionism since the 1930's.

Although the F.A.K. is in theory above or outside politics, its nationalistic orientation, its activities, its membership and its links with other organizations, give it an increasingly political tinge which does not represent the views of that minority of non-Nationalist Afrikaners who still belong to some of its affiliated societies. It has been claimed that the F.A.K. is a direct creation of the Broederbond, in which case there can be little doubt about its basic political affiliations. This is partly borne out by the fact that one of F.A.K.'s founders, Professor J. C. van Rooy of Potchefstroom, who was chairman of F.A.K. from 1941 to 1951, was chairman of the Broederbond during the same period.

In the present climate of Afrikaner nationalism, however, it is increasingly difficult for an individual to be a good Afrikaner or for an association to pursue truly Afrikaans aims without being associated with the tenets of the political party that claims to be the only political representative of Afrikanerdom.

CHAPTER EIGHT

BOERS AND AFRIKANERS

'In the long quietude of the eighteenth century the Boer race was formed. In the vast unmysterious thirsty landscape of the interior lay the true centre of South African settlement. When the trek-boers entered it with their flocks and tented wagons they left the currents of European life and lost the economic habits of the nations from which they had sprung. Though they never became true nomads, the mark of nomadism was upon them, and their dominant traits were those of a restless and narrow existence . . . their life gave them a tenacity of purpose, a power of silent endurance, and the keenest self-respect. But this isolation sank into their character, causing their imagination to lie fallow and their intellect to become inert. Their virtues had their obverse qualities as well. Their tenacity could degenerate into obstinacy, their power of endurance into resistance to innovation, and their self-respect into suspicion of the foreigner and contempt for their inferiors. For want of formal education and sufficient pastors, they read their Bibles intensively, drawing from the Old Testament, which spoke the authentic language of their lives, a justification of themselves, of their beliefs and their habits.'

(C. de Kiewiet, *A History of South Africa*, p. 17).

'Virile, resolute, passionate, with a passion hid far below the surface, they are at once the gentlest and most determined of peoples. Under the rough exterior of the up-country Boer lies a nature strangely sensitive and conscious of a personal dignity; a people who never forget a kindness and do not easily forget a wrong.'

(Olive Schreiner).

THE first recorded use of the term 'Afrikaner'[1] was in 1705. The affirmation 'I am an Afrikaner' was made, significantly enough, by a Huguenot settler called Bibault. For it was the Huguenots far more than the early Dutch

---

[1] 'Afrikander' in the older spelling.

settlers who regarded Africa as their only future home, and who stamped the Boer race with their own religious fanaticism and craving for freedom.

At that time the words meant an attitude of mind, a rejection of Europe and an acceptance of Africa as the homeland. It did not involve a separate language, an exclusive culture or a group consciousnesss other than that of colonists against officials. Still less did it involve the trappings and symbols of modern nationalism. From the start, however, the term Afrikaner meant a Christian, and increasingly it came to mean a white man. Nevertheless, it did not become a universal term until the breakdown of the old homogeneous rural society and the self-conscious period of nationalist revival in recent decades.

In early days the preferred term was 'Burger', as opposed to officials or soldiery. This passed over into 'Boer' on the frontier, when the frontiersmen began to feel aloof from government and civic ties. 'Burger' returned in the republics as a particular function of the Boer, but, as Sarah Gertrude Millin writes: '. . . if one speaks to men who fought the Boer war . . . they say wistfully that of all names they have borne or could think of, they love best the homely name . . . under which they fought for their freedom'.

A song by C. F. Visser called 'O Boereplaas' expresses these late nineteenth century values, concerned with the boereplaas or farm and the mother-tongue. In general, the songs and references of this earlier period stress the Boerevolk, the Boeretaal, the Boer way of life and the national beauties of the homeland. It was only with military defeat and increasing urbanization that the fatherland came to be more closely identified with a lost social and political system.

Of the three terms, 'Burger' was the name of a class or category, 'Boer' became the name of a homogeneous land-owning people, but 'Afrikaner' really came into its own when that people began to leave the land and to think in terms of nationality or even of nationalism. The concept of nationality is here defined, with MacIver, as 'a type of community sentiment, a sense of belonging together, created by historical circumstances and supported by common spiritual possessions, of such an extent and so strong that those who feel it desire to have a common government peculiarly or exclusively their own . . . In another form the sentiment of nationality turns into nationalism, an attitude of profound import for good or for evil in the modern world. Nationalism is the spirit which seeks to make the nation an effective unity'.

At the outset, 'Afrikaner' was not so exclusive a term as it was later to become. Jan Hofmeyr and Hertzog would have equated it with 'South African'. They included in it all whites who regarded South Africa as their home and object of primary loyalty. Botha and Smuts thought in terms of a 'single stream' or 'whole' nation of Boers and Britons; Hertzog believed that a 'whole' nation could only be built out of two whole and complementary groups, South Africans and Suid-Afrikaners. Incidentally, the most tolerant thinkers never considered the possibility of including the other 'nation', the millions of Africans and other non-whites.[1] More liberal members of the English-speaking group, who call themselves South Africans, might tolerate the use of 'African' for the black man. To the Afrikaner, however, the black man was a Kaffir, a Native or, amongst more gently-spoken intellectuals, a Bantu; he could never be an 'African' or 'Afrikaner'. Race purity and a high regard for it were increasingly demanded of the 'ware Afrikaner'. 'White blood' was invested with mystic properties. A writer in the *Cultural History of the Afrikaner* calls it 'the bearer of the Christian West-European life-content (lewensinhoud) and civilization form', while the South African Blood Transfusion Service has to pander to white prejudice by reserving blood from non-white donors for non-white patients.

Gradually the voice of those Afrikaners who wished to equate Volk and Nation and to exclude all non-Afrikaner or volksvreemde elements began to prevail. Afrikanerism became equated not only with whiteness, the language and the Calvinist faith, but with a political creed. Not only did Afrikanerdom

---

[1] At the opening of the Van Riebeeck Festival in 1952 Dr. Malan began by referring to the broader nationhood of a multi-racial state, but later sections of his speech showed that he was in fact limiting its application to the white population.

lose much of its old capacity to absorb outsiders, but it began to look for alien elements within. In turn, national-minded Afrikanerdom extruded the 'loyal Dutch', the collaborationist Handsoppers, and the one-stream holists. Now it is in the process of converting or excluding the moderate two-stream Nationalists.

The national-minded Afrikaner has equated Nation and Volk to the extent that there is an increasing number of Afrikaners who despite all traditional cultural links are excluded from Volk-membership on political grounds. These non-national Afrikaners have incidentally suffered a twofold rejection, for many of their English-speaking political allies accept the Nationalist usurpation of Afrikanerdom and regard all Afrikaners with increasing distrust.

The impetus of continued victory has carried national-minded Afrikanerdom from the egalitarian aspirations and the unforced sense of unity of Anglo-Boer War days to the aggressive exclusiveness and regimented uniformity of so many twentieth-century nationalist movements. The exclusiveness is accentuated by the fact that Afrikanerdom has to share its living-space with another white minority group linked to a world culture, and with a majority group of non-whites of an alien culture, in whom the seeds of nationalism are already quickening. Group unity is therefore threatened both culturally and demographically from without. From within it has for several decades been endangered by the great social and economic revolution which smashed the old Boer way of life and created an Afrikaner urban proletariat.

In the increasing complexity and differentiation of the Western socio-economic structure, man's need for group unity has led him to a sense of nationality. Where groups lived in subjection to or were threatened by other groups, this sense of nationality crystallized into nationalism, the demand for national unity and autonomy.

Afrikaner nationalism was borne out of the bitterness of defeat, and the fear of engulfment. It grew and flourished in a climate of economic insecurity and social and cultural frustration. It was deliberately cultivated by a rising intelligentsia who

rewrote the peoples' myths and refurbished their symbols to suit
the needs of a changing world. The nation was even endowed
with a national soul, which made its care fall within the province of the predikants. As Dr. Theo Wassenaar wrote in a
special song for the 1938 centenary celebrations: 'God has decreed that we should be a nation, a nation with its own language
and soul and will and spirit.'[1]

Science has on occasion been called in to buttress the Old
Testament basis of many group myths. On the whole, however,
science and liberal rationalism are regarded as threats to the
Afrikaner nation and its traditional values. In the selection of
traditional elements that would help to maintain national unity,
considerable realism has been shown. There has however been
an irrational aspect which seems to have much in common with
Ralph Linton's account of magical forms of nativistic movement. In these, he says: 'Moribund elements of culture are not
revived for their own sake or in anticipation of practical advantages from the elements themselves. Their revival is part of a
magical formula designed to modify the society's environment
in ways which will be favourable to it. The society's members
feel that by behaving as their ancestors did they will, in some
usually undefined way, help to recreate the total situation in
which the ancestors lived'.

Behind such reactions are deep-seated fear and insecurity,
which are perhaps the dominant motifs of Afrikaner attitudes
and behaviour today. This fear and insecurity are manifested in
a whole set of responses which show an increasing degree of
aggressiveness, some avoidance, or refusal to accept reality, and
a very low capacity for accommodation to the total situation.
Aggressiveness has from the beginning been a primary response
amongst the Boers, and one generally approved by the group—
amongst whom behaviour is in general characterized by direct-
ness and emotionalism.

---

[1]The Afrikaner nation was not only endowed with a national soul, but
with specific physical attributes. As recently as 1951, a speaker informed the
Science Congress in Durban that: 'The foot of the Afrikaner is distinctly
different from the English foot in length, the joint girth, and the cleavages
and furrows of the sole . . .'

Generalizations about group or national attitudes and traits are in the present stage of socio-psychological inquiry an alluring but highly dangerous pastime. The writer in fact is likely to reveal as much indirectly about himself as about the group he is attempting to describe. It is however possible with Professor Ginsburg to accept the existence of a group or national character, conditioned, he suggests, by special selection and heredity, by historical occurrences and traditions, by institutions, group pressure and selection climate; and possibly even by genetic factors, although little is yet known in this field. To these factors one should perhaps add that of the outside environment, whether natural or human.

To describe such a national character, however, three points must be borne in mind. Firstly, a group character exists not as a totality but as a set of traits shared by the majority of individuals within the group. Secondly, group character is not handed down once for all from on high, *pace* the Calvinist proposition to that effect, but is always in the making. One has only to read the accounts of the English as viewed by foreign observers at various periods of history to realize that groups like everything else are in a state of flux. And finally, social differentiation may emphasize certain rôles and traits and so lead to the creation of sub-group characters. For instance, the traits that are generally ascribed to the Polish nation were in fact typical of the szlachta or nobility of pre-Partition days. These traits survived to some extent in upper-class society until 1939 at least, but they were by no means the dominating characteristics of the large peasant class at any time.

The frontier and Republican Boers were particularly well situated for the development and perpetuation of a distinctive group character. The group consisted of individuals with a similar social and cultural heritage; they were undifferentiated in occupation and were living in isolation from the rest of the civilized world.

Such a group might take a skeletal social and cultural framework with it into the wilderness, but most of its values would be rapidly modified or even superseded under the impact of the new environment. And the difference in environment was that between the neat, fertile, crowded lands of Holland or North Germany and the empty, arid sweep of veld and mountain, where hostile natives lurked; a difference comparable, in the cultural context, to that between Nederlands and the new language, Afrikaans.

Where the Boer group was concerned the change was hastened by the fact that they never fully dominated their natural environment, but accommodated themselves to its demands and limitations just as the black Africans had done before them. Their human environment on the other hand evoked different responses; fear of, and aggressiveness towards, the non-whites, and apprehension and avoidance of the British who periodically followed them up and reasserted their suzerainty.

The Boer was born in the isolation of the veld and out of the turmoil and danger of the expanding frontier. But the pattern of his growth down the generations was conditioned by one trait which was not shed but rather strengthened after the colonists' rejection of Europe—his rigid fundamentalist piety. This led him to regulate his life by the precepts of the Bible, which was as much a part of his equipment as his roer or gun. The Old Testament in particular described similar experiences, and the story of the Israelites encouraged a rough law-abidingness and that belief in vocation in which the Calvinist doctrine of the elect had already inculcated.

In the recently published *Cultural History of the Afrikaner* Professor R. W. Wilcocks described the traits of the 'ware Afrikaner' thus: fondness for order; respect for law and moral precepts; devoutness in his life and in his general outlook; conservative disposition; a strong spirit of freedom and individualism; self-reliance; hospitality; a certain wanderlust or trekgees (not universal); isolationism and quarrelsomeness; a lack of co-operative spirit; self-sufficiency; and personal dignity.

These are the traits that strike the reader of Boer social history or the visitor to isolated parts of the countryside today. In 1856, Mrs. Andrew Murray wrote of the Ceres Boers: 'The manners and customs of the people amused me much, all sitting down together servants and all. But they are very kind and hospitable, and reminded me of the Scotch, a strong sensible, rather slow people, with a great reverence for religion, a great idea of Church-going and psalm singing but ignorant and prejudiced. Still there is a good foundation of common sense to work on'. These traits are not however so apparent amongst the demoralized rural poor, the urbanized Afrikaner proletariat, nor the growing commercial middle-class.

Out of distance and social equality came the traditional freedom-loving independence, self-reliance, conservatism and hospitality of the Boers. Independence could on occasion veer over into egocentrism, factiousness, aversion to all discipline, restlessness and lack of co-operativeness. As the Boers said of themselves: 'Elkeen wou baas en niemand Klaas wees nie'. ('Each wanted to be boss, but nobody the servant'). Self-reliance could generate self-satisfaction, which in turn could sap initiative. Conservatism was a natural development of the slow pastoral rhythm, the lack of formal education or outside cultural contacts, and the felt need to preserve group identity. It could at times degenerate into obstinacy, prejudice, exclusiveness and ancestor-worship.

Other Boer traits were conditioned less by the natural than by the human environment, and these were to prove more deep-seated and permanent. Almost without exception, Boer contacts with other peoples have served to evoke uneasiness and fear, however much these fundamental responses might be masked by superficial aggressiveness.

In Boer contacts with the African, fear has been the underlying reaction from the start. It was born on the frontier and sustained by the endless wars and campaigns of the nineteenth century. It persisted on the eroded veld and in the towns, wherever the impoverished Boer sank helplessly down to the economic and even social level of the unskilled African labourer. Today it has flared again with the rise of black African states and such anti-white movements as Mau Mau. The old fear of cultural and physical swamping in a vast black sea has revived anew, reinforced by an increasing fear of revenge on the part of the black man. This fear was stated in its simplest form by a correspondent to *Die Volksblad* in April 1955. The letter called upon the Minister of Defence to supply all burgers of 16 and over with rifles and about 1,000 cartridges, 'not only for protection against assaults' but because 'the country needs it in the present crisis. Who knows what is still awaiting us?'

To allay their early fears, the Boers first conquered the African tribes, then reduced them to a permanently inferior status. For a few decades this sufficed to blunt the sharp edge of fear and hatred, and many Boers came to treat their Kaffirs with the same kindly condescension they showed towards their coloured servants, in fact as a father treats a rather backward and permanently immature child. Afrikaners still like to compare their own master-servant relationships with those of the English-speaking group, to the latter's detriment. Just over four years ago *Die Burger*'s political correspondent produced a self-righteous 'Blanket-Basuto's version of the difference between Afrikaner and Briton':

'You walk to the Afrikaner's house . . . and you knock carefully on the kitchen door. The baas comes out and shouts: "What you want"! You say what you want and he says what he wants. Everything is clear and done. You know where you stand. Then he shouts: "Wait there"! and then he goes inside and comes out with a mug of coffee, and he shouts: "There, take it"! If you go to the Briton's house then you knock on the front door. He lets you in, says what a fine fellow you are, and you talk in the drawing-room. You get nothing that you wanted, not even the coffee. You are just where you were when you came. He lets you out with a friendly word, and when you are off the step he throws the drawing-room window open for fresh air and says: "Phew"!'

Today the old frontier fears are back in full. But this time the African is a part, though unacknowledged, of the total society, and there is no more land. As Mr. N. C. Havenga said in 1951: 'When we think that we are a small white community of only two million, five hundred thousand, there must be a doubt whether we can maintain our position. As far as the Afrikaners are concerned, we cannot get out. We in South Africa dare not adopt a policy that would make it possible for us to be driven out, because we—the Afrikaners—have no other home in which we can take refuge . . . The other section of the white population (i.e. the English-speaking section) will also have to stand with us, if the Europeans are to maintain their place.'

Prolonged and intimate contact with the African has given the Boer his fear complex. It has also conditioned him in other ways. It has caused him to lower his standards of efficiency, and to accept beliefs which are superstitious in Christian eyes; it has given him an approved outlet for aggressiveness, thereby encouraging arbitrariness, violence and lack of control; and it has set up an inner conflict, usually unadmitted, by virtue of its incompatibility with the egalitarian and Christian values which the Boer has so long accepted for himself.

Boer and Afrikaner attitudes to other non-whites whom they have had no physical reason to fear, have been increasingly marked by a dichotomizing tendency to classify all the country's inhabitants as white or non-white. More indirectly, however, fear has characterized Afrikaner responses to both Coloureds and Indians. In the former case the Afrikaans-speaking and Christian Coloured group by their very origin and existence represent a threat to the purity of the white race. Most cases of race-mixing have, after all, occurred between white and light-coloured people. Furthermore, many Coloureds and Indians threaten the stereotype of the simple child-like non-white by virtue of their cultural level, and, in the case of the Indian, by their economic achievements. Recently, too, the despised South African 'Coolies' have acquired the backing of a powerful and verbally aggressive 'father-land', whose very existence threatens the whole set of values supporting white baasskap.

Boer contacts with other whites have not been so intimate as they have been with the non-white peoples. The group that has exerted most formative influence on the Boer has been the British group. Until recently the underlying motif of all Boer responses to the self-assured Briton and his world culture has been a feeling of insecurity, although this might often combined with an uneasy respect and admiration. This insecurity bred frustration, suspiciousness, a feeling of inferiority and what might be described as the 'porpoise close behind me' mentality. Turn where they might, in Natal or the Transvaal, the Boers soon found the long British arm reaching out after them.

The Anglo-Boer War came to be seen as the crowning act in a series of gratuitous attacks by Imperialist Britain. The effect was augmented by its aftermath of humiliation, bereavement, devastation and impoverishment, and above all, like the War Between the States, by its destruction of the Boer way of life. During this period the apprehension swelled into actual fear, fear that the nation would be physically destroyed in the concentration camps. The Anglo-Boer War was followed by what the Afrikaner viewed as his economic subjection to English-dominated industrial and commercial interests. This subjection evoked the deliberately-inspired Economic Movement described in an earlier chapter.

This feeling of insecurity in the economic field still persists, despite the growing strength of Afrikaner-owned commerce and industry. It persists despite the virtually total victory of Nationalist Afrikanerdom in the political field. Even in the latter, the aggressive truculence of the victorious Nationalists often imperfectly masks a lurking uncertainty and apprehension. This is one of the motives behind the incessant cry for a republic. In addition to being a part of the Trekker tradition, a republic would make it possible to cut the English-speaking South African's ties with his ruler and former homeland overseas. In republican isolation, the English South Africans might, it is hoped, become gradually Afrikanerized.

Such a development would bring a much-needed reinforcement into the ranks of white Afrikanerdom. It would also avert a trend that has been greatly disturbing national-minded leaders. For so far there has been a far greater tendency for Afrikaners to become anglicized, than for the English-speaking to be Afrikanerized. All through Afrikaner history there have been constant defections from the national-minded core. These defections have either been total or partial. Under the latter heading come Botha and Smuts, who, according to Professor Scholtz, worked for anglicization and co-operation with the British on the basis laid down by the latter.

There is no doubt that the world-wide culture and institutions of the English have exerted a powerful influence and even fascination over Afrikaners, and not the least gifted and able of them. National-minded Afrikaners often admit the beauty of the language, but many of them were in youth at least conditioned to regard learning it as a betrayal of the people, whose own language and freedom the 'Brit' had so often tried to destroy.

For generations, some Afrikaners have been fascinated by the scope and maturity of English culture *per se*, and the opportunities it afforded to escape from the increasing constraint of the Boer laager to a wider world. These Afrikaners have come under intensifying fire as traitors to the Volk. W. J. B. Pienaar, writing in the *Cultural History of the Afrikaner*, gives a colourful description of the early version of this type, the Orangeman, as seen by the national-minded today: 'A dwarf-spirited volk-bastard who is faintly explicable from a scientific point of view as the illegitimate victim of Dutch-mania and Dutch-Afrikaner anglicization. He is anti-French and extravagantly pro-English; an unnational phenomenon, who shamelessly joins up with the authorities against his own people . . .'

Other Afrikaners have accepted the British way of life for the sake of economic advantage or for such personal reasons as marriage into the group. Apart from such overt defections national-minded leaders have come to realize that Afrikanerdom faces an even subtler and more profound threat to its identity from within. An official of the F.A.K. told the writer that, in his view, the phase of the struggle against anglicization from without was over, but the struggle against the enemy within had begun. Non-Afrikaner values based on the English and American urban way of life are, in fact, infiltrating Afrikaner society through the radio, the cinema and the popular press. In most cases this is happening through the medium of the Afrikaans language itself.

A Dutch observer, Professor A. J. Barnouw, wrote in 1934 in *Language and Racial Problems in South Africa*; 'The effect of this anglicizing process is a strange anomaly, of which the Afrikaners themselves are apparently unaware. Their outlook on life, their conceptions of a world abroad, their methods of government and business administration, their ideals of sportsmanship, even their manners in forms of social intercourse, bear the trademark "made in England".' This passage was written before the Nationalist-inspired cultural and economic movements had time to take effect. It can, however, be said that Afrikaner-English relations still remain at their closest in the field of sport.

The national-minded Afrikaner's feeling of intellectual frustration in the face of a dominant culture has been intensified by the patronizing and at times grossly arrogant and hurtful attitude of many British and English-speaking South Africans. This attitude was particularly prevalent in earlier days, although it has, since the armed co-operation of both language groups in the last war and the Nationalist political victories, died away in all but a few die-hard bastions. There are, however, some signs of a revival of jingoistic attitudes as a result of the growing feeling of impotent resentment amongst English-speaking South Africans over Nationalist aggressiveness.

The Boers of the Cape were exposed to well over a century of such attitudes. During the first British occupation, Lady Anne Barnard wrote to Henry Dundas: 'We are both very civil and never despise anybody, which I can perceive as being one great error in some of the English'. Seventy years later Andrew Murray's wife described the English in Bloemfontein as 'an unprincipled violent set, with a contempt of the Dutch most irritating, and I am sorry to say their clergyman, to say the least, has acted very foolishly, omitting in the Church service the prayers for the President . . . Through anonymous letters the English have threatened Mr. Boshof's life'. A letter published in the *Eastern Star* of 15th April, 1879, and signed 'John Bull', furnishes an instance of the violent hostilities which were current and openly expressed at this period:

'Who . . . would live in a district . . . inhabited by cowardly, traitorous, yet boasting and senseless Dutch Boers who, although traitors at heart and openly avowing their anti-English feeling and hatred of the Queen's Government, are nevertheless allowed all the privileges and rights of loyal English subjects . . .? I repeat, Mr. Editor, who would remain a day to consort with such brutes, if he could possibly avoid it? . . . I would not for one—and should I afterwards hear, that these hounds, too cowardly to fight for themselves, and too un-manly and ungrateful to thank the English, who have hitherto fought for them had all been cut up and massacred by the natives, I could feel no pity for them . . . It would indeed be a bright day for the Cape if every Dutch Boer was driven out of it, or even if they were deprived of their privileges and treated as the wretched, disloyal, ungrateful foreigners they really are?'

Of a more recent period Sarah Gertrude Millin writes: 'There was a time when the Englishman who came to South Africa completely changed his character so that his nationality stuck out of him like the quills of a porcupine. He lost the smooth and genial charm of the Englishman at home and dis-ported himself with an assertiveness that not only emphasized the difference between himself and the man he called a Colonial, but that was haughtily meant to emphasize this difference'. Many Afrikaners would, in fact, acquiesce in the description of the English given by Augustine Birrell in *Res Judicatae*; 'No foreigner needs to ask the nationality of the man who treads on his corns, smiles at his religion and does not want to know anything about his aspirations'.

Social slights and pricks are at least as important as economic or political discrimination. They also tend to leave a deeper scar on the memory than the many gestures of friendship, such as the Trust set up some years ago under the will of Sir Abe Bailey; its aim was to further South African national unity by such measures as fostering in each group a fluent knowledge of the other official language, through bilingual holiday camps and exchange holiday schemes. It may be that such things as the superior references to the Boer 'patois' or 'kitchen Dutch', harsh jokes about 'Japies' and 'back-veld Boers' and the black-balling of eminent Afrikaners whose names were put up for 'English' clubs, were as much responsible as any other factors for the insecurity that caused the Boer to fight and stimulated Afrikaner Nationalism in the political, economic and cultural fields.

Another factor, and one which is still operative, is the stream of criticism, some of it informed, but much of it superficial, subjective, patronizing and at times even misinformed, that pours out from Britain against the attitudes and the policies of Afrikaner Nationalism. This is felt to be a continuation of the old colonial attitude, and an infringement of the Union's independent status. Such criticism is particularly resented when it comes from English-speaking South Africans. In this case it is taken as an indication that they are not truly South African in feeling.

Afrikaner Nationalism has, over the last two years, moved over from defence to aggression against the English-speaking South African on his own ground. Nationalist Afrikanerdom had come a long way from the equal comradeship for which Jan Celliers pleaded half a century ago in his poem 'Afrikaner-Boer aan Afrikaner-Brit.'

> 'And honour in me what highest stands with you,
> Only thus will, strong and proud,
> Our southern home be built on unifying rock.
> When two hard heads come together, in neighbourly love
> and work,
> Then shall we two be strong against the world, indeed.'

This poem acknowledged a relationship which persists to this day under the surface—the Afrikaners' need of and dependency on the South African and overseas English, who are in the last resort their only real champions in the outside world. Today however, overt national-minded attitudes towards the 'Brit' range from the malicious bullying of the rank-and-file 'rooinek'-baiters to the political group sport of twisting the old lion's tail. On a higher plane, these attitudes have, in view of the need for white unity in place of the black danger, been modified from the crude exclusiveness of the Draft Republican Constitution and Ossewa-Brandwag days. They now take the form of such demands as that made by Dr. Malan in 1951: 'The South African nation we want must not only consist of one race, it must consist of two races speaking two languages. It must be a nation where the English-speaking section, like the Afrikaans-speaking section, must be national in marrow and bone and stand by the principle of South Africa first—in theory and in practice.'

The same demand was later stated at greater length by Professor L. J. du Plessis of Potchefstroom in *Koers*. He wrote: 'I would like to see them (the English-speaking South Africans, or, as Professor du Plessis prefers to call them, English-speaking Afrikaners) wholly absorbed by Afrikanerdom, and not merely absorbed politically into South Africa. This cultural absorption I desire, because I consider an inner union or unification necessary for the maintenance of our civilization in Southern Africa, and because I see Afrikanerdom as the bearer of that civilization, not in South Africa alone, but also further northwards . . . This attitude naturally implies that we must be prepared to enlarge our own "Afrikanership" in this respect, viz., in that we shall have to assimilate also the English-speaking Afrikaner's cultural heritage. This does not mean that we shall have to renounce the Dutch basis of our Afrikanerdom, but only that we are prepared further to enrich it with English blood and culture, as in the past it has already been enriched by it, as well as by German and French and other elements. Personally I am perfectly ready to do this because for me Afrikanerdom is no static conception, but dynamic and expansive. In this connexion I visualize an enrichment of Afrikanerdom similar to that undergone by the English themselves, when, with an Anglo-Saxon background, they assimilated the culture of their Norman conquerors and yet remained Anglo-Saxon in essence . . . For the Europeans in Southern Africa, I see a future with one nationhood or people . . . namely a broadened or rather enriched Afrikanerdom. And within this Afrikanerdom I see, in the political sense, a South African nation, a Rhodesian nation, etc. . . . Furthermore, beside white Afrikanerdom I see in the future various Coloured peoples, progressively developing into separate and independent nations. And finally I see, amongst various national states thus developed, in the distant future, a political federation of the whole of southern Africa, based on the foundation of Afrikanerdom's racial policy and way of life.'

The full significance of Professor du Plessis' urbanely phrased 'Come into my parlour' thesis is brought out by Professor Arthur Keppel-Jones in 'Friends or Foes?' This work is a plea for the substitution of a federal system for the present unitary system prevailing in South Africa. He writes: 'The object of the nationally-minded Afrikaners is to make the state itself the organ of their nationality. There is no room for any other nationality in it. Since the non-Europeans are not thought of as potential Afrikaners, they must be excluded from citizenship. The English, who already have citizen rights, must be absorbed. There is no talk of allowing *them* to 'develop along their own lines' in 'their own areas' . . . Since the State is a unit, the nation must be homogeneous, which means that it must be Afrikaner. Since the Nationalists reject the Monarchy, the English must become Republicans.'

In the next chapter, he writes: 'We of British stock who were born and bred in this country are South Africans as surely as anyone else . . . South Africa is our country, and we love it and we have grown up with the idea of serving it. The only thing that can kill this spirit is an attempt to turn us into Afrikaners. It is not that we feel a special antipathy to Afrikaners. It is merely that whatever contribution we make for the good of South Africa and the world must be our own contribution, derived from our own history and tradition and arising spontaneously in our own breasts. We will not wear the cast-off clothes of another man.'

The other white groups with which the Afrikaner has principally come into contact are the Hollanders, the Germans, and the Jews. In no case however has one of these groups exerted any direct influence on the Afrikaner people comparable to that of the English-speaking group.

The Dutch links are by far the most important, but they were formally cut after 1806, and even before that on the frontier. Hollanders occupied influential posts in the Church, schools and civil service in the Transvaal, but were as widely disliked for what the Boers regarded as their supercilious sophistication and liberal views as the mainland French have often been in Quebec. The mainland Dutch however gave the Boers strong emotional and economic support during the Anglo-Boer war.

Close cultural links have persisted between Holland and the Union. There is now a Chair of Afrikaans literature at the

Dutch University of Amsterdam, while most South African universities, English or Afrikaans-speaking, have Chairs of Nederlands and Afrikaans. The two languages have however moved sufficiently far apart for the Afrikaner man in the street to have difficulty in following High Dutch. There is now no feeling amongst Afrikaners towards Holland as a mother country, and indeed during World War II Nazi sympathies led some national-minded Afrikaners to represent the German invasion and devastation of Holland as a just retribution for her support of the English and godless ways. This attitude was counter-balanced to some extent by such gestures as the building of a home in Holland for Dutch war orphans, and the collection of money to help the flood-damaged areas of Holland in 1953, both organized by the F.A.K.

For their part, the modern Dutch do not appear to feel more than a vague cousinly feeling towards Afrikaners. Those who come to live in the Union often gravitate towards the English-speaking group, whether because many are Catholic or because they find English cultural life more congenial and 'European', or perhaps because they feel bitter about the recent pro-German views and activities of some Afrikaners.

The relationship between Germans and Afrikaners is of a different type. There is a certain feeling of kinship because of the large proportion of Germans who helped constitute the original Boer group. There are similarities of culture and language, but these are far less strong than in the case of the Dutch, despite the number of national-minded Afrikaners who have received their higher education at German universities.

The main bond between Germans and Afrikaners is however a political one. In the old Transvaal, German advisers taught the President and the burgers to look to Germany for help against Britain. Despite the Kaiser's failure to give such help during the Anglo-Boer War, many national-minded Afrikaners became pro-German in the First World War because Germany was the great enemy of Britain and must therefore be their friend. Between the two World Wars National Socialism left its mark on Afrikaner youth and kept the pro-German feeling alive. Today the Germans are at the top of the list of desirable immigrants into the Union. A faint note of disillusionment has however been perceptible of late. As in the Dutch case, some Germans seem to prefer the English-speaking group, while others adopt a critical and superior attitude towards the Afrikaner way of life.

Jewish history and mores, as recorded in the Old Testament, have had a profound influence on the Boers. The present-day descendants of the Israelites have however on the whole served only to provide Afrikaner Nationalism with a two-headed scape-goat. On the one side the Jew has figured as a Kaffir-loving, communistic trade-union organizer or intellectual; on the other the cartoon figure of Hoggenheimer has for decades been the symbol of the bloated foreign capitalist who trod poor Afri-kaners down in their thousands.

Prior to that, however, the Jew had been an accepted though separate part of Boer rural life, performing the rôles of pedlar, shopkeeper and hotel-keeper that the Boer himself found un-congenial. At this period the Jews were still regarded as God's Chosen People, and the Voortrekkers therefore felt some kind of spiritual kinship with them, and received them kindly. The Jewish children learned to speak Afrikaans and some Jews even married Boer women. One such case was Michael Welensky, father of Sir Roy Welensky. Soon, however, Jews began to make their mark in and finally even to dominate the business world and professions. Their numbers rose to well over 4 per cent of the white population. Because of the persecution of their race they had more liberal ideas on the colour question, and they gravitated more and more towards the English-speaking group. Their votes were almost invariably cast against Afrikaner Nationalism, particularly during the later career of the cham-pion of Israel, General Smuts.

Nationalist Afrikanerdom reacted against the Jewish group with a Quota Act, with a ban on their membership of the Nationalist Party in the Transvaal, and, in the 1930's and 1940's, with a Nazi-influenced campaign of vituperation and race hatred. Dr. Verwoerd, then Professor of Applied Psycho-logy at Stellenbosch, joined five other Nationalist professors in a strongly-worded protest against the admittance of Jewish refugees to South Africa; the Dutch Reformed Church Synod at Bloemfontein decided by sixty-four to sixty-one votes that the Jews were not, after all, God's Chosen People; while Dr. Malan accused the Jews of disruptive activities in the trade unions, and called for a Nordic Front to oppose growing Jewish immigration; in 1940 he declared that Smuts had turned South Africa into a 'Jewish-Imperialistic war machine'.

As late as 1946, the present Minister for Economic Affairs, Mr. Eric Louw wrote: 'If the Jews can manage to find a country of their own anywhere, we shall certainly place no difficulties in the way, provided that country is not too near to South Africa! If any of South Africa's surplus Jews wish to go there, our best wishes will accompany them. I hope they will be so happy and successful there that they will never want to come back to South Africa again! We want to build up a population here who know only one loyalty: loyalty to South Africa and to the interests of our country. And this also concerns the English-speaking people in our country'.

Apart from the Jewish group's economic success, their dual loyalty and religious exclusiveness are both likely to offend an aggressive nationalist movement. On the other hand, there has of later years been a certain rapprochement between the Nationalist rulers in South Africa and the new State of Israel, in the building of which South African Jews are playing a conspicuous part. Doctor Malan toured Israel and even had his name inscribed in the Golden Book of the Zionist World Organization, as a token of appreciation, it was said, for the active sympathy shown by his Government to Israel. A party of Dutch Reformed Church predikants, who visited Israel in 1953, were impressed with the strong national feeling in that country. Somewhat significantly, they were also impressed with the results already achieved by Israel by means of a vast master plan intended to affect the whole land and the whole people.

* * * * *

The Boer character was formed in the isolation of the veld and amidst the insecurity and turbulence of the expanding frontier. Then it was a true group character. Today, it has become an ideal. This ideal is constantly being held up to Afrikaner miners, clerks and factory workers, by their predikants, their teachers and their political leaders as the only fitting set of traits for a 'ware Afrikaner' to display.

When Nationalist leaders find such exhortation necessary, it is reasonable to infer that they have noticed serious and widespread back-sliding. Indeed, the predikants and writers often admit this themselves, although they are usually the victims of their own myth-making and will never admit that the lapse represents a permanent change. In February 1955, an editorial appeared in *Die Transvaler* in answer to a defence of the English-speaking section's contribution to the country by the Johannesburg *Star*. This editorial defined the basic elements of love of country: 'A love (of country) which is based on material things is no true love. The true love goes out to the call of the partridge in the early morning, to a pomegranate hedge, to a little pool in the Karoo, a rainbow, a plain in the blazing sun, a farmer or a worker with calloused hands, or the lamenting coloured folk at a white burial. Can drills and hooters, blocks of flats, smoking chimneys and mineshafts, swimming pools, cocktails and dance floors ever weigh against the silence of the bush, the night-sounds of the veld, or the stars?'

Yet it is hardly possible that a group which has experienced so great a social and economic revolution, which has been dragged from the seventeenth to the twentieth century in a few decades, should for ever cherish this nostalgia or preserve an ethos linked with a nearly defunct way of life. The old frontier Boers shed much of their Huguenot and Dutch cultural paraphernalia when they moved into the interior. How then can a Poor White living next to a coloured family in a slum, or a miner in his neat suburban house, or a briskly efficient businessman, be expected to conform to the old patterns of thought and action, except nostalgically once a year, when they put on corduroys and veldskoene and drive in their second-hand jalopies or their glossy new American cars to attend the Ceremony of the Vow? In this situation, one might even expect to find that increasing social differentiation is leading to the formation of a number of new sub-group traits.

It is the traits that arose in the veld that have suffered most as a result of impoverishment, industrialization, the impact of urban values and the regimentation of education and communal life by national-minded leaders. The old independence and love of freedom have withered into an acceptance of authority, or have been distorted into a lust for power which increasingly denies freedom to others. Individualism which could in the veld shade over into egocentrism has now been transformed into ethnocentrism. The patriarchal or authoritarian principle has gradually triumphed over the libertarian one.

Hospitableness and personal dignity are waning traditions. Self-reliance has faded away under the pauperizing impact of relief schemes and sheltered labour policies. In the closer contacts of modern life there has been a considerable increase in co-operativeness, but a tendency to factiousness still persists in personal relations and political life. Under the impact of the outside world, conservatism has tended to rigidify into psychological isolationism, prejudice, worship of the past, and a refusal to compromise with or adjust to new ideas or situations.

The 'ware Afrikaner's' feeling for order and respect for moral precept has shown a tendency either to disappear, or to shrivel into an empty legalism without ethical content. Devoutness has shown greater staying power. In the country districts however it has often dulled into superstition or an almost Islamic fatalism, while in the towns it has tended to be submerged or partially diverted to such objects of worship as the Volk or Nation and its leaders, past or present. The 'Chosen People' complex of old days has degenerated into an uneasy Herrenvolkism. The worship of Calvin's stern God, which formerly supported the patriarchal authority of the father, an authority so common to pastoral, warlike and semi-nomadic societies, has now been diverted to worship of the leader principle.

The Afrikaner is no longer so close to the veld, but he still lives in close contact with the Africans and the English group. In these relationships there has been no significant change in the basic reactions of fear and insecurity, although overt behaviour is increasingly violent and aggressive towards both groups. National-minded Afrikaner aggressiveness towards the other white group is the understandable aftermath of political victory. Aggressiveness towards the African conceals a growing fear and hatred, and a usually unadmitted consciousness of guilt and expectation of revenge. It is accompanied in most Afrikaners' minds by a refusal to consider any change in the established relationship between the two groups. It should be noted here that this underlying fear of the African is continually being played upon by Nationalist speakers. It is in fact one of the main elements in maintaining national cohesion and unity.

Fear of the black man is a real and definite emotion. But the basic insecurity of national-minded Afrikaners in their new environment and in their new proximity to the rest of the world and its values has produced other and more amorphous bogies. Amongst these are Communists, liberals, the overseas press and above all the United Nations Organization, where coloured men may with impunity cast stones at white men. In general, national-minded Afrikaners today see themselves as a unique group proceeding along the path divinely determined for them and struggling to survive against the machinations of a mysterious set of malevolent outside forces. These forces, as a Govern-statement put it in 1953: 'are ever ready to besmirch South Africa . . . (and) pour forth a flood of propaganda based on ignorance, prejudice and hostility against the Union'.

The first reaction of many Nationalist Afrikaners to such a situation is one of avoidance, tempered with counter-aggressiveness for home consumption. The Afrikaners cannot as in the old days trek away physically from the hateful circumstances, but their political leaders can make such 'snook-cocking' gestures as walking out of UNO. In general, they can close their minds and pretend that the offending situation does not exist, or at least have any significance.

This hyper-sensitive 'all the world's against us' attitude serves to distract national-minded Afrikaners from a state of mind which is closely linked with it. This is a profound anxiety and pessimism about the future. It is a feeling that is rarely put into words, for it would involve facing bitter reality. When it is voiced, the responsibility for the approaching doom is transferred to the outside world, whose peoples are represented as having persistently misunderstood, besmirched, oppressed or humiliated the Afrikaner nation. And the statement of this anxiety has all too often the sound of a death-wish. Apartheid in all its forms is a last-ditch policy to save Afrikanerdom from being swamped in the black sea or overwhelmed by the world tide of liberalism that threatens it, but in their hearts many Nationalist Afrikaners do not believe that it will succeed. Rather than adapt or compromise, they are however prepared to go down before the black hordes in glorious sunset defeat, the last lonely champions of White Christian Civilization.

PART THREE

INTO THE FUTURE

CHAPTER NINE

HAS THE AFRIKANER A FUTURE?

'At this point in our history total apartheid appears to be no more than the dream of a Rip van Winkel.'
(Prof. B. B. Keet, *Suid Afrika Waarheen?*)

'When the principle of national liberty has been achieved, the true community inspiration of nationality is fulfilled, and nationality having become the basis of community must cease to be also its ideal.'
(MacIver, *Community*, p. 281.)

SINCE their rise to power, national-minded Afrikaners have been so engrossed with the past that their rare thoughts about the future constitute nothing more than an an extension of this past. This wishful thinking applies to the intellectuals who support total apartheid, as much as to the great majority who wish to perpetuate the prevailing forms of segregation and white baasskap. For what is total apartheid but an imagined return to the old Voortrekker days of co-existing Boer Republics and independent tribal territories?

Of recent years a few national-minded Afrikaners have switched their gaze from the hypnotic symbols of Nationalist Afrikanerdom to inspect the world around them in a more objective manner. One such man is Dr. G. D. Scholtz, the assistant editor of *Die Transvaler*, who in 1954 published an important book in Afrikaans, from whose title the heading of this final chapter is taken. Dr. Scholtz's hard-hitting jeremiads against isolationism, ignorance and complacency among his countrymen have found wide circulation amongst the more thoughtful national-minded Afrikaners.

His book is couched in a somewhat portentous and ethno-centric vein, which recalls the old joke told against themselves by another oppressed national group, the Poles. It concerns an Englishman, a Frenchman and a Pole who were asked to write a work about elephants. The Frenchman produced an elegantly written manuscript on *The Sex Life of the Elephant*; the English-man wrote a brief manual called *The Elephant and How to Shoot It*; while the Pole sent in a bulky work entitled *The Elephant and the Polish Question*.

In this somewhat self-conscious package, Dr. Scholtz has nevertheless succeeded in making his readers chew on a number of unpalatable facts, all of which are said to constitute a 'threat' to Afrikanerdom and an incitement to further national 'struggle'.

The writer points out that South Africa's fate has so far always been determined by outside factors, and that the twentieth technological revolution has made South African isolationalism even more of an impossibility than before. He points out too that despite the growing weakness and decay of Western Christian society, White South Africa needs both European cultural links and even Commonwealth membership to maintain her own culture and identity. On the African con-tinent, continues Dr. Scholtz, South Africa's frontiers are now the Mediterranean, the Red Sea and the Indian Ocean. Here White South Africa faces three rising forces—all hostile to her. They are:—black nationalism, Communism and Indian expansionism.

Within her own frontiers, writes Dr. Scholtz in the accents of doom, South Africa has to contend not only with social threats but with the great natural dangers of drought, desiccation and erosion. In the socio-economic field, Afrikaners are menaced spiritually and culturally by alien secular and urban values, by materialism, proletarianization, isolation and self-satisfaction; they are frustrated by their feeling of inferiority and resentment towards the English; and they are hampered by the legacy of the 'Kaffir work' attitude to manual labour, and by their con-sequent unwillingness to make sacrifices for the sake of the future.

In his analysis of the sombre circumstances which are likely to attend the Afrikaner's future, Dr. Scholtz is clear-sighted enough. It is when he proceeds to consider solutions that his gaze becomes blurred. For his solution is no more than the advocation of total apartheid, in the vague hope that this will satisfy not only non-white discontent within the Union but hostile criticism from outside. As for the Afrikaners themselves, Dr. Scholtz adjures their leaders to lead them back to the Church and their old ways, to prevent the growth of internal class-conflict, and to maintain contact with the best sources of Western culture.

The future of Afrikanerdom and indeed of all South Africa is, as Dr. Scholtz sees, primarily dependent on finding a peaceful solution to the colour problem. Any solution that is found has to satisfy not only the capacities and aspirations of the internal non-white population, but the pressure of outside opinion in a world in which the numerically dominant non-white peoples are playing an increasingly important rôle. Such a solution has also to conform to existing socio-economic and geographical facts, and should even have a certain ethical justification.

The Afrikaners who have faced up to the need for such a solution are not usually to be found within the ranks of the national-minded. They are to be found within the liberal-minded organizations, in inter-racial social welfare work, or scattered through the Commonwealth in voluntary exile. The great majority of national-minded intellectuals and churchmen have salved their own consciences by adopting the cry of 'total apartheid', despite its patent practical impossibility.

In January 1956, however, a lone voice came out of the centre of intellectual Calvinist Afrikanerdom—the voice of Dr. B. B. Keet of the Dutch Reformed Church Theological Seminary at Stellenbosch, one of the five translaters of the Afrikaans Bible. In a short and devastating book called *Whither South Africa?* he accepts a continuation of the present partial segregation as a temporary expedient, without permanent moral justification. Of total apartheid he says:

> Can one be blamed for coming to the conclusion that here is a pipe dream that seeks to solve the problem in the easiest way,

because it is an impossibility? The impossible is the easiest because no one needs to worry about it. He just dreams about it.

There was a time when barbarism and darkness of colour were synonymous, but that time is irrevocably past.

No matter how convinced we may be that our apartheid policy is in the interest of the coloured races, because it develops their independence, the fact remains that its consequences are always greater alienation and enmity . . .

We must acknowledge that in the end result colour has no essential significance in our human relations. The fight we must wage is not between black and white, but between barbarism and civilization, or, if you wish, between heathenism and Christendom.

The antithesis—black versus white—which in human relations is indeed ridiculous, must make way for the only antithesis that has any meaning, namely, that between good and evil, right and wrong, in which black and white are both concerned and stand shoulder to shoulder.

The fulfilment of our calling to bring evangelism to the non-whites and to act as their guardians has nothing to do with the colour of our skin. It certainly has to do with our existence as a Christian people, but whether it will please the Almighty to keep us white as a Christian people is another matter . . .

One swallow does not make a summer. It may be however that Dr. Keet's challenge will encourage other Afrikaner churchmen and intellectuals to peer through the rosy mists of total apartheid into a realistic future. Nevertheless, whatever its long-term consequences, any such development towards a more liberal approach would almost certainly decrease the direct influence of intellectual and Church circles in Nationalist politic life, while it would probably not filter down into the rank-and-file ministry, or teachers' training colleges, and thence to the younger generation, for many years to come, if at all.

The leaders of Nationalist Afrikanerdom came to power on a combination of anti-British chauvinism and white baasskap. The unpopularity of total apartheid among the Nationalist rank-and-file has become increasingly evident, and every measure instituted by Dr. Verwoerd in the direction of positive apartheid has been counter-balanced by another aimed at segregation with integration, or at more complete police control.

Positive apartheid is doled out in doses sufficient only to soothe national-minded Afrikaners whose consciences are not clear; to cause dissension amongst the non-white groups by favouring one above the other and creating sufficient opportunities for their more docile and co-operative members; and to produce a smoke-screen of achievement to foil outside criticism.

Amongst political leaders a different leaven is working, that of political realism and responsibility. First Malan and then Strijdom faced the fact that the electorate would not stand for total apartheid, with its attendant loss of cheap labour and lowered living standard. Outside the Union, Nationalist political leaders have begun to appraise the rising power of the non-white peoples. Willem van Heerden, editor of *Dagbreek*, said at the S.A.B.R.A. Conference in Port Elizabeth in January, 1956, a conference devoted to the theme of 'the Asiatic in Africa':

'The time has come for us to face up to the fact that white supremacy is fast disappearing in Africa, and that our approach to matters in this sphere must be modified accordingly. Unless we do this, tragedy may be nearer to our door than we think . . . All the signs indicate that the era of white authority is ending fast.'

In the same month, Mr. Strijdom said in Parliament that it was his policy to maintain and foster good relations with other States in Africa, including the Gold Coast and Nigeria. This attitude was supported by the retiring Chairman of S.A.B.R.A., Dr. Gerdener, at the Port Elizabeth Conference. He warned delegates to modify not only their ideas but their language, and to avoid such words as 'Coolie' when referring to Indians. It should be added here that two Indians who wished to attend the Conference were turned away by the management of the hotel where the Conference was held, an hotel in a predominantly English-speaking city; while the Executive Committee of S.A.B.R.A. failed to reach agreement on whether Non-European observers should be allowed to attend future Congresses.

At about the same time, the Minister of External Affairs, Mr. Eric Louw, who used to make considerable use of such epithets, as 'Kaffir' and 'Coolie', was quoted by *Die Burger* as saying that the Government had for a long time been considering

the matter of the accommodation of prominent Non-Europeans who visited the Union as delegates to international conferences: 'If South Africa wants to play a leading rôle in the
affairs of Africa, especially south of the Sahara, we will have to
make contact with the Non-European states.'

Such statements are justified by reference to the total apartheid policy, which calls for separate white and black states.
These statements are not however likely to have much effect on
the Indian or Nigerian Governments or to affect the ordinary
Union citizen directly for some time to come. Meanwhile,
Nationalist political leaders must, if they are to retain power,
study and follow the prejudices of the electorate, prejudices
which have often been either inculcated or deepened by the
earlier oratory of Nationalist leaders themselves.

Nationalist leaders now find themselves in a difficult situation. After the political victory of Afrikanerdom, they must
drive in triple harness an increasingly diversified electorate of
farmers, urban workers and entrepreneurs.

In the immediate future the Union's destiny lies with the
Nationalist Party. Great attention should therefore be paid to
the stresses and shifts to which a victorious political party that
aspires to represent a whole nation is subject. It is to the rising
influence of the entrepreneur group as much as to the fruits of
intellectual and spiritual unrest that optimistic observers of the
South African scene pin most of their hopes for the Union's
peaceful development. Enlightened self-interest amongst employers has certainly been a potent ally of Christian fervour in the
past development of liberal attitudes towards the colour problem.

Whether such economic motives will prove of any more consequence against the deep-rooted prejudices of rural and urban
workers than did the earlier attempts of the English-speaking
magnates and industrialists remains to be seen. Prestige usually
counts for as much in human life as financial advantage, and the
whiteness of the worker is at present usually more evident than
his working-class status. One thing however seems certain, that
neither Afrikaner farmers, nor urban workers, nor entrepreneurs
are in the mass willing to consider the implementation of total
apartheid, with its consequent loss of a cheap labour force and

of the status that the lowest white possesses in the presence of a permanently inferior non-white population.

It seems likely therefore that total apartheid will not form part of the foreseeable future in the Union. The pattern of development will therefore proceed on its customary lines of continued economic integration and social segregation, reinforced with increased police control. Such a development cannot continue indefinitely without provoking a series of non-white explosions. It is difficult to predict whether the factors for change within Nationalist Afrikanerdom will, before it is too late, succeed in countering the old prejudices, the consolations of Herrenvolkism and predestination and the impetus of uncompromising extremism.

Out of these stresses and strains will emerge the answer to the question posed by this chapter—whether the Afrikaner has a future or only a past? It is a question of vital importance not only for the Afrikaner himself but for all white settlers in Southern Africa.

For the Africa of today is clearly following in the path of Asia. The era of colonialism is passing and the era of nationalism has begun. If the bulk of the Afrikaner nation persists in its arrogant and uncompromising white nationalism, it will inevitably be overwhelmed by the black nationalism that surrounds it. And its downfall will be accompanied by so much violence and hatred that the tentative experiments in multi-racial living to the north will be wrecked, and a white skin will become unacceptable anywhere in Southern and East Africa.

If the mentality portrayed in the following song sung at the 1938 centenary persists, it can prove to be the swan-song of Nationalist Afrikanerdom:

"We look into the future, our symbols stand we by;
We shall continue our onward trek, no struggle will we shun;
We think of blood-steeped rivers,[1] we see the enemies stand.
O God, knit up our strength, with valour fill our hearts,
That we yet may for true freedom offer up our hearts."

---

[1]Blood River—the battle in which the Boers avenged the murder of Piet Retief by Dingaan the Zulu.

The next decade or so will show whether the future holds any place for the Afrikaner. The national-minded Afrikaner has no future in the world of today. His uncompromising values and attitudes are too directly in conflict with those of the outside world and with the conditions of survival. A future might perhaps be predicted for him in the event of atomic war and devastation leading to the resumption of isolated tribal life far from the main centres of urban civilization.

Otherwise, the Afrikaner's future must lie in increased adaptibility, in economic integration, and in a radical revision of his basic values so that they cease to be based on insecurity, fear and hatred. For national-minded Afrikaners the next years represent the last trek—a trek into the twentieth century world, where no man nor nation can be an island, or a trek away from it into a barren and deadly wilderness which leads to no Promised Land.

1652
Dutch East India Company settlement of the Cape under Jan van Riebeeck.

1657
First free burgers settled in the Cape.

1658
Introduction of slaves.

1658–60
Hottentot War.

1688
Huguenot settlers begin to arrive.

1705–10
Burger agitation under Adam Tas against William Adrian van der Stel. Dutch East India Company's decision to stop assisted immigration.

1714–15
Commando system evolved against Bushmen. First great commando raid.

1717
Official decision to rely on slave rather than white labour.

1775
Cape Eastern frontier reaches the Little Fish River.

1777–9
First Kaffir War.

1779
Cape Patriots protest to Amsterdam.

1781–3
Unofficial French occupation of the Cape brings prosperity.

1792
Second Kaffir War.

1794
Dutch East India Company goes bankrupt.

1795
Great campaign against Bushmen.
Graaff-Reinet and Swellendam burgers rise. British occupy Cape for the first time.

1798
First representatives of the London Missionary Society arrive in the Cape.

1799
Burgers of Graaff-Reinet and Swellendam rise again.

1803–6
Batavian Republic.

1806
Second British occupation of the Cape.

1807
Act prohibiting the Slave Trade.

1811
Circuit Courts established.

1812
Fourth Kaffir War. 'Black Circuit.'

1813
English made compulsory in the Cape Civil Service.

1815
Slagter's Nek Rebellion.

1819
Fifth Kaffir War.

1820
Arrival of 5,000 British settlers in the Eastern Cape.

1822
Legal reforms start. Lord Charles Somerset sets up free English-medium State schools. Proclamation enforcing the exclusive use of English in the Courts is issued.

1828
Ordinance 50.

1830
De Zuid Afrikaan started.

1833
Emancipation Act.

1834
Sixth Kaffir War.

1835–8
The Great Trek.

1836
Battle of Vegkop.

1837
Battle of Kapain. Annexation of the Transvaal by Potgieter. Nine Articles of first Trekker Republic.

1838
Foundation of Vootrekker Republic of Natal.
Piet Retief murdered by Dingaan. Dingaan overthrown at Blood River. First Day of the Vow or Covenant.

1839
Use of English promoted in the Dutch Reformed Church of the Cape.

1843
British occupy Natal. The Second Trek starts. Dutch Reformed Church of the Cape gains its autonomy.

1845
Natal proclaimed British territory. British treaties with Adam Kok (Griqua) and Moshesh (Basuto).

1846
Seventh Kaffir War.

1848
British sovereignty proclaimed over the Orange River Territory.

1850–52
Eighth Kaffir War.

1852
Sand River Convention. End of Great Trek.
Cape Constitution promulgated without reference to colour. English made sole Parliamentary language in the Cape.

1853
N.H.K. set up in the Transvaal.

1854
Bloemfontein Convention and abandonment of the Orange River Sovereignty.

1856
Transvaal Grondwet.

1858
Theological College opens at Stellenbosch.

1859
G.K. (Doppers Church) of the Transvaal breaks away from the Transvaal N.H.K.

1865
English becomes sole medium of instruction in Cape schools.

1868
British annex Basutoland.

1869
G.K. Theological College founded at Burgersdorp (Cape).

1870

Diamonds discovered in Kimberley. Griqualand West annexed by the British.

1872

The Cape gets responsible government.

1875

Hofmeyr founds 'Farmers Protection Association'. 'Genootskap van Regte Afrikaners' founded. First Language Movement. Annexation of the Transvaal by Shepstone

1876

Di Patriot (first periodical in Afrikaans) begins to appear in Paarl.

1880

Burgers proclaim the independence of the South African Republic at Paardekraal. The first War of Independence starts.

1881

Dutch Reformed Mission Church of the Cape set up. Battle of Majuba.

1882

Dutch becomes an optional Parliamentary language at the Cape. School regulations modified. Pretoria Convention ends war.

1882–90

Increasing restrictions on naturalization and citizenship in the Transvaal Republic.

1884

Transvaal Education Act (single-medium, religious basis). Dutch becomes equal language in Cape Magistrates' Courts.

1886

Discovery of gold on Witwatersrand. Dutch becomes obligatory in Cape Civil Service.

1890

Die Taalbond founded.

1893

Language Monument unveiled at Burgersdorp.

1895

Jameson Raid.

1896

Ons Klintji started. Chief Justice Kotze dismissed by President Kruger.

1899–1902

Anglo-Boer War (Second War of Independence).

1902

Peace of Vereeniging. Renewed anglicization in Cape and north.

1902–7

Christian National Education schools started in the Transvaal and Orange River Colony.

1904

The A.C.V.V. (Cape) founded. Pan-South African Language Conference.

1906

Afrikaanse Taalvereniging and other organizations founded to promote Afrikaans.

1907–8

Responsible government granted to the former Republics. Boers win political victory.

1908

Hertzog's Orange River Colony Education Act.

1909

Suid-Afrikaanse Akademie vir Taal, Lettere en Kuns founded.

1910

Union of South Africa. English and Dutch languages entrenched in the Act. Louis Botha becomes Prime Minister.

1912

Hertzog leaves the South African Party to form the Nationalist Party.

1914

Armed rebellion under Maritz. 'Helpmekaar' organization founded.

1915

Die Burger founded. Dr. Malan is appointed its first editor.

1916

First Afrikaanse Studentebond. Afrikaans becomes primary school medium.

1917

Theological Faculty (N.H.K.) set up at Pretoria.

c. 1918

Afrikaner Broederbond founded. Voortrekker Movement begins.

1919

Cape Dutch Reformed Church Synod accepts Afrikaans as Church language.

1921

Federale Vroueraad founded.

1924–33

Nationalist-Labour 'Pact Government'.

1925
Afrikaans is finally recognized as a second official language, replacing Dutch.

1926
Mines and Works (Amendment) 'Colour Bar' Act.

1927
Nationality and Flag Act. Immorality Act.

1929
F.A.K. set up.

1931
Economic depression. Statute of Westminster.

1932
Carnegie Poor White Commission's Report published.

1933-39
Hertzog-Smuts 'Fusion' Government.

1933
'Purified Nationalist Party' set up by Dr. Malan. Bible published in Afrikaans.

1935
Noodhulpliga founded.

1938
Ceremonial Centenary of the Great Trek. Foundation of the Ossewa-Brandwag and of the Handhawersbond. A.T.K.V. set up for Afrikaans-speaking railwaymen.

1939
Beginning of Volkspele Movement. First Economic Conference. Education Conference. Reddingsdaadbond and Handelsinstituut founded. War. Hertzog breaks with Smuts on the war issue, and seeks rapprochement with Malan.

1940
Hertzog leaves Reunited Nationalist Party and sets up the Afrikaner Party.

1942
'Draft Constitution of the Republic' published by *Die Transvaler*.

1943
Smuts returns with an increased majority.

1947
British Royal Family visits the Union.

1948
Nationalist Party under Malan returns to power, in co-operation with the Afrikaner Party.

1949

Dedication of the Voortrekker Monument near Pretoria. Prohibition of Mixed Marriages Act. Christian National Education programme issued by F.A.K. Transvaal Language Ordinance passed, making mother-tongue instruction compulsory. SABRA founded.

1950

Immorality Amendment Act. Population Registration Act. Group Areas Act. Blue-print for apartheid issued by Stellenbosch intellectuals and Dutch Reformed Church. Greyshirts dissolved. Dutch Reformed Bantu Church established.

1951

Afrikaner Party amalgamates with Nationalist Party. South West African representatives enter Union Parliament. Potchefstroom is raised to university status. The Suppression of Communism Amendment Act. Torch Commando founded.

1952

Van Riebeeck Tri-centenary.

1953

Nationalist Party returns to power with an increased majority. Malan and Havenga retire. Strijdom becomes Prime Minister. New uniforms for armed forces. Public Safety Act. A.K.T.B. set-up for Afrikaans-speaking postmen.

1954

Free State's Centenary. Inter-racial religious conference called by N.G.K.

1955

A.K.P.O.L. founded for Afrikaans-speaking policemen. Appeal Court Quorum Amendment Act. Bantu Education Act. Pretoria Centenary.

BIBLIOGRAPHY

'Adamastor', *White Man Boss*, Gollancz, 1950.

Agar-Hamilton, J. A. I., *Native Policy of the Voortrekkers*, Maskew Miller, Cape Town, 1928.

Albertyn, J. R. (and others), *Kerk en Stad*, Stellenbosch, 1947.

Armstrong, F. C., *Grey Steel* (General Smuts), Baker, London, 1937.

Barnouw, A. J., *Language and Race Problems in South Africa*, Nijhoff, The Hague, 1934.

Baumann, G., and Bright, E., *The Lost Republic*, Faber, 1937.

Beyers, C., *Die Kaapse Patriotte 1779–91*, Cape Town, 1929.

Böeseken, A. J., Kieser, A. and Krüger, D. W., *Ons Drie Eeue Reeks*, Nasionale Pers, Cape Town, 1951.

Bosman, D. B., *Oor die Ontstaan van Afrikaans*, Amsterdam, 1928.

Botha, C. Graham, *Social Life in the Cape Colony in the Eighteenth Century*, Juta, Cape Town, 1926.

The French Refugees at the Cape, Cape Town, 1921.

Breytenbach, J. H., *Die Tweede Vryheidsoorlog*, Nasionale Pers, Cape Town, 1948–9.

Calpin, G. H., *There Are No South Africans*, Nelson, 1941.

Cloete, H., *The History of the Great Boer Trek*, Murray, 1900.

Coetzee, Abel and Hattingh, S. C., *Die Afrikaanse Letterkunde*, Voortrekkerpers, Johannesburg, 1951.

Cory, G. E., *The Rise of South Africa, 1820–53*, Longmans 1910–30.

De Kiewiet, C. W., *A History of South Africa, Social and Economic*, Oxford University Press, 1942.

De Kock, M. H., *The Economic Development of South Africa*, King, London, 1936.

De Wet, C. R., *Three Years War*, Constable, 1902.

Diederichs, N., *Die Reddingsdaadbond in die Toekoms van ons Volk*, F.A.K. pamphlet (Johannesburg), 1943.

Douglas, W. M., *Andrew Murray and His Message*, Oliphants, 1926

Du Plessis, J., *The Life of Andrew Murray of South Africa*, Marshall, 1920.

A History of Christian Missions in South Africa, Longmans, 1911.

Du Plessis, L. J., *Die Moderne Staat*, South Africa.

Dvorind, E. P., *Racial Separation in South Africa*, University of Chicago Press, 1952.

Engelbrecht, S. P., *History of the Nederduits Hervormde Kerk*, Pretoria, 1925, and *Thomas Francois Burgers*, De Bussy, Cape Town, 1933.

Engelenberg, F. V., *General Louis Botha*, Harrap, 1929.

Erlank, W. J. du P. (Eitemal), *Die Patroon van Ons Volkskarakter*, F.A.K. 1952.

Faure, D. P., *My Life and Times*, Juta, Cape Town, 1907.

Fouché, L., *Die Evolusie van die Trekboer*.

Frankel, S. H., 'Whither South Africa', *S.A. Journal of Economics*, vol. 15, p. 23, 1947.

Franklin, N. N., *Economics in South Africa*, Oxford University Press, 1948.

Haarhoff, T. J., *Stranger at the Gates*, Blackwell, 1948.

Afrikaans, Its Origin and Development, Oxford University Press 1936.

and van den Heever, C.M.

The Achievement of Afrikaans, Central News Agency.

Heese, J. de V., *Die Voortrekkers en andere Suid-Afrikaanse Jeugverenigings*, Nasionale Pers, Cape Town, 1940.

Hepple, Alex., *Trade Unions in Travail*, Unity Publications Ltd., Johannesburg, 1954.

Hofmeyr, J. H., *The Life of Onze Jan*—van der Sandt de Villiers, Cape Town, 1913.

Keet, B. B., *Suid Afrika, Waarheen?*, Stellenbosch University Press, 1955.

Keppel-Jones, A., *South Africa*, Hutchinson.

Friends or Foes, Shuter and Shooter, Pietermaritzburg.

Kestell, J. D., *Through Shot and Flame*, Methuen, 1902.

My Nasie in Nood, Tweede Trek-Reeks, Bloemfontein, 1941.

and van Velden, *The Peace Negotiations*.

Keyter, J. de W., *Die Huwelik en Gesin*, Tweede Trek-Reeks, Bloemfontein, 1940.

Kotzé, D. J. (ed.), *Letters of the American Missionaries 1835–38*, Van Riebeeck Society, 1951.

Leipoldt, C. Louis, *Jan van Riebeeck*, Longmans, 1936.

Bushveld Doctor, Cape, 1937.

Die Groot Trek, Cape Town, 1938.

Lindsay Smith, H., *Behind the Press in South Africa*, Stewart, Cape Town.

Long, B. K., *In Smuts Camp*, Oxford University Press, 1945.

M'Carter, J., *The Dutch Reformed Church in South Africa*, Inglis, Edinburgh, 1869.

McCord, J. J., *South African Struggle*, J. H. de Bussy, Pretoria.

MacCrone, I. D., *Race Attitudes in South Africa*, Oxford University Press, 1937.

McKerron, M. E. *History of Education in South Africa, 1652–1932*.

MacMillan, W. M., *Bantu, Boer and Briton*, Faber, 1929.

Complex South Africa, Faber, 1930.

The South African Agrarian Problem, Johannesburg, 1919.

Malan, F. S., *Konvensie-Dagboek* (ed. J. H. Preller), Van Riebeeck Society, Cape Town, 1951.

Malherbe, E. G., *Education in South Africa, 1652–1922*, Juta, Cape Town, 1925.

Marais, B. J., *Colour, Unsolved Problem of the West*, Howard B. Timmins, 1953.

Marquard, L., *The Peoples and Policies of South Africa*, Oxford University Press, 1952.

Millin, S. G., *General Smuts*, 2 vols., Faber, 1936.

Cecil Rhodes, Harper, New York, 1933.

The People of South Africa, Central News Agency, 1951.

Moorrees, A., *Die Nederduits Gereformeerde Kerk in South Africa*, Cape Town, 1937.

Murray, Joyce (Ed.), *Young Mrs. Murray Goes to Bloemfontein, 1856–60* (Letters), Balkema, Cape Town, 1954.

Neame, L., *White Man's Africa*, Stewart, 1952.

Nepgen, C. C., *Die Sosiale Gewete van die Afrikaanssprekende*, Johannesburg, 1938.

Nienaber, P. J., *Bibliografie van Afrikaanse Boeke, 1691–1948*, 2 vols, Skrywer., 1943, 1948.

Bronnegids by die Studie van Afrikaans, 2 vols, Skrywer., 1948, 1952.

Dr. J. D. Kestell, Vader van die Reddingsdaad, 1946.

Die Opkoms van Afrikaans as Kultuurtaal, Van Schaik, Pretoria, and Nienaber, G. S., *Geskiedenis van die Afrikaanse Letterkunde*, Van Schaik, Pretoria, 1941.

Pauw, S., *Die Beroepsarbeid van die Afrikaner in die Stad*, Stellenbosch, 1946.

Philip, John, *Researches in South Africa*, 2 vols., Duncan,1828.

Pohl, Victor, *Adventures of a Boer Family*, Faber, 1944.

Preller, G. A., *Piet Retief*, Nasionale Pers, 1920.
  Voortrekkermense, 6 vols., Nasionale Pers, 1918–38.

Reitz, D., *Commando*, Faber, 1929.
  Trekking On, Faber, 1933.
  No Outspan, Faber, 1943.

Robbins, Eric, *This Man Malan*, South Africa Scientific Publishing Co., Cape Town, 1953.

Roberts, M., and Trollip, A. E. G., *The South African Opposition*, Longmans Green, 1947.

Sachs, E. S., *The Choice Before South Africa*, London, 1953.

Scholtz, G. D., *General C. F. Beyers, 1869–1914*, Johannesburg, 1941.
  Het Die Afrikanervolk 'n Toekoms?, Voortrekkerpers, Johannesburg, 1954.

Schreiner, Olive, *The Story of an African Farm*, Hutchinson, 1883.
  Thoughts on South Africa, Unwin, 1923.

Schumann, C. W. G., *Die Reddingsdaadbond as Volksopbou*, F.A.K., Johannesburg, 1941.

Spoelstra, B., *Ons Volkslewe*, Pretoria, 1924.

Tawney, R. H. *Religion and the Rise of Capitalism*, Allen & Unwin.

Theal, G. M., *History of South Africa*, Allen & Unwin, 1892, and later edns.

Theron, Erika, *Fabriekwerksters in Kaapstad*, Nasionale Pers, Cape Town, 1944.

Van den Heever, C. M., *Generaal J. B. M. Hertzog*, 1943.

Van der Merwe, P. J., *Die Trekboer in die Geskiedenis van die Kaapkolonie*, Cape Town, 1938.

Van der Merwe, Andries, *Die Huwelik*, Sacum, Bloemfontein, 1953.

Van der Merwe, W. J., *Missionary Attitudes in the Dutch Reformed Church in South Africa*, Nasionale Pers, 1936.

Van der Poel, Jean, *The Jameson Raid*, Oxford University Press, 1951.

Van der Walt, and Ploeger, Jan B., *Afrikaner, wees u'seef*, Haneker and Wormser (Amsterdam), 1897.

Walker, Eric A., *Lord de Villiers and his Times*, Constable, 1925.
  The Frontier Tradition in South Africa, Oxford University Press, 1930.

Walker, Eric A., *W. P. Schreiner*, Oxford University Press, 1937.
  The Great Trek, Black, 1938.
  A History of South Africa, Longmans, 1947.
  For historical references see also the works of Barrow, Borcherdts,
  Colenbrander, Lichtenstein and Thompson.
  Literature.—See in particular the works of S. J. du Toit, Eugene
  Marais, Jan Celliers, Totius, C. Louis Leipoldt, D. F. Malherbe,
  A. G. Visser, C. J. Langenhoven, W. E. G. Louw, I. D. du
  Plessis, N. P. van Wyk Louw, Uys Krige, Mikro, C. M. van den
  Heever, Sangiro, Hobson, H. C. Bosman, Pauline Smith, L.
  Prance, etc., etc.—also the Afrikaanse Boekelyste published by
  F.A.K., Johannesburg in 1952, and the list of books on South
  Africa compiled for the South African Department of External
  Affairs in 1954.

COLLECTIVE PUBLICATIONS

Cambridge History of the British Empire, Vol. VIII, Oxford University
  Press, 1936.
Coming of Age: Studies in South African Citizenship and Politics, Maskew
  Miller, 1930.
Groote Verseboek, Nasionale Boek., 1951.
Kultuurgeskiedenis van die Afrikaner (3 vols.) ed. van den Heever, C. M.,
  and Pienaar P. de V., Nasionale Pers (Cape Town), 1947.
F.A.K. Volksangbundel, H. A. U. M. and J. de Bussy, Cape Town,
  Pretoria, 1954.
F.A.K. Silver Jubilee Book, 1954.
My Jeugland, ed. C. M. van den Heever, A.P.B., 1953.
The South African Way of Life, ed. G. H. Calpin, Heinemann, 1953.
Voortrekker Monument, Programme and Memorial Album of Inauguration,
  Pretoria, 1949.
  See also *The Archives Year Book* and publications of the Suid-
  Afrikaanse Akademie vir Wetenskap en Kuns, the Patriot-
  vereniging and the Van Riebeeck Society.

REPORTS, YEARBOOKS AND OFFICIAL PUBLICATIONS

Carnegie Commission on the Poor White Problem in South Africa, (5 vols.),
  Pro. Ekklesia Drukkery (South Africa), 1932.
Christian Principles in Multi-Racial South Africa, ed. Federal Mission
  Council of the Dutch Reformed Church, Pretoria, 1953.

BIBLIOGRAPHY

Economic Conferences (First), F.A.K., 1939, (Second), Voortrekkers-pers, Johannesburg, 1950.

God's Kingdom in Multi-Racial South Africa, report of the Inter-Racial Conference of Church Leaders, Johannesburg, 1954.

Commission in Re Pretoria Indigents, 1905.

Transvaal Indigency Commission, (1906–8).

African Press and Advertising Journal.

N.G.K. Yearbooks.

See also *Union of South Africa Yearbooks,* Census Reports (1904–51), etc. etc.

PERIODICALS

Dailies.—*Die Burger, Die Transvaler, Die Vaderland, Die Oosterlig, The Cape Times,* the *Cape Argus,* the *Rand Daily Mail,* the *Argus,* the *Friend.*

Sunday papers, weeklies, monthlies, etc.—*Dagbreek en Sondagnuus, The Sunday Times, Die Kerkbode, Standpunte, Rooi Rose, Fyngoed, The Forum, Ons Eie Boek, Lantern, Tydskrif vir Volkskunde en Volkstaal, Inspan, Koers, Trek,* publications of S.A.B.R.A. and S.A. Institute of Race Relations, etc., etc.

INDEX

A.C.V.V. (Afrikaanse Christelike Vrouevereniging), 261–2
Acts of Parliament;
  Appeal Court Quorum Act, 91
  Bantu Authority Act, 108
  Bantu Urban Authority Act, 108
  Group Areas Act, 85, 105
  Mixed Marriages Act, 211, 242
  Nationalities Act, 79, 81
  Native Building Workers Act, 108
  Natives (Abolition of Passes) Act, 108
  Passport Act, 92
  Population Registration Act, 108
  Prohibition of Mixed Marriages Act, 108
  Public Safety Act, 92
  Quota Act, 290
  Reservation of Separate Amenities Act, 108
  Riotous Assemblies and Suppression of Communism Amendment Act, 92
  Separate Representation of Voters Act, 108
Address, Boer forms of, 240, 246
Adultery, D.R.C. attitude to, 190
Africa (general), 134, 273, 300, 303–6; influence on Boers, 16–17, 217
African Press and Advertising Journal, 126
Africans (see also Non-Whites), 22, 79, 85, 102, 107–9, 119, 147–8, 151, 161–2, 200f, 211, 252; numbers, 67; and Afrikaners; 11, 22, 38, 129, 146, 274, 278–

81, 293–5, and Afrikaans language, 43, 49
Afrikaans Language (see also Language, Education and Press), Ch. II *passim*. 111, 117, 124, 130, 182, 187–8, 212, 224, 260–1, 264–71, 273, 278, 283, 285
Afrikaanse Nasionale Kultuurraad, 270
Afrikaanse Taalgenootskap, 55
Afrikaanse Taalvereniging, 55
Afrikander (see Afrikaners)
Afrikaner Bond (Cape), 29, 31, 97, 117
Afrikanerdom (see also Nationalism), 98, 99, 100, 106, 111, 112, 116, 119, 133, 172, 180, 188, 269–71; definition of, 274–5, 287; and political nationalism, 39, 104–6f, 131, 133, 156, 274–5; beyond Union, 43, 127–34, 263
Afrikanerization (of English-speaking), 100, 212, 282
Afrikaner Party, 81, 101, 102, 104, 113, 116, 126
Afrikaners (see also Boers); statistics, 67–71, 85–87; definitions, 211, 272–5, development of group, 16, 26, 52; traits, 48, 95, 110, 166, 172, 207, 259–60, 276–81, 292–5; way of life, 189–92, 209, 264, 292, attitudes, 230, 276f; unity, 26, 115, 133, 145, 173, 238, 275–6, anti-Nationalists, 86, 117, 118, 125, 188–9, 228–31, 236–7, 301; un-Afrikaans, non-national, 41, 61, 97, 116–8, 133, 154, 168, 256–7, 274–5

320

Agriculture (see also Farmers), 6, 10, 16–17, 19, 24, 70, 136, 137–142, 144–50, 232; co-operatives, 166–7; women's unions, 262

Ahlefeld-Bille, Count, 130

Akademie, see S.A. Akademie

A.K.P.O.L., 269

Amalgamated Engineering Union, 161–2

America (see also U.S.); frontier expansion, 178; religious influence, 182–3, Americanization, 190, 214, 238, 254, 255f, 283

Albert, 53–54

Amiens, Treaty of, 8

Amsterdam, 289; Classis of, 178–9

Anglican Church, 14, 181, 202, 208–9, 270; Afrikaner members, 69, 212

Anglicization, 4, 12, 14, 51–54, 190, 219, 222–3, 254–7, 265, 282; of Afrikaans language, 48–49, of D.R.C., 181–2

Anglo-Boer War(s), 31–36, 37, 41, 77, 96, 135, 139, 188–9, 222, 234, 241, 261, 273, 275, 281–2, 288; economic consequences, 137; and education, 219–20; source of literary inspiration, 46

Angola Boers, 36

Annexation; of Transvaal by British, 98; of Bechuanaland and Northern Natal, 27; of Basutoland and Griqualand W., 25

Antonissen, R., 48

Apartheid (see also Segregation, Separate Development), 9, 78, 102, 105–9, 120, 128, 129, 131–2, 201, 295, 299; and Bible, 207, 237; and churches, 205–10; total, 205–10, 299, 301–5; intellectual, 236, 266; political, 95; educational, 215; economic, 151, 155, 162, 165–6, 171, 173–5; negative, 133; in voluntary

organizations, 262–4; white, 62, 64, 224, 256–7

Apostolic Faith Mission Church, 69–70, 202, 213–4

Appeal Court, 83, 91, 92, 105

Apprenticeship, 151

Archbell, Rev. W., 182

Argus Printing Company, 127

Argentine, Boers in, 36

Armed forces, 87–89, 152, 189

Arnot, D., 25

Arts, Afrikaners in, 257–8

Asia, 134, 305

Asiatics, see Indians

Assembly, House of (see also Parliament), 79, 102, 112

Associations, Afrikaner, 39, 55–56, 77, 111, 158, 229–30, 260–71

A.T.K.B., 269

A.T.K.V., 263–4, 267–8

Authoritarianism (Afrikaner), 76, 94, 96, 101, 104–5, 122, 199, 225, 292

Azikiwe, Dr., 208

Bailey, Sir Abe, 285

Bamangwato, 13

Banks (see also Volkskas), 164–5

Bantu (see also Africans, Kaffirs), 7, 10, 17, 21, 44, 137, 205, 274; education, 108, 210–1; Bantustan, 174

Barclays Bank, 165

Barkly, Sir Henry, 25

Barnard, Lady Anne, 284

Barnouw, Professor A. J., 283

Barolong, 22

Barrow, J., 10

Basutoland, 13, 25, 89, 211

Batavian Republic, 8, 74, 179, 180

Bechuanaland, 13, 27

Bekker, A. J., 116

Benade, J. G., 113

Benn, Wedgewood, 32

Berlin Conference, 27

Besluits, 75

Beyers, C. R., 96, 98
Bezuidenhout, F., 15
Bezuidenhout, J., 16
Bibault, 272
Bible (see also Old Testament), Ch.
  V passim, 18, 45, 182, 190, 205–6,
  216–8, 222, 225, 240, 272, 278;
  in Afrikaans, 46, 167, 188, 301;
  and apartheid, 78, 206–7, 237
Bilingualism, 49, 53, 56–58, 60, 68–
  69, 86, 100, 171, 222, 227–8, 232,
  265; in armed forces, 89; in com-
  merce, 152, 270
Birrell, Augustine, 285
Birthrate (comparative), 67, 101, 103
'Bitter-enders', 34–36
'Black Circuit' (1812), 15
Black Nationalism (see also Nation-
  alism), 208, 275, 279, 300
'Black Peril', 102, 105, 158, 160
Blankewerkersbeskermingbond, 159
Blockhouses, 33
Bloemfontein, 83, 113–14, 180, 252;
  Conference, 31
Blood, Afrikaner, 131, 239, 274
Blood River, 22, 39, 98, 204, 305
Boer Republics, see Republics
Boeremusiek, 256–8
Boeren Beschermings Vereeniging,
  53
Boers (see also Afrikaners), 4, 6, 7,
  17; definition, 6, 273; traits, Chs.
  VII–VIII passim, 4, 12, 14, 17,
  18, 21, 136, 141, 198–9, 246, 251–
  2; way of life, Ch. VIII passim, 16–
  17, 28, 36, 45, 47, 89, 136, 138,
  144–5, 148–9, 182, 189f., 195, 216–
  17, 239, 244, 256, 260, 270; on
  frontier, 10, 14, 16, 19; nation-
  hood, 25–6, 241, 250; attitudes,
  8, 11–14, 37, 78, 143, 203
Bondgenoot, Die, 269
Bond van Dienaresse (N.G.K.), 262
Bonuscor, 169–170
Borcherdts, P. B., 243
Boshoff (mining interests), 149

Bosman, H. C., 241–2
Botha, Louis, 29, 36, 38, 41, 93, 96–
  98, 100, 111, 117, 123, 223, 274,
  282
Bouwerker, Die, 155
Boy Scouts, 264–5
Brand, J. H., 25, 29
Brazil, 243
Brebner, J., 222
Brink, C. B., 200
Brink, G. E., 124
British, 8, 11, 14, 19, 25, 88, 97, 99,
  104, 111, 118, 121, 135, 178, 181,
  183, 203, 219, 284; and Boers or
  Afrikaners, 22–23, 25, 30, 32–33,
  88, 93–94, 98, 105, 116, 129–30,
  281–2, 285–6, 302
Broederbond, 103, 110–13, 118, 196,
  254, 271
Building Societies, Afrikaner, 165
Building Workers Industrial Union,
  156, 160
Bulawayo, 131
Burger, Die, 125–7, 164, 194, 196,
  249, 303
Burger, Schalk, 29, 35
Burgers, 3, 4, 5, 7, 24, 28, 73, 76, 78,
  273
Burgers, T. F., 23, 36, 186, 220
Burgersdorp, 54, 184, 188
Burns, John, 32
Bushmen, 7, 10, 136
Bywoners, 36, 138–9, 145, 217, 246,
  251–2

Calvinism, Ch. V passim, 4, 69, 70,
  73, 110, 133, 173, 176–8, 193, 198,
  267, 277
Campbell, Rev. J., 12
Canaan, 176, 181
Cape (Colony and Province), 3, 6,
  8, 25, 29, 30, 32, 33, 35, 41, 51–52,
  61, 62, 67–68, 74, 83–84, 89, 97,
  99, 119, 127, 139–40, 153, 161,
  185–6, 192, 209, 218–20, 226, 242,
  261–2; Eastern Cape, 105, 113,

139, 263; Western Cape, 201, 219, 236, 243–4, 251

Cape Coloured Liquor Commission, 191

Cape Coloured People (see also Non-Whites), 10–11, 67, 83, 108, 124, 137, 200–2, 209, 258; labour, 150, 158, 191, in trade unions, 161–2; voters, 75, 79–85, 91, 105, 119, 122–3; and Afrikaners, 281; and Afrikaans Language, 42–43, 49

Cape Dutch, Ch. II passim, 5, 15–16, 26–27, 30–32, 133, 243–4, 251, 258, 284–5

Cape Patriots, 7

Cape Town, 6, 40, 68, 83, 84, 123–4, 178, 187, 236, 251–3; University, 237

Capital(ism), 110, 140, 166, 173, 290; and Afrikaners, 109, 135, 167

Capital (cities), 83

Carnegie Poor White Commission Report, 140, 141, 166, 180, 181, 193–4, 245, 247, 251–2

Catholic Times, 210

Catholics (see Roman Catholics)

Cattle, 3, 5, 6, 7, 10, 17

Celliers, Jan, 46, 285

Celliers, Manie, 121

Censorship, 93, 190

Central African Federation, see Federation

'Century of Wrong', 36, 135

Chamber of Mines, 149

Chamberlain J., 21, 31, 38

Champion, Rev., 203

Chosen People, 176–8, 290–1, 293

Christelik (Gereformeerde) Afge-skeie Kerk, 186

Christian Council of South Africa, 208

Christian National Education, 55, 60, 61, 63, 184, 192, 195, 212, 215, 220–6, 270; principles, 93, 228–9, 237, 264, 267

'Christian Trusteeship', 107, 201–2, 205

Christianity (see also Churches), Ch. V. passim, 218; and colour, 9, 177, 202, 273, 281, 302

Churches (see also under separate denominations), Ch. V passim, 247, 269, 301

Cinema, 172, 191, 217, 238, 249, 255, 258, 283

Civilized labour policy, 86, 142–3, 149

Clans, Boer, 244–6

Class (socio-economic), 9, 109, 153–4, 159, 173, 250, 255, 262

Clergy; D.R.C., 106, 112, 152, 158, 178–82, 184, 187–9, 195–6, 229–30, 237, 253–4; Anglican, 11–12

Climate (and character), 136

Cloete, Hendrik, 38, 240

Coal, 170

Coalitions (political), 95–96, 99, 102

Coat of Arms, 81–82

Co-education, 225

Colenso, 33

Collaborators, 33, 38, 104, 183

'Colloquium doctum', 187

Colonialism, 305

Colour (see also Non-Whites, and status), 8–10, 136, 143, 206, 302

Colour-Bar, 8–9, 87, 119, 158

Comic Books, 217

Commandant-General (office of), 89

Commando, 18, 21, 32, 33, 87, 96, 114, 250, 260

Commerce, 56, 70, 73, 86, 107, 111, 148, 151–3, 164–74

Commonwealth (British), 99, 105, 106, 113, 118, 123, 132, 210, 300

Communists, 109, 122–3, 145, 154, 156, 159–61, 187, 195, 198, 208, 237, 290, 293, 300

Competition (white and black), 137, 141, 174–5

Concentration Camps, 32, 34, 37, 222, 241–2, 261, 282

Confederate Party, 131–2
Congregational Union, 209
Conradie, Rev. J., 168
Conservative Party, 103, 118–19
Constitution, 74, 76, 80, 95, 103, 105, 122, 210
Consumers, 109, 152, 163, 171–3
Co-operatives, 109, 164–7
Cornelius, Johanna, 159
'Corner House', 125
Corporal Punishment, 93
Cory, G. E., 16, 19
Courts, 7, 14, 90–92
Cradock, Governor, 202
Crime, 151
Cronjé, Prof. G., 248
Culture; Afrikaans, Ch. VII *passim*, 113, 114, 117, 119–20, 124, 136, 154, 190, 192, 225, 233, 238, 253–6, 260–2, 273, 275; American, 172; English, 282–3; West European, 300–1; organizations, 266–71
Currency (reforms), 14

Dagbreek, 125
De Kiewiet, C. W., 20, 136, 138, 148, 272
De Klerk, J., 73, 108, 173, 190, 199, 235
de Kock, M. H., 175
de la Rey, Dolf, 96, 123–4
de Mist, J. A., 19, 180, 182
de Villiers, Lord, 53
de Vos, D. V., 188
de Vos, J. J., 188, 254
de Wet, General C., 35, 96, 98, 241
de Wet, N. J., 123–4
de Wildt (Hertzog's speech at), 97
Defence Force (see also Armed Forces), 87–89, 101
Delagoa Bay, 23, 27
Delimitation (of constituencies), 80–81
Delius, Anthony, 46
Democratic Party (S. Rhodesia), 131

Depression (1906), 138, (1929–32), 99, 140
Diamonds, 25, 137, 139, 140, 150
Diederichs, N., 119, 167, 169
Dingaan, 21–2, 39, 204, 305
Dingaan's Day (see also Vow, Day of the), 38, 98, 190
Distillers Corporation, 170
Divine destiny, 104, 110, 176, 177, 196, 225, 276
Divorce, 190, 248
Dominion Party, 100–1
Dominion Status, 99
Dönges, T. E., 112, 155, 236, 241
Doppers (see also G. K.) 27, 183–6, 234
Draft Constitution of the Republic, 42, 77, 82, 85, 105, 112, 286
Drakensberg, 22, 23, 240
Drakenstein, 178
Drama, 48, 256, 259
Drink, 191, 247, 249
Drought, 19, 137, 177
Du Plessis, D. J., 160
Du Plessis, Rev. J., 187
Du Plessis, Louis, 117, 196
Du Plessis, Professor L. J., 125, 287
Du Plessis, Otto, 93, 97
du Preez, A. B., 155, 248
du Toit, D. J., see Totius
du Toit, E. S. (Betty), 160
du Toit, Dr. S., 186
du Toit, Rev. S. J., 46, 52, 187, 220
Dundas, General, 19
Durban, 68
D'Urban, Sir Benjamin, 19
Dutch (see also Holland(er)), 4, 27, 130, 148, 211, 252, 288–9
Dutch (language) (see also Cape Dutch and Schools), Ch. II *passim*, 43, 44, 50, 51, 52, 63, 125, 187–8, 218, 219, 221, 222, 224, 266, 278, 289
Dutch East India Company (D.E.I. C.), 3, 5, 6, 7, 14, 17, 43, 136, 178, 202, 213

Dutch Reformed Churches (see also G.K., N.G.K., N.H.K.), 9, 13, 22, 51–53, 55, 62, 69, 70, 75, 77–79, 82, 88, 95, 107–8, 113, 117, 128, 130, 145, 154, 178–215, 217–18, 223–5, 227–30, 260, 262–4, 268, 270, 291

Dutch Reformed Mission Church (D.R.M.C.), 200–2, 205–6; D.R. Bantu Church, 205

East Africa, 128, 184
East London, 68
Eastern Star, 284
Ecology, 17
Economic Conference, 154, 167–9, 171
Economic Movement, 56, 104, 109, 163–73, 282
Economy (S.A.), 8–9, 95, 99, 109; competition, 279; change, 279; and apartheid, 107
Education (see also Schools and Language), Ch. VI *passim*, 53, 55–56, 59–62, 69, 142, 144, 179, 217, 248, 262, 270; and language, 59–60; Non-White, 209, 211
Edwards, Rev. R., 13
Eendrag, 262
Egalitarianism (Boer) see also Equality, 74, 136, 180, 246, 250–1, 253, 255, 278
Ekonomiese Instituut, 167, 171
Eldoret, 129
'Elect', Doctrine of, 176–7, 215, 278
Elections, 98–103; (1910), 97; (1948), 81, 106; (1953), 110, 124, 231–2; Federation, 132; Provincial, (1954), 102
Ellis, D. E., 155, 157
Emancipation, 11, 20
Employers, 99, 136, 143, 153, 194
English-speaking South Africans, 41, 57–58, 63, 67, 71, 73, 78, 89, 93–95, 100, 102, 105, 112, 117–18, 124, 126, 130, 132, 148, 151, 173, 208–9, 212, 217, 223–4, 226, 227, 252–6, 260–2, 267, 277, 280–8, 300; language, Chap. II *passim*, 42, 49, 50, 51, 125–6, 130, 132–3, 152, 163, 223; and Africans, 280; voters, 97–98, 163–5; at Afrikaans universities, 232, 234, 236; and Afrikaners, 96, 230, 252–3, 259, 260–1, 264, 282, 285–8, 293–4
English War—see Anglo-Boer War
Entrenched Clauses, 56, 63, 91, 93
Entrepôt, 3
Entrepreneurs, 133, 304–5
Environment, 17–18, 277f
Equality; econ., 141, 158; political and legal, 11, 15, 20, 154, 204
Erasmus, F. C., 89
Erosion, 148, 300
Ethnocentrism, 77, 133, 172, 292
Europe, 174, 300
Evanston (churchmen meet, 1954), 206
Evolution, Theory of, 225
Expansion (see also Great Trek); Boer, 3, 5, 20, 26, 173, 287; British, 25, 182
Ex-servicemen (see also Torch Commando), 122

F.A.K. (Federasie van Afrikaanse Kultuurverenigings), 56, 77, 111, 131, 154, 166–7, 225, 250, 268–71, 289
Faku, Pondo chief, 13
Family (Boer and Afrikaner), 189–90, 216–17, 239–50, 260–2
Farmers (see also Agriculture), 6, 7, 10, 80–81, 95, 96, 99, 107, 112, 118, 136–7, 146–7, 217–19, 239f, 253–5, 304–5
Farmers Protection Association (see Boeren Beschermings Vereniging)
Faure, Rev. D. P., 187
Fear (dominant motive), 207, 215, 276, 278, 279–81, 293
Federal Party (C.A.F.), 129

Federal Party (S.A.), 118, 124
Federale Mynbou, 149
Federale Vroueraad, 261–2
Federation, Central African (see also Afrikanerdom), 127–34
Federation (plans), 25–26, 29, 97, 118, 287–8
Feminism, 261
Finance (Afrikaners in), 164–75
Fisheries, 170
Flag, national, 81–82, 228
Flemish language, 43
Forum, 92
Franchise, 24, 28, 31, 75, 76, 79, 84, 93–94, 103, 119, 198–9
Franzsen, D. G., 148
Free Protestant Church, 187
Free State (see Orange Free State)
Free State Express, 26
Freemasons, 209
French Canadians, 43, 73, 90, 127, 244
French; language, 4, 43, 51; traits, 300; in Cape, 6; Revolution, 7
Frontier (and Boers), 7, 9–11, 41, 136, 177–8, 216, 218, 240f, 243, 256, 277–80, 291–2
Fundamentalism, 225
Fusion Government, 99–100, 115
F.V.B. (Federale Volksbeleggings Bpk.), 169–70

Garment Workers Union, 122, 154–6, 158–60, 162, 195
Geneva, 176, 178, 188, 190, 192, 194–5, 199
Genootskap van Regte Afrikaners, 45–6, 52, 219–20, 261, 269
George VI, 82
Gerdener, Dr. G. B. A., 303
Germans, 4, 29, 43, 81, 98, 101, 115, 178, 209, 211, 288–90; language, 43
Germany, 27, 89, 100, 210, 232, 278
Germiston (strike), 158, 195
Gey van Pittius, E. F., 74–78

Girl Guides, 264–5
Ginsberg, M., 277
G. K. (Gereformeerde Kerk) (see also Doppers), 181, 183–6, 204, 233, 262
Gleisner, J., 155
God (see also Divine destiny), 18, 22, 31, 41, 81, 128, 199, 305
Gold, 27, 137, 139, 140, 150
Gold Coast, 303
Gordonia, 126
Goudriaan, J., 148
Governor-General, 79, 92, 254–5
Graaff-Reinet, 7, 51, 179, 184, 219
Graham, Billy, 213
Great Trek (see also Voortrekkers), 20–24, 37–38, 41, 181–2, 204, 218, 239, 240; Centenary Celebrations, 38–40, 114, 268, 276, 305
Griqualand West, 25
Griquas, 12, 25
Grondwet (of the Transvaal), 13, 24, 73, 74, 90

Handelsinstituut, 169, 175, 270
Handhawersbond, 114
Handsoppers, 33, 275
Hansard, 57
Harlow, V, 3
Harris, C., 157
Havenga, N. C., 81, 101–3, 113, 116, 280
Hay, F. J., 213
Heemraden, 51, 85, 90
Heidelberg Catechism, 13, 179
Heilbron, 35
Helpmekaar, 164, 263
Hereniging (see Reunion)
Hertzog, Dr. A., 155, 157, 169
Hertzog, J. B., 35, 62, 81, 93, 96, 97, 99, 100–1, 103, 112–13, 123, 188, 197, 274
Hervormde Nederduits Gereformeerde Kerk, 188
'Het Volk', 97
High Dutch, see Dutch

History (Afrikaner), 133; partisan teaching of, 14, 36, 133, 219–21, 227–8

Hobhouse, Emily, 32, 34

Hofmeyr, Jan (senior), 25–26, 29–31, 38, 42, 45, 52–53, 97, 102, 117, 187, 212, 219, 274

Hofmeyr, J. H. (junior), 236

'Hoggenheimer', 135, 290

Holism, 93, 274–5

Holland (see also Dutch), 181, 183, 186, 210, 218, 221, 223, 232, 252, 278

'Hollander Clique', 27, 29, 76, 251–2, 288

Hottentots, 3, 8–12, 15, 18, 20–21, 44, 202, 242

Huddleston, Father Trevor, 14

Huggins, Sir Godfrey (see Malvern, Lord)

Huguenot College, 237; Seminary, 219

Huguenots, 5, 43, 51, 178–9, 218, 272–3, 292

Huisgenoot, Die, 127

Humanitarianism, 14

Huyser, P. J., 156, 160

Ideas, New, 8, 19, 27

Immigration, 3, 5, 67, 79, 269–70, 289–91

Immorality Act, 242; Amendment, 50, 108, 242

Imperial Preference, 171

Imperialism, 28–29, 98

Inbreeding (Boer), 244–5

Incomes, 144, 163

Independent Labour Party (I.L.P.), 32

Independent United Party (see Conservative Party)

India, 281, 300, 304

Indians, (see also Non-Whites), 42–43, 67, 129, 151, 162, 281, 303

Indies, route to, 3, 8

Industrial Development Corporation, 150

Industrial legislation, 151, 161–3

Industrialists, 95, 99, 107, 118

Industrialization, 104, 109, 144, 150–1

Industry, 56, 70, 73, 86, 107, 112, 143–4, 148, 150, 164–74

Inglis, Rev. W., 13

Inspan, 168

Institute for National Welfare (Instituut vir Volkswelsyn), 270

Integration (black-white), 24, 106, 143, 174–5, 200, 201, 206, 267, 302, 305–6

Intelligentsia (Afrikaner), 254f, 275–6

Interior, Ministry of, 85

Inter-marriage; Afrikaner-English, 69, 99–100, 128; white-coloured, 192, 281

In-marriage (Boer), 244–5

International League of Country-women, 262

Irish settlers, 211

Isolation (Boer), 44–45, 48, 63, 247, 256–7, 266, 278, 299–300

Israel, 290–1

Jameson, Dr. S., 30

Jameson Raid, 27, 29–31

Jansen, Hon. E. G., 131, 254

Jengbond, 103, 110, 174, 231, 265

Jerling, J. D., 116

Jerusalemgangers, 177

Jews, 91, 109, 168, 221, 234, 252-3, 288, 290–1

Jingoism, 29, 37, 83, 113, 120, 227, 284–5

Johannesburg, 27, 68, 85, 111, 252, 254, 262, 269–70

Jongeliedverenigings, 265

Jongspan, Die, 127, 227–8

Joubert, P. J., 29

Journalists, S. A. Society of, 127

Judiciary, 14, 59, 90–2

Jukskei, 90, 114–5, 235, 268

Jury System, 90

'Kafferboeties', 120, 187
Kaffir Wars, 10–11, 136, 228
'Kaffir Work', 8, 136–7, 142, 300
Kaffirs (see also Africans), 7, 17, 19–20, 142, 274, 280, 303
Kafue, 129, 132
Kaiser, 27, 289
Kariba Gorge, 132
Keet, B. B., 206, 237, 299, 301
Kenya, 128–131, 263
Keppel-Jones, A., 287–8
Kerkbode, Die, 82, 193, 197, 213
Kerkjengvereninging, 265
Kestell, J. D., 167
'Khaki Election' (1900), 32
Kimberley, 33, 68
Kitchener, Lord, 33
Klerewerkersnuus, Die, 155–6
Knox, John, 199
Koers, 286
Kotzé, Chief Justice J., 29, 90
Kotzé, Rev. J. J., 186, 197
Krige Uys, 47
Kruger, Paul, 27–30, 40–41, 73–74, 76, 82, 90, 94, 105, 114, 139, 184, 185, 199, 246, 251, 289
Krugerism (see also Neo-Krugerism), 29, 32, 111, 115, 133, 197, 199
Ku Klux Klan, 206
Kultuurgeskiedenis van die Afrikaner, 98, 254, 274, 278, 283
Kultuurraad (see Afrikaanse Nasionale Kultuurraad)
Kultuurverenigings, 115, 269
K.W.V., 164

Labour (see also Trade Unions and 'Kaffir Work'), Ch. IV passim, 86, 95, 99-100, 107, 109–10, 118, 120–2, 136, 138–9, 143, 145, 147, 151, 161, 173–5, 218, 252, 267, 302–5
Labour Party, 97, 99, 101–2, 110, 120–2, 124, 153, 160, 172
Ladysmith, 33

Land, 7, 10, 18, 21, 24, 107, 136–7, 144–8, 239–40, 245, 251–2, 253f, 260, 273, 280
Land en Volk, 29
Landdrosts, 7–8, 90
Langenhoven, C. J., 81, 240
Language (see also Afrikaans Education), 42–43, 63, 91, 96, 225, 276; Official, 19, 43, 50, 51, 56, 132, 224, 266; Home, 67–71; Language Movements, 46, 55, 196, 233; African, 108; Monument, 54
Law (S.A. legal system) 89–93
Lawyers, 112, 253–4
Le Boucq, 179
Le Roux, Le Roux Smith, 258
Legal Profession, 59, 90, 152–3
Legislation (see also Acts), 79, 92, 108, 242
Leipoldt, C. Louis, 31, 46–47, 174
'Lekker Lewe,' 136, 239
Leyds, W. J., 29
Liberal Party, 35, 118–20, 236; in U.K., 32
Liberalism, 14, 36, 74, 77, 83, 94, 102, 118–20, 123, 212, 220, 244, 267, 276, 295, 302, 304; religious, 178, 180–1, 186–7, 295, 302, 304
Liberals, 91, 118, 121, 133, 235, 237, 290, 293, 301
Lindley, Daniel, 182
Lindsay Smith, H., 127
Linton, R., 276
Literature, Afrikaans Ch. II, 45, 257–8, 288–9
Livingstone, David, 13
'Loading' (of parliamentary constituencies), 80–81, 102
'Loan-places', 14, 17
Loebser, S. M., 207
London Missionary Society, 12–13, 15
Louw, C. R., 169
Louw, Eric, 74, 175, 291, 303–4
Louw, M. S., 166, 168–9
Louw, N. P. van Wyk, 47

'Loyal Dutch', 32, 33, 275
Lutherans, 178, 180, 213

M'Carter, Rev. J., 178–9
MacCrone, I. D., 38
Macdonald, Ramsay, 32
MacIver, R. M., 273–4, 299
Mackenzie, Rev. J., 13, 38
MacMillan, W. M., 140
Magersfontein, 33
Magic, African, 214–15
Magistrates, 85, 90
Magnates, (mining), 28, 30
Majuba, 26
Malan, A. G. ('Sailor'), 96, 117, 122
Malan, A. I., 169
Malan, D. F., 39, 77, 81–83, 99–104,
    106, 108, 112–13, 125, 133, 163,
    176, 188, 194, 204, 231, 236, 262,
    274, 286, 302; Clan, 245; Malan-
    ites, 100–1, 105
Malay-Portuguese, 44
Malvern, Lord (Sir G. Huggins),
    129, 131–2
Manchester Guardian, 32
Mansvelt, Dr., 53, 221
Marais, Dr. B. J., 206
Marais, Eugene, 29, 46
Marais, Mrs. J., 157
Maria van Riebeeck Club, 254, 262
Maritz, Gert, 22, 98
Marquard, 86, 146, 189, 198, 237
Marriage (see also Intermarriage
    and Mixed Marriages), 181, 189–
    90, 244–5, 248–9
Marx, Karl, 176
Master-servant relations, 11, 20, 92,
    204, 207, 217, 280
Matabele, 22–23
Materialism, 104, 154, 172, 213,
    249, 270, 300
Mau Mau, 279
Maynier, H. C., 38
Mayors, 85
Medical Service, 113
'Meesters', 218, 253

Methodists, 69, 83, 208–9
Meyer, C., 159
Meyer, Lukas, 35
Meyer, P. J., 172
'Mfecane', 24
Migrant Labour, 108
Military Service, 87
Millin, S. G., 255, 273, 285
Milner, Sir Alfred (Lord), 33–35,
    38, 51, 54–55, 222
Mineworkers Union, 153–9, 161–2
Mining Industry (see also Gold), 28,
    70, 128, 143, 148–50
Miscegenation (see also Mixed
    Marriages), 242–3, 281
Mission Work, 181, 186, 188, 199–
    205, 208–9, 215
Missionaries, 9–13, 15, 25, 27, 201–3
Mixed Marriages (see also Inter-
    marriage), 205–6, 242–3; Act,
    211, 242
Mocke, I., 255
Monarchy (in S.A.), 79, 82–83, 131
Moral Rearmament (M.R.A.), 208
Morgenster, 204
Morkel, Rev. I. D., 201
Morley, John, 32
Mother, Boer concept of, 217, 240–
    2, 246–8
Mother-tongue instruction (see
    Language and Education)
Municipal Government, 83–85
Murray, Rev. A., (1) 182, (2) 203,
    222
Murray, Mrs. A., 12, 180, 184, 278
Music, 256–8, 270
Mynwerker, Die, 155
Mythology (Boer and Afrikaner),
    10, 15–16, 22, 36–41, 78, 204,
    228, 239, 242–3, 275–6

Nagmaal, 75, 179–80, 250
Napier, Sir G. T., 181
Napoleon, 8
Nasionale Party (see Nationalist
    Party)

Nasionale Pers, 164

Natal, 13, 21–23, 25, 27, 59, 62, 67–69, 84, 88–89, 105, 113, 124, 182, 240, 242, 263, 281

National Anthems, 81–82

National Council of Women, 261–2

National Income, 168, 171

National Production, 147

National Scouts, 32–33, 138, 189

National Socialism, 100–1, 103, 110, 114–16, 188, 197, 199, 206, 289–291

National Theatre, 259

National Union of South African Students (N.U.S.A.S.), 237

Nationalism, 28, 39, 41, 93–124, 131, 212, 214–15, 230, 236, 256, 268, 273–6, 285; economic, 163, 171, 173–4; language, 63, Ch. II passim; non-white, 119, 133, 166, 306

Nationalist-Labour Coalition, 142, 153–4

Nationalist Party, 39, 59–62, 74, 81–82, 84, 86, 88–89, 91–124, 126–8, 140, 146, 149, 153–60, 170, 172, 175, 195–7, 208, 211, 218, 224, 226, 228–32, 237, 253–4, 282, 290–1, 302–6

Nationality and Nationhood (see also Nationalism), 25, 95, 99, 132–3, 154, 273–5, 299; national-minded, 106, 111, 130, 153, 157, 159, 224, 227, 282

Native Affairs Department, 85, 92

Natives, see Africans

Naturalization, 79

Navy, South African, 89

Nederlands, (see Dutch)

Negrophilism, 154

Nel, Veld-Kommandant, 16

Nel, M. C. de Wet, 174

Neo-Calvinism, 183

Neo-Krugerism (see also Kruger-ism), 77, 93, 100, 110, 115, 125, 133, 193

Netherlands (see also Holland), 95, 130, 206

New England, 136

'New Order', 101–2, 115

N.G.K. (Nederduits Gereformeerde Kerk), (see also Dutch Reformed Churches), Ch. V passim, 69–70, 131, 167, 249, 262, 265; N.G. Bantu Church, 200–1

N.H.K. (Nederduitsch Hervormde Kerk van Afrika), 155, 183–5, 195

Nicol, W., 42, 60, 196, 229

Niemeyer, Dr., 97

Nigeria, 303–4

Nine Articles (1837), 13

Non-Whites (see also Africans, Cape Coloured, Indians), 37, 78, 87, 89, 92–94, 106–9, 118, 120–1, 124, 133, 151, 153, 158–60, 165–6, 171–3, 199–209, 226, 242–3, 246, 261, 301, 303, 305–6

Noodhulpliga, S. A. 263–4

North-South Antithesis, 41, 48, 83–4, 103, 133

Northern Rhodesia (see Federation, C.A.)

Nurses, 58, 71–72

Nyasaland, 204

Nylstroom, 177

Nywerkor, 170

O.B. (Ossewa-Brandwag), 39, 77, 102, 104, 114, 123–4, 197, 237, 268, 286

O.B., Die, 116, 154, 239

Oblates, 211

Occupations, 70–1, 150, 233

Odendaal, F. H., 82

Officials (and colonists), 4–8, 18, 21, 273

Ohrigstad, 74

Old Testament (see also Bible), 18, 22, 177, 276, 278, 290

Olivier, P. J., 61

One-Party State, 95, 133, 199

'One-stream' principle (see also

'single-stream' and 'two-stream'), 99, 116, 123, 125, 133, 274–5

Ons Klintji, 55, 125

Ons Land, 125

'Oom Gert Vertel', 31

Oost, Harm, 60

Oosterlik, Die, 126, 154

Opperman, Dirk, 47–48

Orange, House of, 81

Orange Free State (see also Republics), 13, 23–6, 29, 30–35, 37, 40, 56, 62, 67–69, 73–8, 83–4, 88–9, 97, 102, 140, 145, 161, 182, 184–5, 209, 222, 226, 242, 284; Centenary 40, 268; University 14, 191, 232, 237

Orange River, 13, 19, 21

Orange River Colony (Sovereignty), 56, 182, 223

Ordinance, 50; (1828), 12, 20

Organizations (see Associations)

Outstryders, 146

Paardeberg, 33

Paardekraal, 26, 75, 98

Paarl (see also Genootskap), 45, 164

Pact Government (1924–33), 99

Paris Evangelical Mission, 13

Parliament, 57, 74, 80, 83, 91–2, 112, 146; occupational structure, 253–4; parliamentary system, 98, 104, 118, 123

Pass Laws, 146

Passports, 93

Pastoralism, 17, 136, 148, 177, 278

Paton, Alan, 206

Patriarchalism, 18, 76–77, 94, 189, 216, 239, 246, 248, 292

Patriot, Di, 45, 52, 125, 164

Pellissier, H. S., 268

Pensions, 146, 190

Pentecostal Churches, 213–4

Philanthropists, 12, 203

Philip, John, 38, 208–9

Pienaar, W. J. B., 283

Pierneef, J. H., 258

Pietermaritzburg, 22, 68

Pirow, 101–2, 104, 115, 155

Platteland, see Rural Areas

Plewman, R. P., 92

Poetry, 45 f, 257–9

Poles (national character), 277, 300

Police, South African, 114, 152, 269, 302

Politics Ch. III *passim*; political parties, 76–77, 79, 93–124, 133, 195–9, 231–2, 269

Pondoland, 27

Poor Whites (see also Poverty), 36, 136–43, 167–8, 172, 192–4, 213, 251–2, 270, 279, 292

Port Elizabeth, 68, 84, 303

Post Office, (S.A.), 85, 269

Postma, Rev. D. 186

Potchefstroom, 23, 103, 114, 125, 184, 232–5, 271

Potgieter, A. H., 23, 74

Poverty (see also Poor Whites), 9, 137–43, 190, 192–3, 245–8

Predestination, doctrine of, 176–8, 225, 293, 305

Preller, A., 258

Press, Afrikaner, 45, 83, 89, 124–7, 144, 154–6, 158, 161, 164, 172, 209, 255, 283

Pretoria, 27, 38–39, 82–83, 139, 252–3; Centenary 40, 245; University 74, 103, 113, 184, 234–7

Pretorius, A., 98

Pretorius Clan, 245

Pretorius, M. W., 24

'Prikkel-lektuur', 48

Prinsloo, H., 16

Professions, Afrikaners in, 112, 119, 128, 133, 148, 152, 233, 235, 252–4

Proletariat, Afrikaner, 99, 109, 145, 154, 180, 194, 199, 213–4, 217, 252, 275, 278

Protectorates, 107, 128

Protestant Churches (non-Afrikaner), 76

Provinces (administration), 79, 80, 83–85, 102, 117; education, 59, 117, 224, 228–30

Public Service, 57, 71–2, 73, 85, 112, 128, 142, 148, 151–2, 267

Purchasing power, Afrikaner, 56, 163

Purified Nationalist Party (see also Nationalist Party), 99, 104, 106

Quebec, 4, 51, 127, 288

Queen (see Monarchy)

Queen Adelaide Land, 19

Quit-rent tenure, 14

Racialism, 36–41, 93, 94, 109

Radio (see also S.A. Broadcasting Corporation), 172, 255, 283

Railways (see S.A. Railways and Harbours)

Rand (see Witwatersrand)

Rand Daily Mail, 40, 117

Rape, 243

Read, Dr. James, 12, 15

Rebellions (eighteenth century), 7–8; (1914), 96, 98, 164

Reconstruction, 33, 137

Reddingsdaadbond (R.D.B.), 56, 77, 111, 131, 167–8, 172, 268, 270

Reform Organization, 157–9

Reitz, Denys, 33–34, 96, 139

Religion, (see also Churches, Sects.) 69, 192–4, 212–4, 217, 220–2, 239, 250, 255, 278–9; press, 126; organizations, 264

Rembrandt Tobacco Co., 169, 170, 172

Republicanism (see also Draft Constitution of the Republic), 74–78, 82, 84, 98–100, 102–6, 115–16, 118, 171, 210, 254, 282, 288

Republics (see also Transvaal, Natal, S.A. Republic and Orange Free State), 7, 13, 23–41, 54, 73–78, 81–82, 93, 111, 137, 183, 195, 204, 216, 218, 222–3, 239, 256, 273, 277f

Reserves, African, 107–8

Retief, Magdalena, 244

Retief, P., 20–22, 23, 98, 204, 244, 305

Reunion (Hereniging), 113, 117

Reunited Nationalist Party (see Nationalist Party)

Revivalism (see Sects)

Reyneke, H. J., 189

Rhodes, C. J., 28, 30, 38

Rhodesias (see also Central African Federation), 184, 263

Rifle Commandos, 87

Rinderpest, 139

Robbins, Eric, 176

Roberts, General, 33

Roberts, Michael, 116

Roman Catholic Church, 202, 208–212, 214, 221, 289

Roman-Dutch Law, 15, 89f, 137

Roodezand, 179

Rule of Law, 8, 90, 197

Rupert, Anton, 169

Rural areas, 68, 80–81, 87, 93, 96, 99, 104, 109, 121, 137, 140, 144–8, 151, 217, 226, 234, 246–7; (voters), 95, 102, 133

Rustenburg, 185

Saambou, 169

(S.A., see South Africa)

S.A.B.R.A. (Suid-Afrikaanse Buro vir Rasse-Aangeleenthede) 107–8, 236, 266–7, 303

Sachs, E. S., 36, 109, 121–2, 154–60, 195

Sakekamers (Afrikaans Chambers of Commerce), 175

Sand River Convention (1852), 22–23

Sanlam, 164, 169–70

Santam, 164

Sauer, Paul, 85

Scheepers, Anna, 156, 159

Schoeman, Rev. A. J., 214

Schoeman, B. J., 158, 160, 175

Scholtz, G. D., 48, 154, 256, 282, 301

Schools (see also Education, Teachers), 28, 41, 53, 60, 110, 111, 117, 168, 181, 192, 212, 219, 223–5, 257, 264, 268; English-medium, 60, 212, 219, 221–2, 227; School Boards, 196, 223–4, 228–30, 269

Schreiner, Olive, 53

Schriener, W., 32

Schumann, C. G. W., 169, 171

Scotland (and Scots), 181, 183, 185, 199, 278

Scott, Rev. M., 14, 38

Sculpture, 258

Sects, Religious, 194, 199, 213–4

Secularization, 180–1, 190–2, 220, 300

Segregation, 78, 95, 106, 118, 174–5, 183, 204, 207, 237, 299, 301–2, 305

Senate, 79–80, 105; legislation re, 74–75, 80, 91, 103, 210, 235–6

Separate development (see also Apartheid), 106–7, 199–208, 225

Sex (D.R. Church attitudes), 190–1

Shaka, 21, 24

Shepstone, Sir T., 26, 38

'Single-stream' policy (see also 'one-stream' and 'two-stream'), 36, 39, 41, 93–94, 96, 111

Skakelkomitees, 229, 269–70

Slagters Nek (1815), 15–16

Slavery (Slaves), 5–6, 8–11, 13, 18, 20, 44, 136, 202, 218, 243, 251

Smit, Erasmus, 182, 240

Smith, Rev. P. E. S., 201

Smuts, J. C. 30–31, 36, 38, 41, 56, 81, 86, 93, 96, 98–102, 112, 116–18, 123, 125, 135, 223, 227, 236, 246, 265, 274, 282, 290–1

Snowdon, Philip, 32

Social Structure (see also Class), Ch. VII passim

Social Welfare, 71–72

Socialism, 99, 109

Somerset, Lord Charles, 38, 51, 181

Sonop, 166

Sons of England, 113

South Africa Act, see also Union, Act of, 63, 91, 125

S.A. Blood Transfusion Service, 274

S.A. Bond, 103

S.A. Broadcasting Corporation, 255–6

S.A. Calvinist Protestant Church, 201

S.A. Congress of Trade Unions, 162

S.A. Federation of Trade Unions, 161–2

S.A. Institute of Race Relations, 267

S.A. Party (see also United Party), 97–98, 125

S.A. Police, 87

S.A. Press Association, 127

S.A. Railways and Harbours, 85–87, 110, 142, 151, 264, 267–8; Rail-waymen, 128, 263, 267–8

S.A. Republic (see also Transvaal, Republics), 23, 26–36, 58, 73–8, 183, 218, 220

S.A. Teachers Association, 226

S.A. Trades and Labour Council, 156, 160–2, 195

S.A. Trade Union Council, 162

South Africanism, 42, 227, 248, 257, 274

South-West Africa, 79, 81, 102, 129, 184

Southern Cross, 210, 212

Southern Rhodesia (see Federation, Central African)

Sovereignty, 73–74, 76, 79, 90–91, 198–9

Sports, 217, 235, 249, 255–6, 283–4

Standard Bank of South Africa, 165

Standpunte, 48

Star, 49, 57, 91, 256, 292

State Information Department, 108

Status (see Class)

Steed, H. Wickham, 32

Stellenbosch, 107, 164, 169, 178, 219, 232, 236, 243, 266; University 149, 232, 236–7, 290–1; Theological Seminary, 182, 187, 237

Steyn, President, M. J., 30, 34–35, 55, 223, 266

Steynberg, C., 258

Stockenstrom, A., 38

Strauss, J. H., 117

Strauss, Professor, H. J., 74

Strijdom, J. G., 77, 83, 99, 103–4, 108, 112–13, 126, 128, 231, 303

Strikes, 156–8

Strydmakkertjies, 110, 231

Studentebond, Afrikaanse, 103, 163, 235, 237, 264

Students' Christian Association of South Africa, 264–5

Sub-division (of land), 137, 139, 144

Subsistence economy, 17, 136, 138, 147, 164, 217

Sustersbond (G.K.), 262

Sustersvereniging (N.H.K.), 262

Suid-Afrikaanse Akademie, 48, 55, 266

Suid-Afrikaanse Onderwysersunie (S.A.O.U.), 226

Suiderstem, Die, 125

Suidwester, Die, 129

Suzerainty, 26, 30

Swart, C. P., 92, 155

Swart, C. W. P., 62

Swaziland, 22, 107

Swellendam, 7, 179

Taal, Die (see Afrikaans Language)

Taalbond, 53–54

Taalgenoot, Die, 267

Tanganyika, 128–30, 263

Tas, Adam, 5, 135

Tawney, R. H., 176, 199

Taxes, 21, 26, 76, 145

Te Water, Charles, 210

Teachers, 71–72, 111–12, 146, 179, 181–2, 220–7, 231, 253–4, 262

Tegniese Beleggings, 170

Theal, 18–19, 25

Theocracy, 74, 103, 188, 199, 215

Theology, 233, 235, 257

Torch Commando, 96, 122–4

Tot System, 191

Totalitarianism, 93–94, 115

Totius, 46, 97

Toynbee, A., 215

Trade Unions, 122, 143, 151–63, 167–8, 195, 198, 270, 290–1

'Traitors' (to the Volk), 16, 38, 93, 98, 104, 117, 283

Transorangia, 23, 203

Transvaal Indigency Commission, 139

Transvaal (Province), 60, 69, 82, 84, 99, 213; language, 58, 60; education, 220–4, 227–30

Transvaal (Republic), 9, 13, 22–23, 26, 53, 67–68, 73–78, 97–98, 139, 182–3, 185–6, 196, 265, 281, 289

Transvaalse Onderwysersvereniging (T.O.), 226–7

Transvaler, Die, 42, 77, 82, 126, 145, 149, 174, 193, 229, 234, 255–6, 292, 299

Trek-Boers, 180, 193, 240, 244, 272

Trek-gees, 17, 141, 278, 294

Trekkers (see also Great Trek, Voortrekkers), 10–11, 19, 83, 96, 128–9, 204; Costume, 38–39, 41, 115

Trichardt, L., 23

Trollip, A. E., 3, 116

'Two-stream' principle (see also 'one-stream'), 93–94, 98–100, 102–4, 116, 118, 120, 125, 133, 224, 274–5

Uitenhage, 15

Uitlanders, 27–31, 75–76, 92, 221

Unie Volkspers, 125

Uniewinkels, 166–70

Unilingualism (see also Language), 68–69, 152

Union, (1910), (see also South Africa Act), 36, 56, 83, 97, 104–5, 224

Union Jack (see also Flag), 81–82, 228, 264
Unionist Party, 97–98
United Nations, 198, 293
United Party 59–62, 81, 86, 93–125 *passim*, 231, 236; Junior U.P., 231
United States (Calvinist Churches), 206
Universities (see also O.F.S., Stellenbosch, Witwatersrand, Potchefstroom, Pretoria, etc.), 110, 211, 226, 232–8, 253
Urban areas, 56, 67–68, 85, 93, 99, 109, 111, 117, 139–144, 148, 151, 154, 163, 172–3, 180, 193–4, 199, 209, 213–4, 238, 247–9, 252, 269–70; (society) 178, 252, 255f; voters 80–81, 95, 102, 119, 133, 143, 153, 159–60
Urbanization, 99, 107, 109, 174, 191–2, 194–5, 198–9, 215, 217, 246–8, 273, 292, 300.

Vaderland, Die, 126, 154
Van den Berg, Martinus, 121
Van der Hoff, Rev. D., 183
Van der Kemp, Dr., 12
Van der Merwe, Dr. A. J., 200, 249
Van der Merwe, Dr. C. F., 113
Van der Merwe, Schalk Willem, 249
Van der Poel, Dr. Jean, 29
Van der Stel, S., 4–5, 51, 179
Van der Stel, W. A., 5
Van der Walt, G. H., 159
Van Eck, H. J., 150
Van Eeden, Guillaume, 129, 132
Van Heerden, W., 303
Van Niekerk, G. L. H., 159
Van Rensburg, J. F., 114
Van Rhijn, A. J. R., 149, 175
Van Riebeeck, Jan, 89; Tricentenary, 40–41, 268, 274
Van Rooy, J. C., 271
Van Wyk, Arnold, 258
Vegkop, 22
Veldkornets, 90

Venter, J. J., 156
Verburg, Commissioner, 5
Vereeniging, 35, 229; Peace of, 138
Vereniging; Policy of Unity, 116–17
Verwoerd, H. F., 59, 77, 108, 126, 173, 175, 290, 302
Vierkleur, 81–82
Viljoen, Dr. P. R., 48
Visser, C. F., 273
Volk (see Afrikaners, Boers)
Volksblad, Die, 37, 126, 145, 172, 279
Volksgaderings, 75
Volksgenoot, Die, 131, 132
Volkskas, 111, 165–6, 169
Volkskeuring, 116
Volkspele, 190, 268
Volksraad, (Transvaal), 24, 30, 40, 75
Volkstem, Die, 29, 125
Volksvriend, Die, 52
Volkswil, 74, 82, 90–91, 105–6, 199
Voorligter, Die, 196
Voortrekker Monument, 22, 39, 167, 241, 258, 268
Voortrekker Press, 154–6
Voortrekkers (see Trekkers, Great Trek), 20–22, 41, 110, 115, 135–6, 167, 181–2, 203–4, 240, 264–5, 299
Voters, Ch. III *passim*, 79, 101, 129, 153-63, 262, 302–5
Vow, (see also Covenant), 38, 41, 292
Vredefort, 35
Vrou en Moeder, 262
Vroue Sendingbond (N.G.K.), 262

Wages (differentials), 143, 207, 249
Walker, Eric, 6, 12–13, 21, 138, 179, 187
War Veterans Torch Commando (see Torch Commando)
'Ware Afrikaners', 39, 102, 182, 278
Wars of Independence, see Transvaal and Anglo-Boer Wars
Wassenaar, T., 276

Waterboer, N., 25
Wealth (as status determinant), 246, 249–55
Weenen, 22
Welensky, Sir Roy, 132, 290
Welfare associations, 261f, 267–70
Wepener, Louw, 89
Werda, 163
Werkerspers, Die, 155–6
Wesleyans, 13, 182
Westdene, 116
Western Areas Removal, 50, 85
Western Province Federation of Labour Unions, 161
Westminster, Statute of, 99
Whites; statistics, 67–71; White baasskap or supremacy 94, 104, 281, 302–3; White-Black dichotomy, 255, 281; White-Black relationships, 78, 242–3; White Christian Civilization, 105, 128, 133, 177, 215, 237, 295; 'White Man's Law', 92; White prestige, 139, 141, 191, 240, 304; White Woman concept, 9, 242–3; White, Workers, 86, 95, 99
Wiid, J. J., 98

Wilberforce, W., 12
Wilcocks, R. W., 278
Witwatersrand, 27, 68, 143, 192, 229, 234–5, 237; (University), 235
Wodehouse, Sir P., 25
Wolmarans, H. P., 155
Women (see also White Women); Boer, 22, 34–35, 43, 189, 217, 239–44, 262; Afrikaner, 69, 71, 83, 190–1, 261–2; in politics, 75, 254; workers, 144, 150, 247, 249, 262; English-speaking, 69
Wool-farming, 144
Workers (see Labour, and Whites)
World Council of Churches, 206–7
World Wars; (1914–18), 98, 150, 289; (1939–45) 88, 100, 143, 186

Youth, Ch. VI *passim*, 59–64, 95, 110, 117, 207, 265, 289
Yssel, Gert, 114

Zionism, 291
Zuid Afrikaan, De, 52–53
Zulus, 22–24, 26, 98, 291